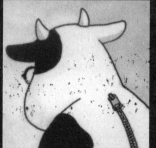

Apparently, when my neighbor's 3-year-old daughter found out that I'm a manga artist, she said with a sparkle in her eyes, "I wonder if she draws princesses and stuff?" Sorry little girl, I only draw grubby old men.

—*Hiromu Arakawa, 2003*

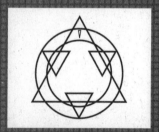

Born in Hokkaido (northern Japan), Hiromu Arakawa first attracted national attention in 1999 with her award-winning manga *Stray Dog*. Her series *Fullmetal Alchemist* debuted in 2001 in Square Enix's monthly manga anthology *Shonen Gangan*.

FULLMETAL ALCHEMIST
VOL. 6

Story and Art by Hiromu Arakawa

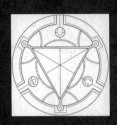

Translation/Akira Watanabe
English Adaptation/Jake Forbes
Touch-up Art & Lettering/Wayne Truman
Design/Amy Martin
Editor/Jason Thompson

Editor in Chief, Books/Alvin Lu
Editor in Chief, Magazines/Marc Weidenbaum
VP, Publishing Licensing/Rika Inouye
VP, Sales & Product Marketing/Gonzalo Ferreyra
VP, Creative/Linda Espinosa
Publisher/Hyoe Narita

Printed in U.S.A.

Published by VIZ Media, LLC
P.O. Box 77010
San Francisco, CA 94107

10 9 8 7 6 5 4
First printing, February 2006
Fourth printing, September 2008

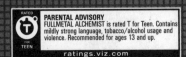

鋼の錬金術師

FULLMETAL ALCHEMIST

6

荒川弘

HIROMU ARAKAWA

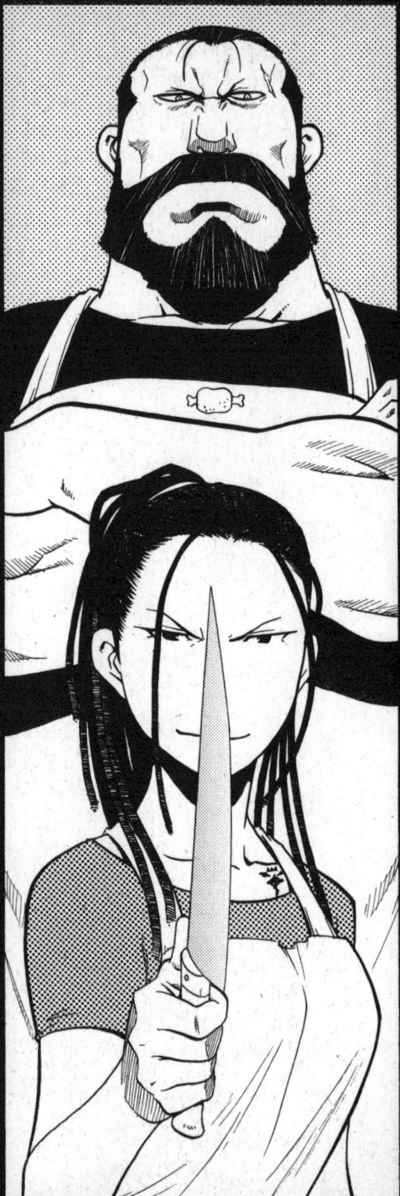

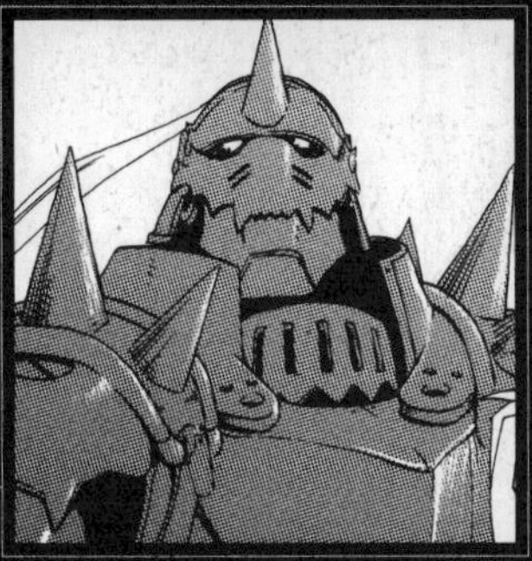

アルフォンス・エルリック

Alphonse Elric

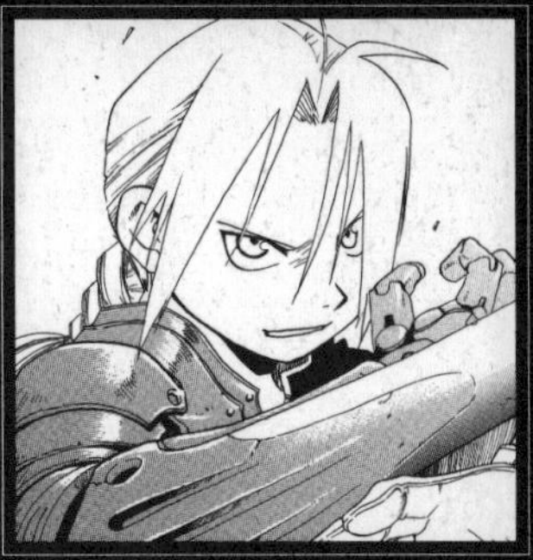

エドワード・エルリック

Edward Elric

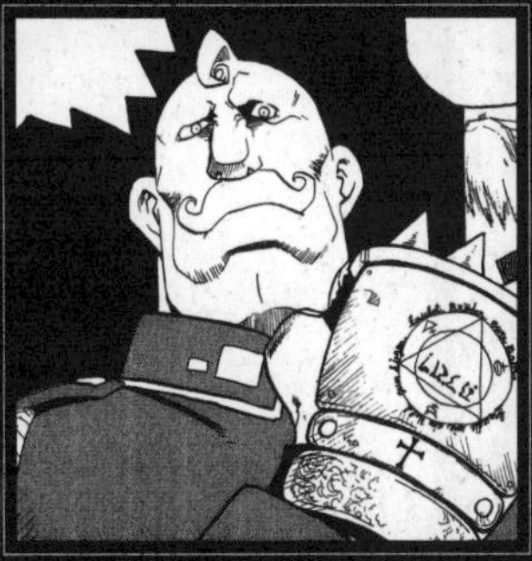

アレックス・ルイ・アームストロング

Alex Louis Armstrong

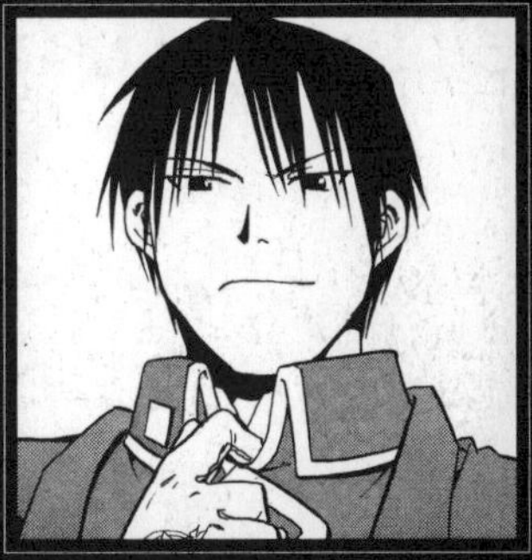

ロイ・マスタング

Roy Mustang

Using a forbidden alchemical ritual, the Elric brothers attempted to bring their dead mother back to life. But the ritual went wrong, consuming Edward Elric's leg and Alphonse Elric's entire body. At the cost of his arm, Edward was able to graft his brother's soul into a suit of armor. Equipped with mechanical "auto-mail" to replace his missing limbs, Edward becomes a state alchemist, serving the military on deadly missions. Now, the two brothers roam the world in search of a way to regain what they have lost...

Feeling unprepared to face the dangers ahead, the Elric brothers return to their old alchemy teacher, Izumi Curtis, for advice. In a flashback to the past, we see how the Elric brothers first met their teacher, shortly after the death of their mother. Reluctant to take on apprentices, but impressed by the brothers' determination, Izumi agrees to train them...but only if they can survive for one full month on a dangerous island...

鋼の錬金術師
FULLMETAL ALCHEMIST

CHARACTERS
FULLMETAL ALCHEMIST

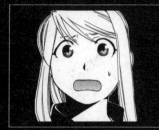

□ ウィンリィ・ロックベル

Winry Rockbell

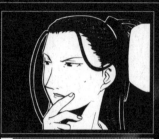

□ イズミ・カーティス

Izumi Curtis

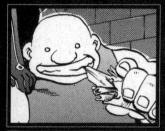

□ グラトニー

Gluttony

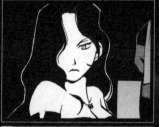

□ ラスト

Lust

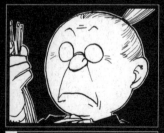

□ ピナコ・ロックベル

Pinako Rockbell

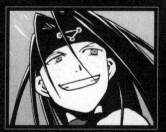

□ エンヴィー

Envy

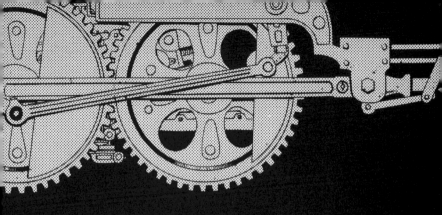

CONTENTS

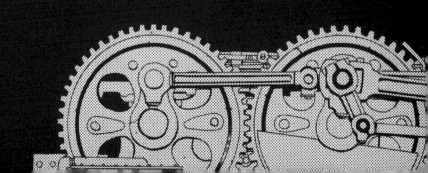

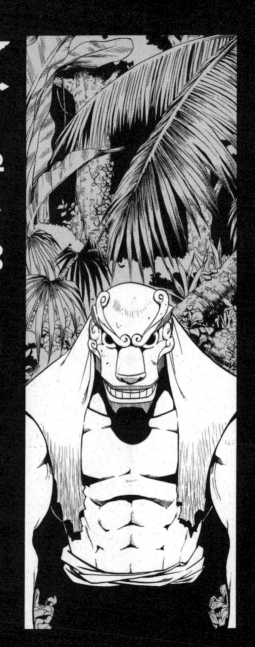

Chapter 22:
The Masked Man

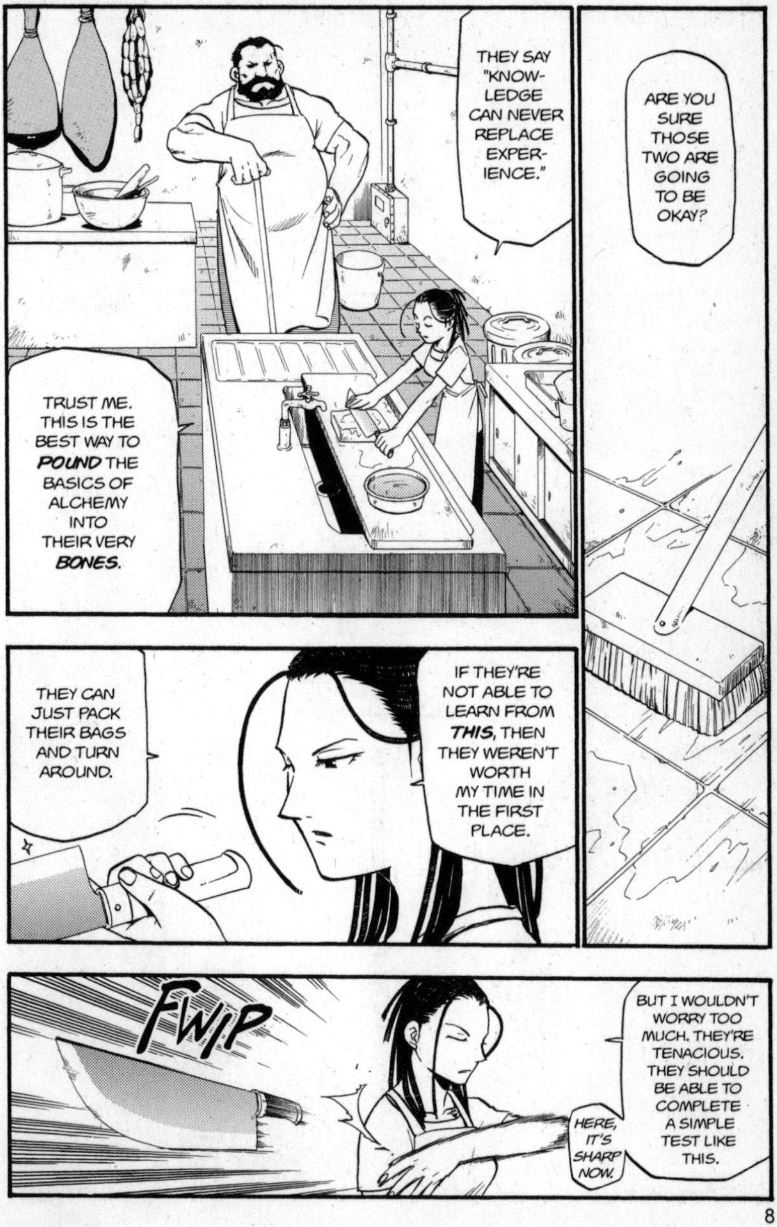
ARE YOU SURE THOSE TWO ARE GOING TO BE OKAY?
THEY SAY "KNOW-LEDGE CAN NEVER REPLACE EXPER-IENCE."
TRUST ME. THIS IS THE BEST WAY TO ***POUND*** THE BASICS OF ALCHEMY INTO THEIR VERY ***BONES***.
IF THEY'RE NOT ABLE TO LEARN FROM ***THIS***, THEN THEY WEREN'T WORTH MY TIME IN THE FIRST PLACE.
THEY CAN JUST PACK THEIR BAGS AND TURN AROUND.
BUT I WOULDN'T WORRY TOO MUCH. THEY'RE TENACIOUS. THEY SHOULD BE ABLE TO COMPLETE A SIMPLE TEST LIKE THIS.
HERE, IT'S SHARP NOW.
FWIP

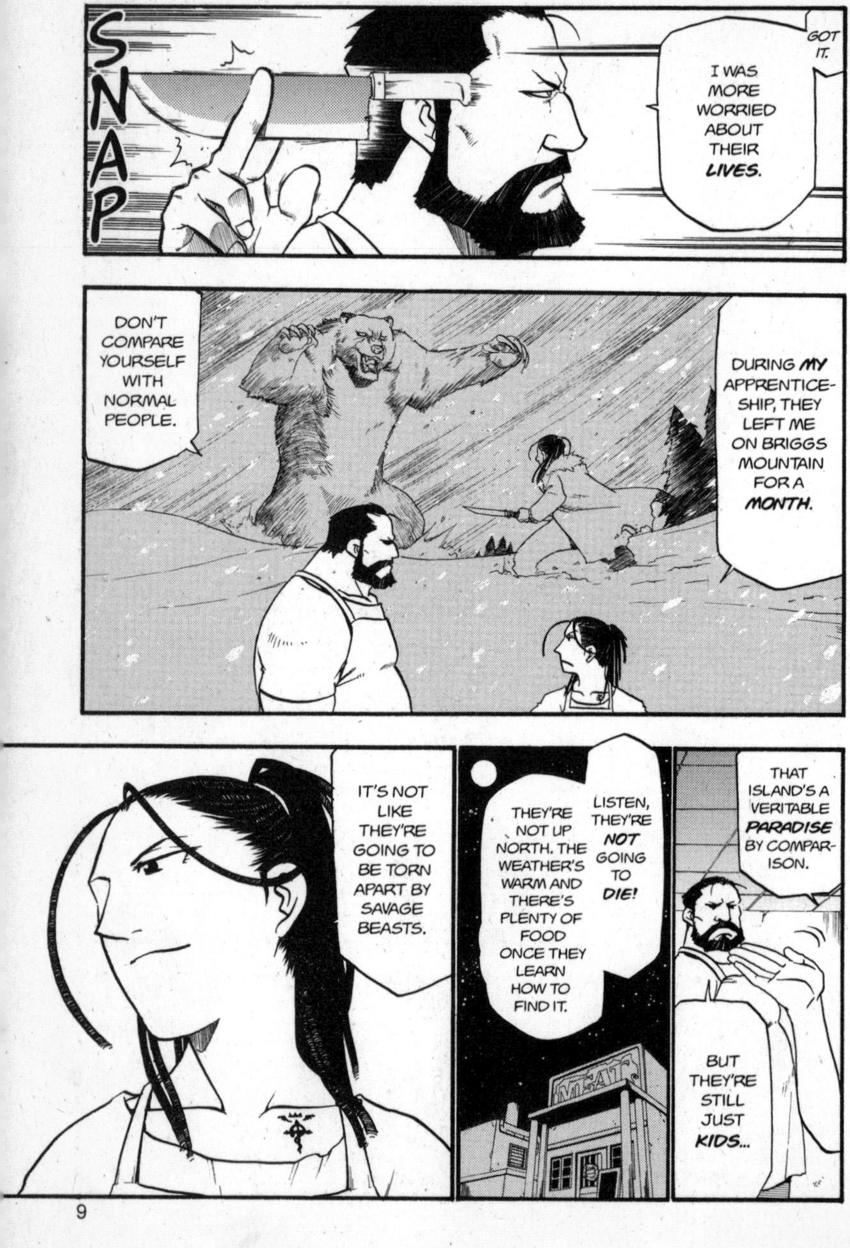
GOT IT.
I WAS MORE WORRIED ABOUT THEIR LIVES.
SNAP
DURING MY APPRENTICESHIP, THEY LEFT ME ON BRIGGS MOUNTAIN FOR A MONTH.
DON'T COMPARE YOURSELF WITH NORMAL PEOPLE.
THAT ISLAND'S A VERITABLE PARADISE BY COMPARISON.
BUT THEY'RE STILL JUST KIDS...
LISTEN, THEY'RE NOT GOING TO DIE!
THEY'RE NOT UP NORTH. THE WEATHER'S WARM AND THERE'S PLENTY OF FOOD ONCE THEY LEARN HOW TO FIND IT.
MEAT
IT'S NOT LIKE THEY'RE GOING TO BE TORN APART BY SAVAGE BEASTS.

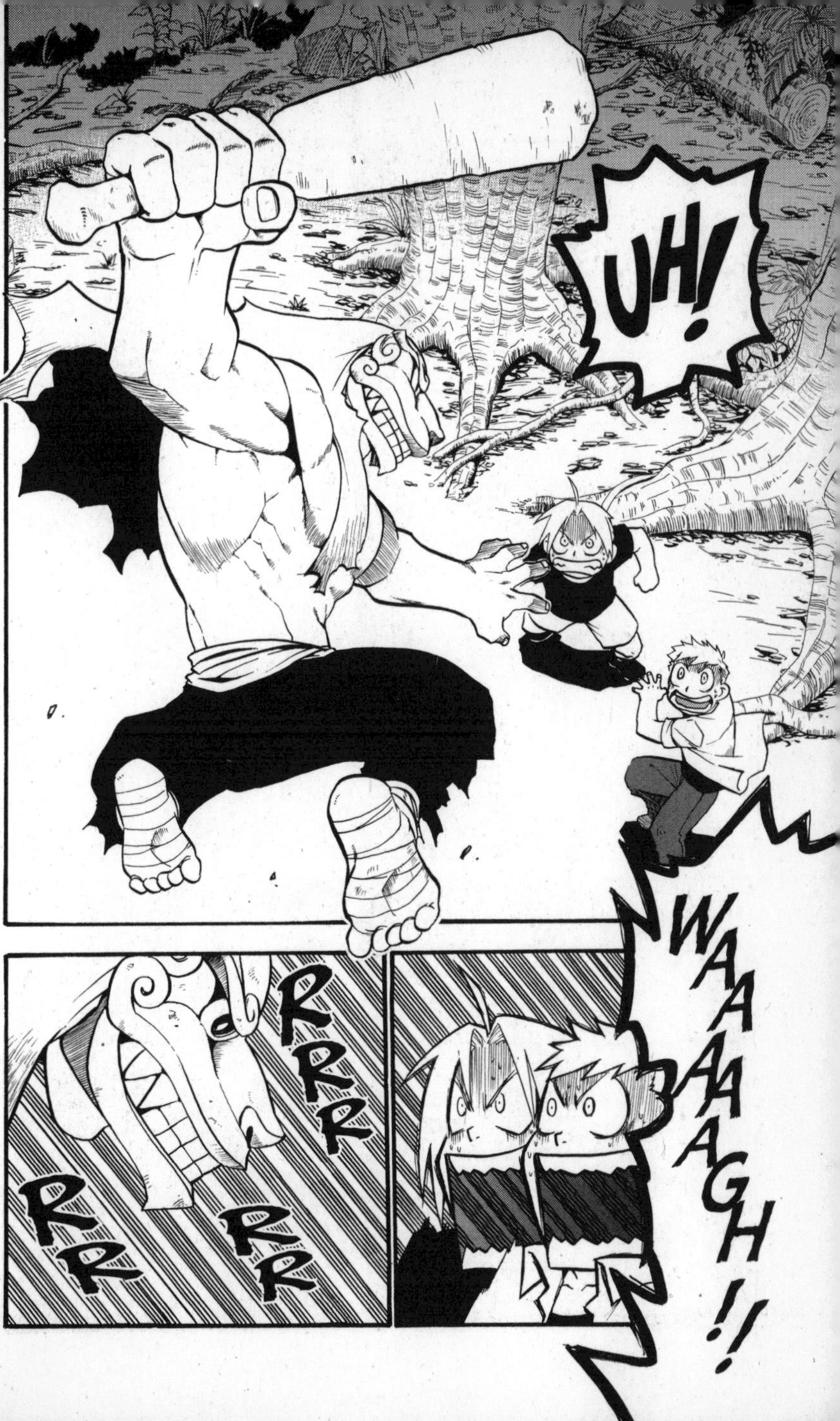
UH!
WAAAAGH!!
RRRR
RRR
RRR

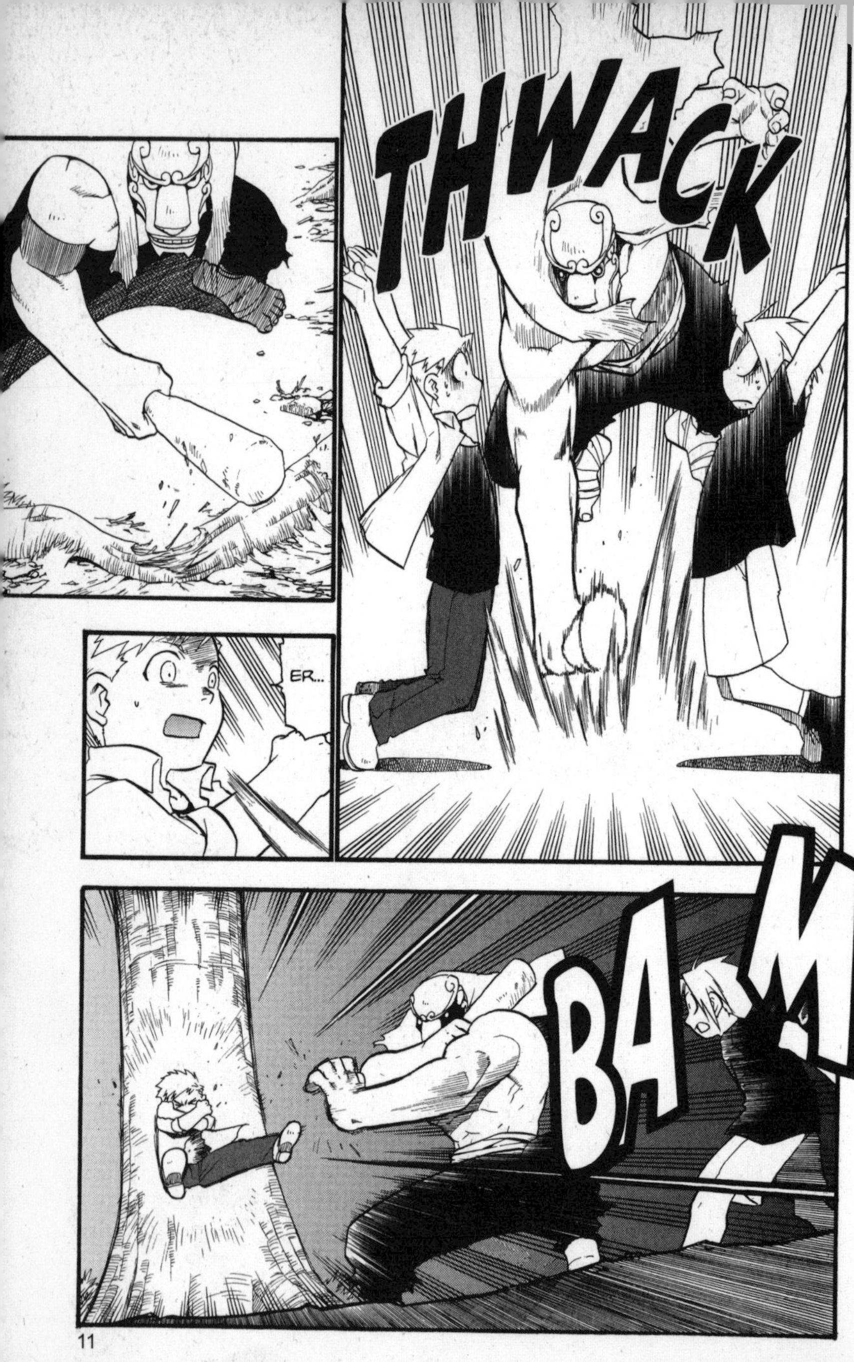
THWACK
ER...
BAM

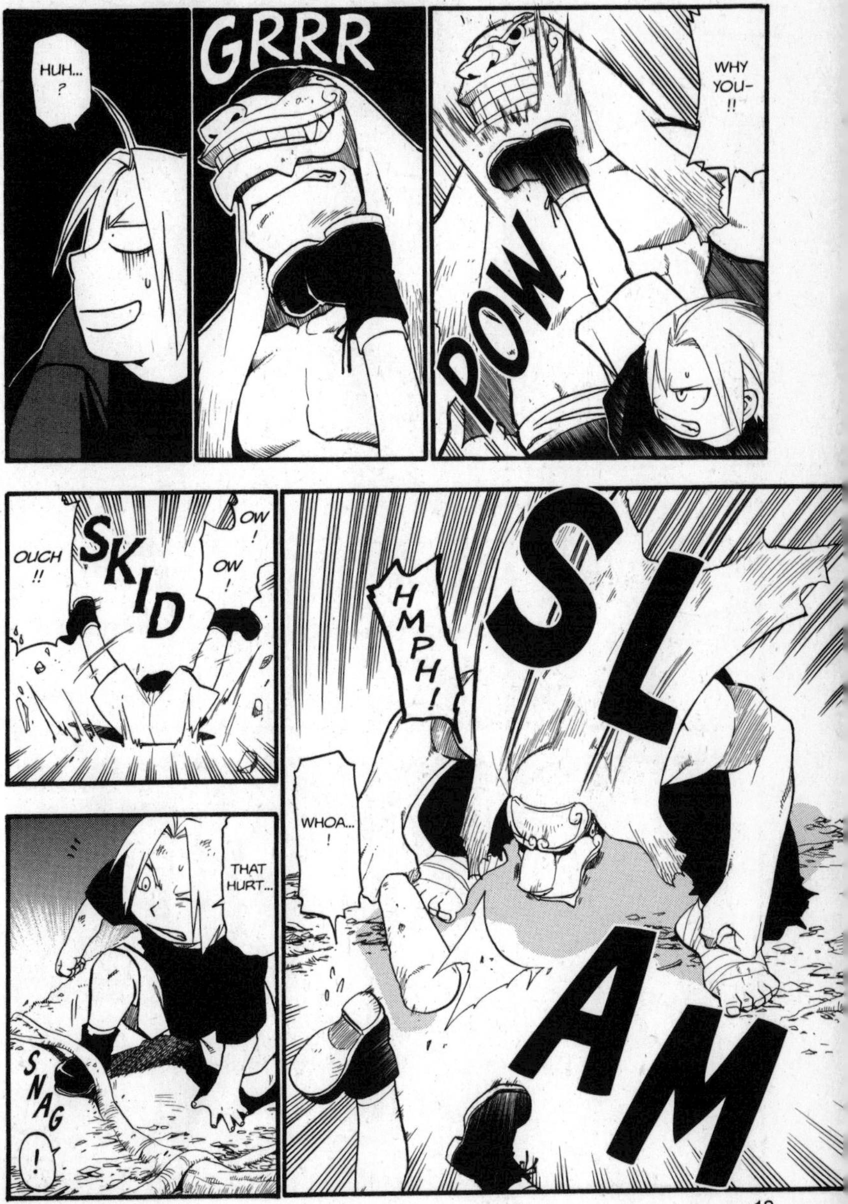
WHY YOU-!!
POW
GRRR
HUH... ?
SLAM
HMPH!
WHOA... !
OW!
SKID
OW!
OUCH!!
THAT HURT...
SNAG!

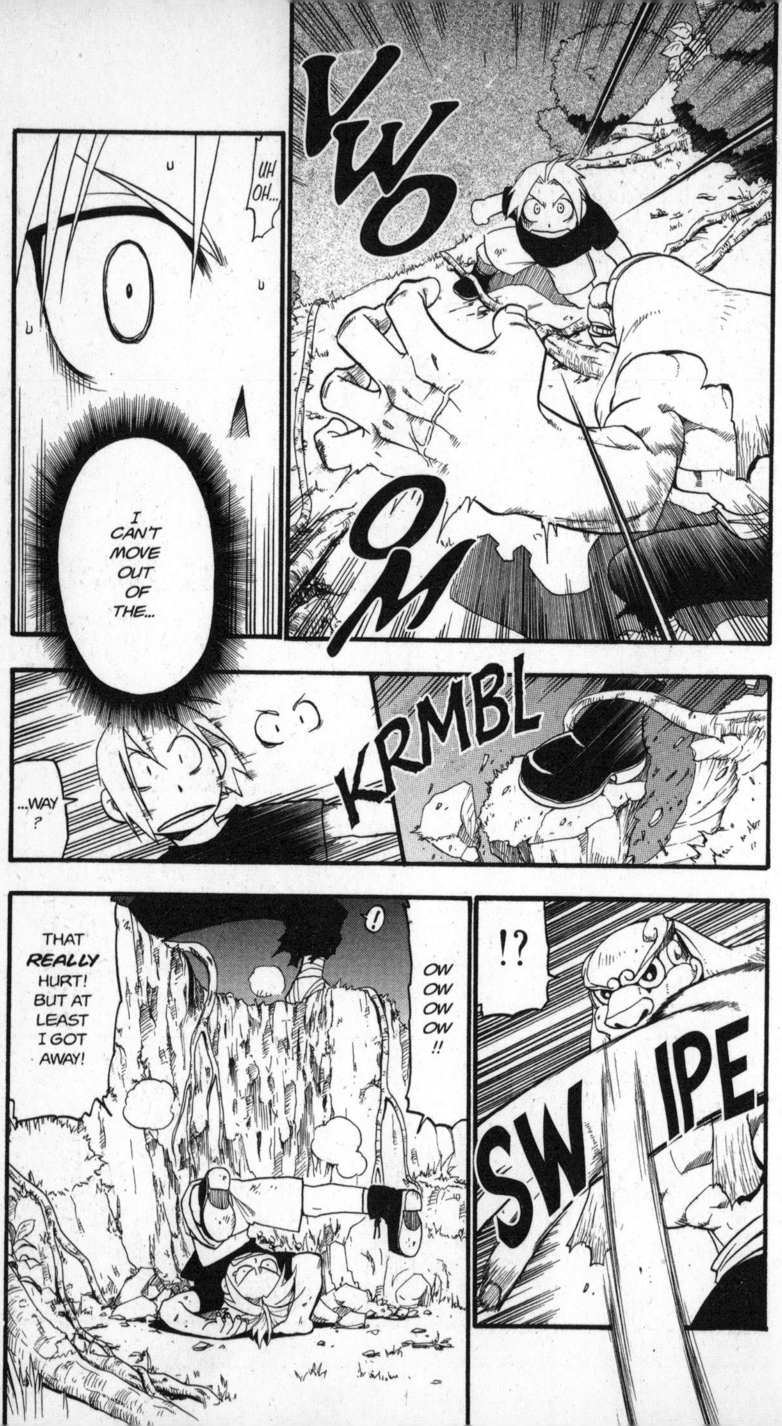
VWO
OM
UH OH...
I CAN'T MOVE OUT OF THE...
KRMBL
...WAY ?
!?
SW IPE.
!
OW OW OW OW !!
THAT *REALLY* HURT! BUT AT LEAST I GOT AWAY!

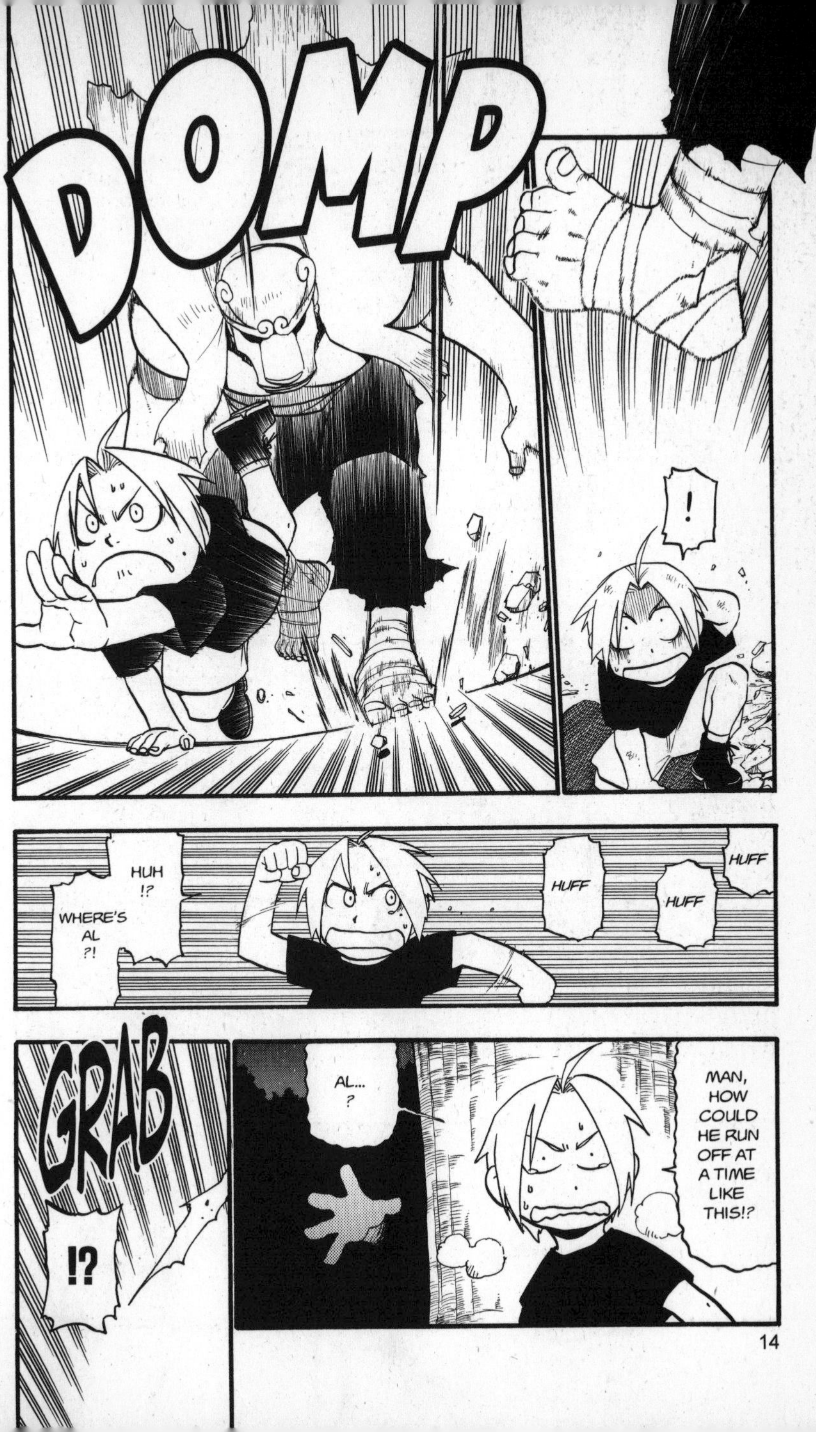
!
DOMP
HUFF
HUFF
HUFF
HUH !?
WHERE'S AL ?!
MAN, HOW COULD HE RUN OFF AT A TIME LIKE THIS!?
AL... ?
GRAB
!?

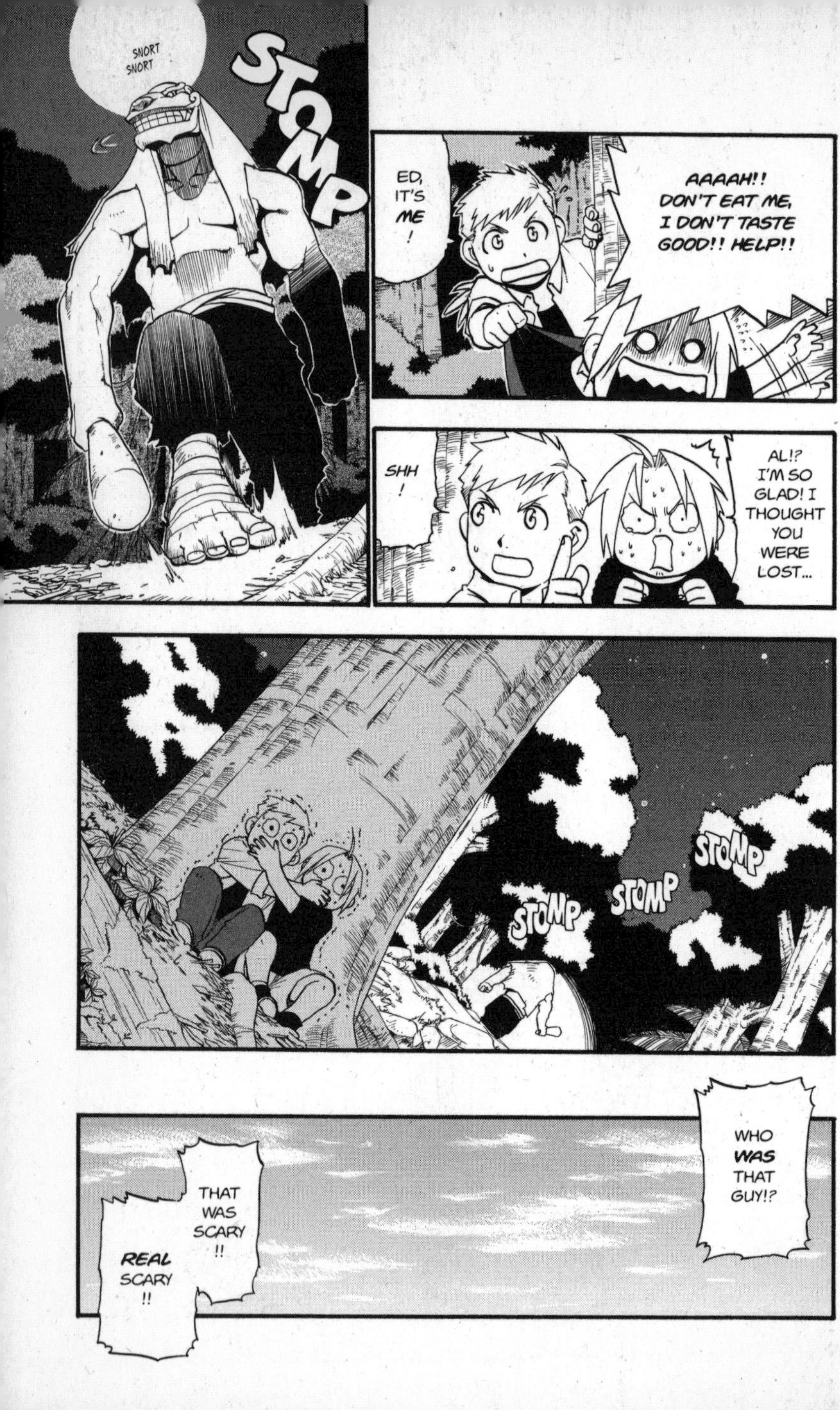
AAAAH!! DON'T EAT ME, I DON'T TASTE GOOD!! HELP!!
ED, IT'S ME!
AL!? I'M SO GLAD! I THOUGHT YOU WERE LOST...
SHH!
STOMP
SNORT SNORT
STOMP
STOMP
STOMP
WHO WAS THAT GUY!?
THAT WAS SCARY!!
REAL SCARY!!

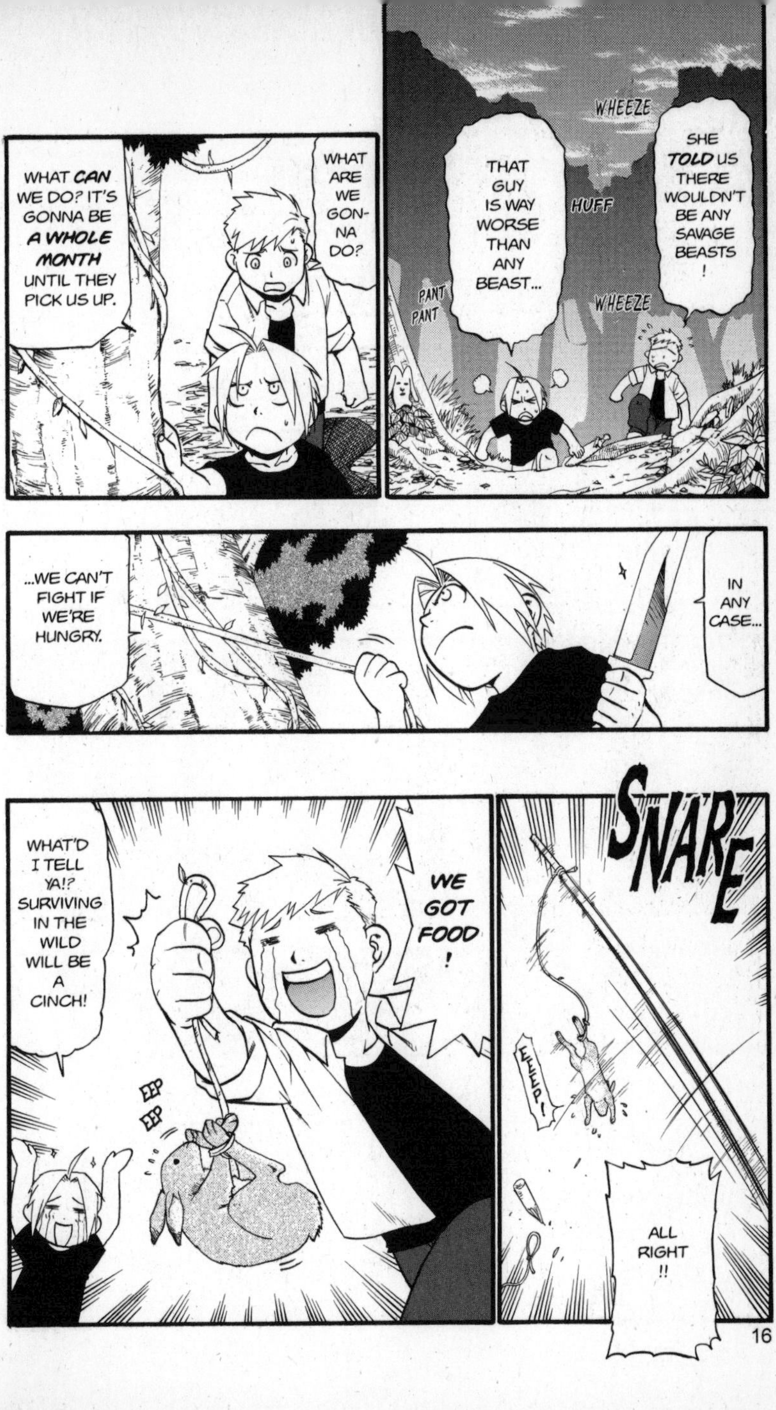

WHEEZE
SHE TOLD US THERE WOULDN'T BE ANY SAVAGE BEASTS!
HUFF
THAT GUY IS WAY WORSE THAN ANY BEAST...
PANT PANT
WHEEZE
WHAT ARE WE GONNA DO?
WHAT CAN WE DO? IT'S GONNA BE A WHOLE MONTH UNTIL THEY PICK US UP.
IN ANY CASE...
...WE CAN'T FIGHT IF WE'RE HUNGRY.
SNARE
EEEP!
ALL RIGHT!!
WE GOT FOOD!
WHAT'D I TELL YA!? SURVIVING IN THE WILD WILL BE A CINCH!
EEP EEP

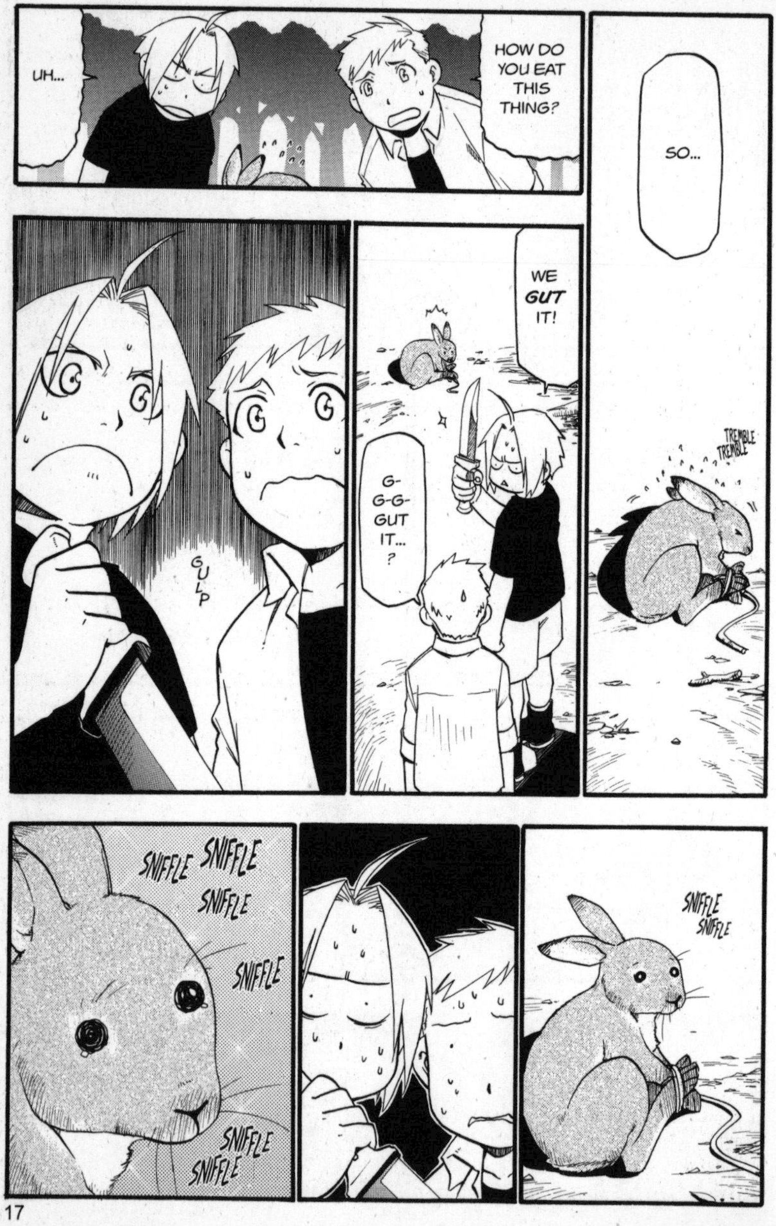
SO...
TREMBLE TREMBLE
HOW DO YOU EAT THIS THING?
UH...
WE **GUT** IT!
G-G-G-GUT IT...?
GULP
SNIFFLE SNIFFLE
SNIFFLE SNIFFLE
SNIFFLE
SNIFFLE
SNIFFLE SNIFFLE

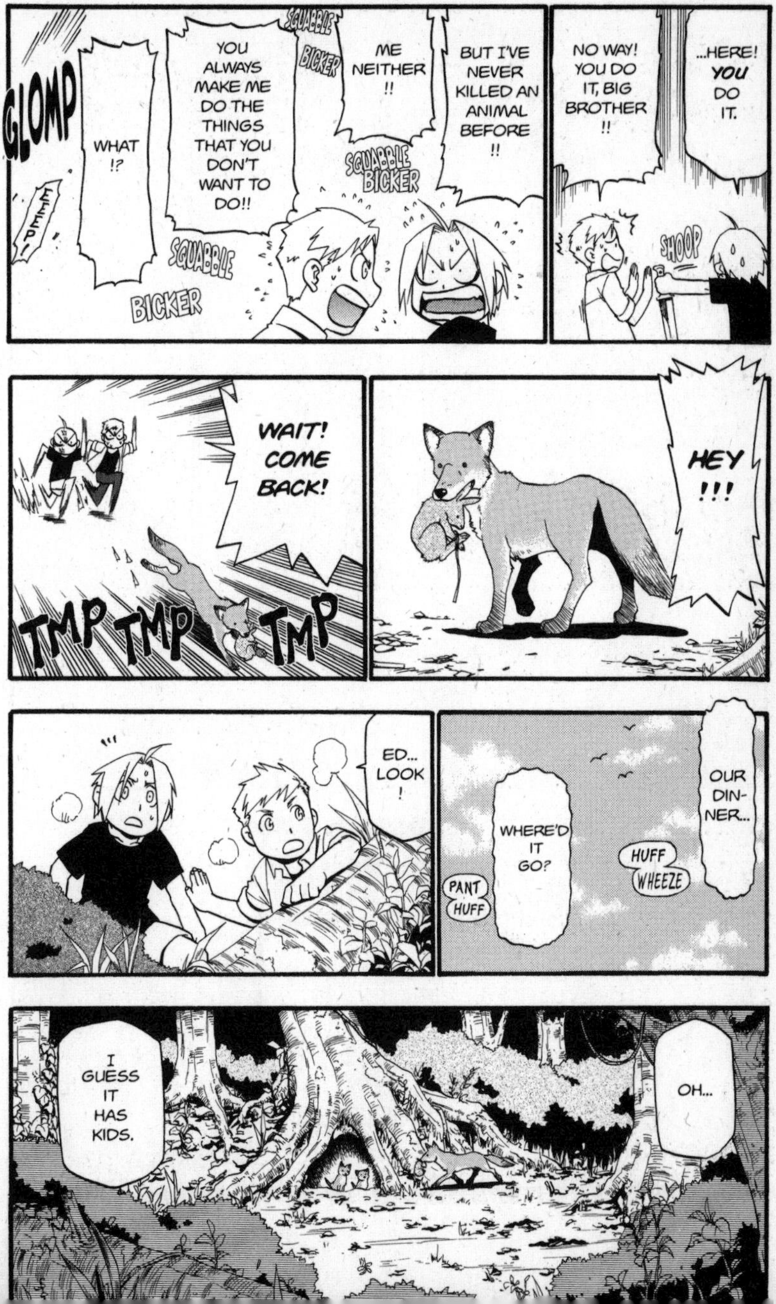
...HERE! YOU DO IT.
NO WAY! YOU DO IT, BIG BROTHER !!
SHOOP
BUT I'VE NEVER KILLED AN ANIMAL BEFORE !!
ME NEITHER !!
SQUABBLE BICKER
SQUABBLE BICKER
YOU ALWAYS MAKE ME DO THE THINGS THAT YOU DON'T WANT TO DO!!
SQUABBLE BICKER
WHAT !?
GLOMP
HEY !!!
WAIT! COME BACK!
TMP TMP TMP
OUR DINNER...
HUFF WHEEZE
WHERE'D IT GO?
PANT HUFF
ED... LOOK !
OH...
I GUESS IT HAS KIDS.

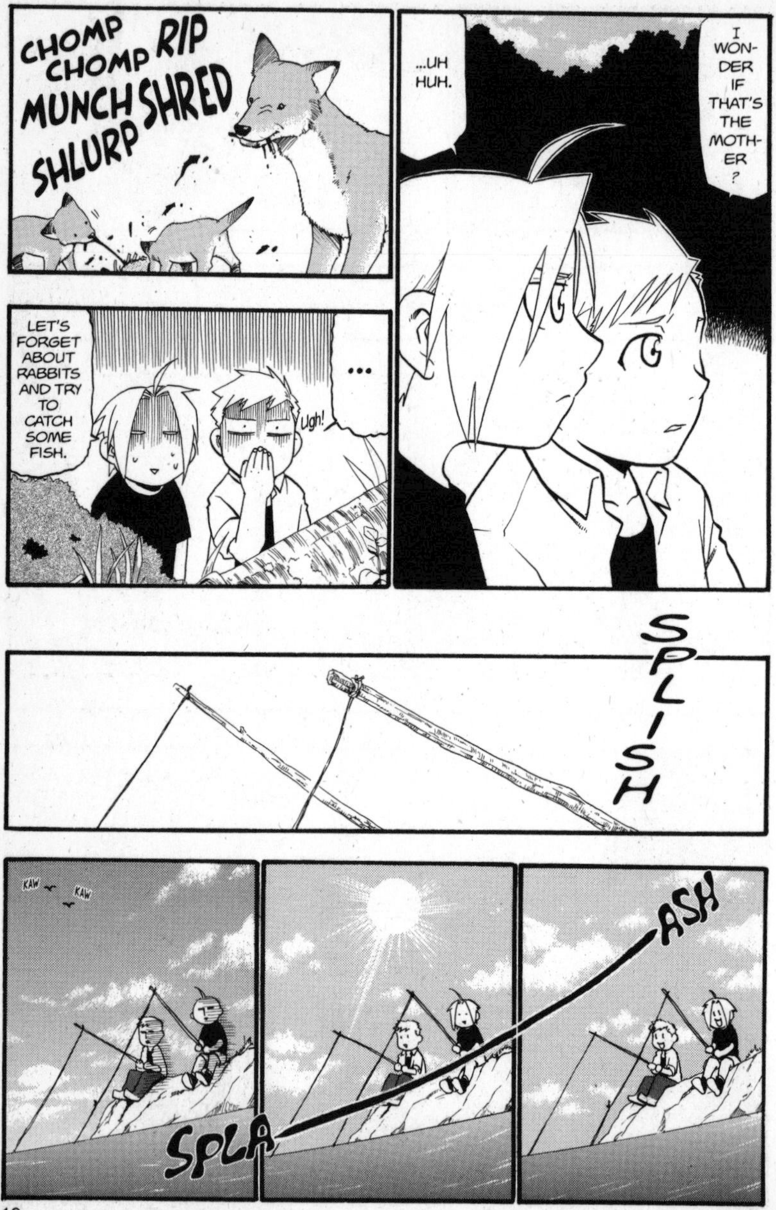
I WONDER IF THAT'S THE MOTHER?
...UH HUH.
CHOMP CHOMP RIP MUNCH SHRED SHLURP
LET'S FORGET ABOUT RABBITS AND TRY TO CATCH SOME FISH.
Ugh!
...
SPLISH
SPLA ASH
KAW KAW

...DO YOU THINK FOXES ARE EDIBLE?
MMMMBBBB
GRRMM
RE-LAX.
HEH HEH.
TUG
WHOA!
FISH!!
SHF
SHF-SHF
FIRE!!
FOOD!!
AT LAST! LET'S EAT!
STOMP

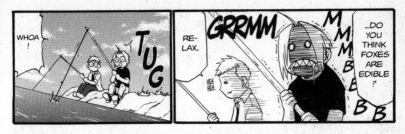

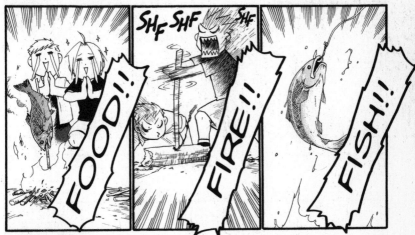

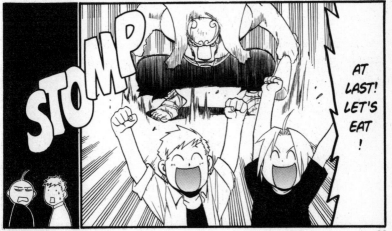

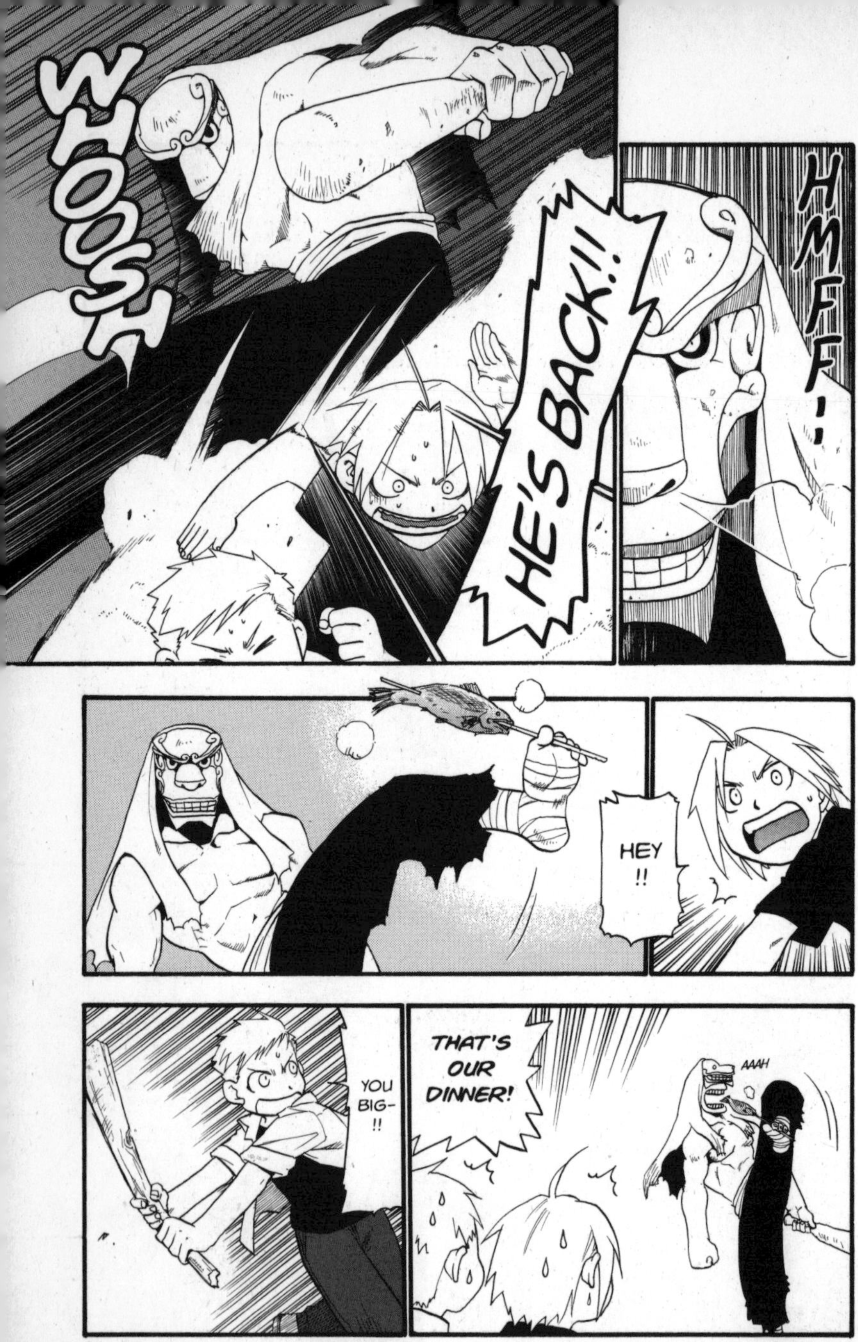
HMFF!!
HE'S BACK!!
WHOOSH
HEY!!
THAT'S OUR DINNER!
AAAH
YOU BIG-!!

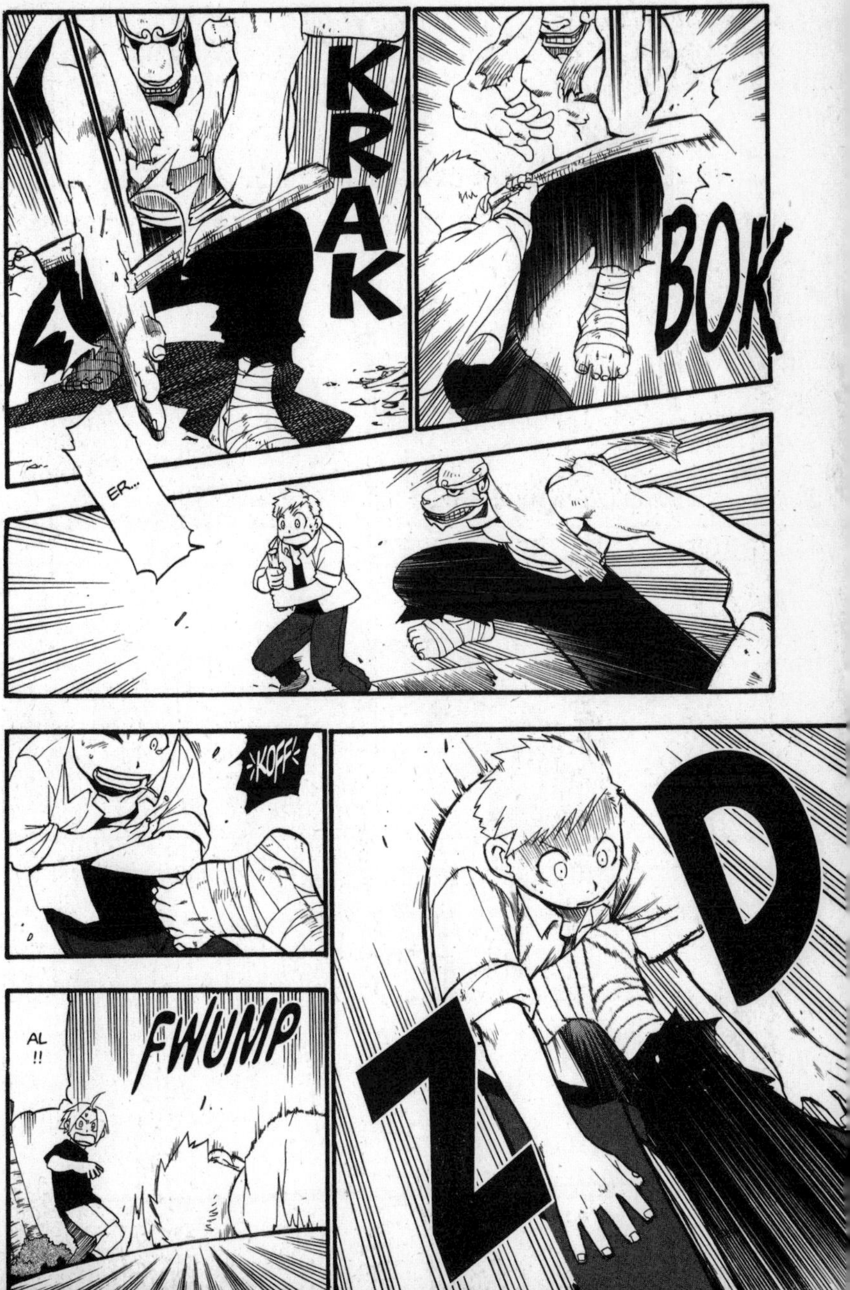
BOK
KRAK
ER...
Z
D
KOFF
FWUMP
AL !!

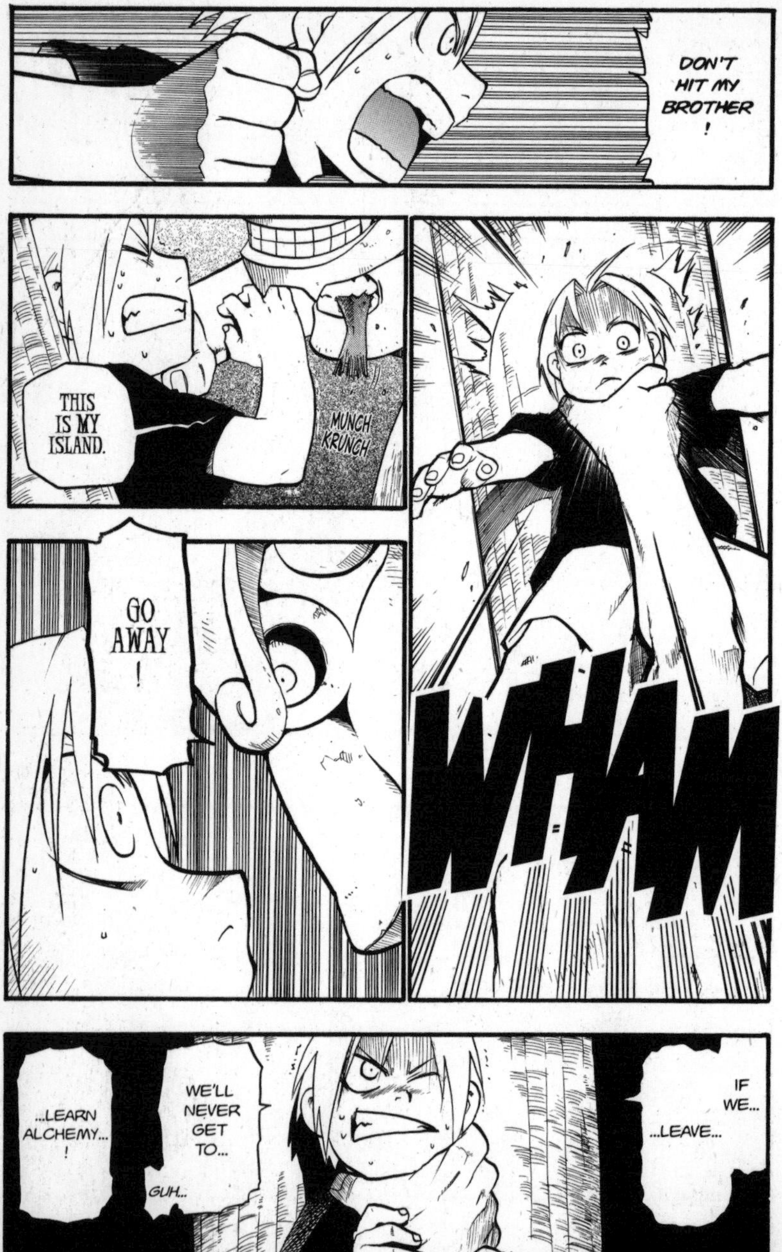
DON'T HIT MY BROTHER!
WHAM
THIS IS MY ISLAND.
MUNCH KRUNCH
GO AWAY!
IF WE...
...LEAVE...
WE'LL NEVER GET TO...
GUH...
...LEARN ALCHEMY...!

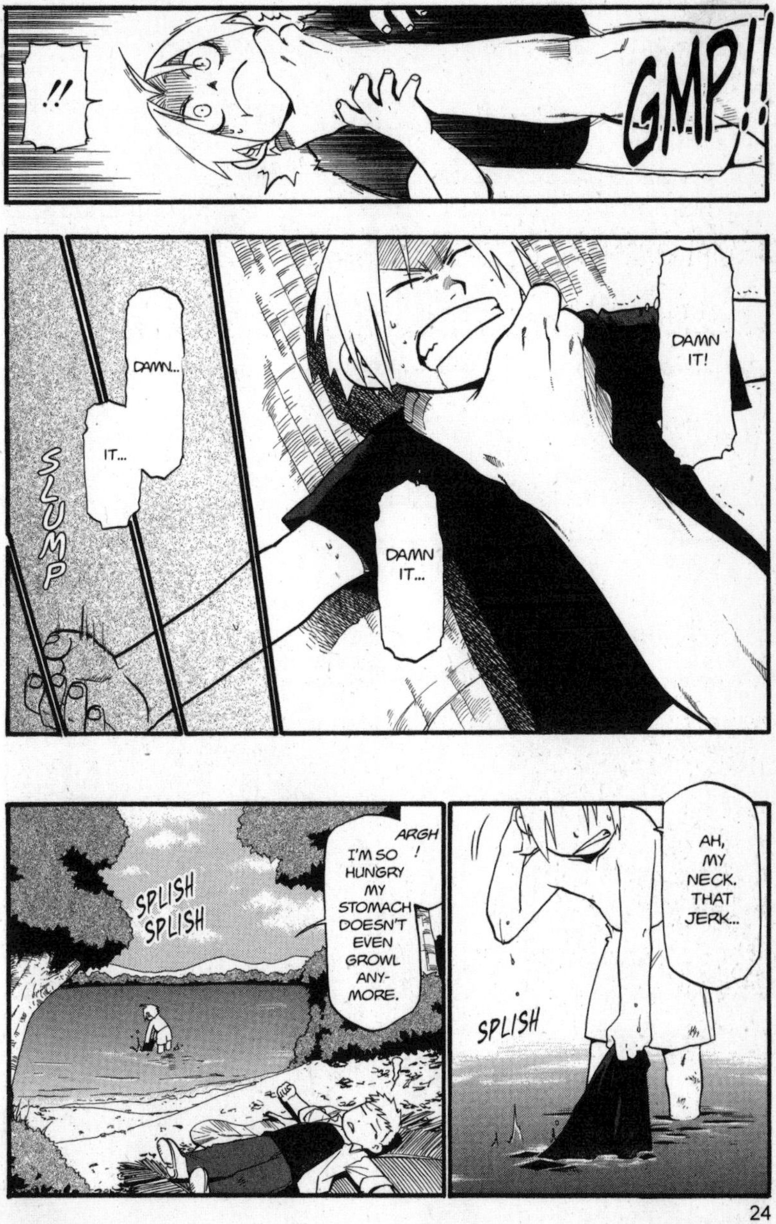
GMP!!
!!
DAMN IT!
DAMN IT...
DAMN...
IT...
SLUMP
AH, MY NECK. THAT JERK...
SPLISH
ARGH!
I'M SO HUNGRY MY STOMACH DOESN'T EVEN GROWL ANY-MORE.
SPLISH SPLISH

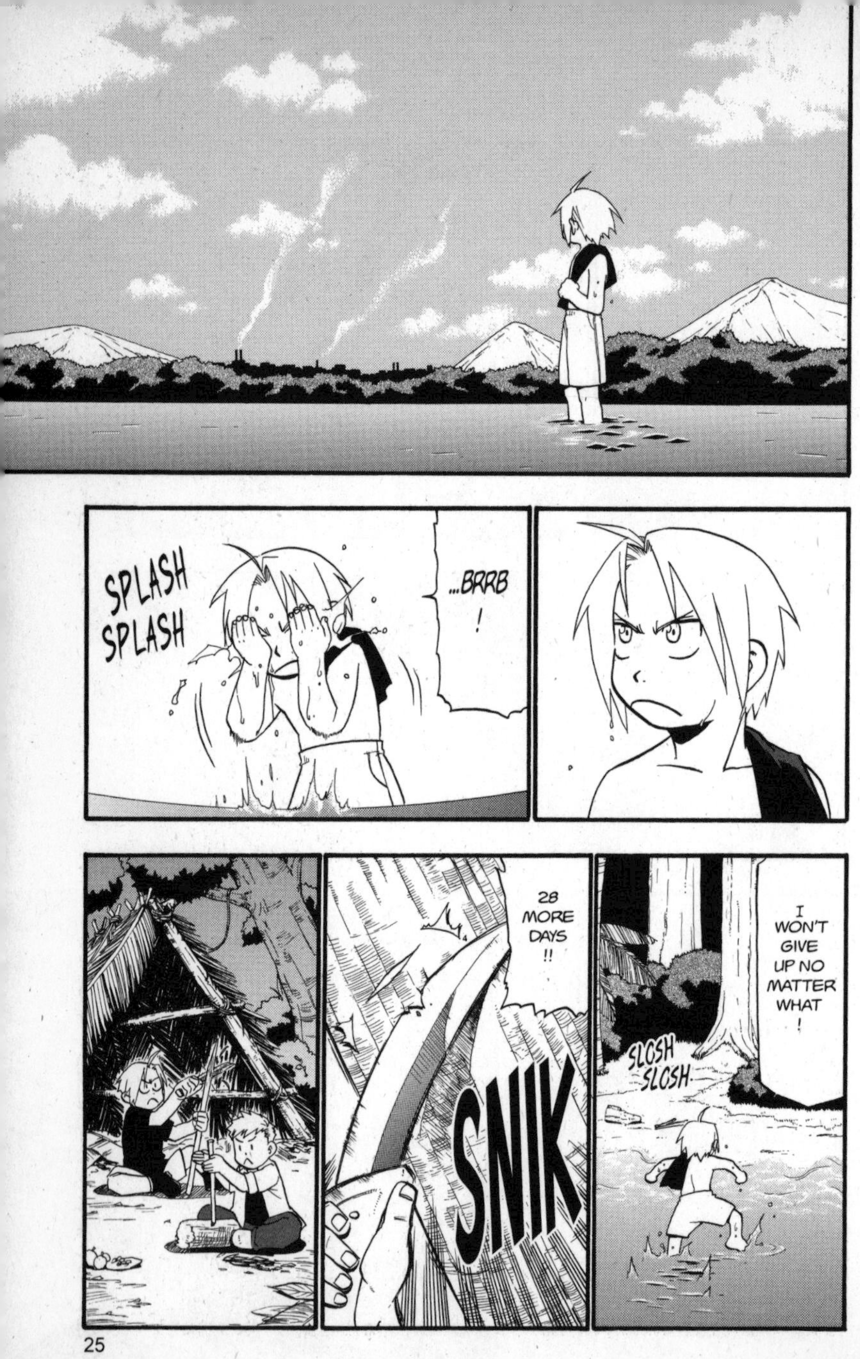
...BRRB
!
SPLASH
SPLASH
I WON'T GIVE UP NO MATTER WHAT !
SLOSH SLOSH
28 MORE DAYS !!
SNIK

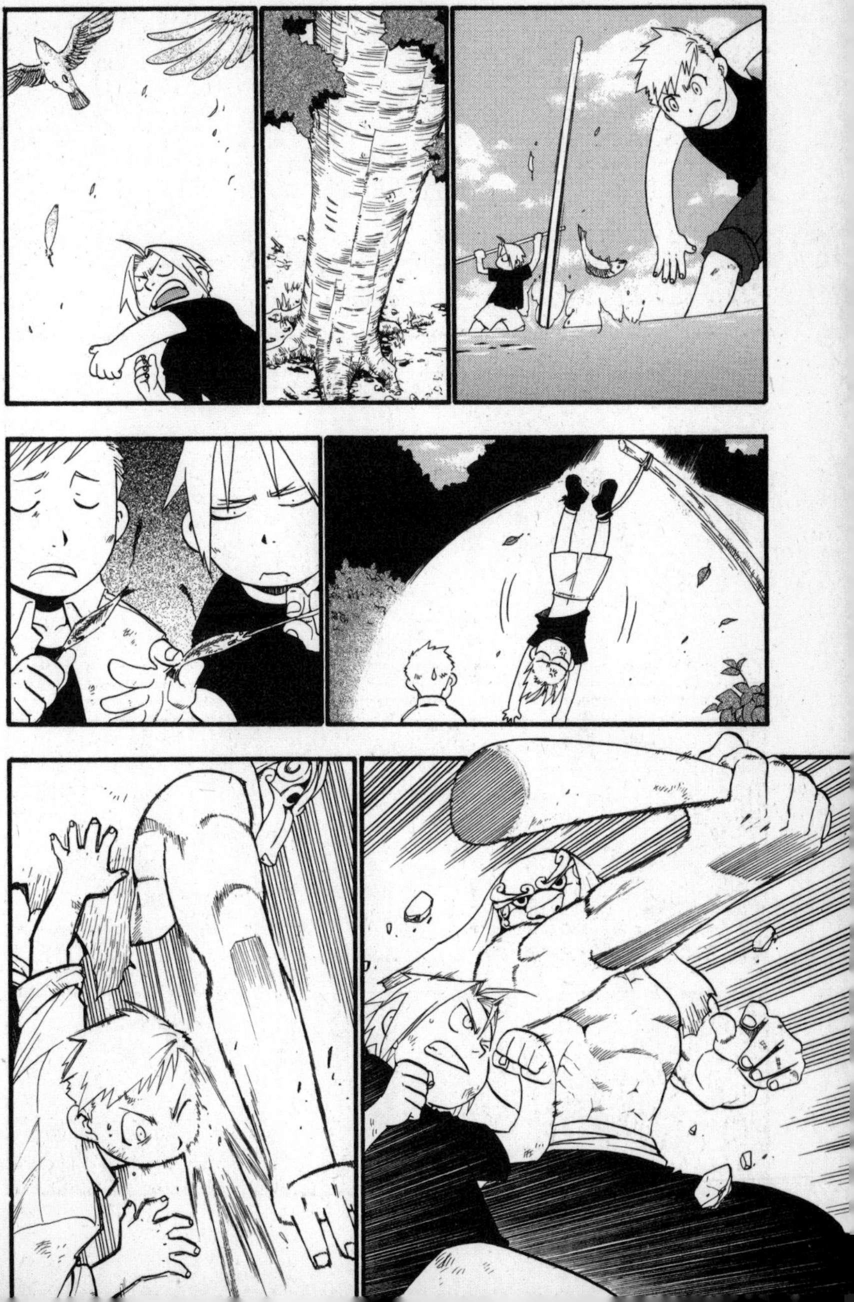

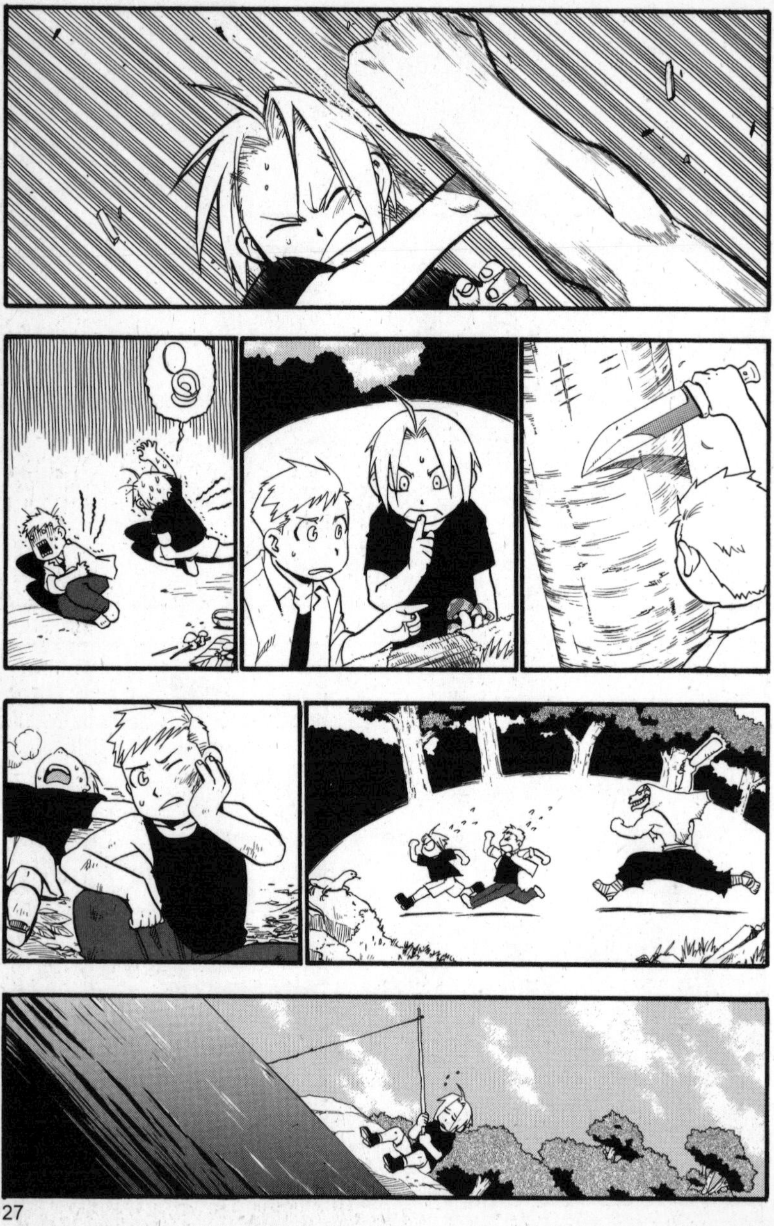

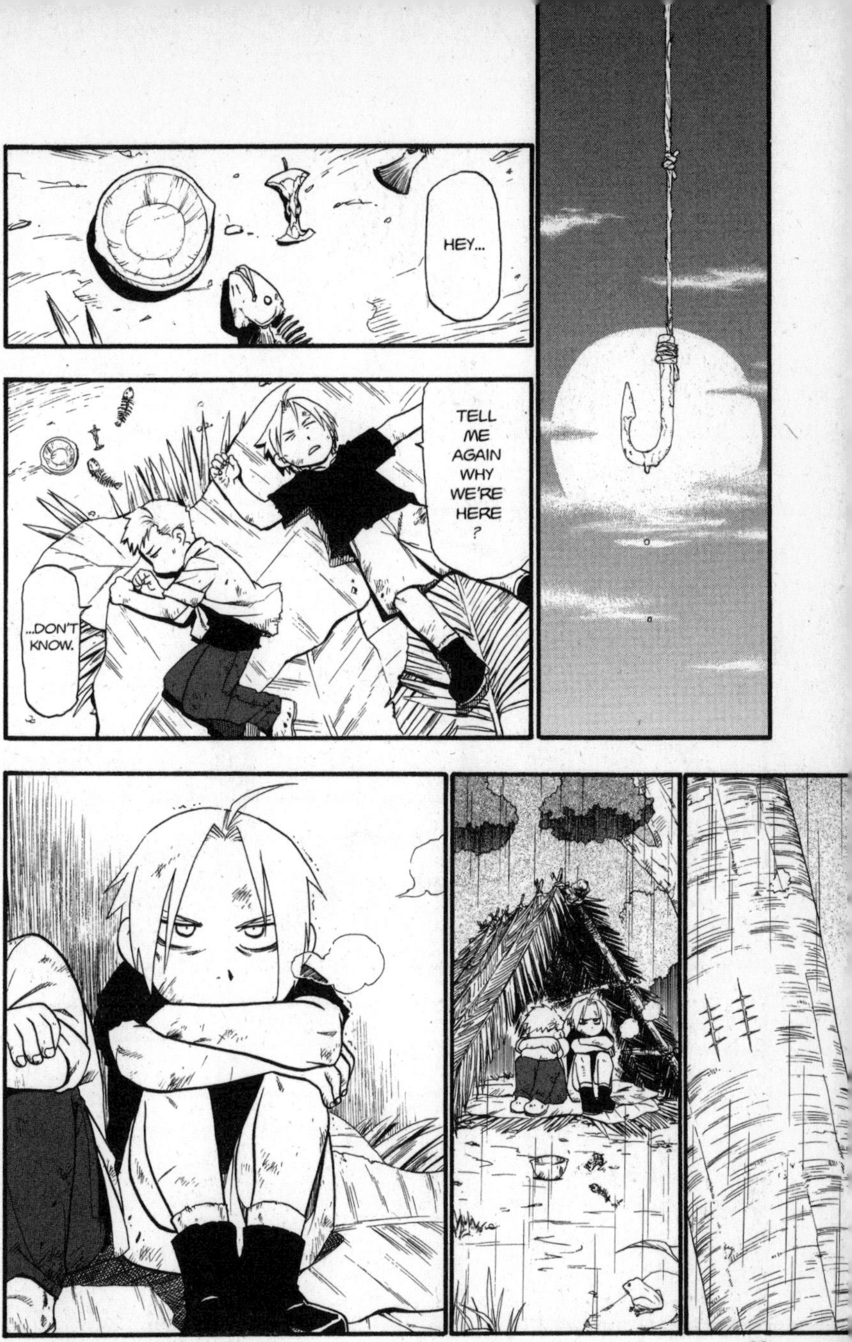
HEY...
TELL ME AGAIN WHY WE'RE HERE?
...DON'T KNOW.

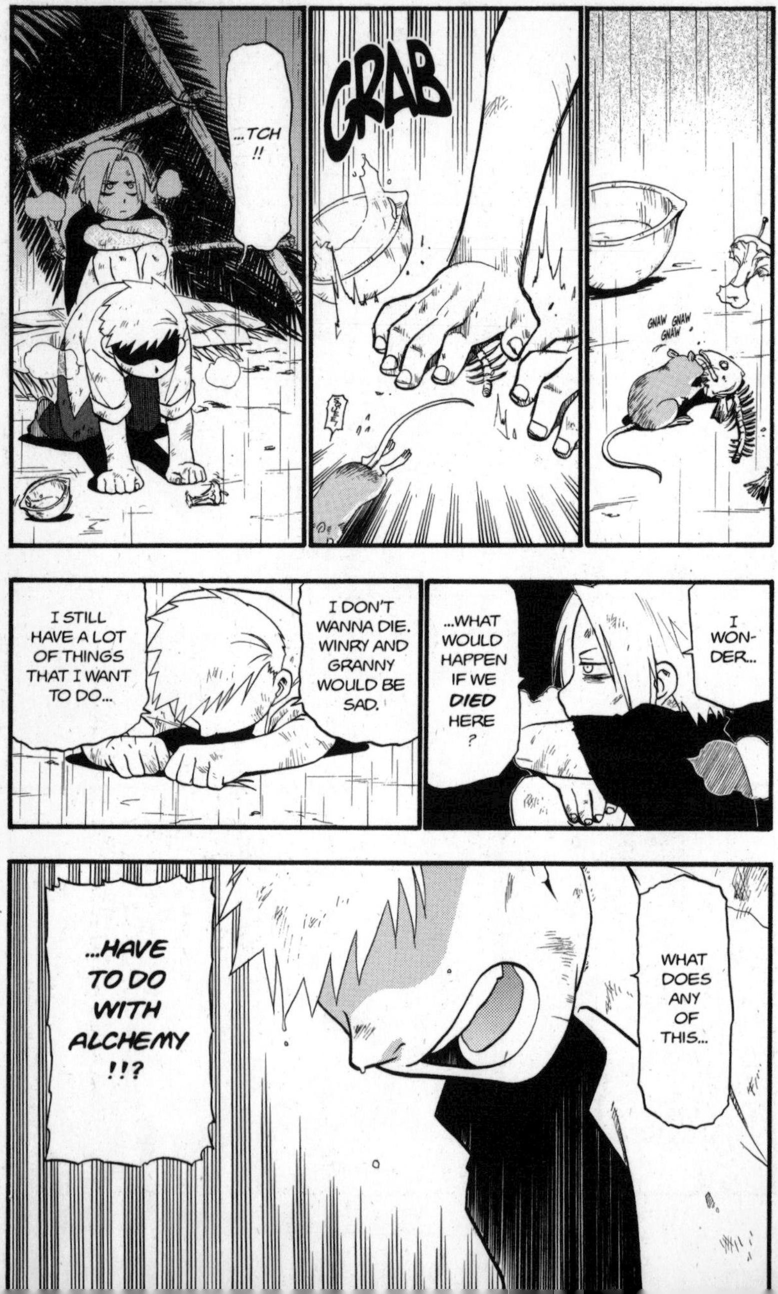
GNAW GNAW GNAW
GRAB
...TCH !!
I WON-DER...
...WHAT WOULD HAPPEN IF WE DIED HERE ?
I DON'T WANNA DIE. WINRY AND GRANNY WOULD BE SAD.
I STILL HAVE A LOT OF THINGS THAT I WANT TO DO...
WHAT DOES ANY OF THIS...
...HAVE TO DO WITH ALCHEMY !!?

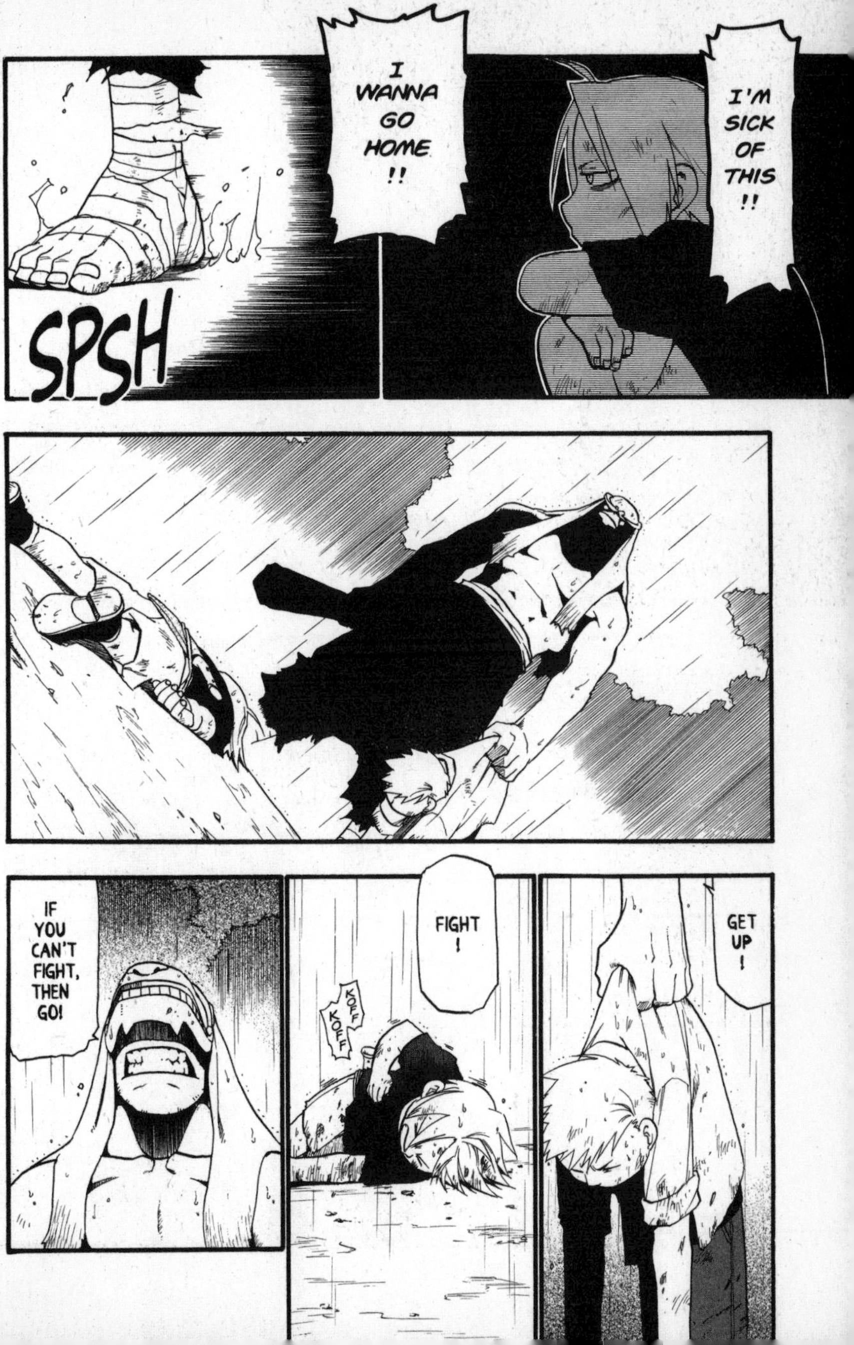
I'M SICK OF THIS!!
I WANNA GO HOME!!
SPSH
GET UP!
FIGHT!
KOFF KOFF
IF YOU CAN'T FIGHT, THEN GO!

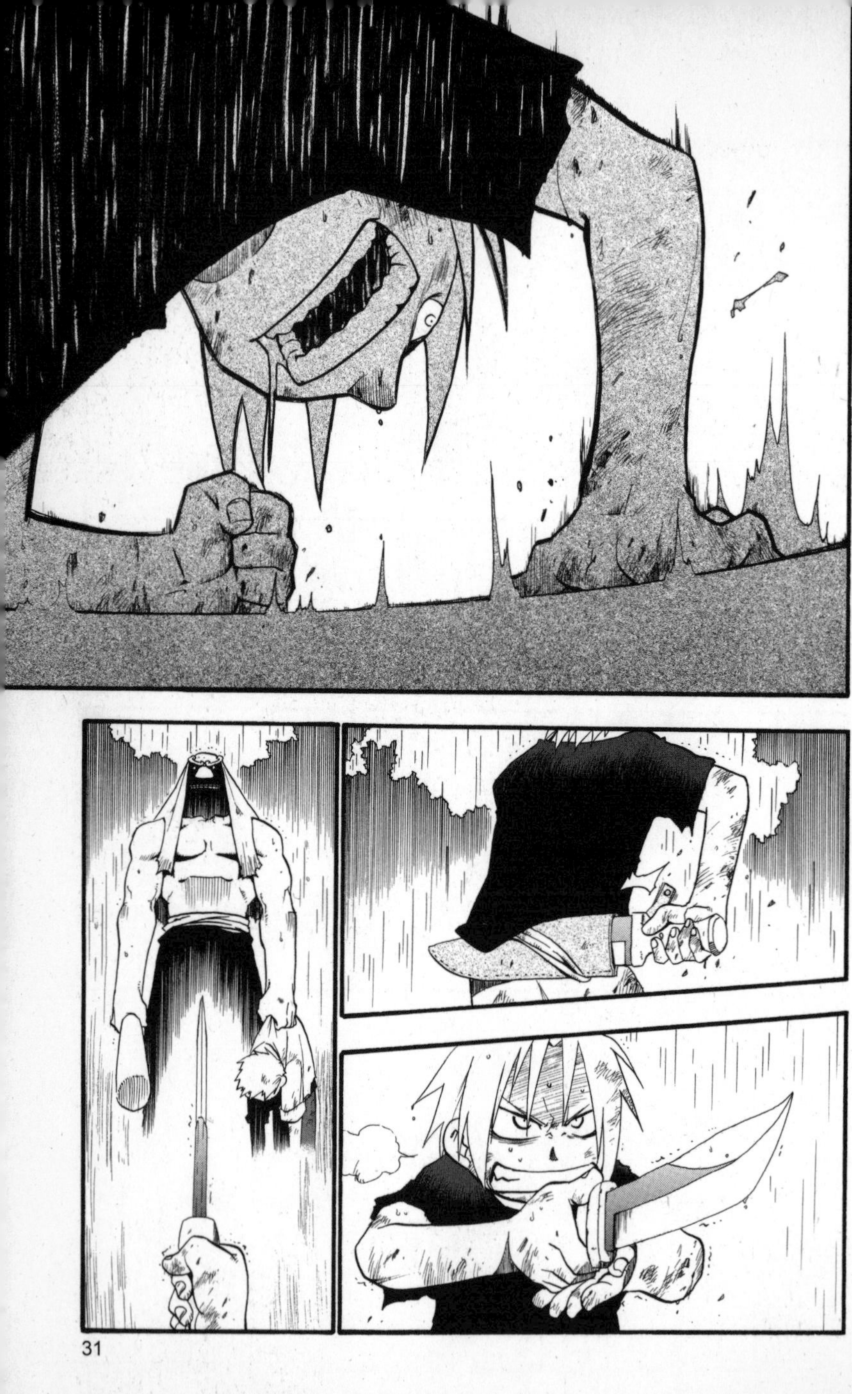

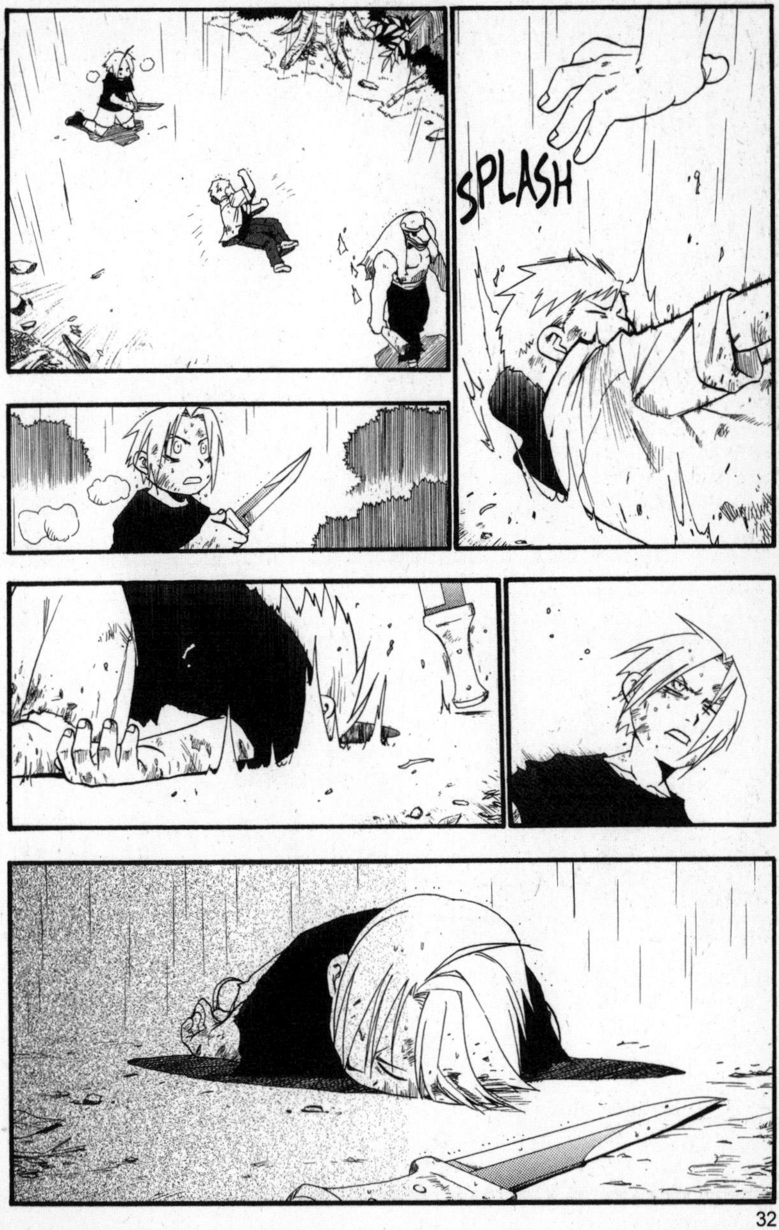
SPLASH

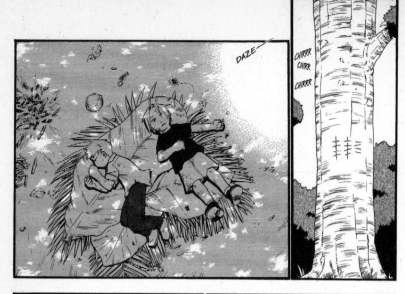

DAZE——

CHIRRR
CHIRR

CHIRRR

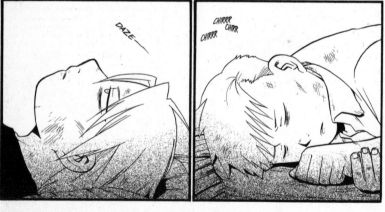

DAZE——

CHIRRR CHIRR
CHIRRR

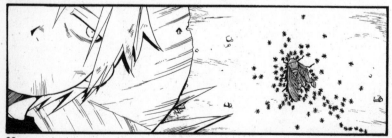

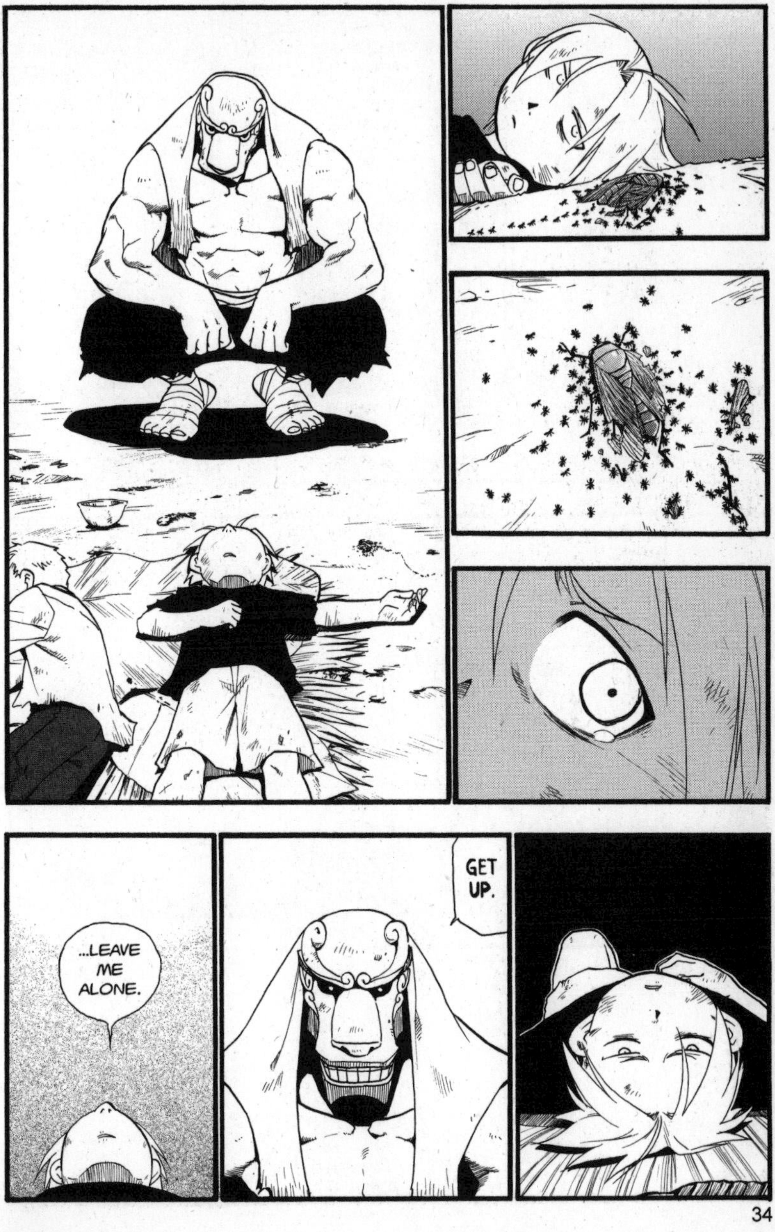
GET UP.
...LEAVE ME ALONE.

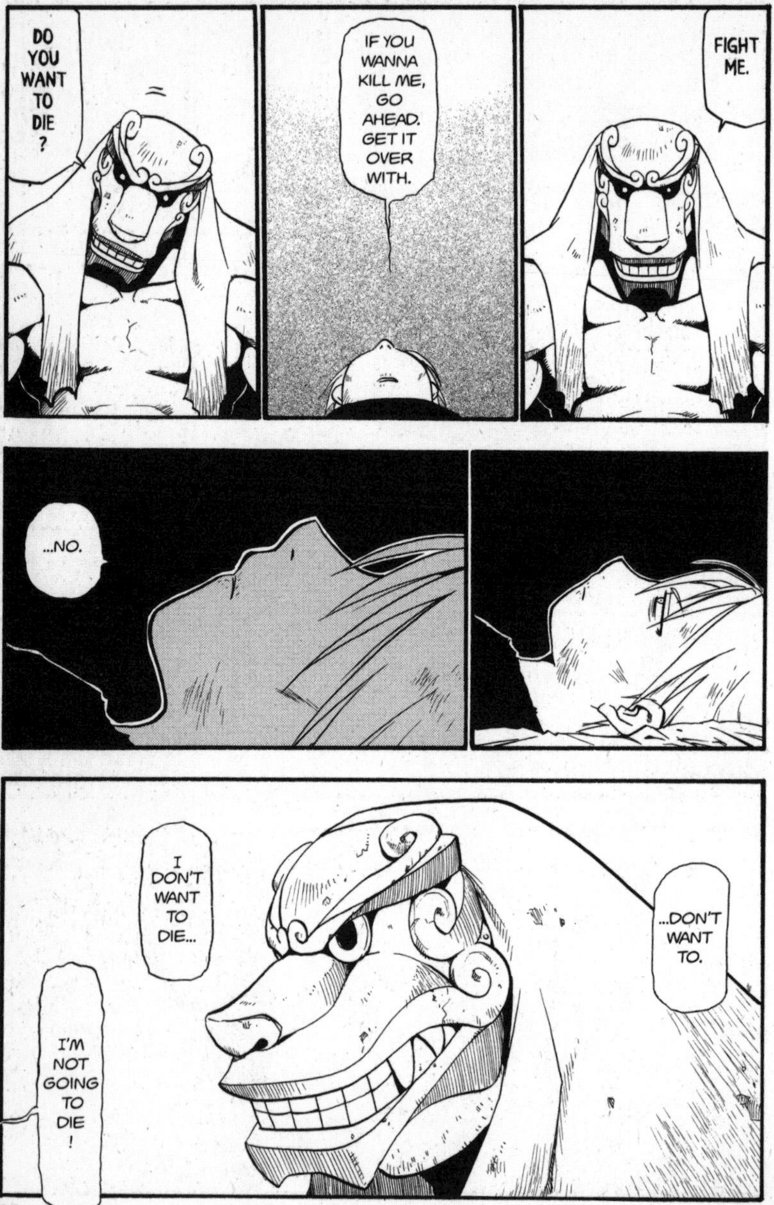
FIGHT ME.
IF YOU WANNA KILL ME, GO AHEAD. GET IT OVER WITH.
DO YOU WANT TO DIE?
...NO.
...DON'T WANT TO.
I DON'T WANT TO DIE...
I'M NOT GOING TO DIE!

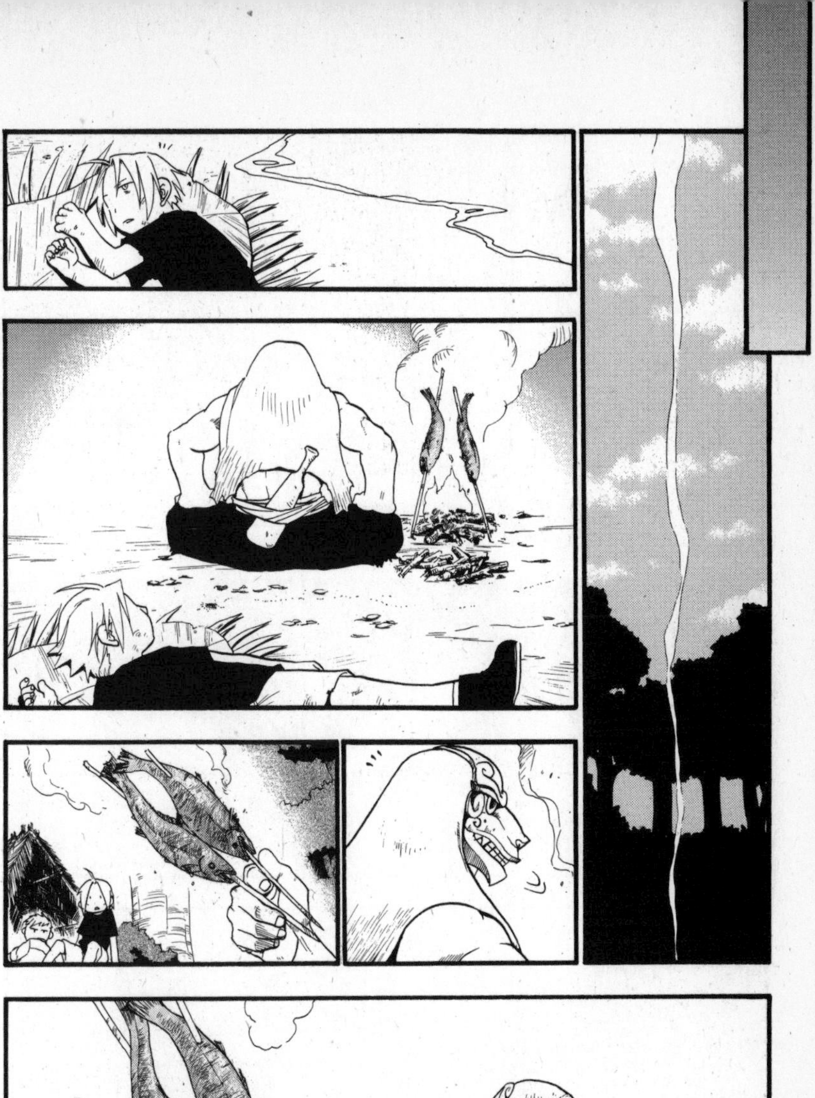

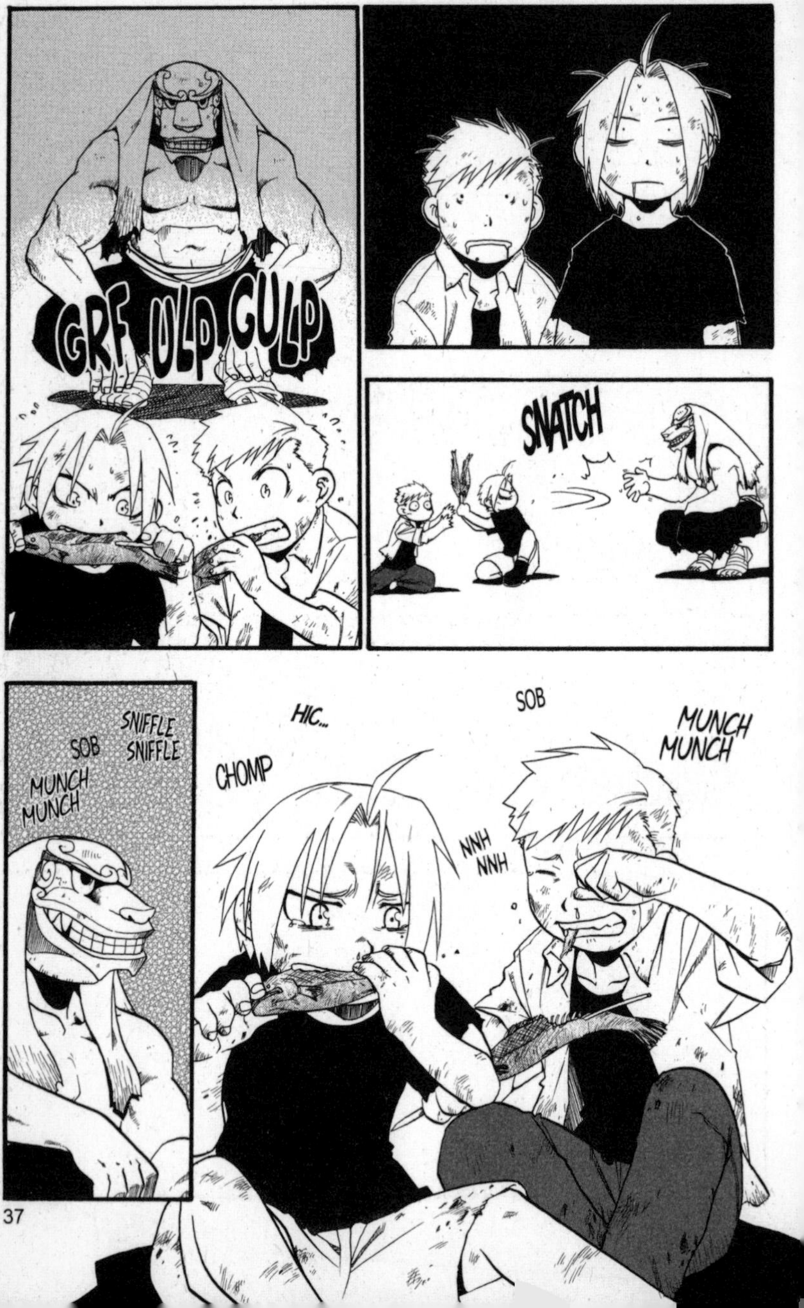
SNATCH
GRF ULP GULP
MUNCH MUNCH
SOB
HIC...
CHOMP
NNH NNH
SNIFFLE SNIFFLE
SOB
MUNCH MUNCH

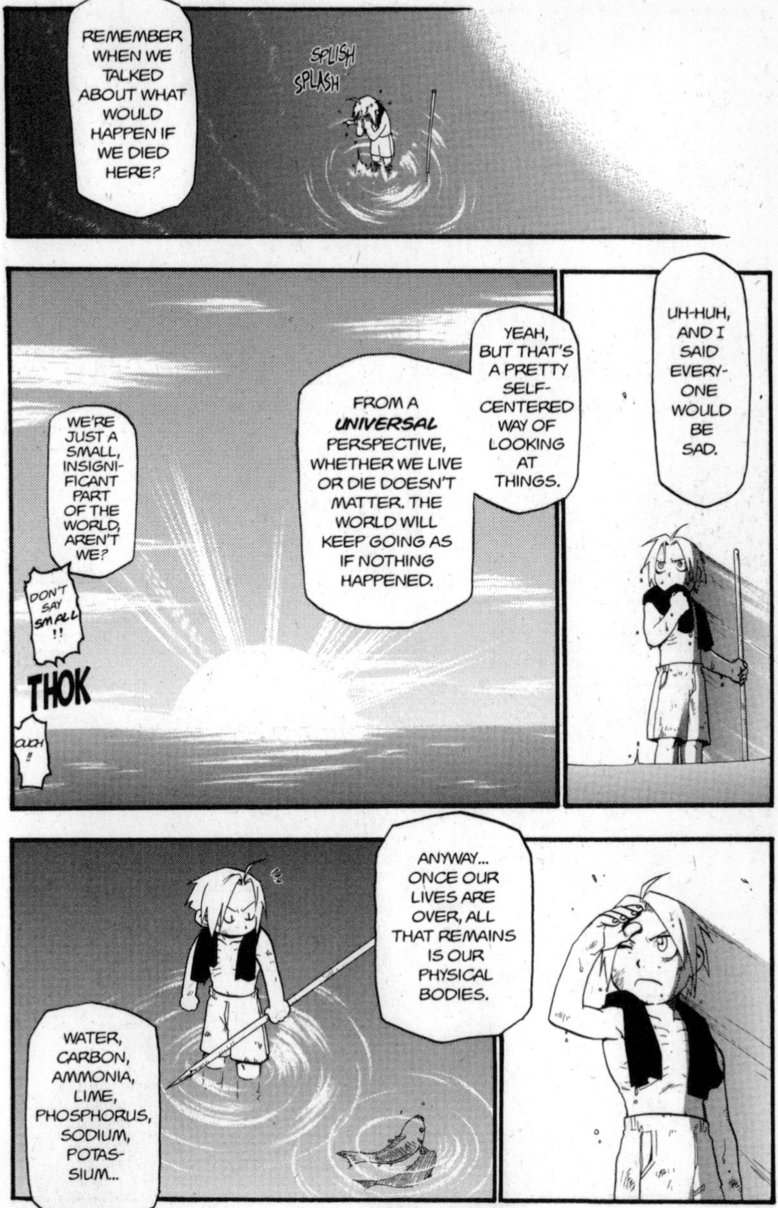
REMEMBER WHEN WE TALKED ABOUT WHAT WOULD HAPPEN IF WE DIED HERE?
SPLISH
SPLASH
UH-HUH, AND I SAID EVERYONE WOULD BE SAD.
YEAH, BUT THAT'S A PRETTY SELF-CENTERED WAY OF LOOKING AT THINGS.
FROM A UNIVERSAL PERSPECTIVE, WHETHER WE LIVE OR DIE DOESN'T MATTER. THE WORLD WILL KEEP GOING AS IF NOTHING HAPPENED.
WE'RE JUST A SMALL, INSIGNIFICANT PART OF THE WORLD, AREN'T WE?
DON'T SAY SMALL!!
THOK
OUCH!!
ANYWAY... ONCE OUR LIVES ARE OVER, ALL THAT REMAINS IS OUR PHYSICAL BODIES.
WATER, CARBON, AMMONIA, LIME, PHOSPHORUS, SODIUM, POTASSIUM...

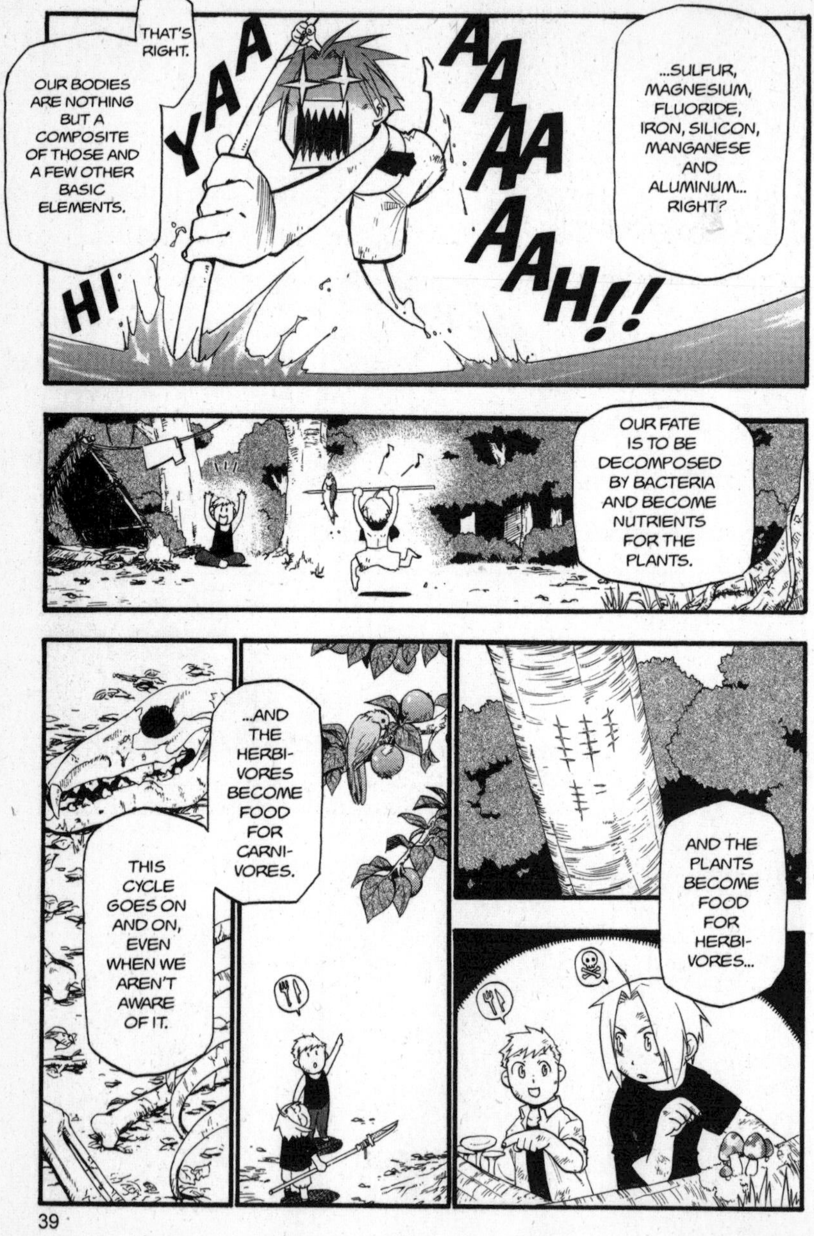
...SULFUR, MAGNESIUM, FLUORIDE, IRON, SILICON, MANGANESE AND ALUMINUM... RIGHT?
HI YAA AAAAAAH!!
THAT'S RIGHT.
OUR BODIES ARE NOTHING BUT A COMPOSITE OF THOSE AND A FEW OTHER BASIC ELEMENTS.
OUR FATE IS TO BE DECOMPOSED BY BACTERIA AND BECOME NUTRIENTS FOR THE PLANTS.
AND THE PLANTS BECOME FOOD FOR HERBI-VORES...
...AND THE HERBI-VORES BECOME FOOD FOR CARNI-VORES.
THIS CYCLE GOES ON AND ON, EVEN WHEN WE AREN'T AWARE OF IT.

EEP EEP
I'M SORRY.
SHUNK
DROOL...

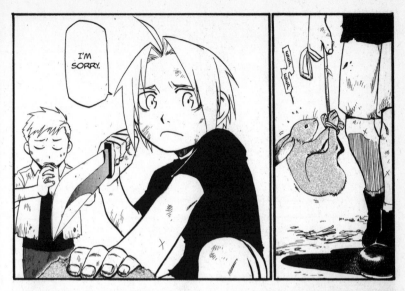

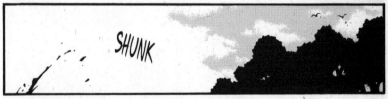

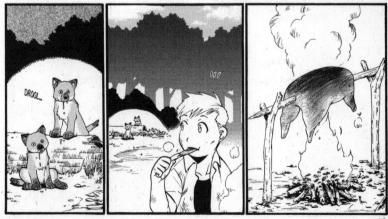

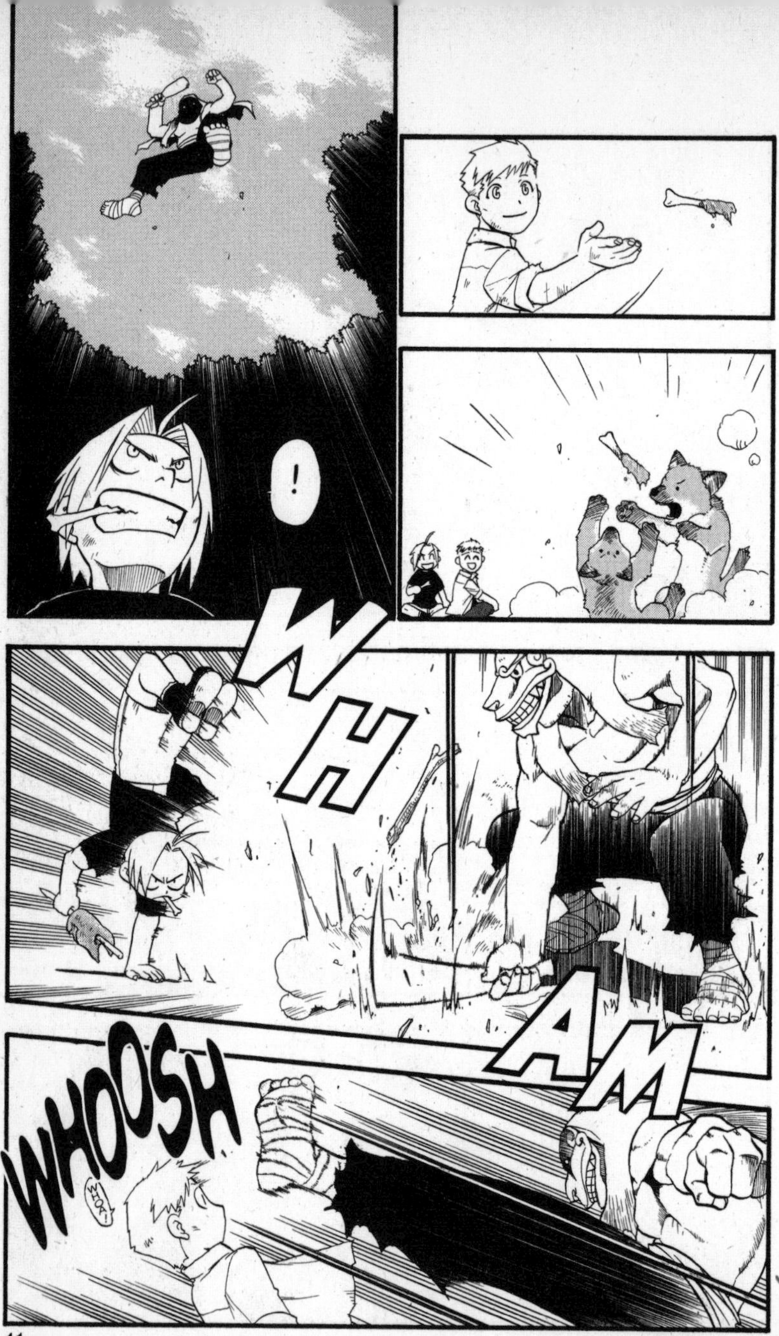
!
WHAM
WHOOSH
WHOA!

TAKE THAT !
LEAP
BAM BAM BAM BAM BAM BAM
KICK
HEY !!
I GOT IT!

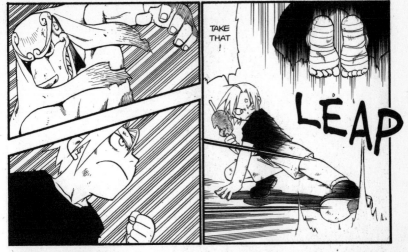

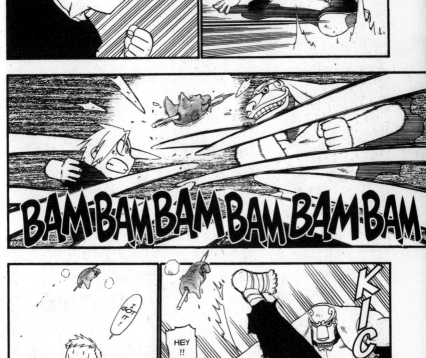

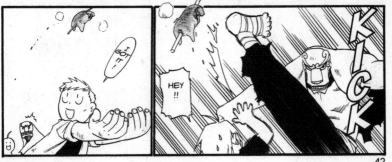

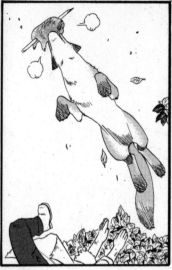

LIFE IS A *COMPLEX CYCLE,* SO VAST THAT WE CAN'T SEE IT WITH OUR OWN EYES.

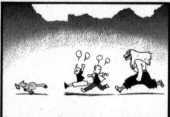

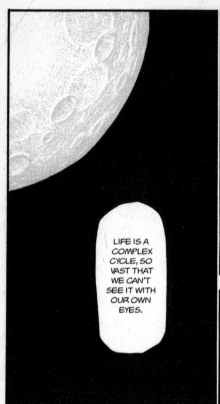

MAYBE IT'S "THE WORLD," MAYBE IT'S "THE UNIVERSE"...

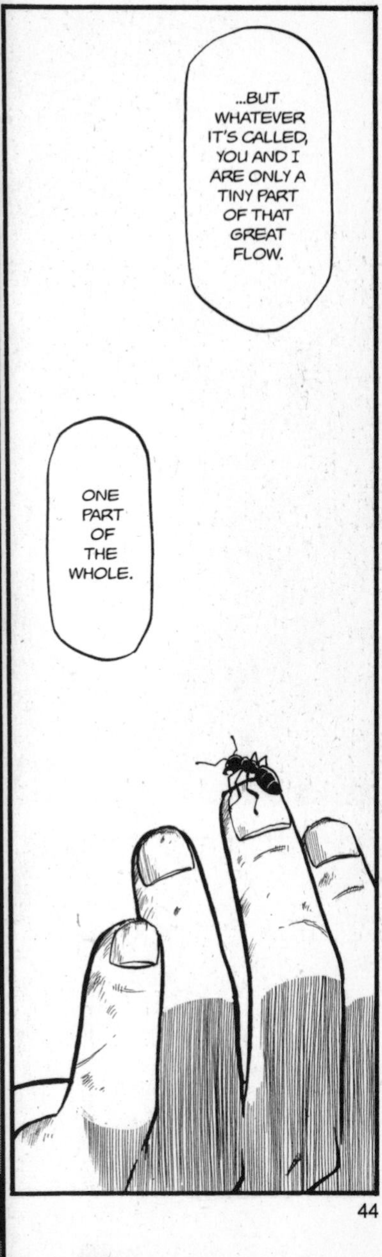
...BUT WHATEVER IT'S CALLED, YOU AND I ARE ONLY A TINY PART OF THAT GREAT FLOW.
ONE PART OF THE WHOLE.

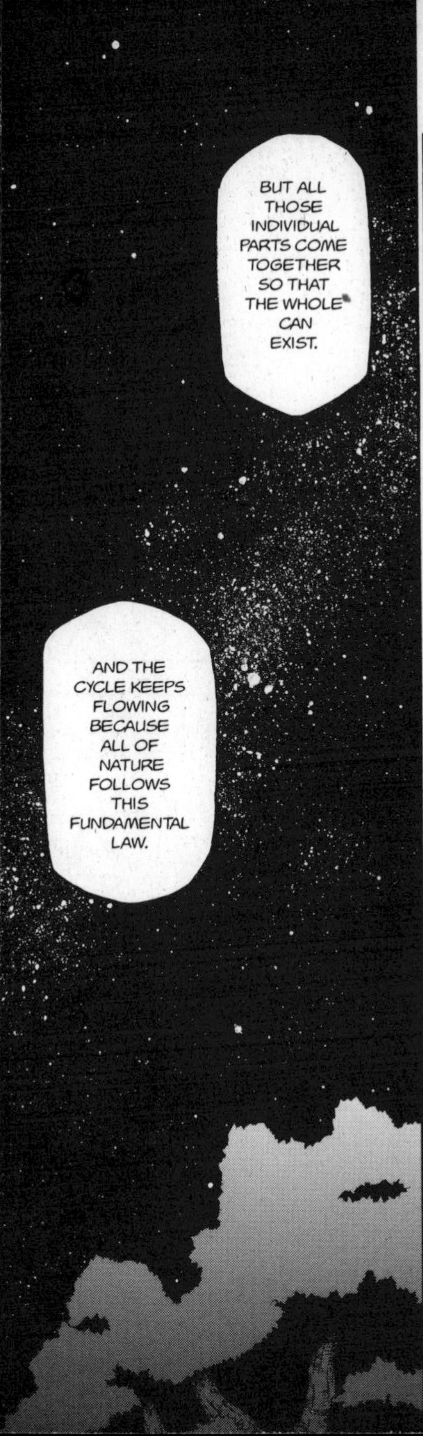
BUT ALL THOSE INDIVIDUAL PARTS COME TOGETHER SO THAT THE WHOLE CAN EXIST.
AND THE CYCLE KEEPS FLOWING BECAUSE ALL OF NATURE FOLLOWS THIS FUNDAMENTAL LAW.

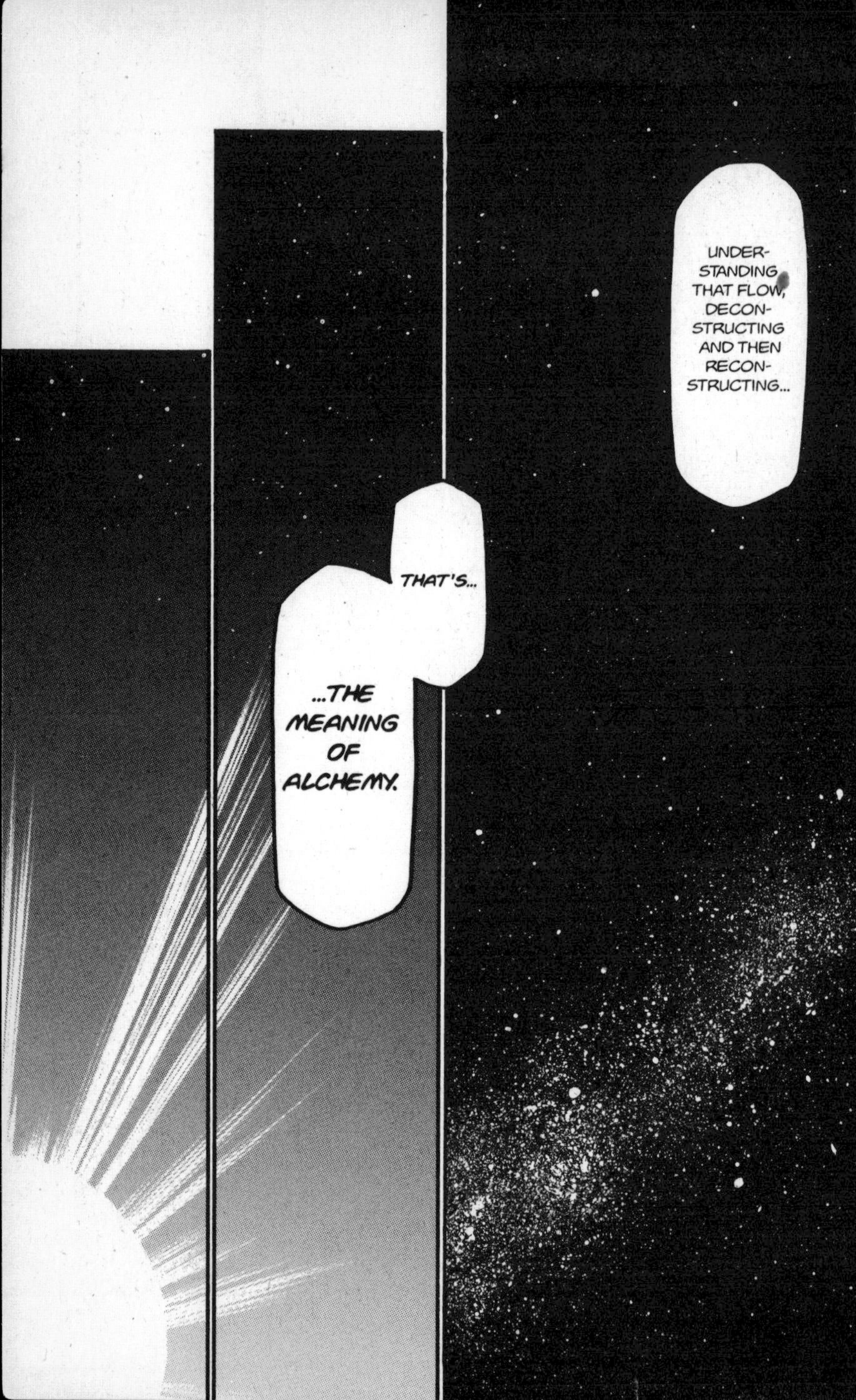
UNDER-STANDING THAT FLOW, DECON-STRUCTING AND THEN RECON-STRUCTING...
THAT'S...
...THE MEANING OF ALCHEMY.

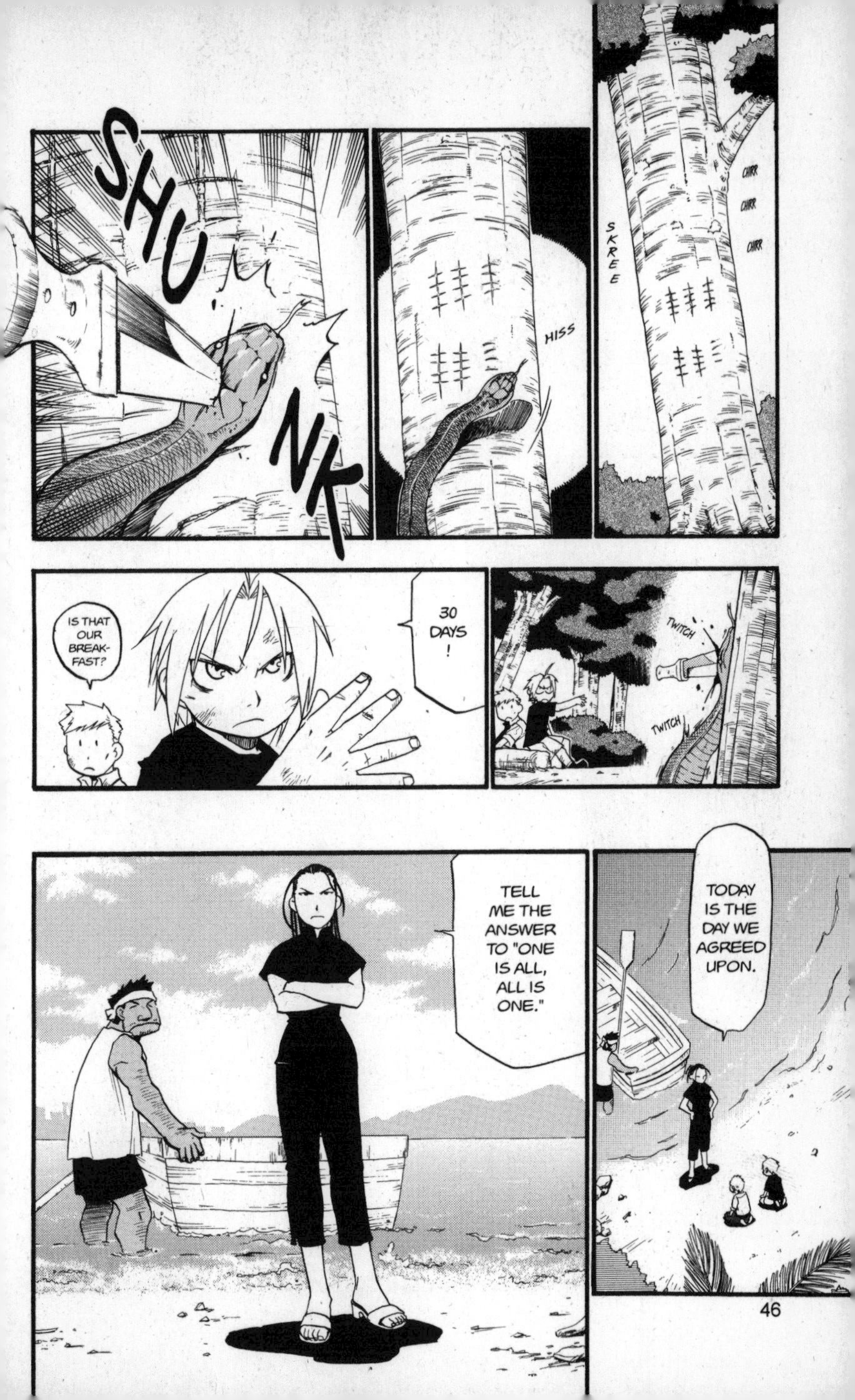
SKREE
CHIRR
CHIRR
CHIRR
HISS
SHU
NK
TWITCH
TWITCH
30 DAYS!
IS THAT OUR BREAK-FAST?
TODAY IS THE DAY WE AGREED UPON.
TELL ME THE ANSWER TO "ONE IS ALL, ALL IS ONE."

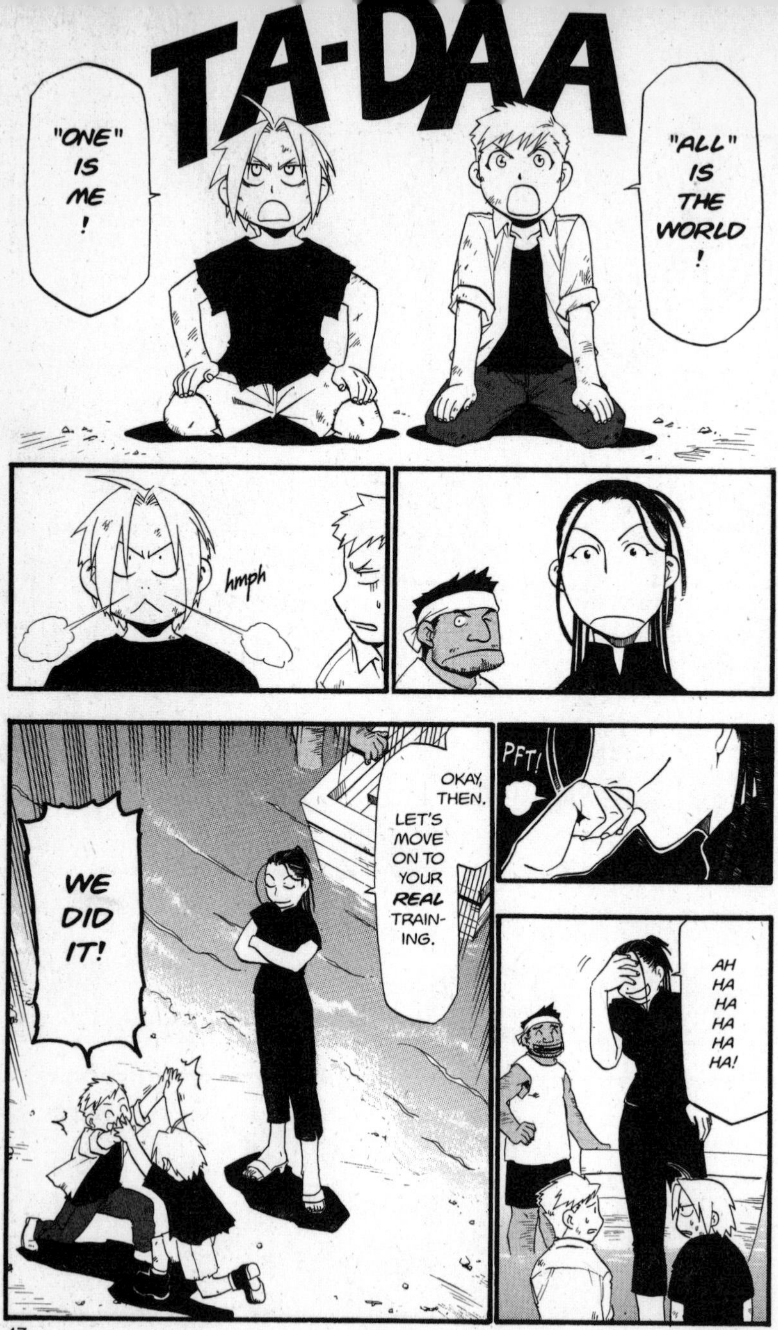
TA-DAA
"ALL" IS THE WORLD!
"ONE" IS ME!
hmph
PFT!
AH HA HA HA HA HA!
OKAY, THEN. LET'S MOVE ON TO YOUR REAL TRAINING.
WE DID IT!

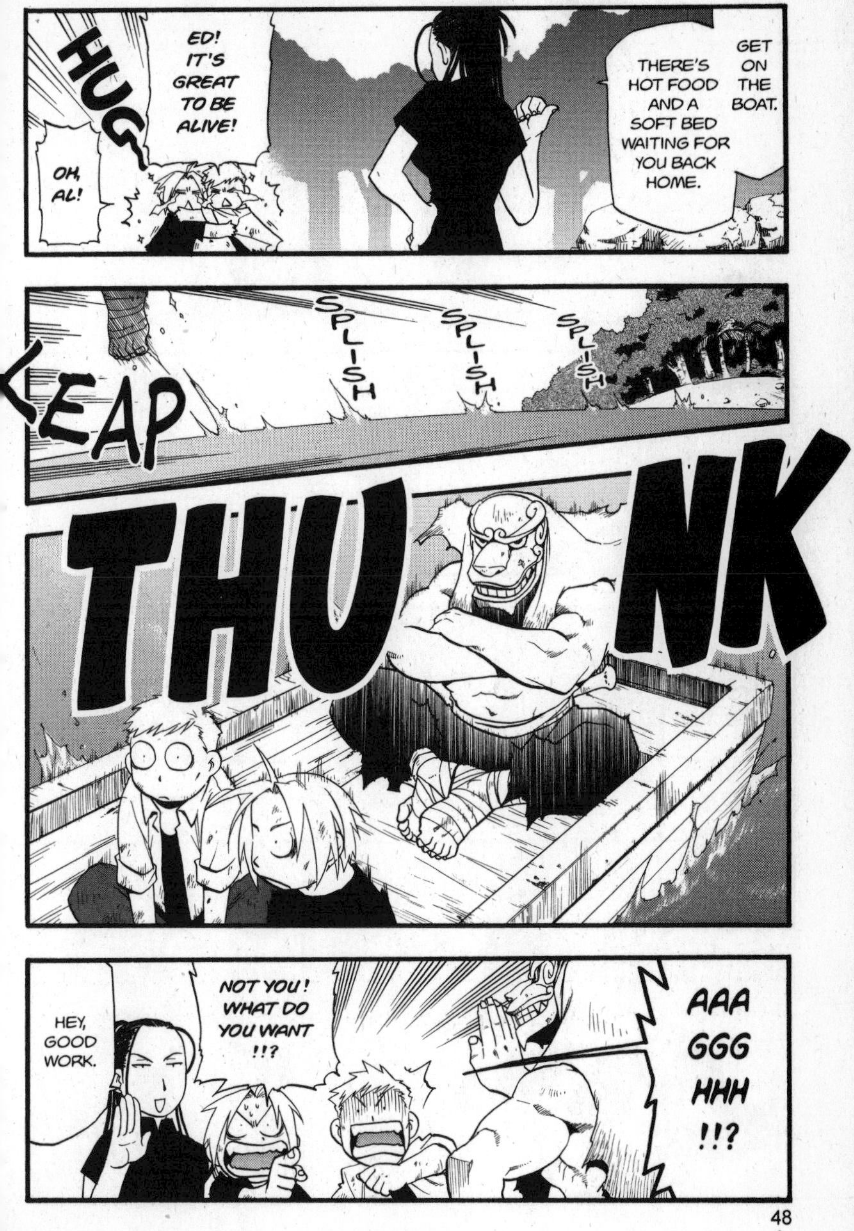
GET ON THE BOAT.
THERE'S HOT FOOD AND A SOFT BED WAITING FOR YOU BACK HOME.
ED! IT'S GREAT TO BE ALIVE!
HUG
OH, AL!
SPLISH
SPLISH
SPLISH
LEAP
THUNK
AAAGGGHHH!!?
NOT YOU! WHAT DO YOU WANT!!?
HEY, GOOD WORK.

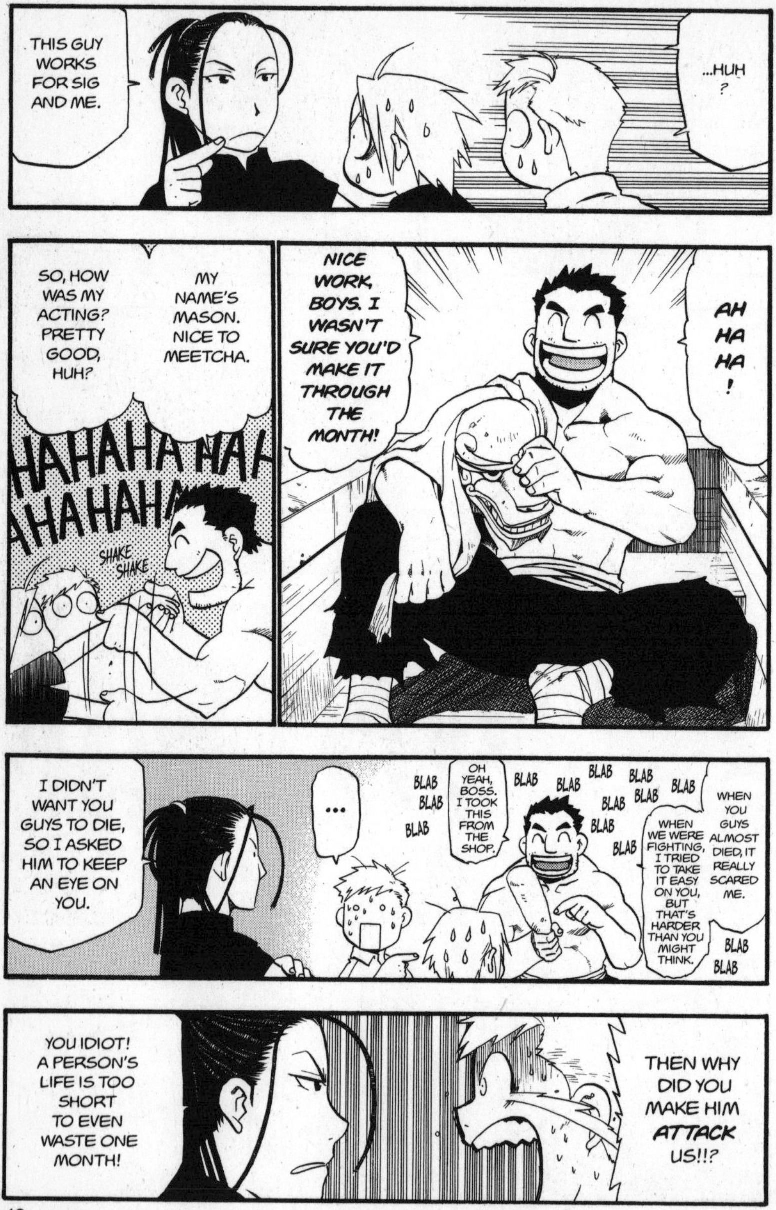
...HUH ?
THIS GUY WORKS FOR SIG AND ME.
AH HA HA !
NICE WORK, BOYS. I WASN'T SURE YOU'D MAKE IT THROUGH THE MONTH!
MY NAME'S MASON. NICE TO MEETCHA.
SO, HOW WAS MY ACTING? PRETTY GOOD, HUH?
HAHAHA HAH AHAHAHA
SHAKE SHAKE
WHEN YOU GUYS ALMOST DIED, IT REALLY SCARED ME.
WHEN WE WERE FIGHTING, I TRIED TO TAKE IT EASY ON YOU, BUT THAT'S HARDER THAN YOU MIGHT THINK.
BLAB BLAB
BLAB BLAB BLAB BLAB BLAB BLAB BLAB BLAB
OH YEAH, BOSS. I TOOK THIS FROM THE SHOP.
BLAB BLAB BLAB
...
I DIDN'T WANT YOU GUYS TO DIE, SO I ASKED HIM TO KEEP AN EYE ON YOU.
THEN WHY DID YOU MAKE HIM ATTACK US!!?
YOU IDIOT! A PERSON'S LIFE IS TOO SHORT TO EVEN WASTE ONE MONTH!

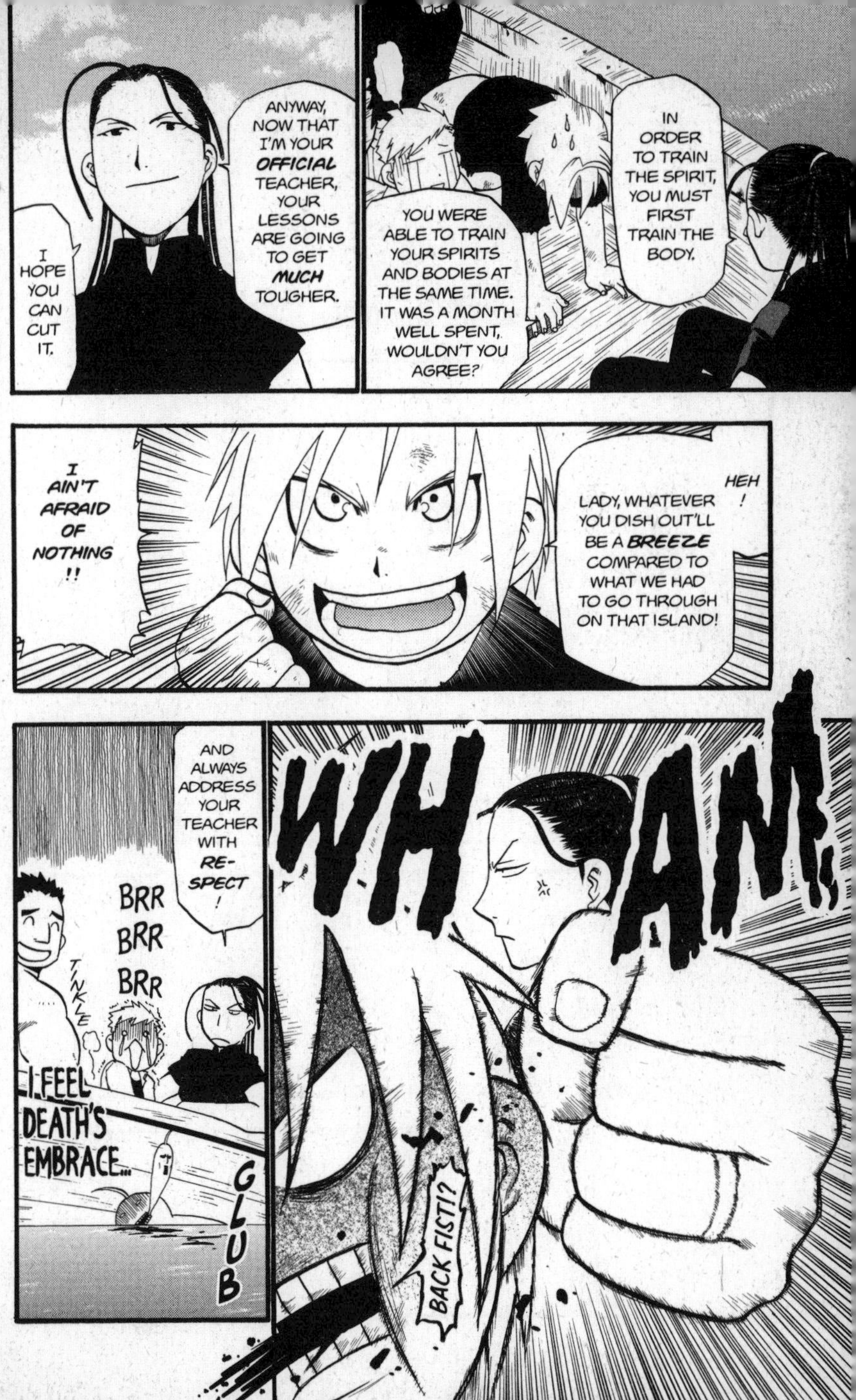
IN ORDER TO TRAIN THE SPIRIT, YOU MUST FIRST TRAIN THE BODY.
YOU WERE ABLE TO TRAIN YOUR SPIRITS AND BODIES AT THE SAME TIME. IT WAS A MONTH WELL SPENT, WOULDN'T YOU AGREE?
ANYWAY, NOW THAT I'M YOUR OFFICIAL TEACHER, YOUR LESSONS ARE GOING TO GET MUCH TOUGHER.
I HOPE YOU CAN CUT IT.
HEH!
LADY, WHATEVER YOU DISH OUT'LL BE A BREEZE COMPARED TO WHAT WE HAD TO GO THROUGH ON THAT ISLAND!
I AIN'T AFRAID OF NOTHING!!
WHAM!
BACK FIST!?
AND ALWAYS ADDRESS YOUR TEACHER WITH RE-SPECT!
BRR BRR BRR
TINKLE
I FEEL DEATH'S EMBRACE...
GLUB

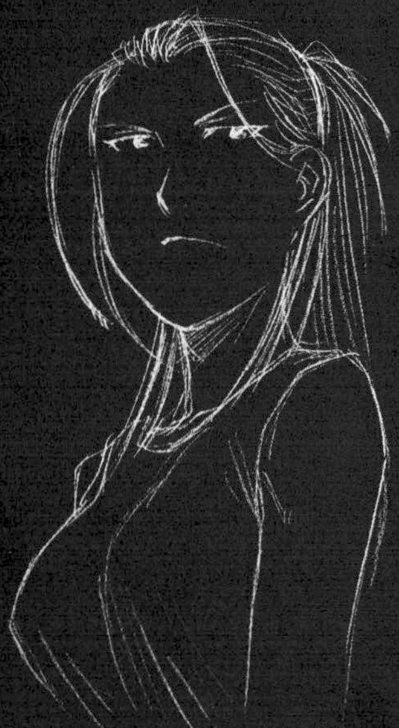

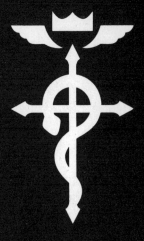

FULLMETAL
ALCHEMIST

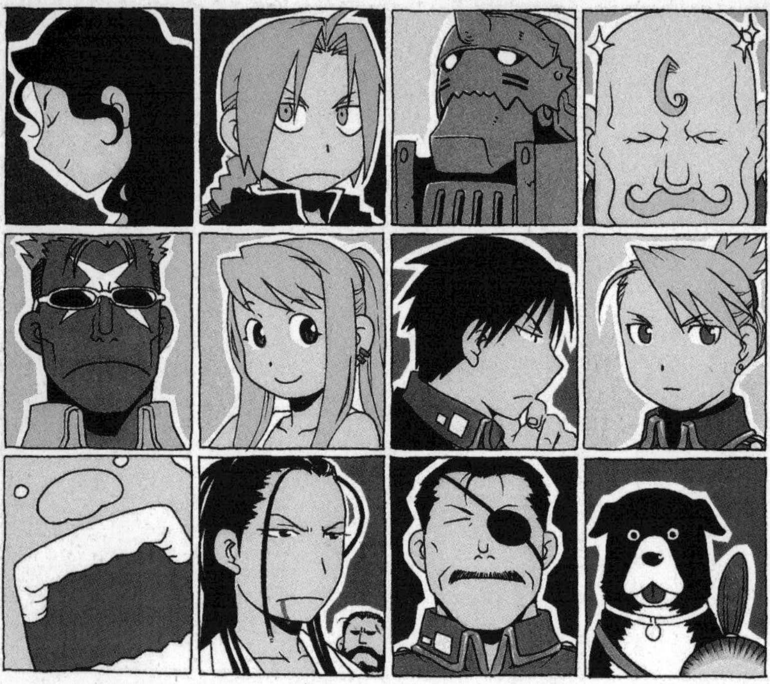

Chapter 23: Knocking on Heaven's Door

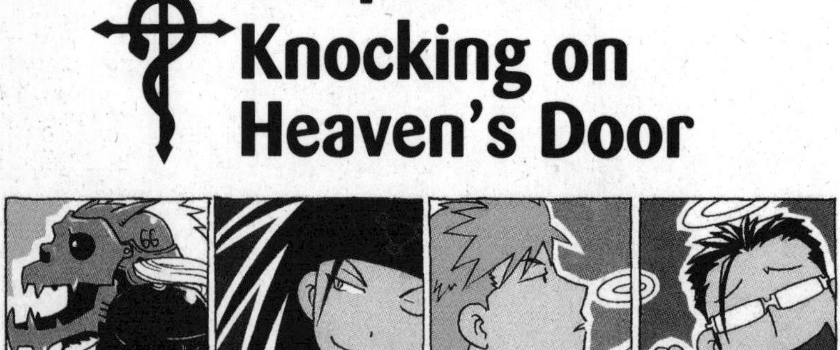

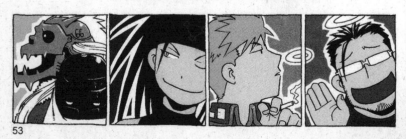

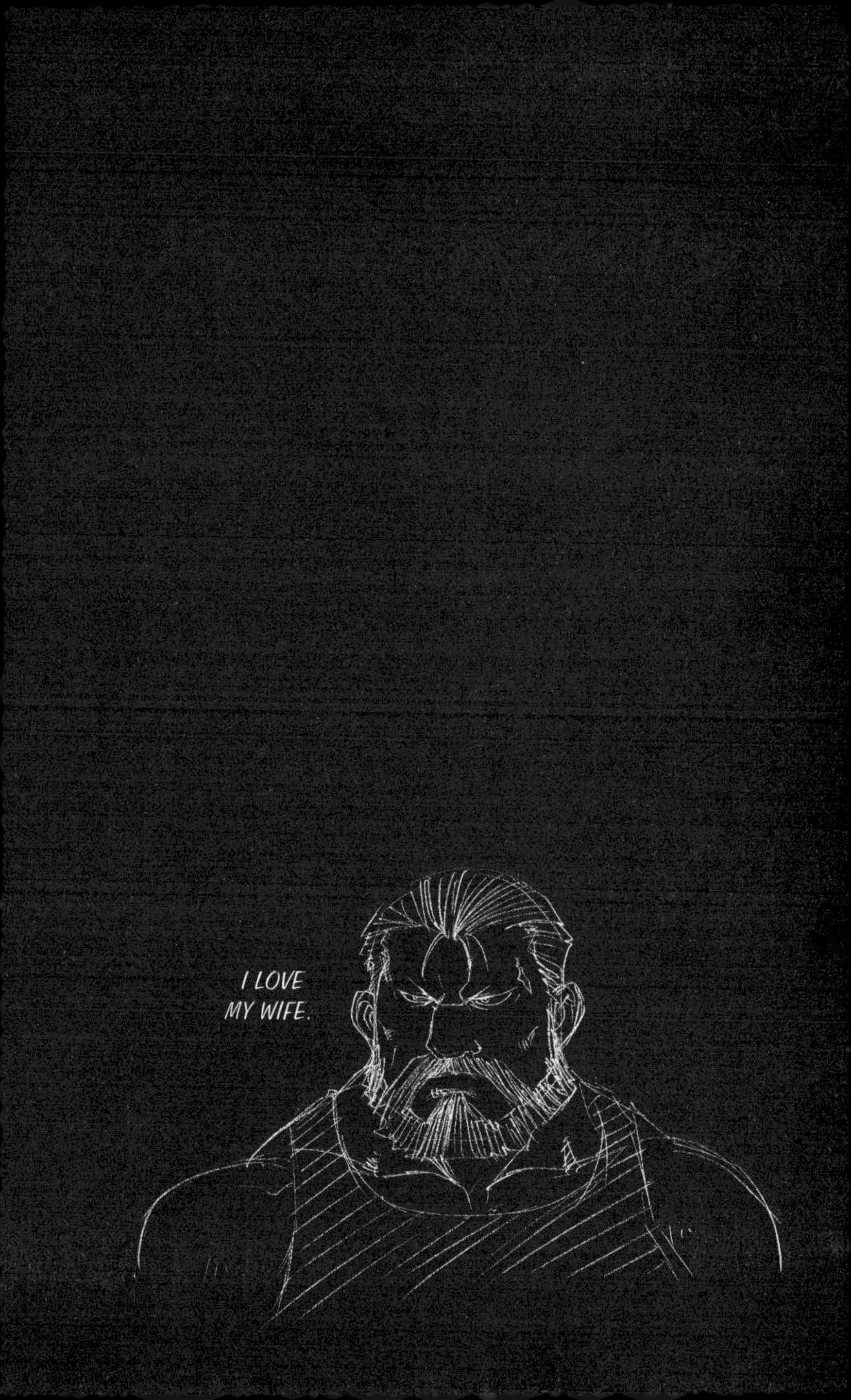
I LOVE MY WIFE.

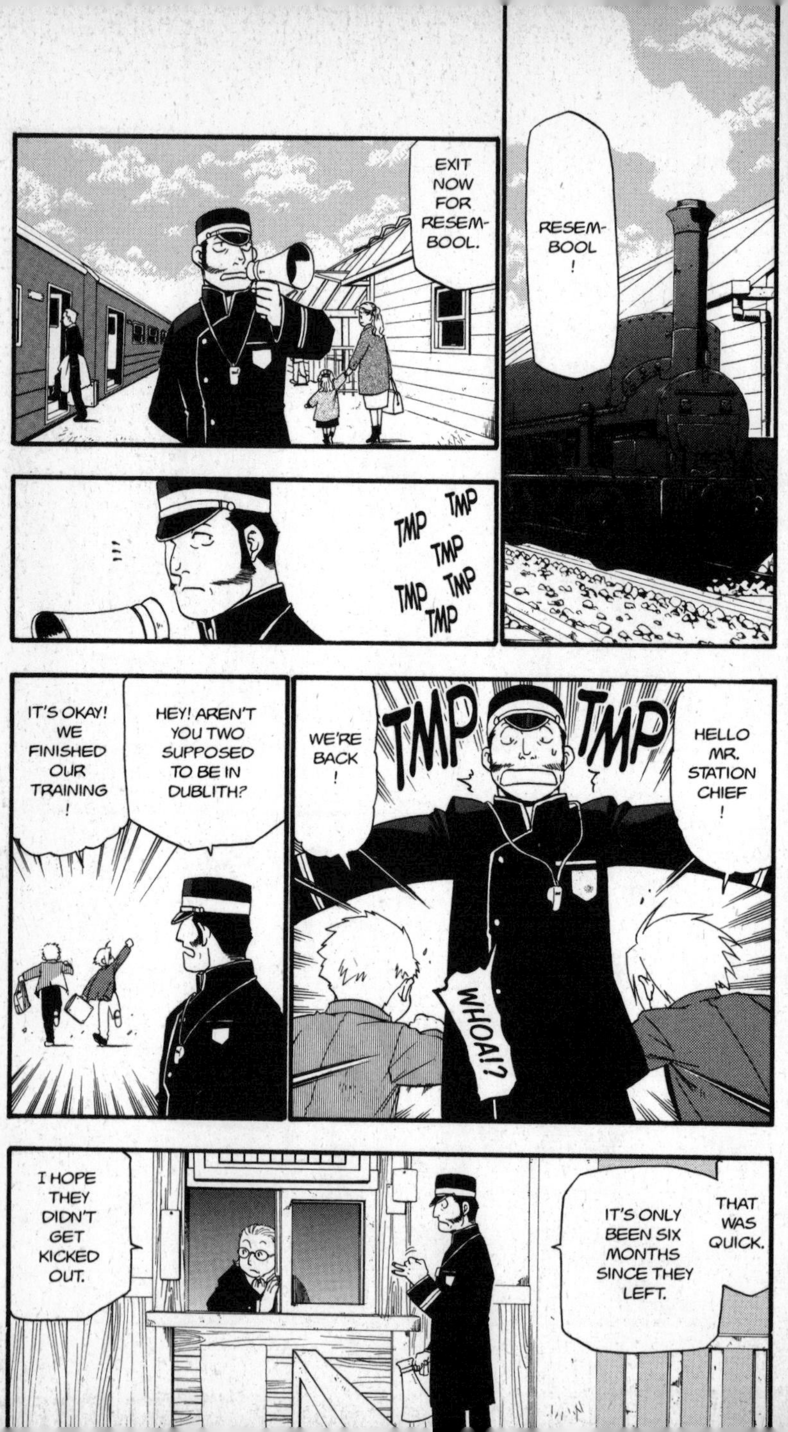
RESEMBOOL!
EXIT NOW FOR RESEMBOOL.
TMP TMP TMP TMP TMP TMP
HELLO MR. STATION CHIEF!
TMP TMP
WE'RE BACK!
WHOA!?
HEY! AREN'T YOU TWO SUPPOSED TO BE IN DUBLITH?
IT'S OKAY! WE FINISHED OUR TRAINING!
THAT WAS QUICK.
IT'S ONLY BEEN SIX MONTHS SINCE THEY LEFT.
I HOPE THEY DIDN'T GET KICKED OUT.

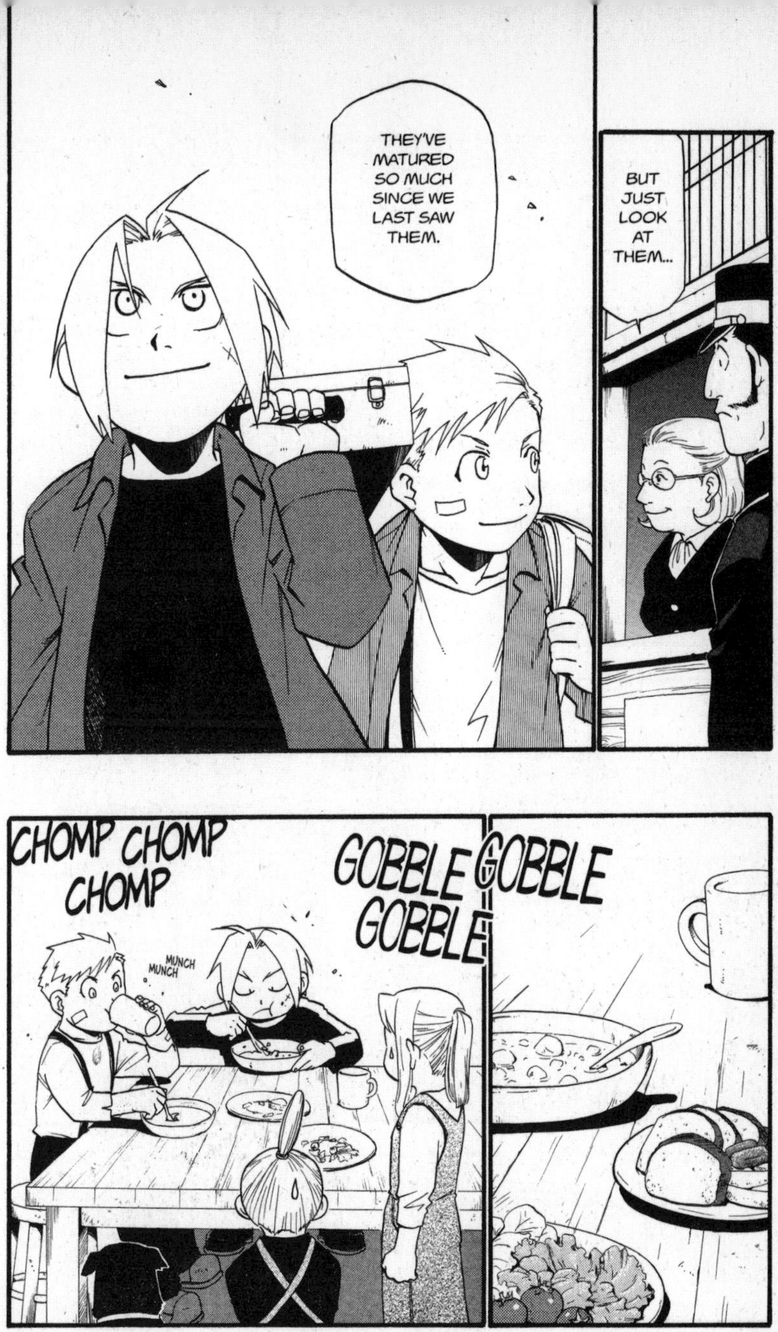
BUT JUST LOOK AT THEM...
THEY'VE MATURED SO MUCH SINCE WE LAST SAW THEM.
GOBBLE GOBBLE GOBBLE
CHOMP CHOMP CHOMP
MUNCH MUNCH

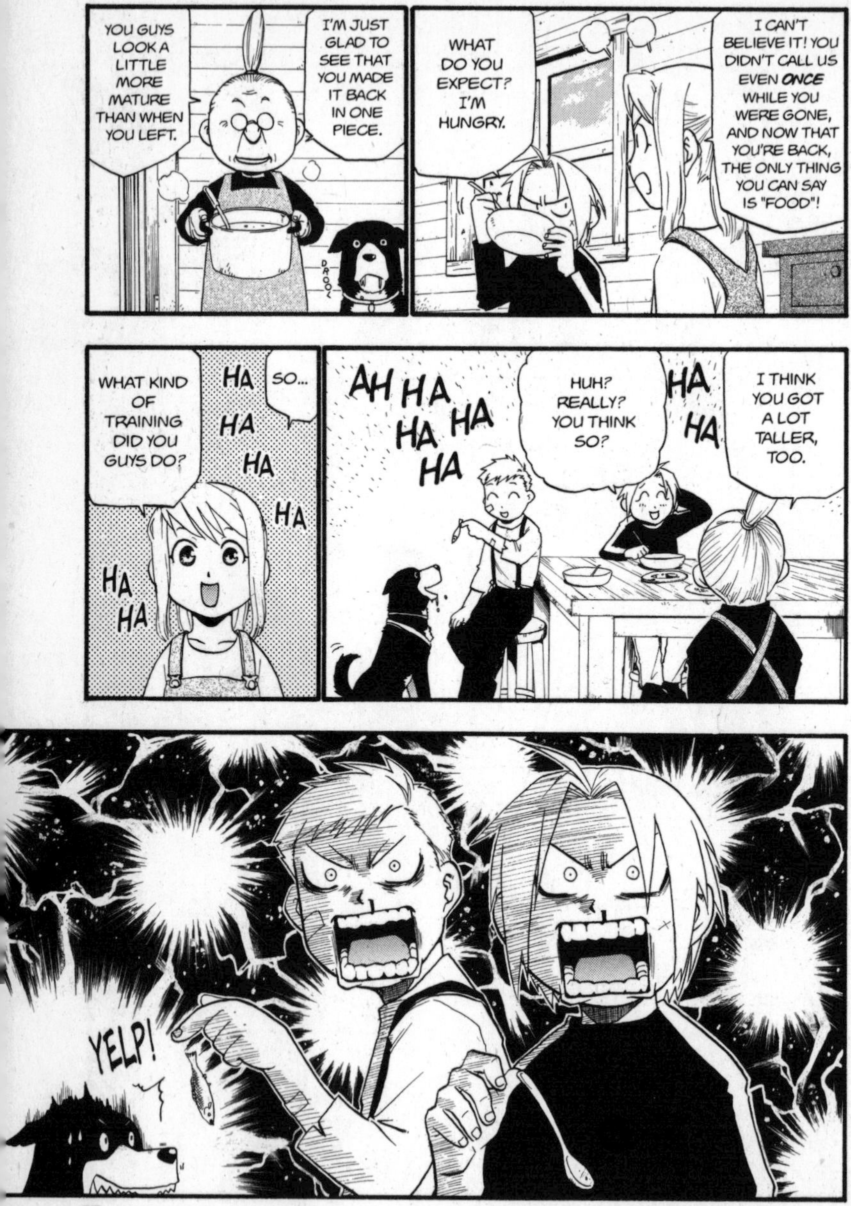
I CAN'T BELIEVE IT! YOU DIDN'T CALL US EVEN ONCE WHILE YOU WERE GONE, AND NOW THAT YOU'RE BACK, THE ONLY THING YOU CAN SAY IS "FOOD"!
WHAT DO YOU EXPECT? I'M HUNGRY.
I'M JUST GLAD TO SEE THAT YOU MADE IT BACK IN ONE PIECE.
YOU GUYS LOOK A LITTLE MORE MATURE THAN WHEN YOU LEFT.
DROOL
I THINK YOU GOT A LOT TALLER, TOO.
HA HA
HUH? REALLY? YOU THINK SO?
AH HA HA HA HA HA
SO...
HA HA HA HA
WHAT KIND OF TRAINING DID YOU GUYS DO?
HA HA
YELP!

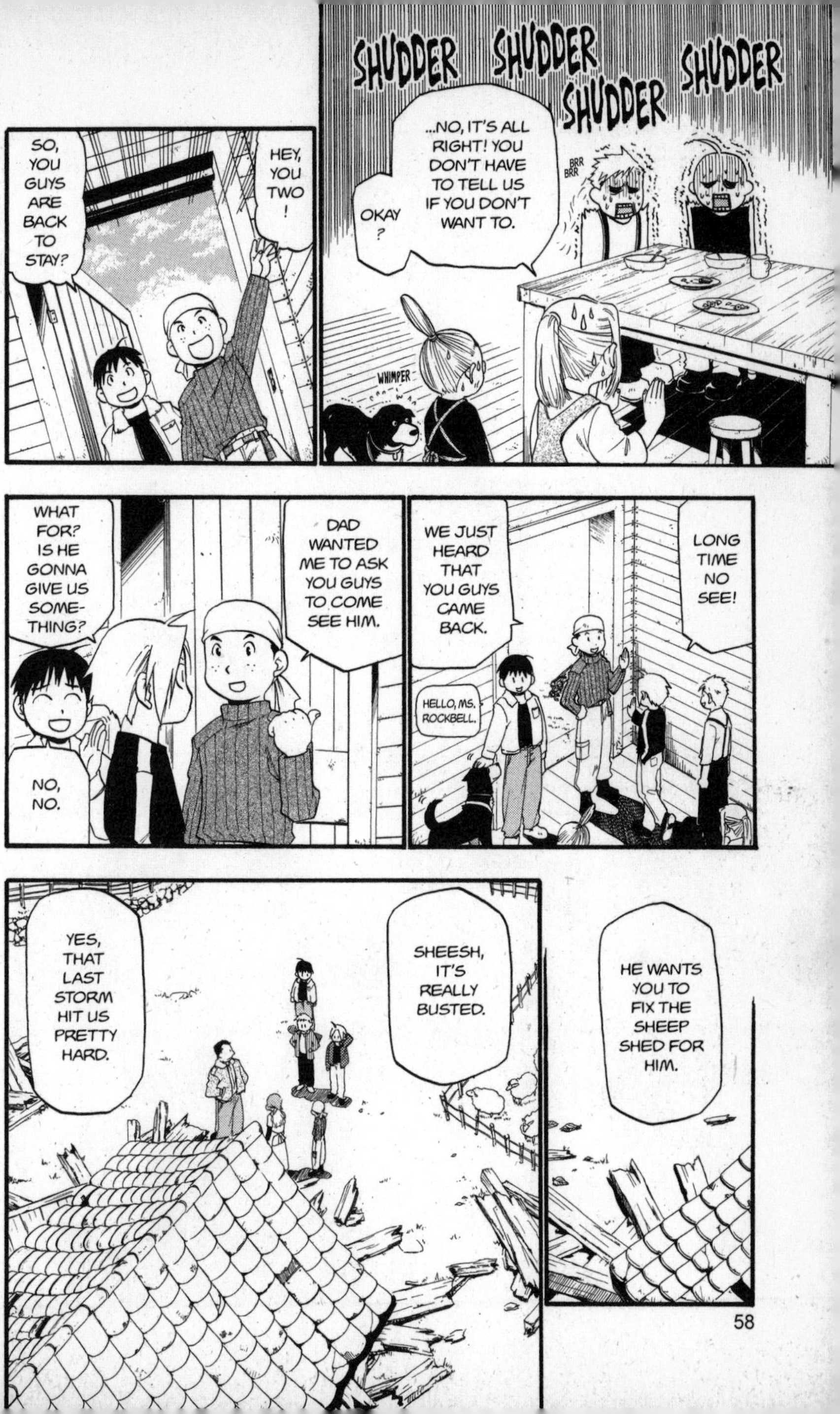
SHUDDER SHUDDER SHUDDER SHUDDER
BRR BRR
...NO, IT'S ALL RIGHT! YOU DON'T HAVE TO TELL US IF YOU DON'T WANT TO.
OKAY ?
WHIMPER
HEY, YOU TWO !
SO, YOU GUYS ARE BACK TO STAY?
LONG TIME NO SEE!
WE JUST HEARD THAT YOU GUYS CAME BACK.
HELLO, MS. ROCKBELL.
DAD WANTED ME TO ASK YOU GUYS TO COME SEE HIM.
WHAT FOR? IS HE GONNA GIVE US SOME-THING?
NO, NO.
HE WANTS YOU TO FIX THE SHEEP SHED FOR HIM.
SHEESH, IT'S REALLY BUSTED.
YES, THAT LAST STORM HIT US PRETTY HARD.

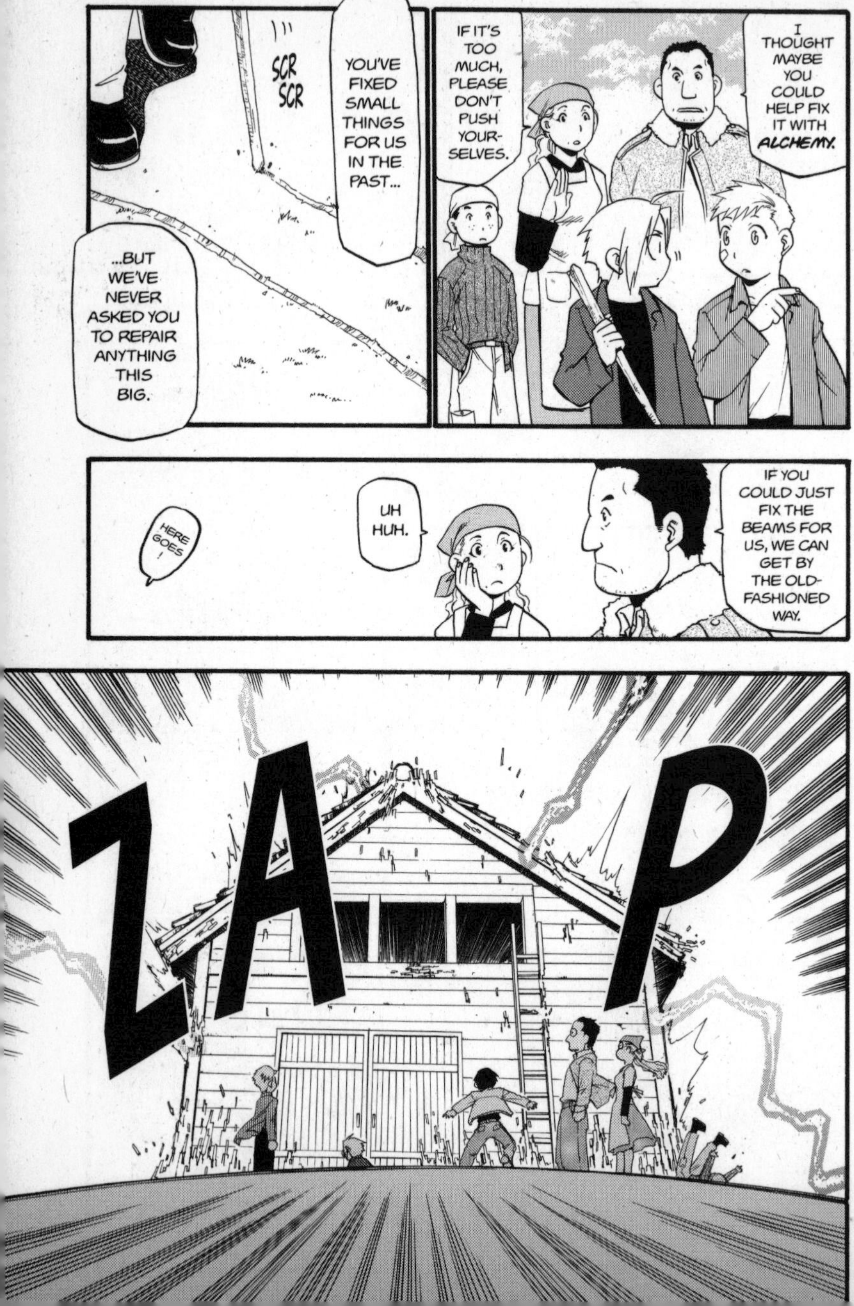
I THOUGHT MAYBE YOU COULD HELP FIX IT WITH ALCHEMY.
IF IT'S TOO MUCH, PLEASE DON'T PUSH YOUR-SELVES.
YOU'VE FIXED SMALL THINGS FOR US IN THE PAST...
SCR SCR
...BUT WE'VE NEVER ASKED YOU TO REPAIR ANYTHING THIS BIG.
IF YOU COULD JUST FIX THE BEAMS FOR US, WE CAN GET BY THE OLD-FASHIONED WAY.
UH HUH.
HERE GOES!
ZAP

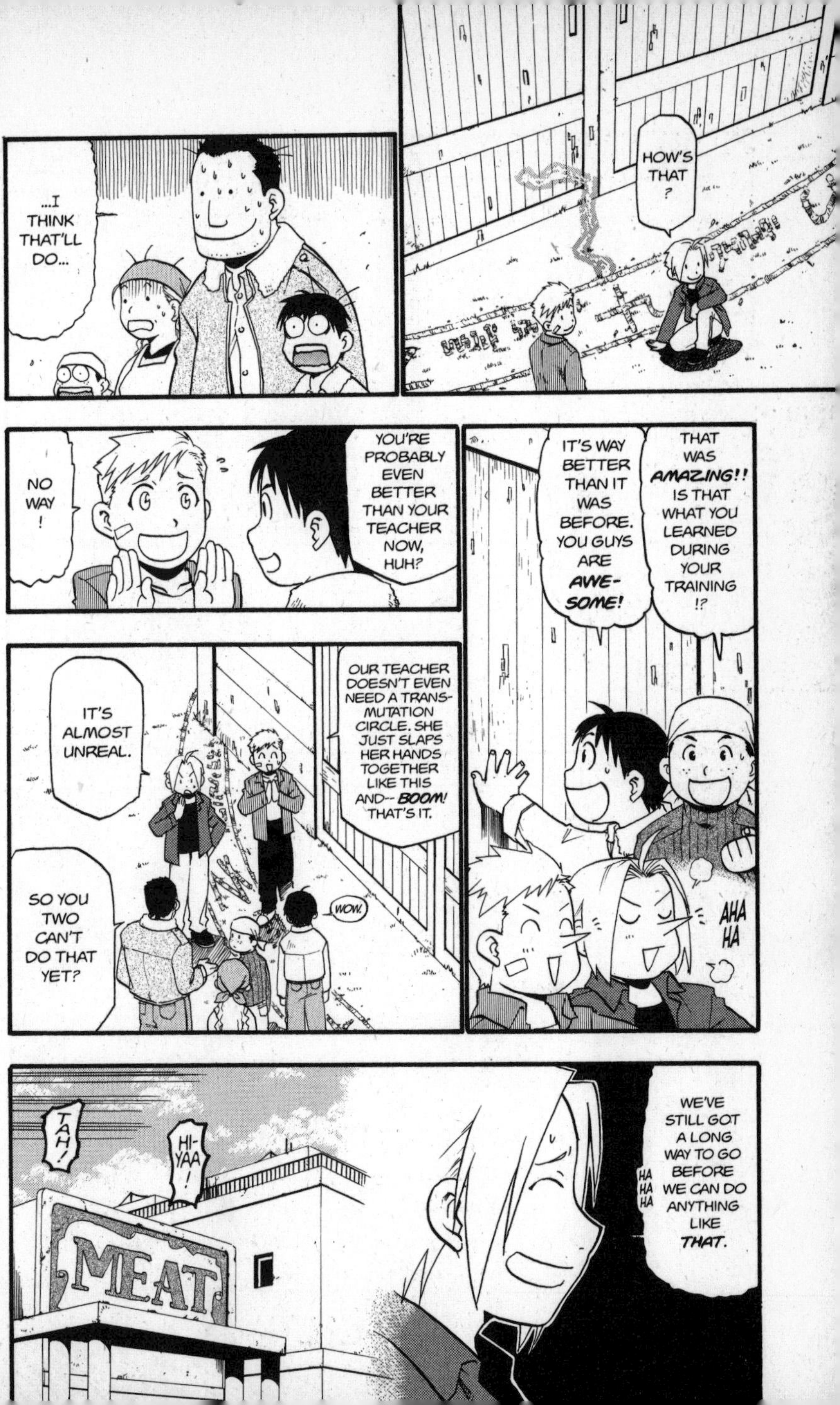
HOW'S THAT ?
...I THINK THAT'LL DO...
THAT WAS **AMAZING!!** IS THAT WHAT YOU LEARNED DURING YOUR TRAINING !?
IT'S WAY BETTER THAN IT WAS BEFORE. YOU GUYS ARE **AWE-SOME!**
AHA HA
YOU'RE PROBABLY EVEN BETTER THAN YOUR TEACHER NOW, HUH?
NO WAY !
OUR TEACHER DOESN'T EVEN NEED A TRANS-MUTATION CIRCLE. SHE JUST SLAPS HER HANDS TOGETHER LIKE THIS AND-- **BOOM!** THAT'S IT.
IT'S ALMOST UNREAL.
WOW.
SO YOU TWO CAN'T DO THAT YET?
WE'VE STILL GOT A LONG WAY TO GO BEFORE WE CAN DO ANYTHING LIKE **THAT**.
HA HA HA
HI-YAA !
TAH!
MEAT

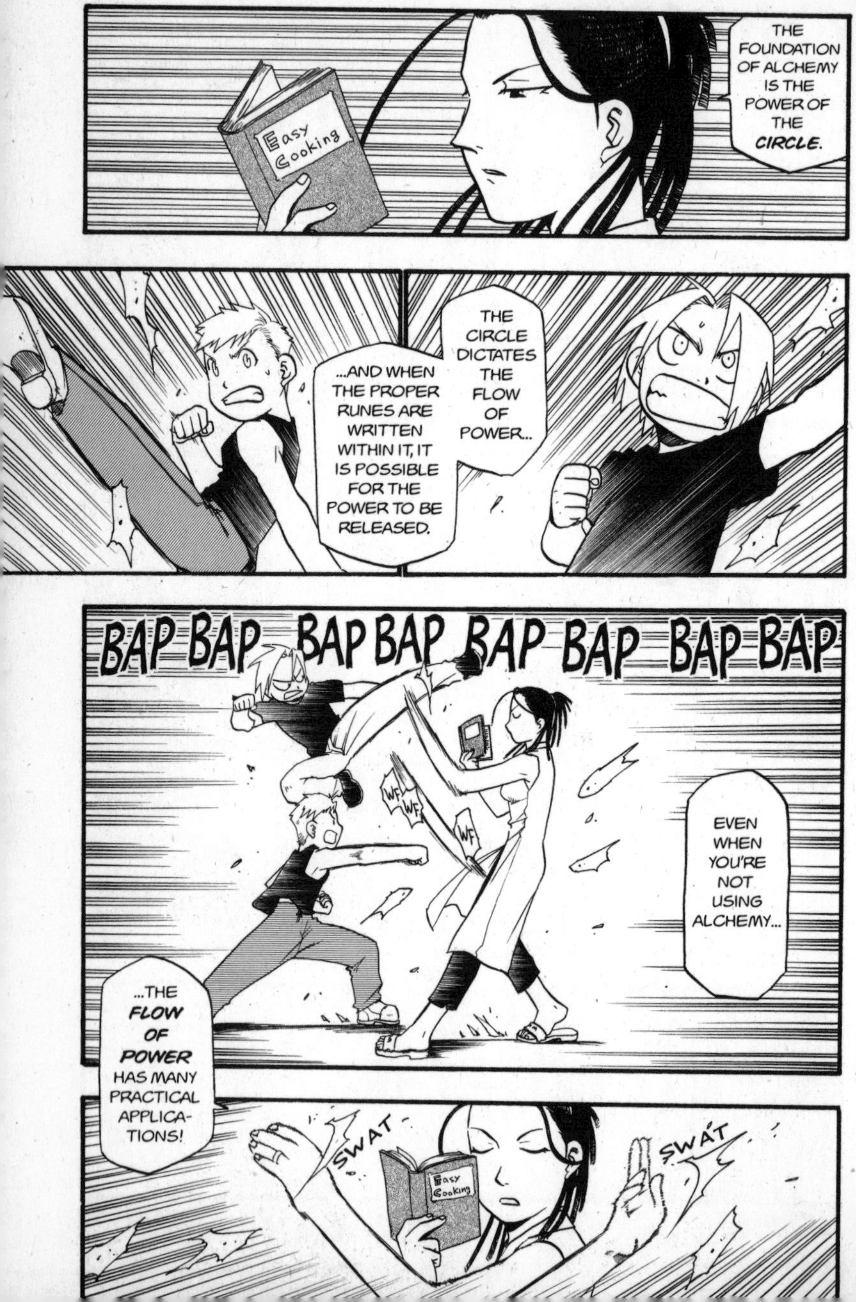
Easy Cooking
THE FOUNDATION OF ALCHEMY IS THE POWER OF THE CIRCLE.
THE CIRCLE DICTATES THE FLOW OF POWER...
...AND WHEN THE PROPER RUNES ARE WRITTEN WITHIN IT, IT IS POSSIBLE FOR THE POWER TO BE RELEASED.
BAP BAP BAP BAP BAP BAP BAP BAP
WF
WF
WF
EVEN WHEN YOU'RE NOT USING ALCHEMY...
...THE FLOW OF POWER HAS MANY PRACTICAL APPLICA-TIONS!
SWAT
Easy Cooking
SWAT

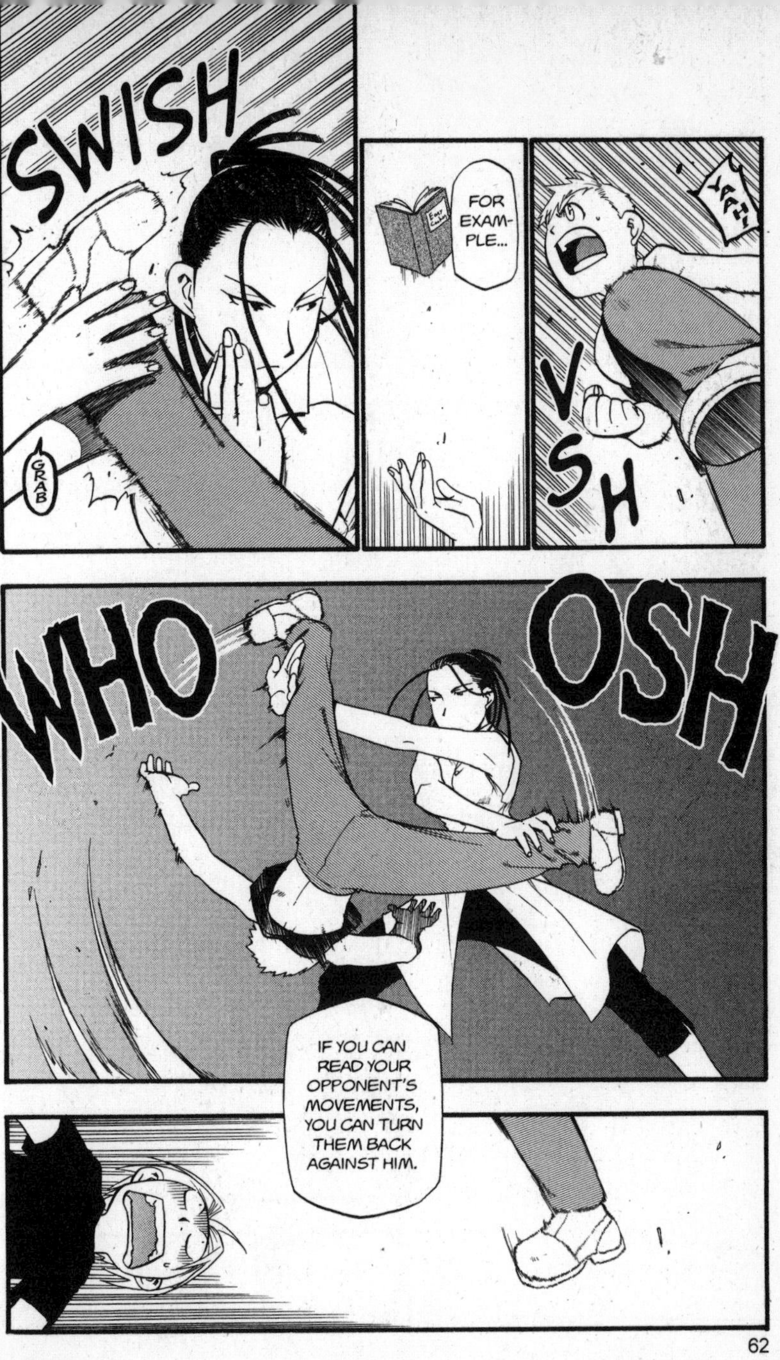
YAAH!
VSH
FOR EXAMPLE...
SWISH
GRAB
WHOOSH
IF YOU CAN READ YOUR OPPONENT'S MOVEMENTS, YOU CAN TURN THEM BACK AGAINST HIM.

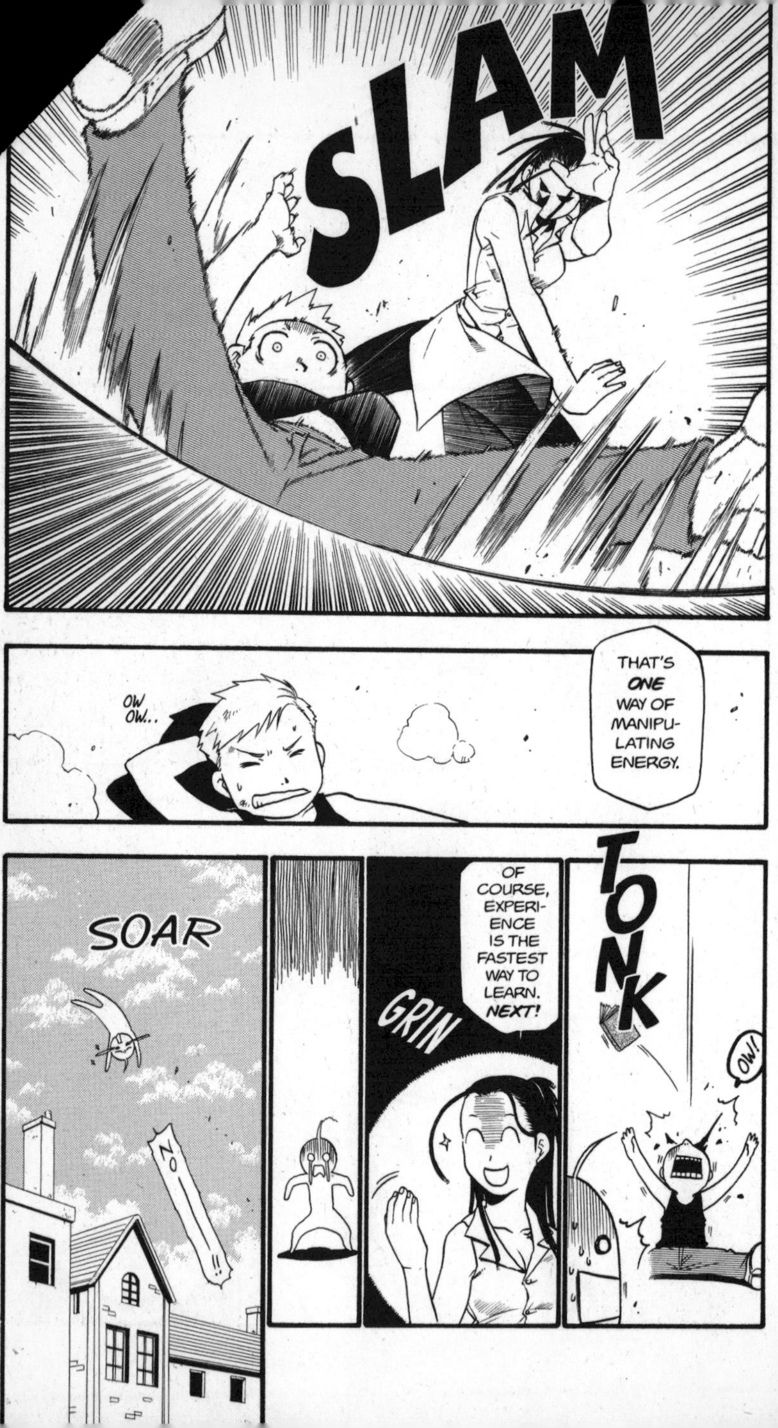
SLAM
THAT'S ONE WAY OF MANIPULATING ENERGY.
OW OW...
TONK
OW!
OF COURSE, EXPERIENCE IS THE FASTEST WAY TO LEARN. NEXT!
GRIN
SOAR
NO!!

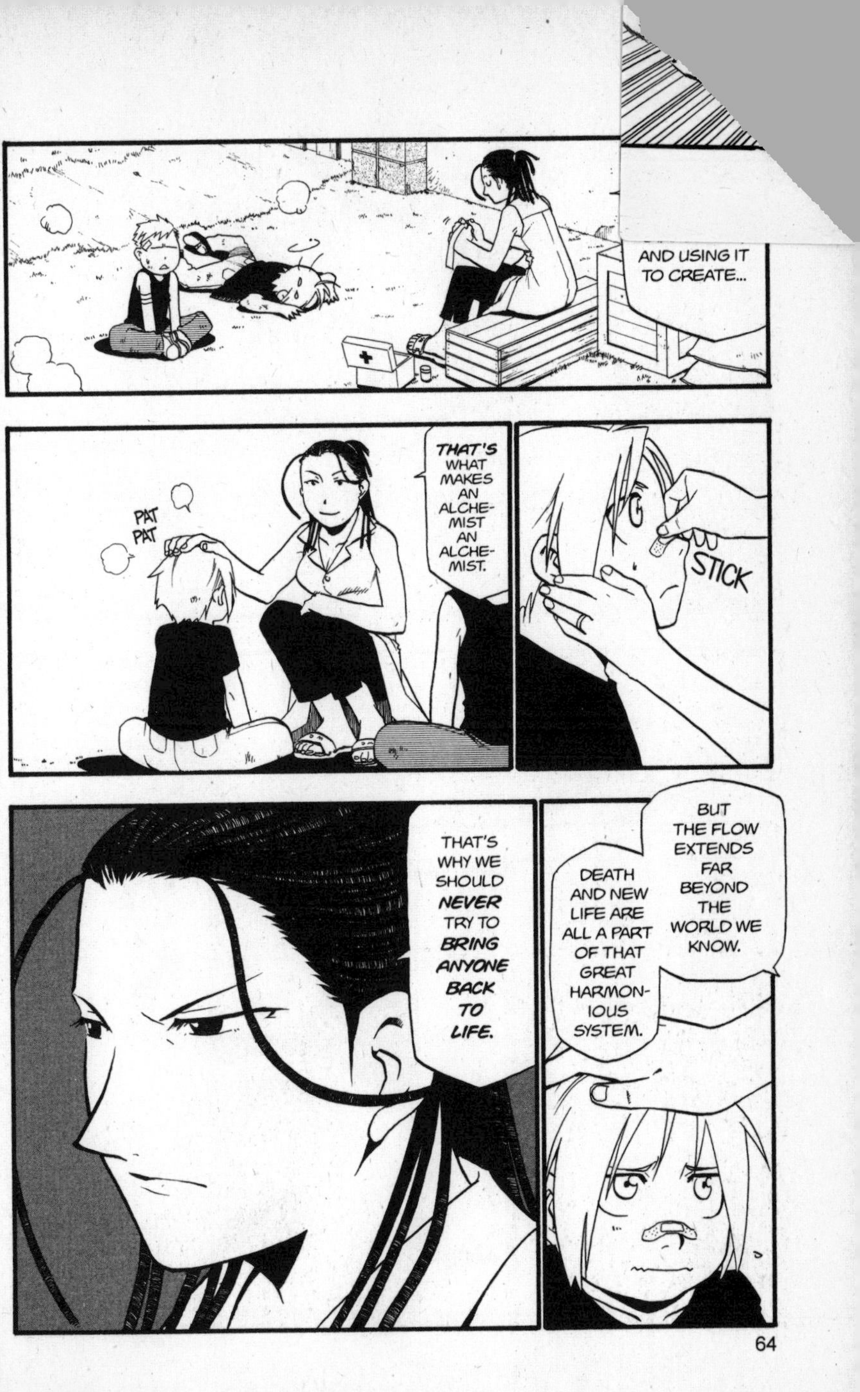
AND USING IT TO CREATE...
STICK
THAT'S WHAT MAKES AN ALCHEMIST AN ALCHEMIST.
PAT PAT
BUT THE FLOW EXTENDS FAR BEYOND THE WORLD WE KNOW.
DEATH AND NEW LIFE ARE ALL A PART OF THAT GREAT HARMONIOUS SYSTEM.
THAT'S WHY WE SHOULD NEVER TRY TO BRING ANYONE BACK TO LIFE.

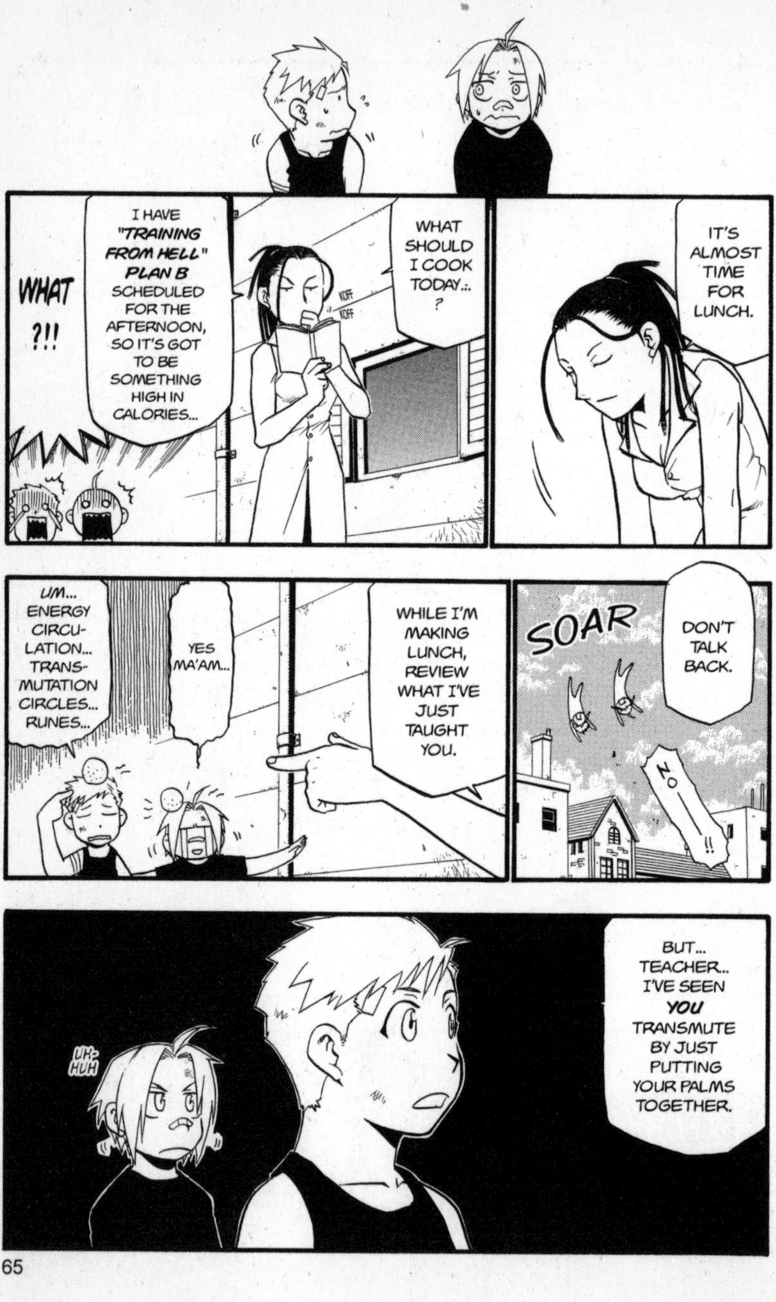
IT'S ALMOST TIME FOR LUNCH.
WHAT SHOULD I COOK TODAY...?
KOFF KOFF
I HAVE "TRAINING FROM HELL" PLAN B SCHEDULED FOR THE AFTERNOON, SO IT'S GOT TO BE SOMETHING HIGH IN CALORIES...
WHAT?!!
DON'T TALK BACK.
SOAR
NO...!!
WHILE I'M MAKING LUNCH, REVIEW WHAT I'VE JUST TAUGHT YOU.
YES MA'AM...
UM... ENERGY CIRCULATION... TRANSMUTATION CIRCLES... RUNES...
BUT... TEACHER... I'VE SEEN YOU TRANSMUTE BY JUST PUTTING YOUR PALMS TOGETHER.
UH-HUH

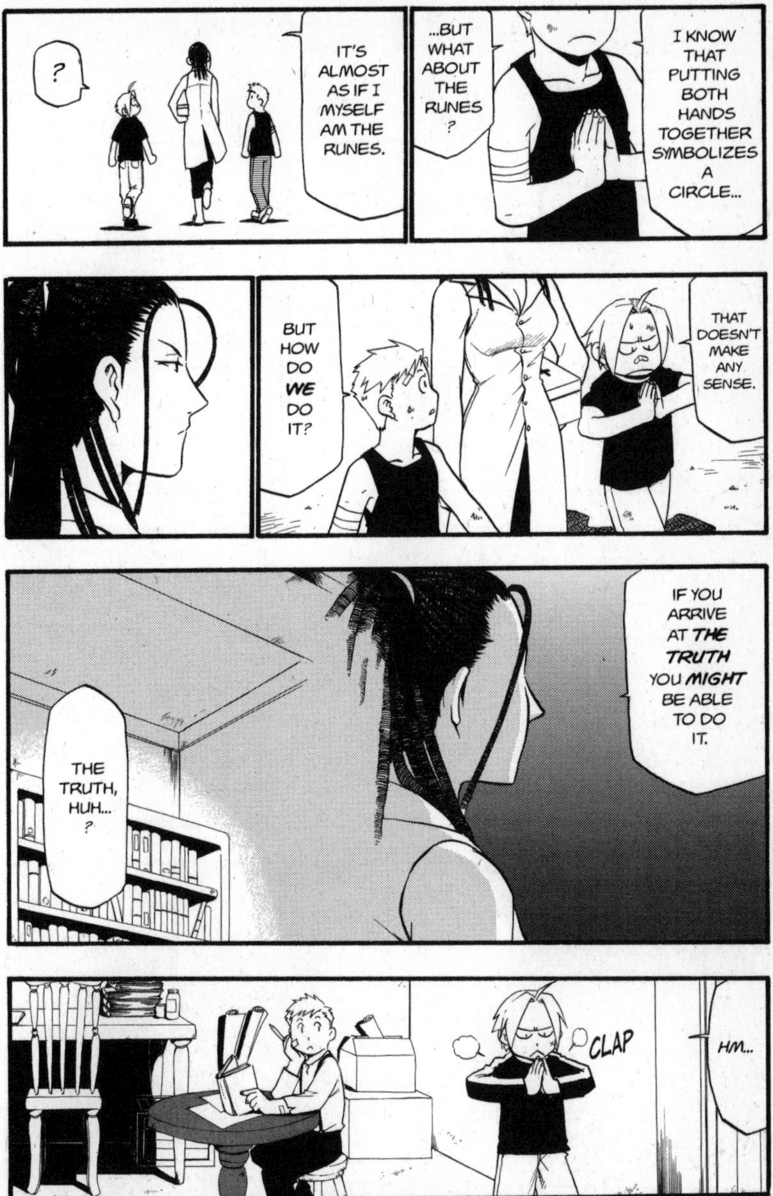
I KNOW THAT PUTTING BOTH HANDS TOGETHER SYMBOLIZES A CIRCLE...
...BUT WHAT ABOUT THE RUNES?
IT'S ALMOST AS IF I MYSELF AM THE RUNES.
?
THAT DOESN'T MAKE ANY SENSE.
BUT HOW DO WE DO IT?
IF YOU ARRIVE AT THE TRUTH YOU MIGHT BE ABLE TO DO IT.
THE TRUTH, HUH...?
HM...
CLAP

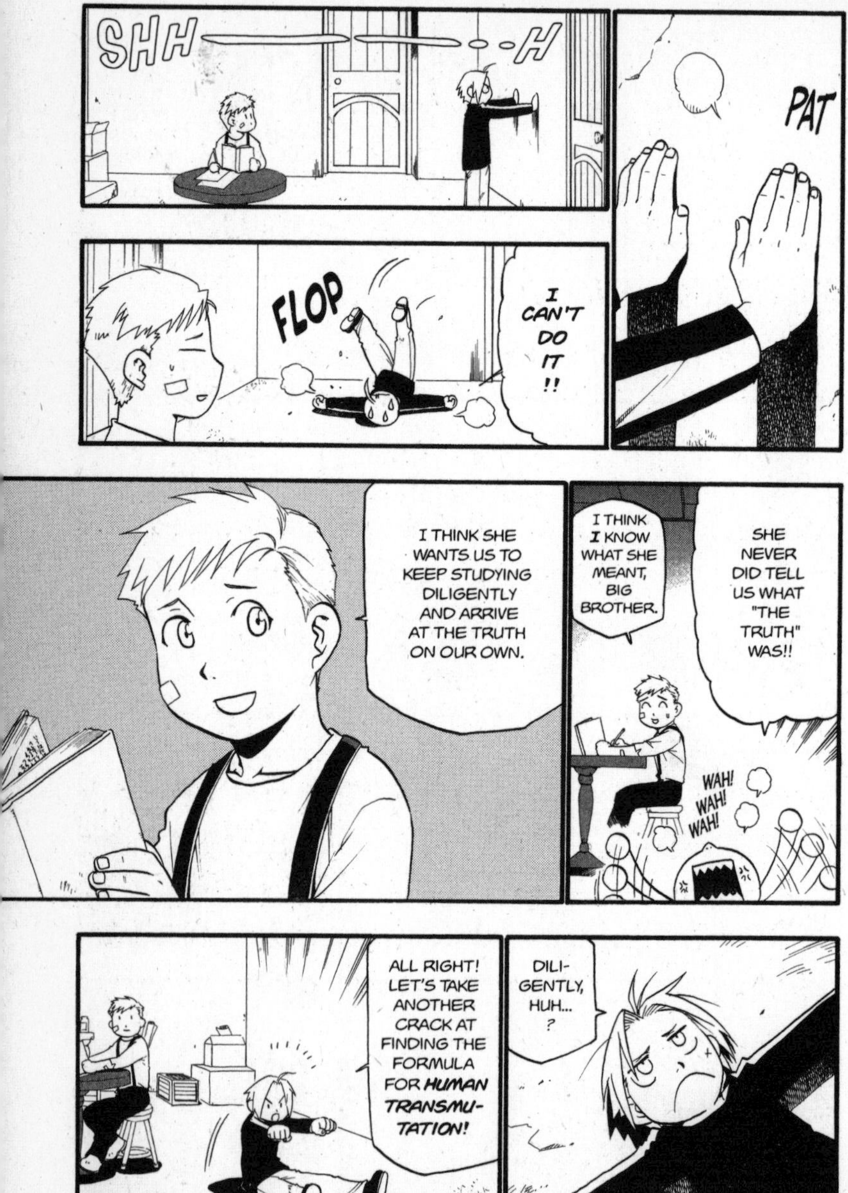
PAT
SHH———H
FLOP
I CAN'T DO IT!!
SHE NEVER DID TELL US WHAT "THE TRUTH" WAS!!
I THINK I KNOW WHAT SHE MEANT, BIG BROTHER.
WAH! WAH! WAH!
I THINK SHE WANTS US TO KEEP STUDYING DILIGENTLY AND ARRIVE AT THE TRUTH ON OUR OWN.
DILI-GENTLY, HUH...?
ALL RIGHT! LET'S TAKE ANOTHER CRACK AT FINDING THE FORMULA FOR HUMAN TRANSMU-TATION!

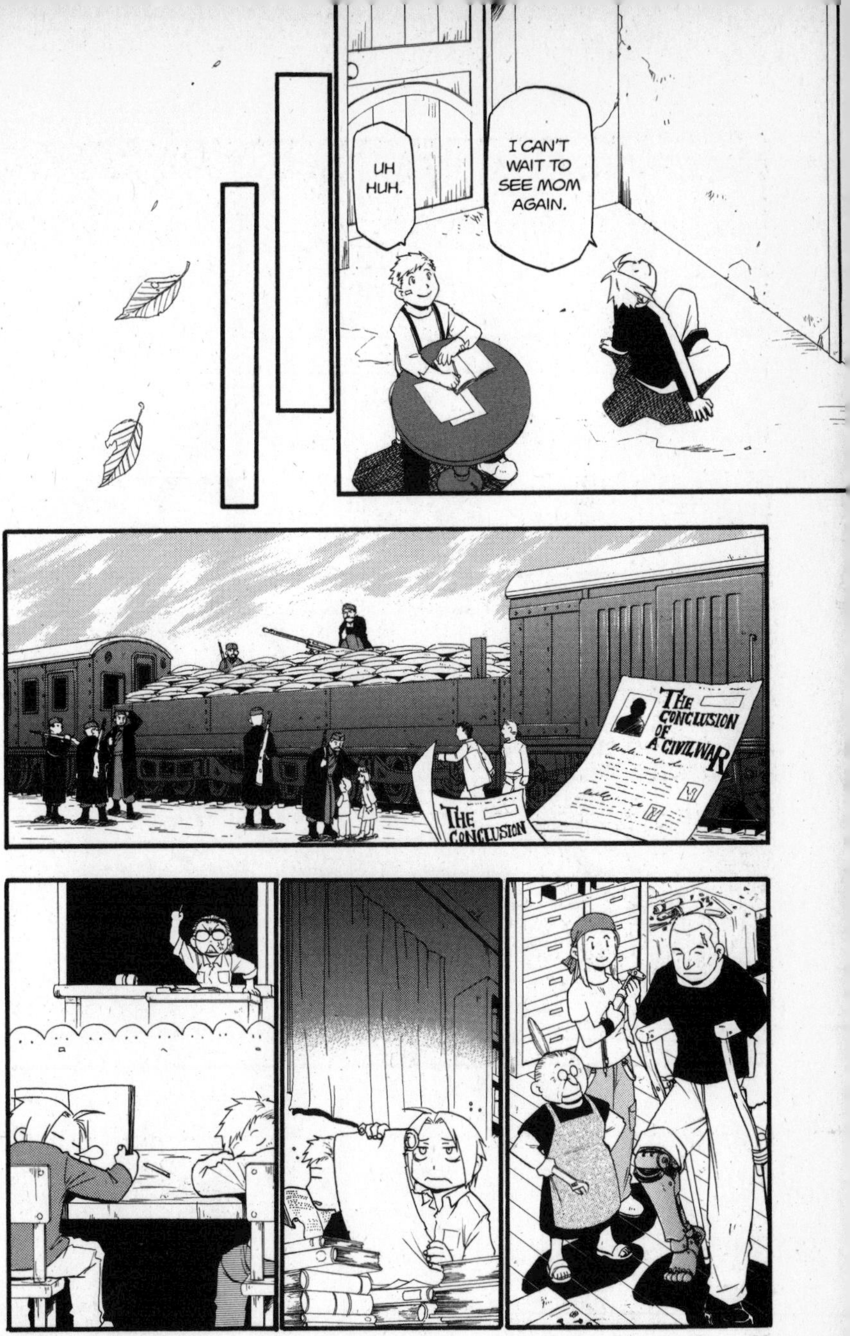
I CAN'T WAIT TO SEE MOM AGAIN.
UH HUH.
THE CONCLUSION OF A CIVIL WAR
THE CONCLUSION

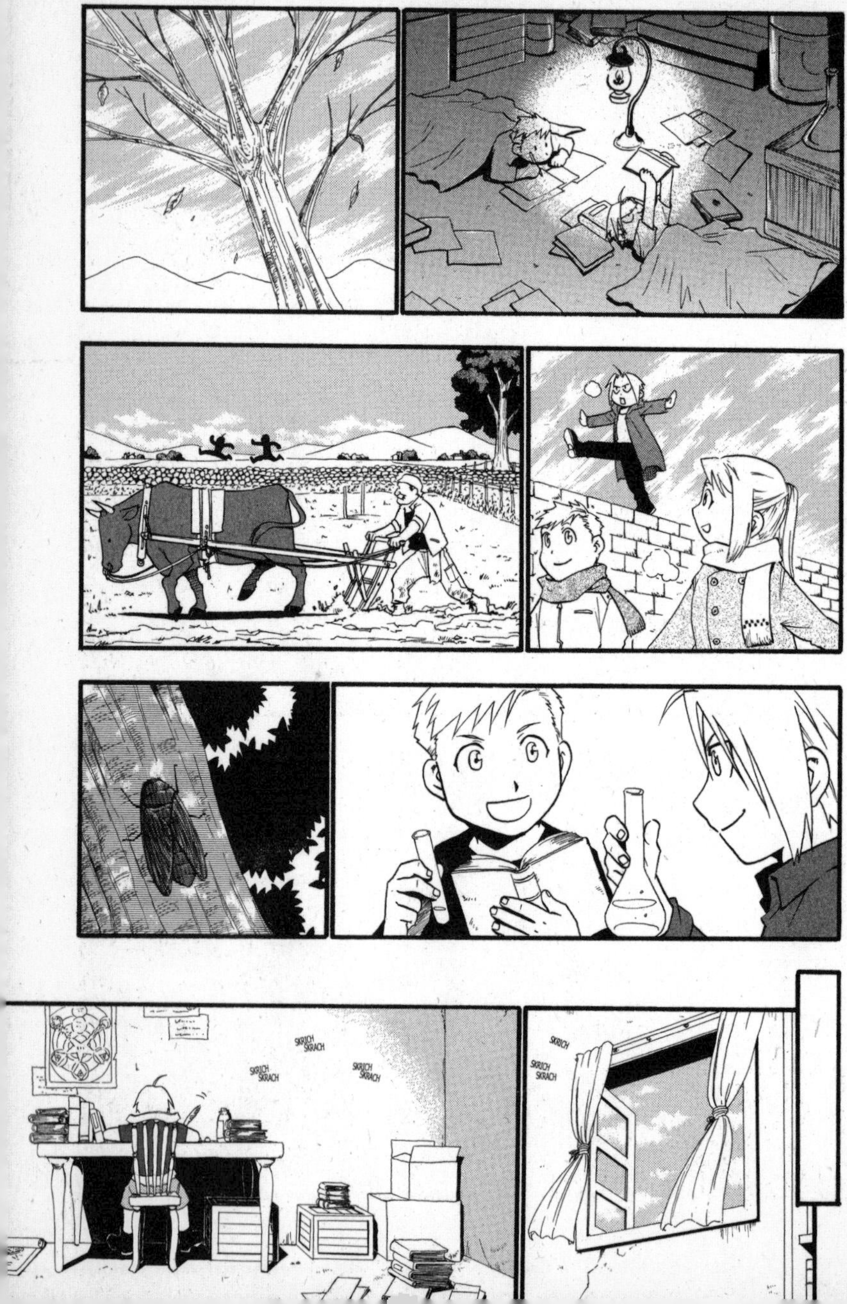
SKRICH
SKRICH SKRACH
SKRICH SKRACH
SKRICH SKRACH
SKRICH SKRACH

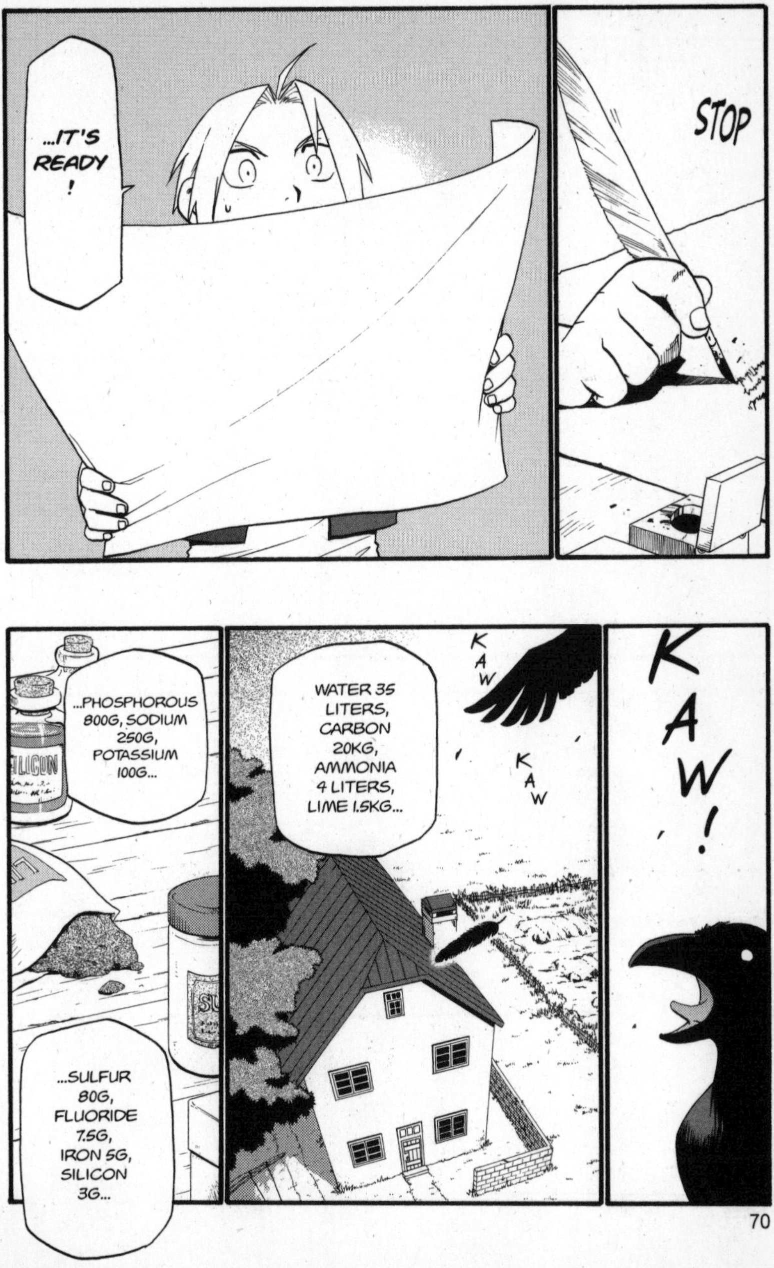
STOP
...IT'S READY!
KAW!
KAW
KAW
WATER 35 LITERS, CARBON 20KG, AMMONIA 4 LITERS, LIME 1.5KG...
...PHOSPHOROUS 800G, SODIUM 250G, POTASSIUM 100G...
SILICON
...SULFUR 80G, FLUORIDE 7.5G, IRON 5G, SILICON 3G...

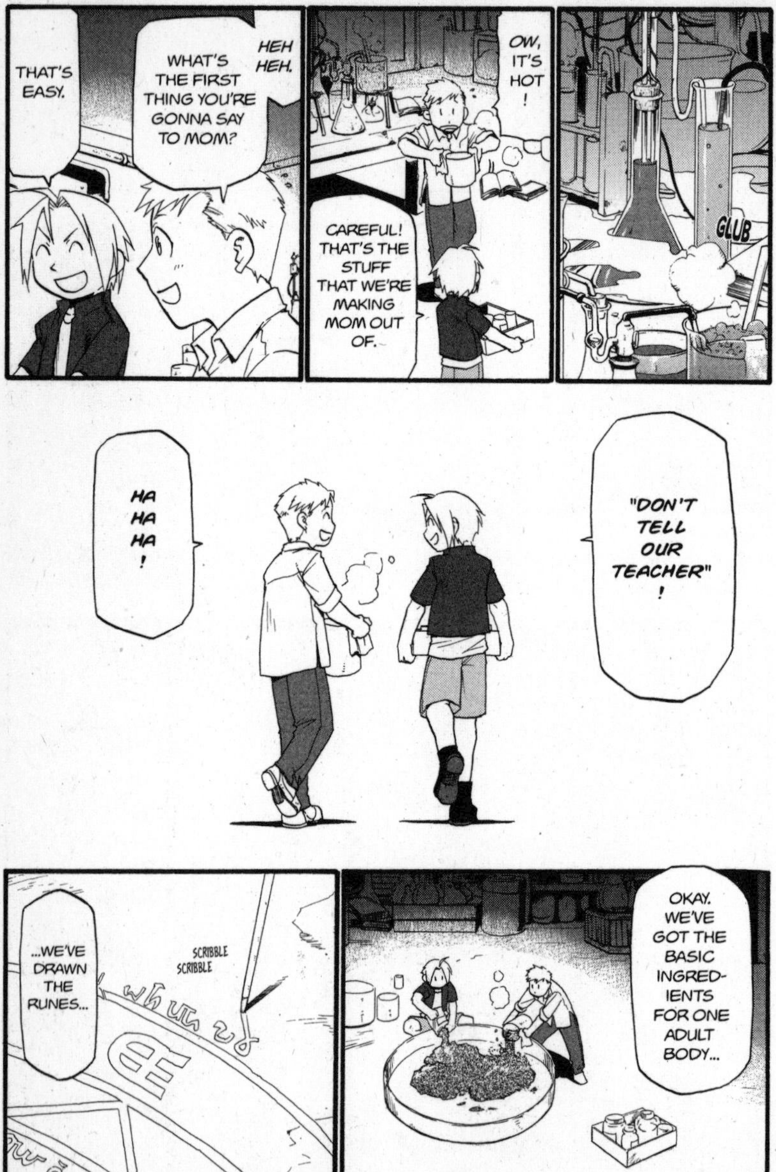
GLUB
OW, IT'S HOT!
CAREFUL! THAT'S THE STUFF THAT WE'RE MAKING MOM OUT OF.
HEH HEH.
WHAT'S THE FIRST THING YOU'RE GONNA SAY TO MOM?
THAT'S EASY.
"DON'T TELL OUR TEACHER"!
HA HA HA!
OKAY. WE'VE GOT THE BASIC INGRED-IENTS FOR ONE ADULT BODY...
SCRIBBLE SCRIBBLE
...WE'VE DRAWN THE RUNES...

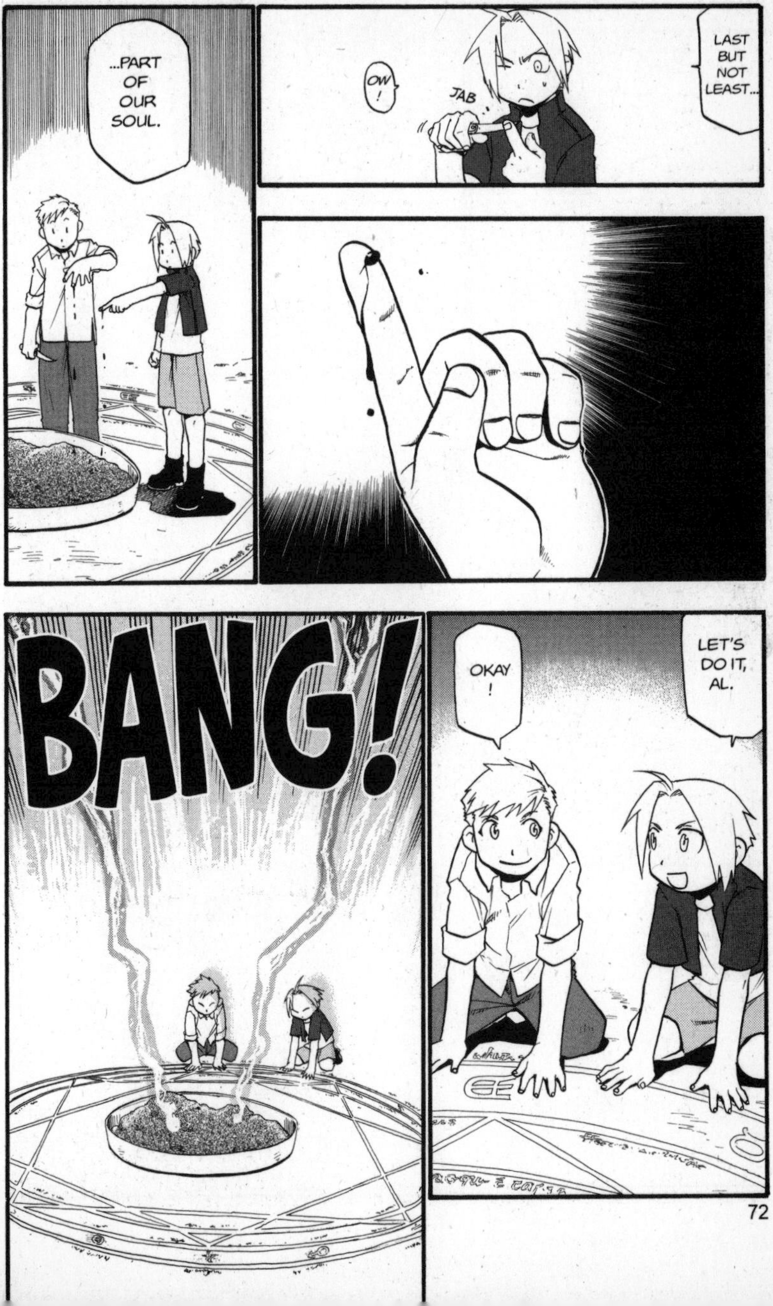
LAST BUT NOT LEAST...
OW!
JAB
...PART OF OUR SOUL.
LET'S DO IT, AL.
OKAY!
BANG!

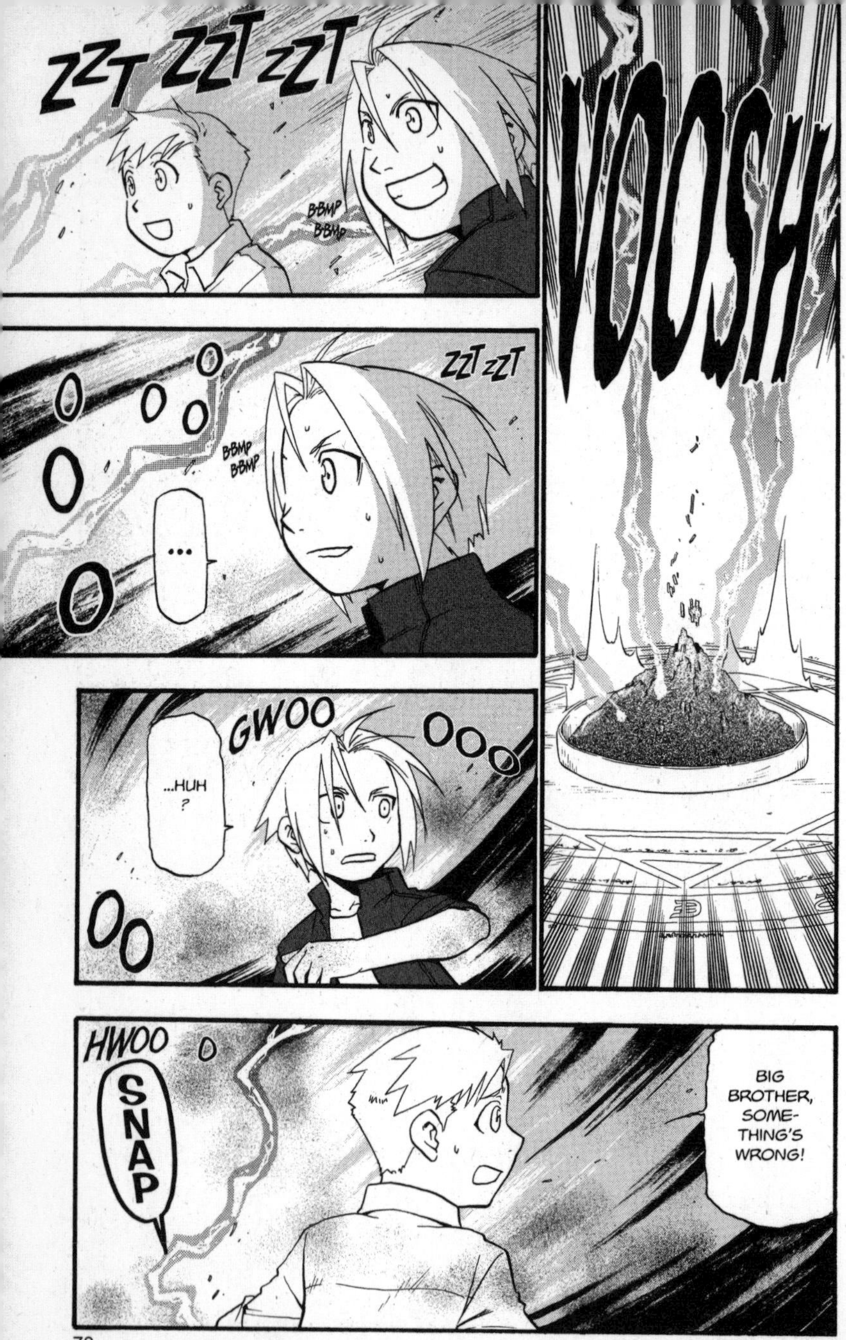
VOOSH
ZZT ZZT ZZT
B-BMP B-BMP
ZZT ZZT
B-BMP B-BMP
...
GWOOOOOOO
...HUH?
HWOO O
SNAP
BIG BROTHER, SOME-THING'S WRONG!

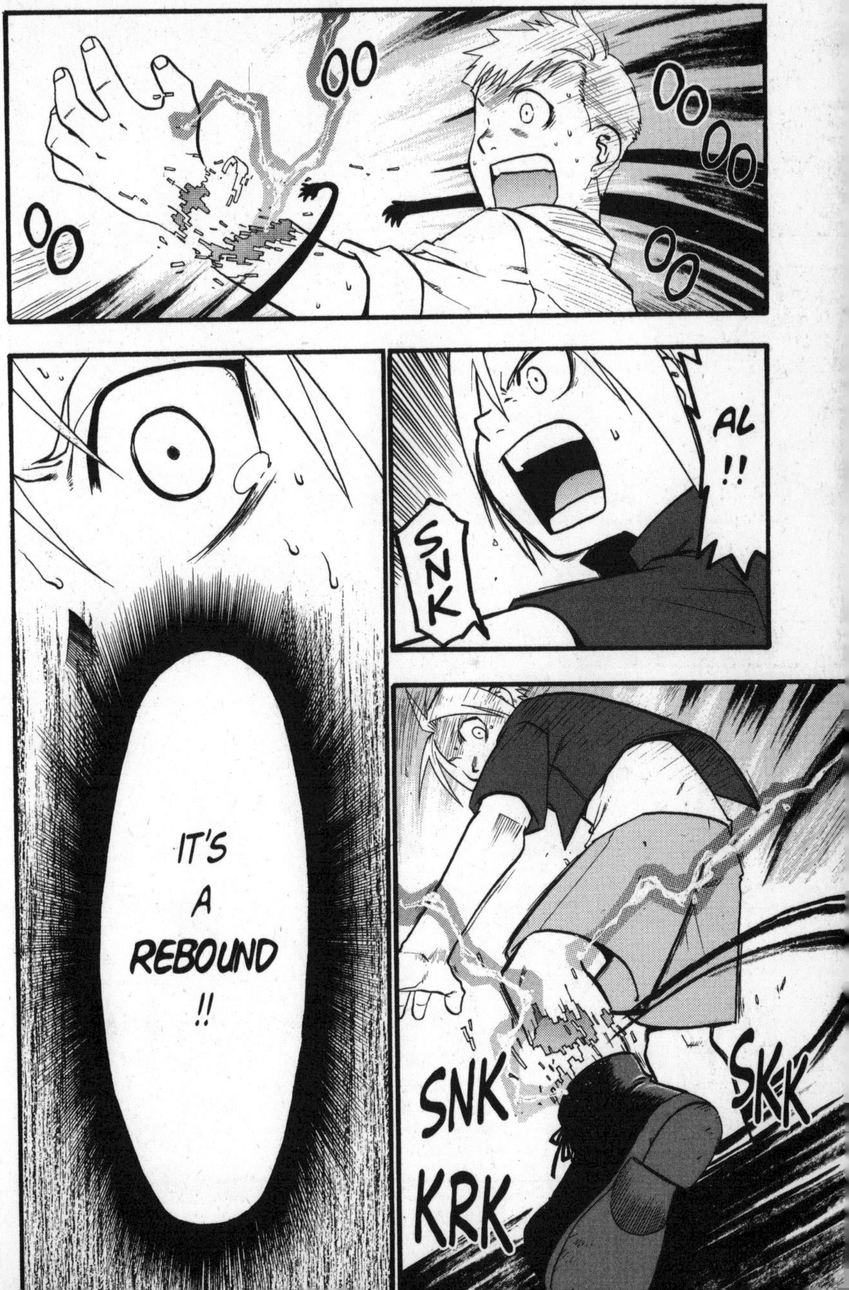
OOOOO
OO
OO
OO
AL !!
SNK
SKK
SNK
KRK
IT'S A REBOUND !!

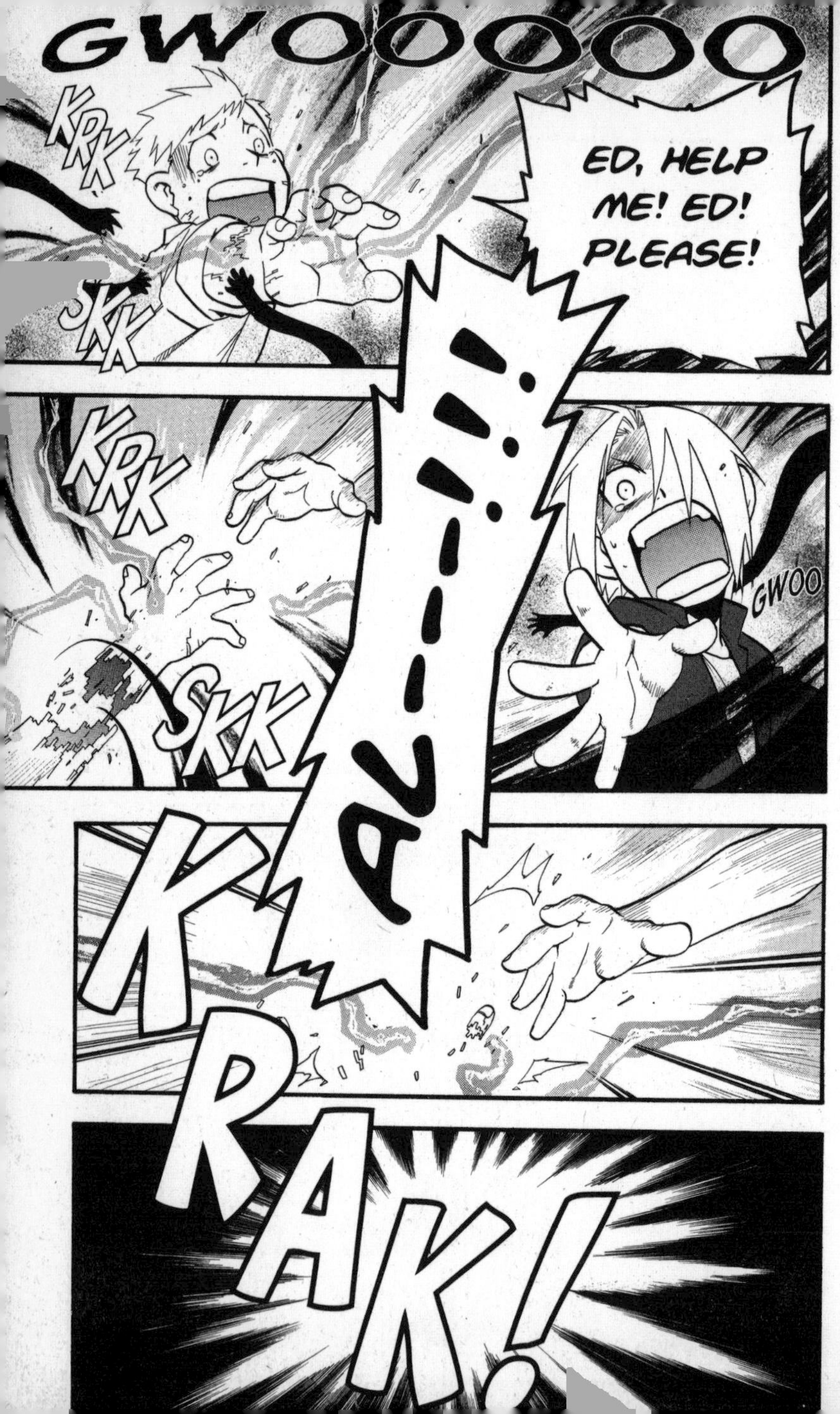
GWOOOOOO
ED, HELP ME! ED! PLEASE!
KRK
SKK
AL--!!
GWOO
KRK
SKK
KRAK!

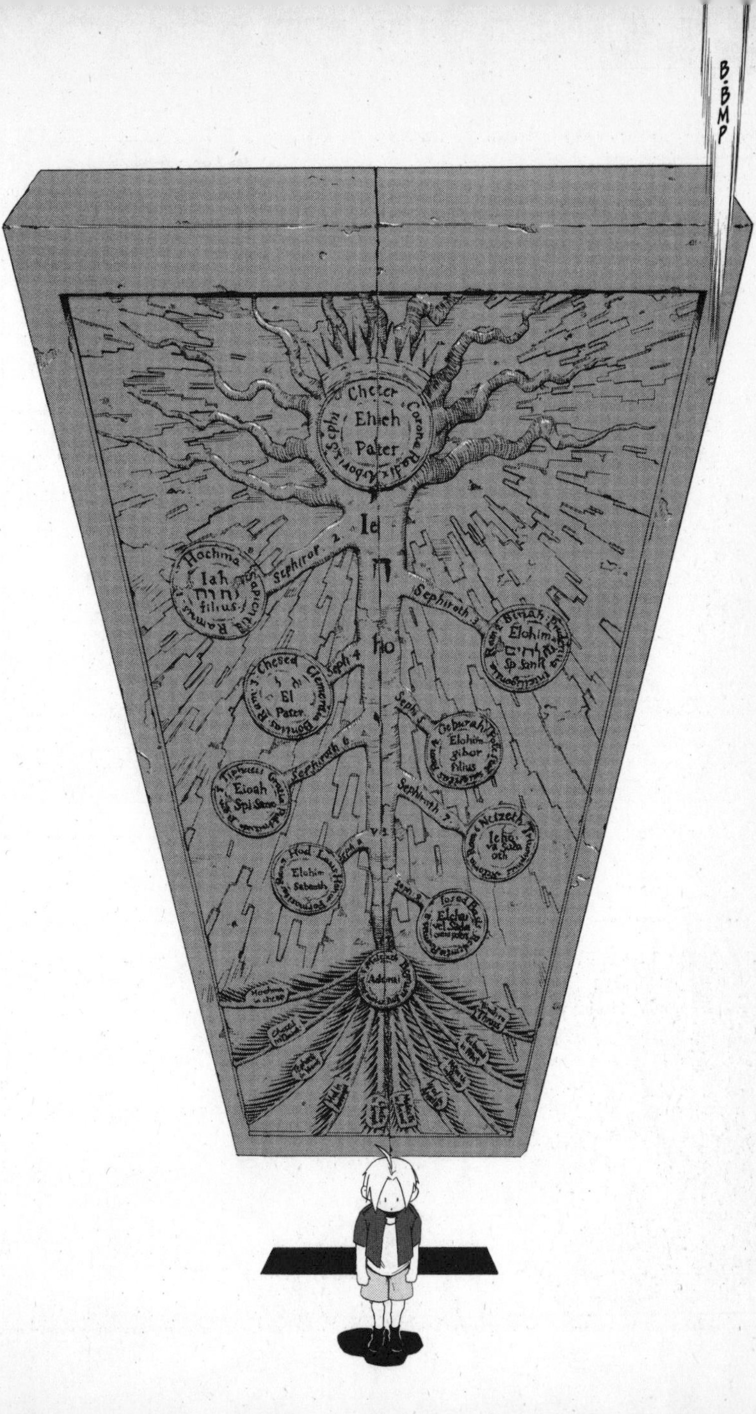
B-BMP

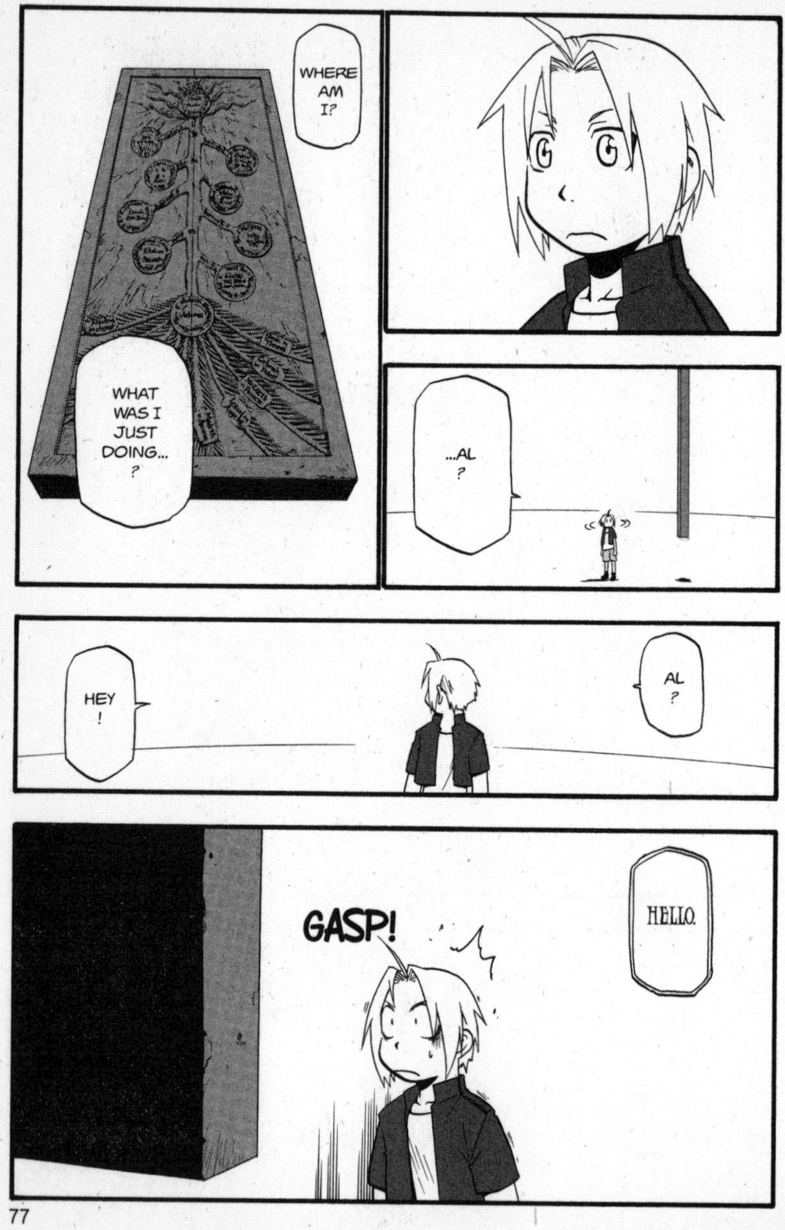
...AL ?
WHERE AM I?
WHAT WAS I JUST DOING... ?
AL ?
HEY !
HELLO.
GASP!

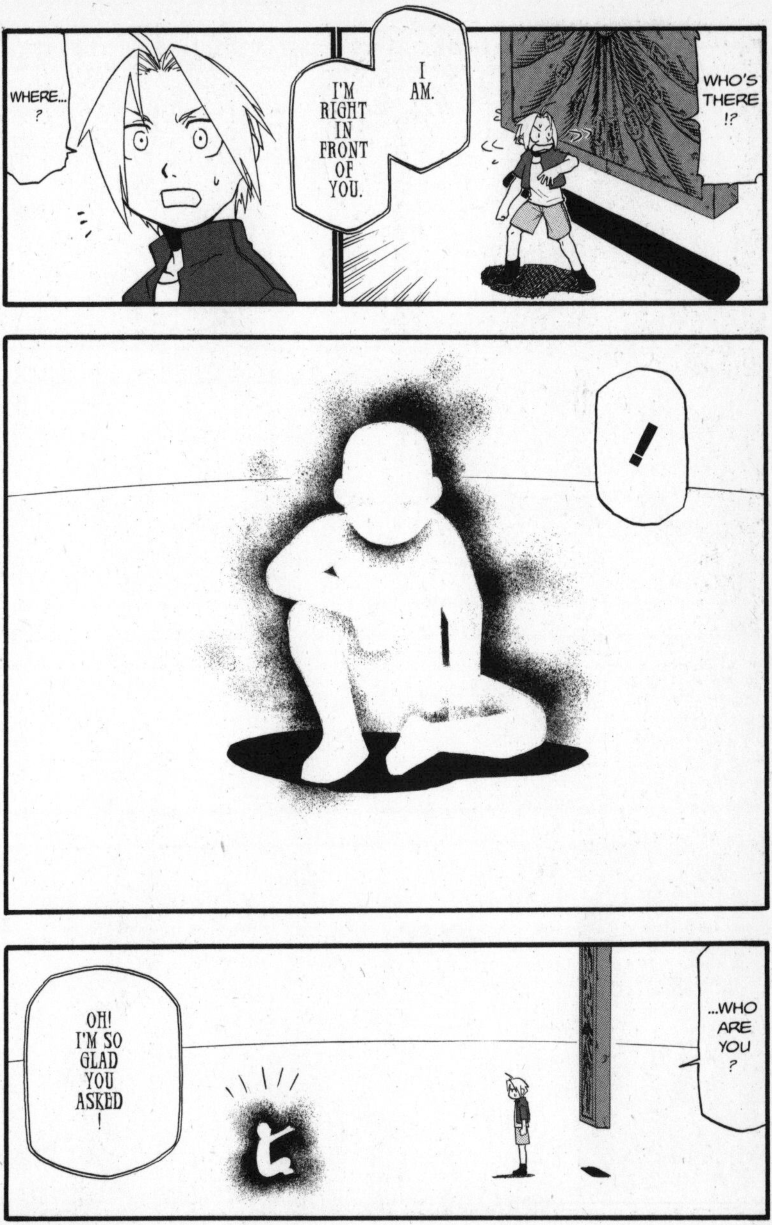
WHO'S THERE!?
I AM.
I'M RIGHT IN FRONT OF YOU.
WHERE...?
!
...WHO ARE YOU?
OH! I'M SO GLAD YOU ASKED!

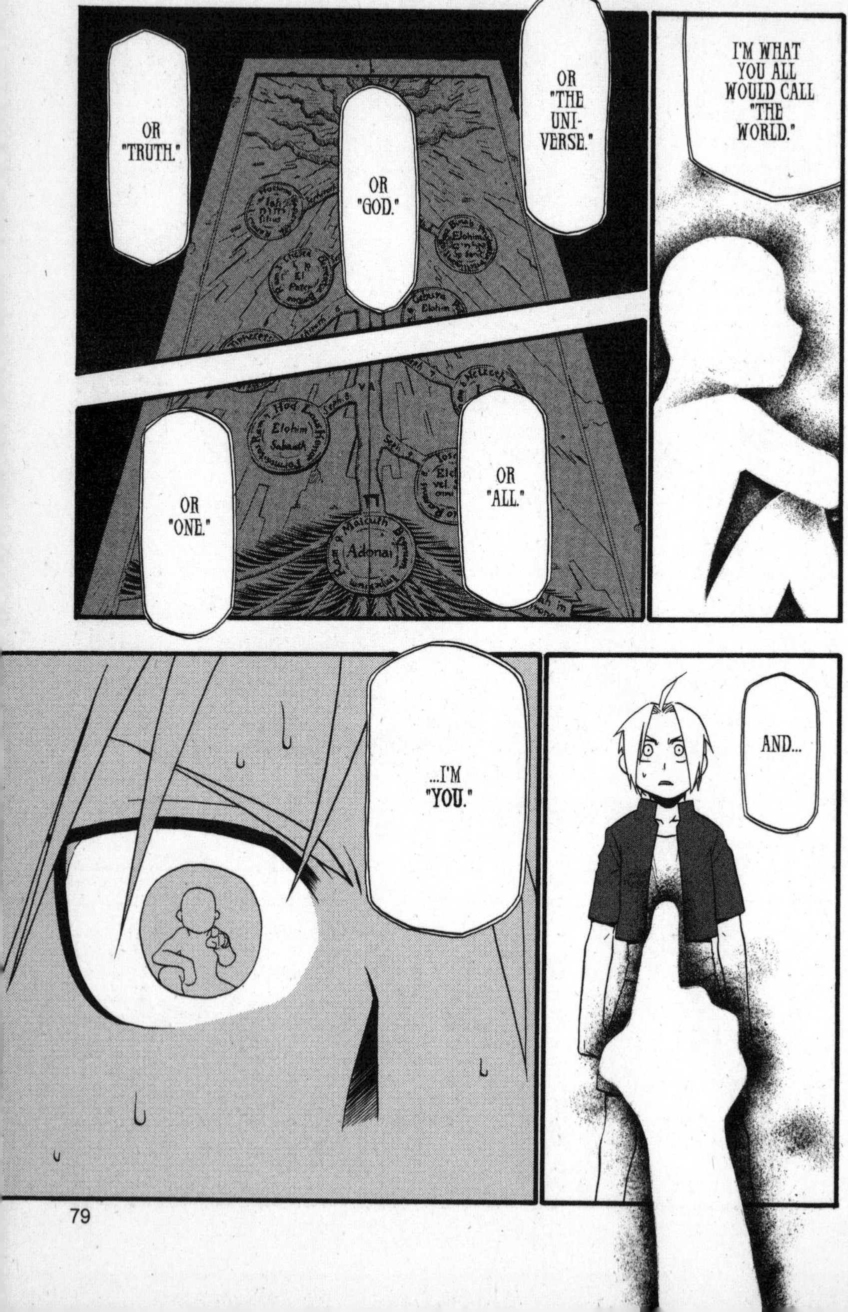
I'M WHAT YOU ALL WOULD CALL "THE WORLD."
OR "THE UNI-VERSE."
OR "GOD."
OR "TRUTH."
OR "ALL."
OR "ONE."
AND...
...I'M "YOU."

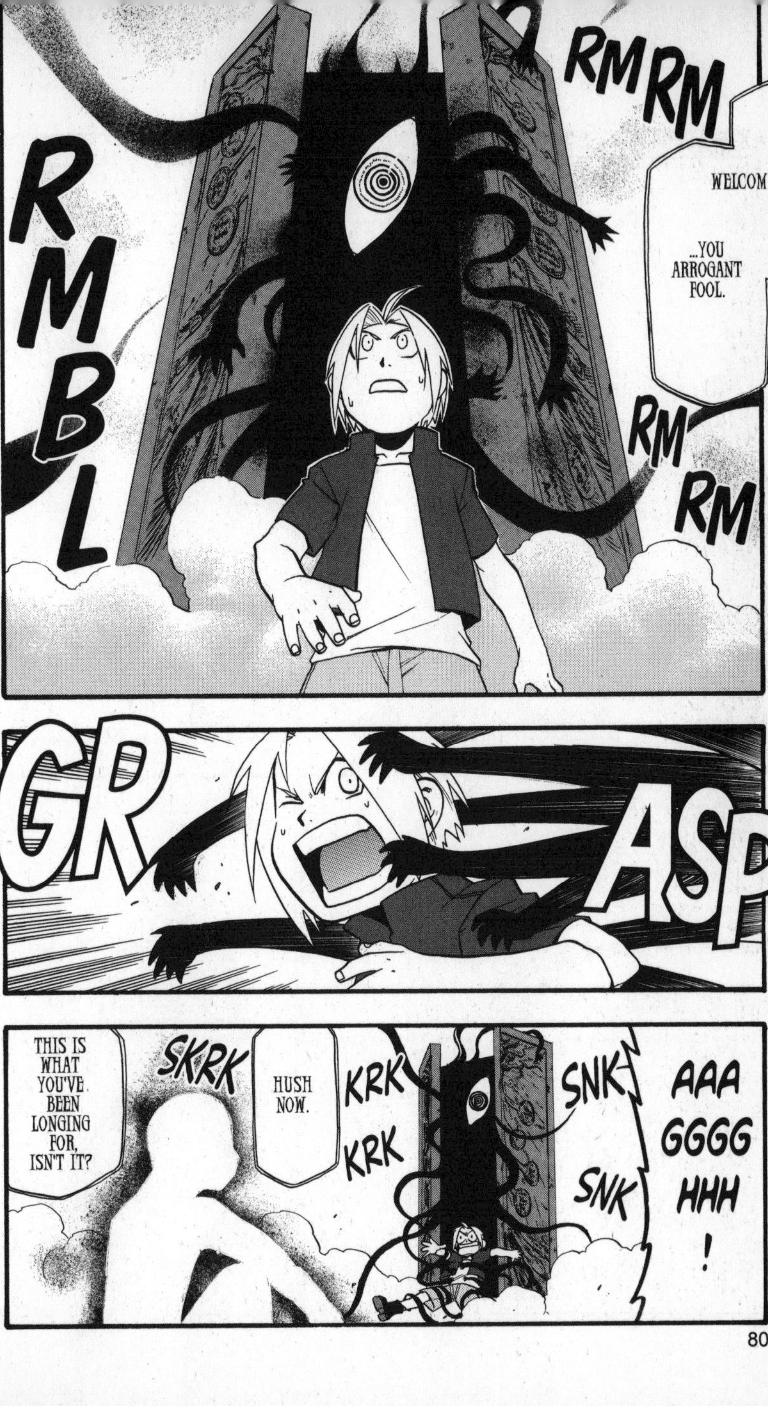
RMRM
WELCOME...
...YOU ARROGANT FOOL.
RM RM
RMBL
GR ASP
AAAGGGGHHH!
SNK SNK
KRK KRK
HUSH NOW.
SKRK
THIS IS WHAT YOU'VE BEEN LONGING FOR, ISN'T IT?

AAAAAAAAH!!
KRIK
KRIK
KRIK
KREEK
I'LL SHOW YOU THE TRUTH.
SLAM

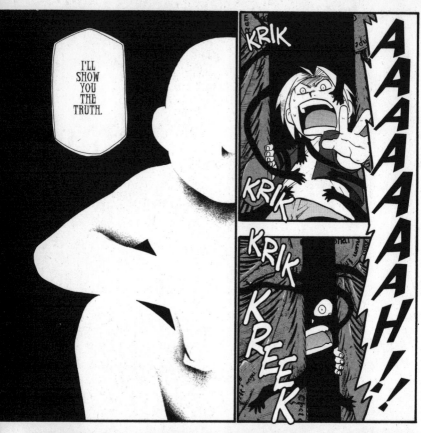

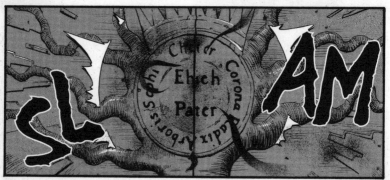

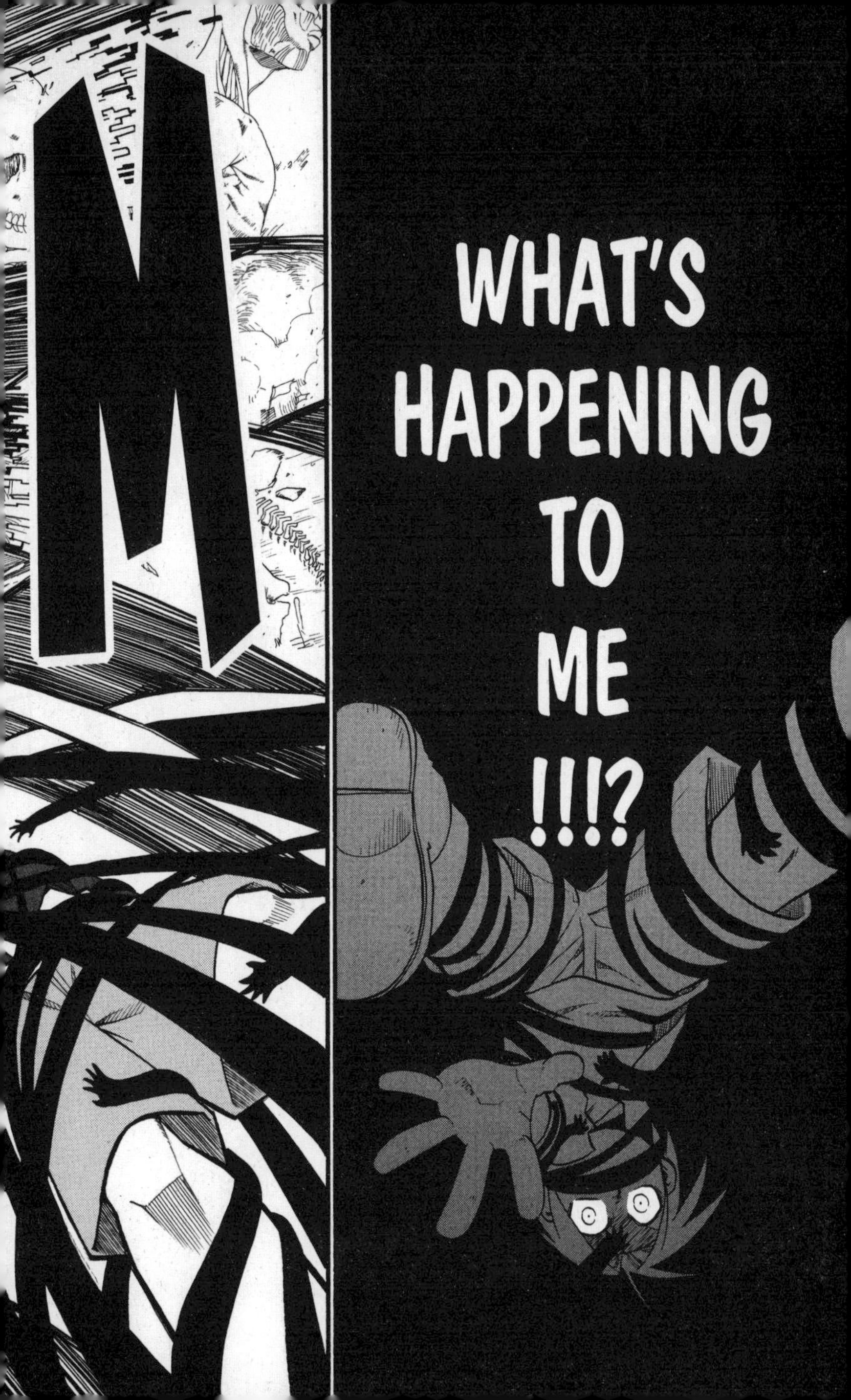
WHAT'S HAPPENING TO ME !!!?
M

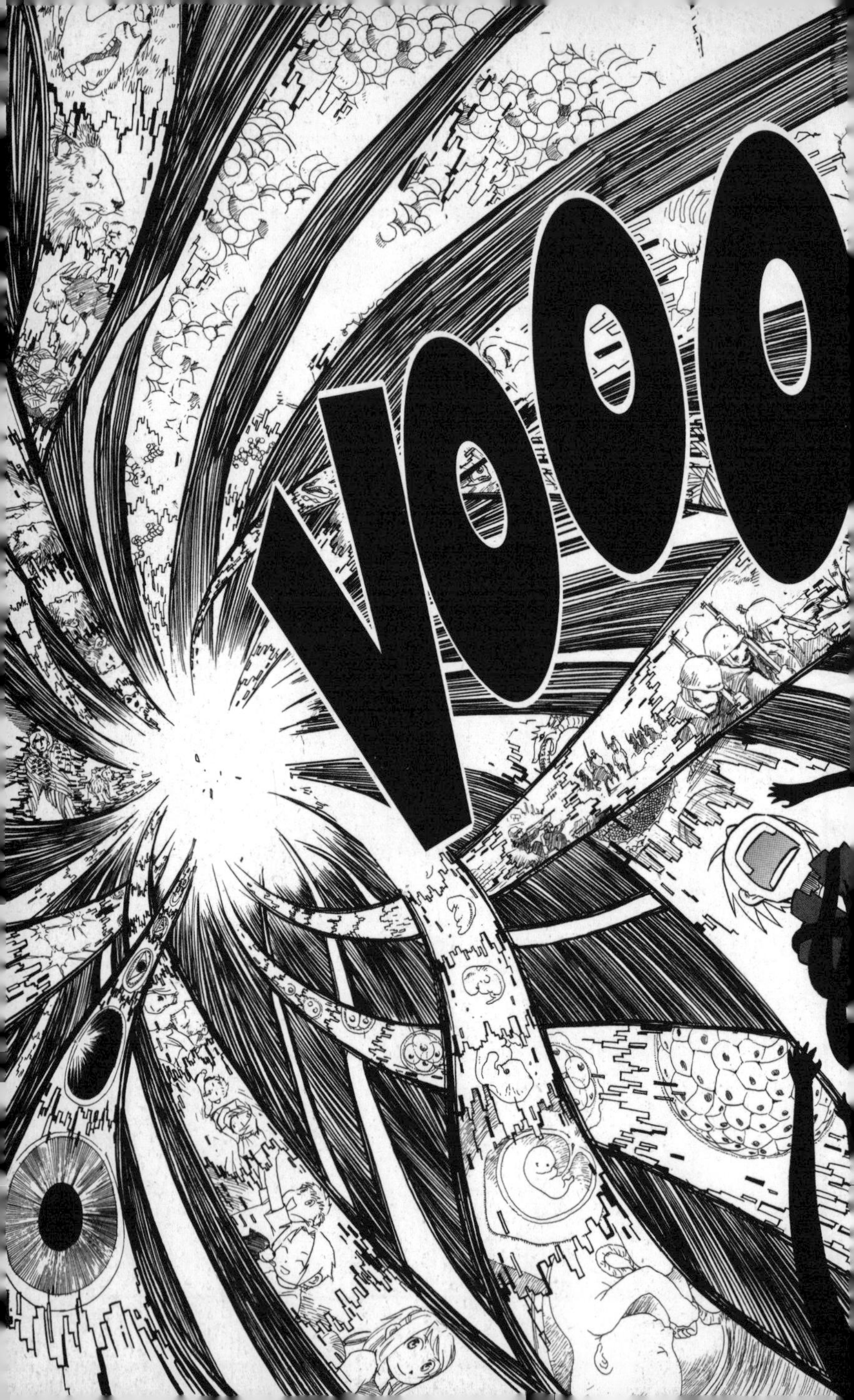
VOOO

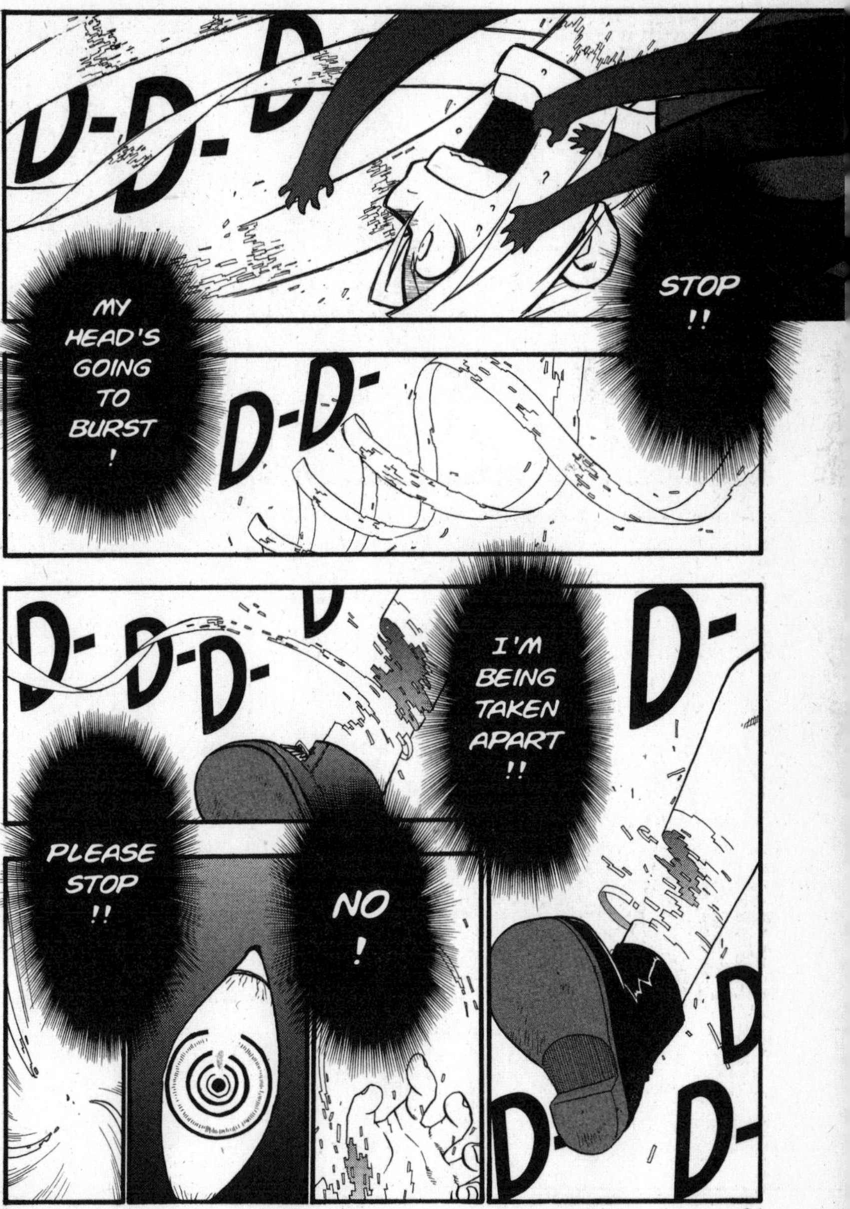
STOP !!
D-D-D-D
MY HEAD'S GOING TO BURST !
D-D-
D-
I'M BEING TAKEN APART !!
D-D-D-D
D
D-
D-
D-
NO !
PLEASE STOP !!

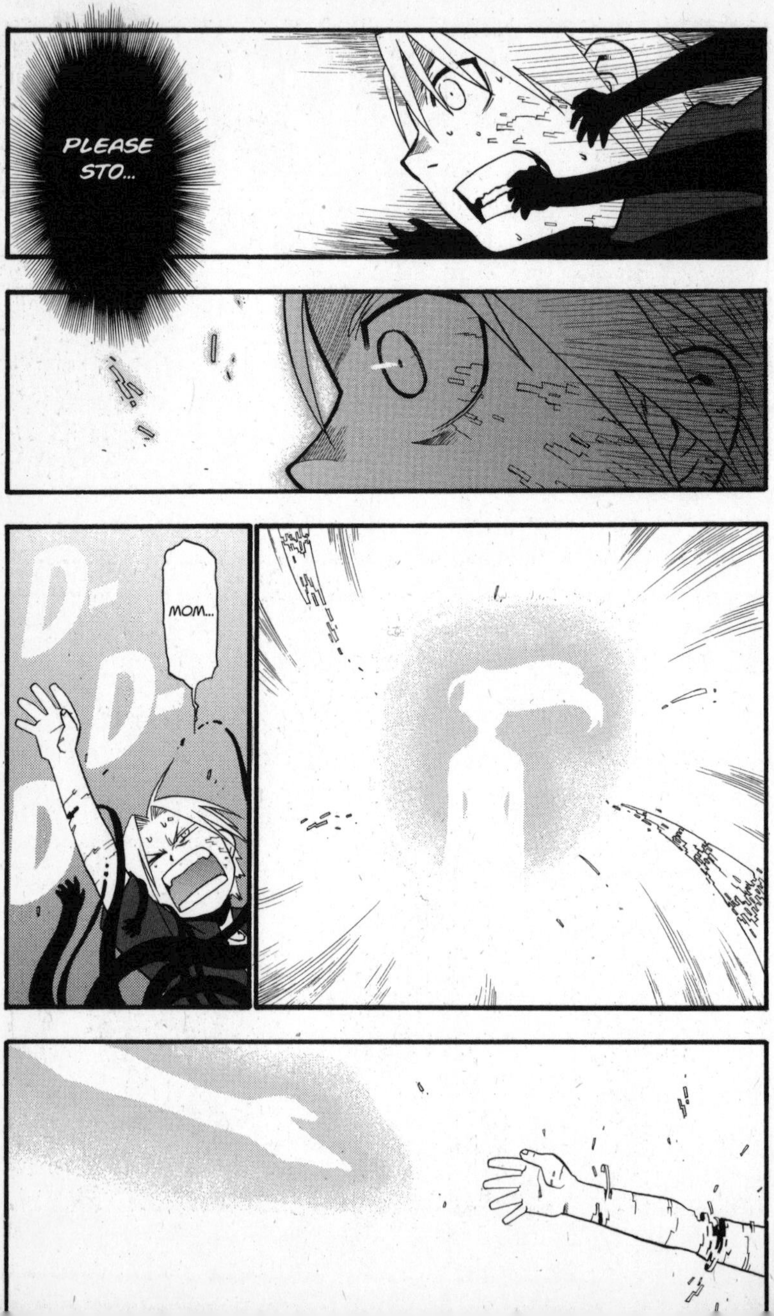
PLEASE STO...
MOM...
D- D- D-

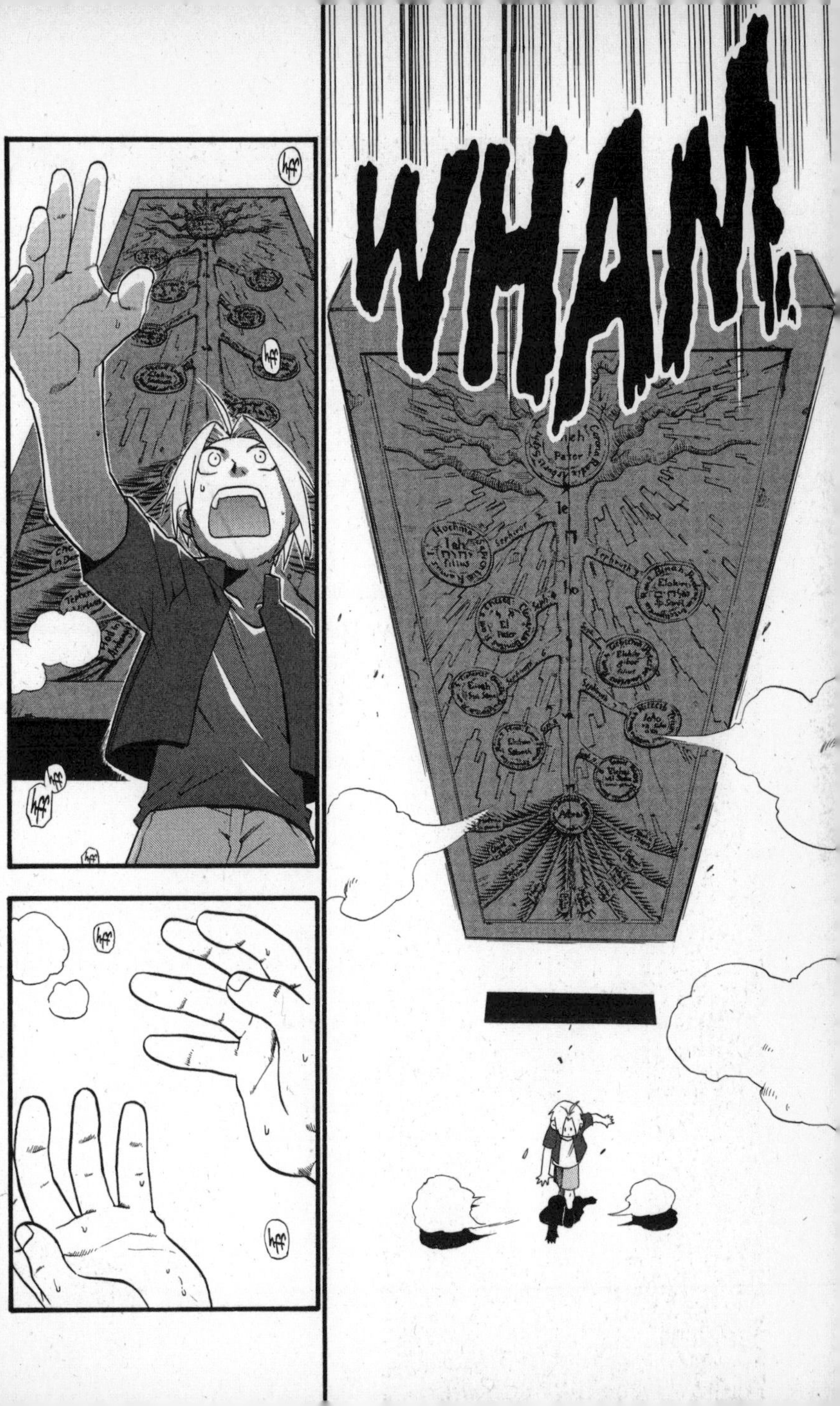
WHAM!
hff
hff
hff
hff
hff
hff
hff

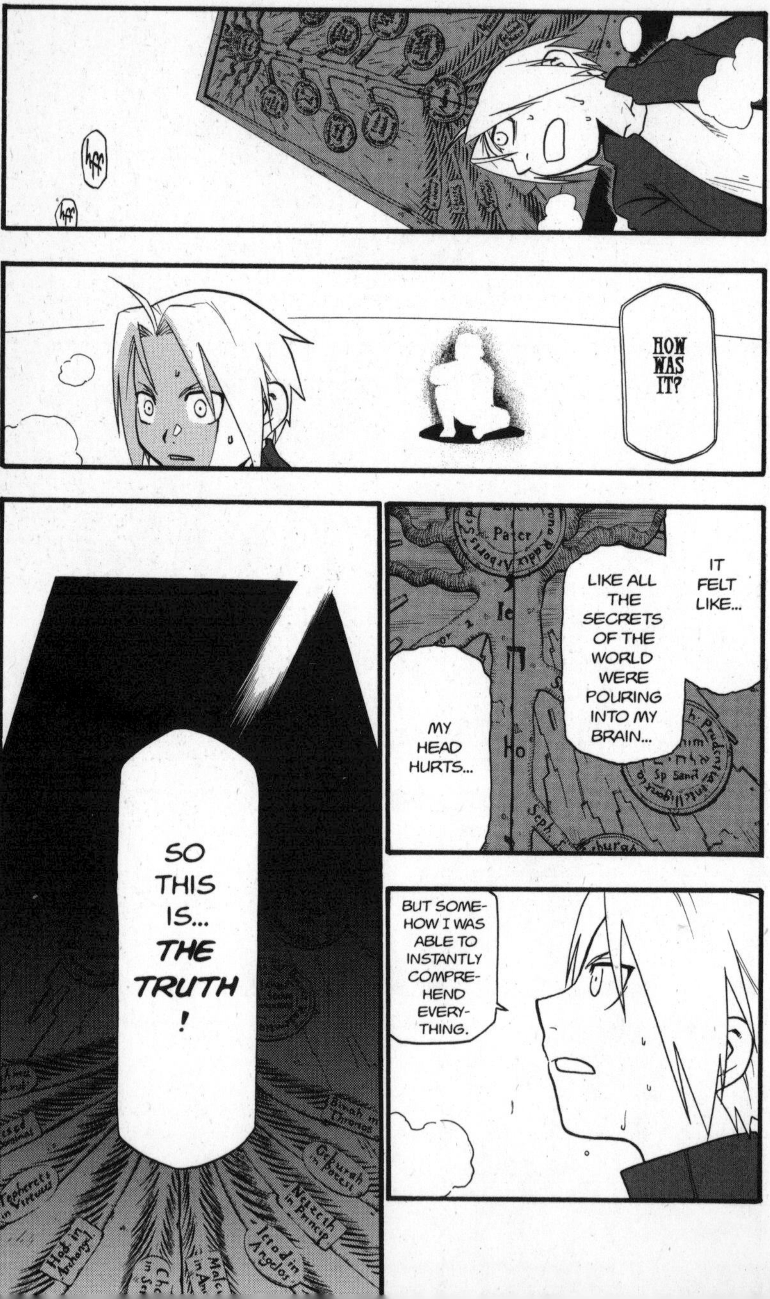
hff
hff
HOW WAS IT?
IT FELT LIKE...
LIKE ALL THE SECRETS OF THE WORLD WERE POURING INTO MY BRAIN...
MY HEAD HURTS...
BUT SOMEHOW I WAS ABLE TO INSTANTLY COMPREHEND EVERYTHING.
SO THIS IS... THE TRUTH!

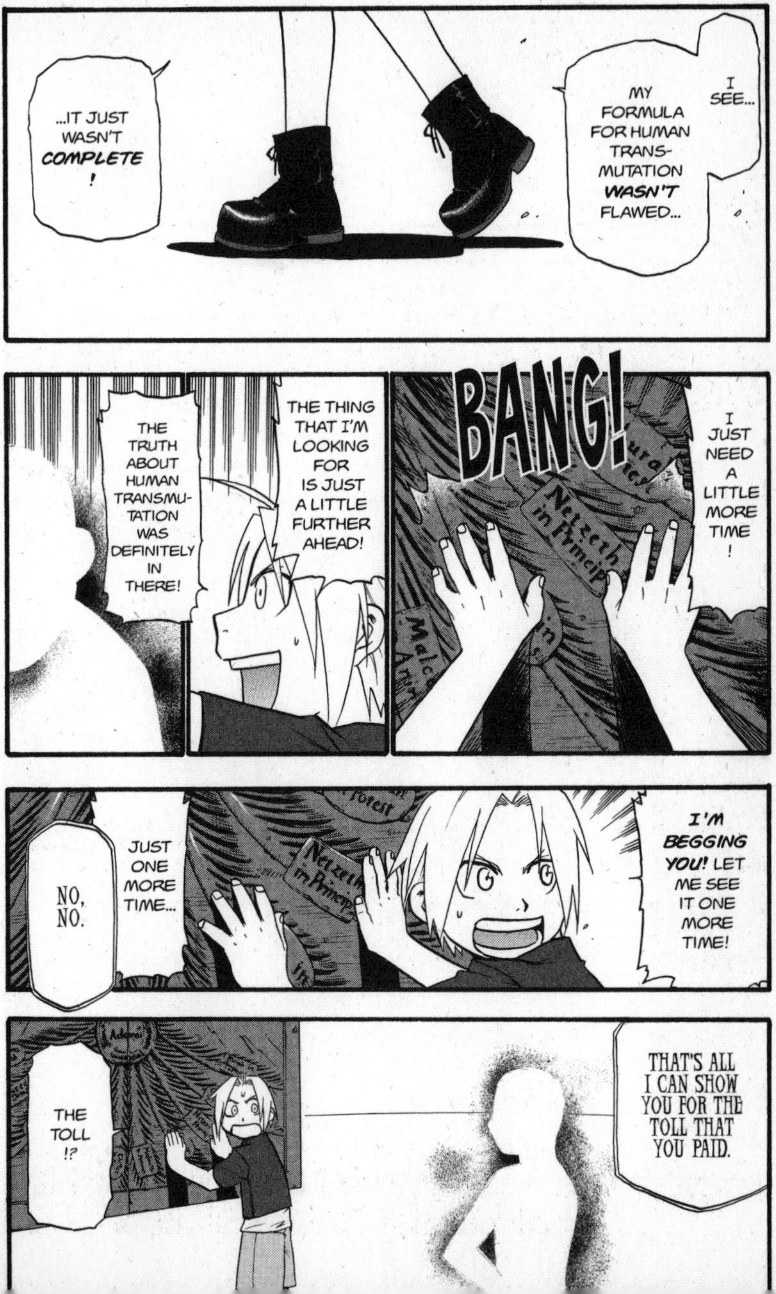
I SEE...
MY FORMULA FOR HUMAN TRANS-MUTATION WASN'T FLAWED...
...IT JUST WASN'T COMPLETE!
BANG!
I JUST NEED A LITTLE MORE TIME!
THE THING THAT I'M LOOKING FOR IS JUST A LITTLE FURTHER AHEAD!
THE TRUTH ABOUT HUMAN TRANSMU-TATION WAS DEFINITELY IN THERE!
I'M BEGGING YOU! LET ME SEE IT ONE MORE TIME!
JUST ONE MORE TIME...
NO, NO.
THAT'S ALL I CAN SHOW YOU FOR THE TOLL THAT YOU PAID.
THE TOLL!?

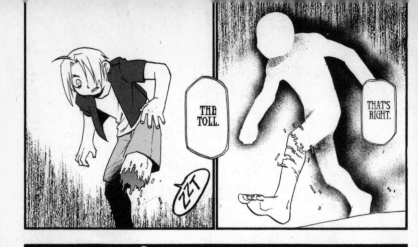

THE TOLL.

THAT'S RIGHT.

ZZT

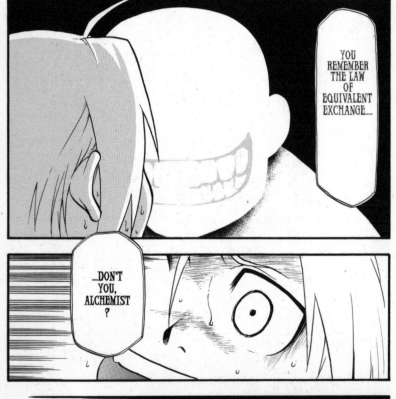

YOU REMEMBER THE LAW OF EQUIVALENT EXCHANGE....

...DON'T YOU, ALCHEMIST?

BBMP

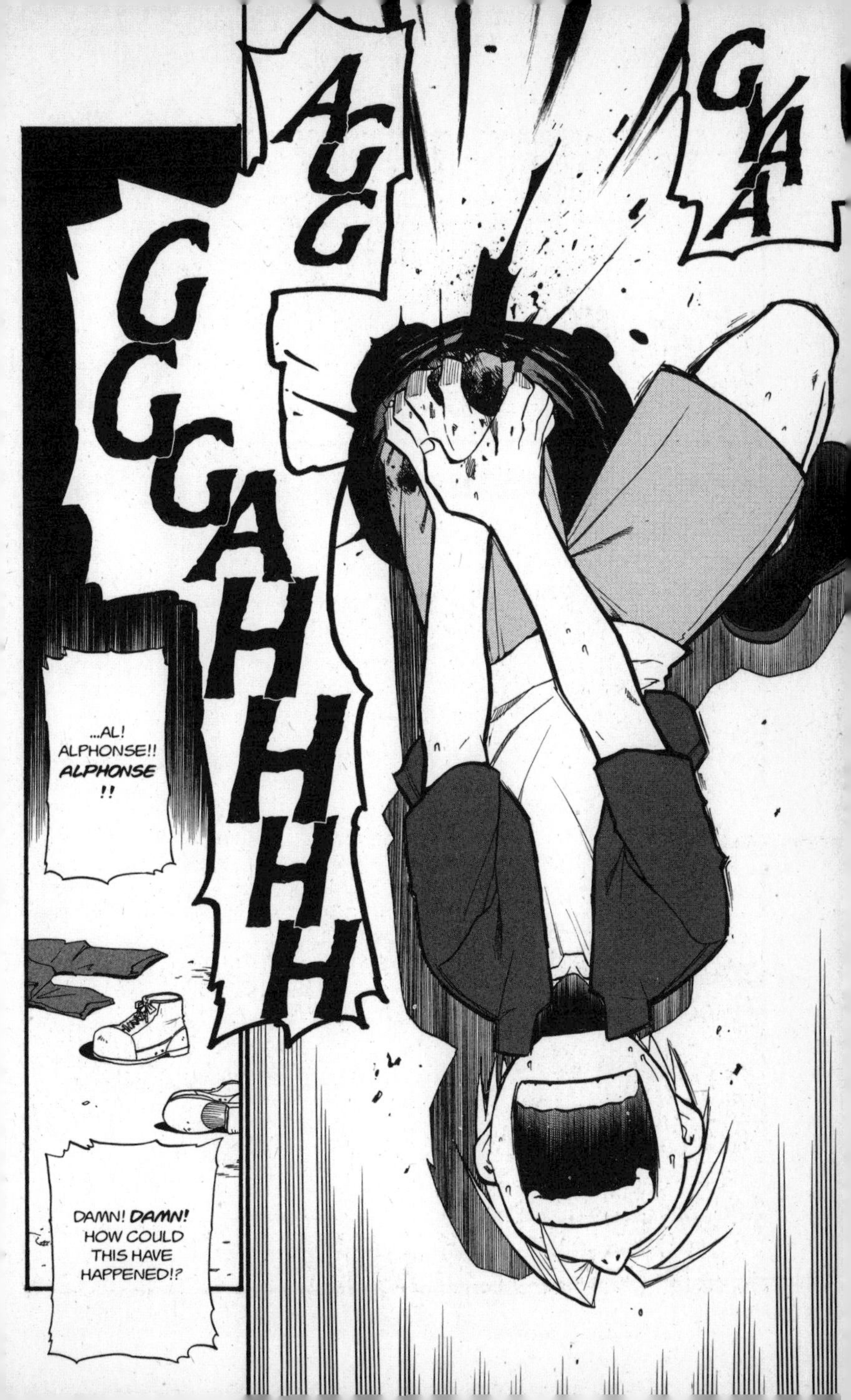
GYAA
AUGGGGGAHHHHHH
...AL! ALPHONSE!! ALPHONSE!!
DAMN! DAMN! HOW COULD THIS HAVE HAPPENED!?

DRAG
IT...IT WASN'T SUP-POSED TO BE LIKE THIS...
OH NO... HE'S GONE!
SOME-BODY...
HELP ME...
MOM !!
MOM...
WHEEZE
WHEEZE
WHEEZE
WHEEZE

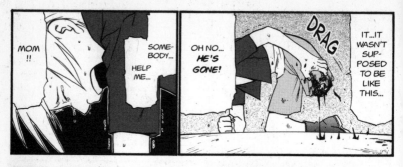

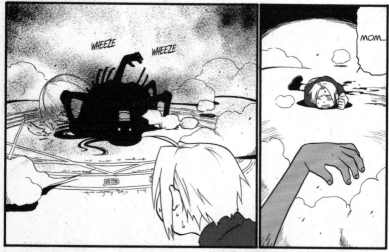

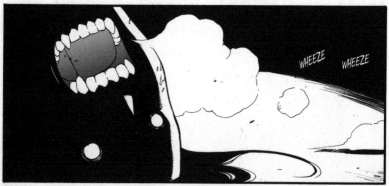

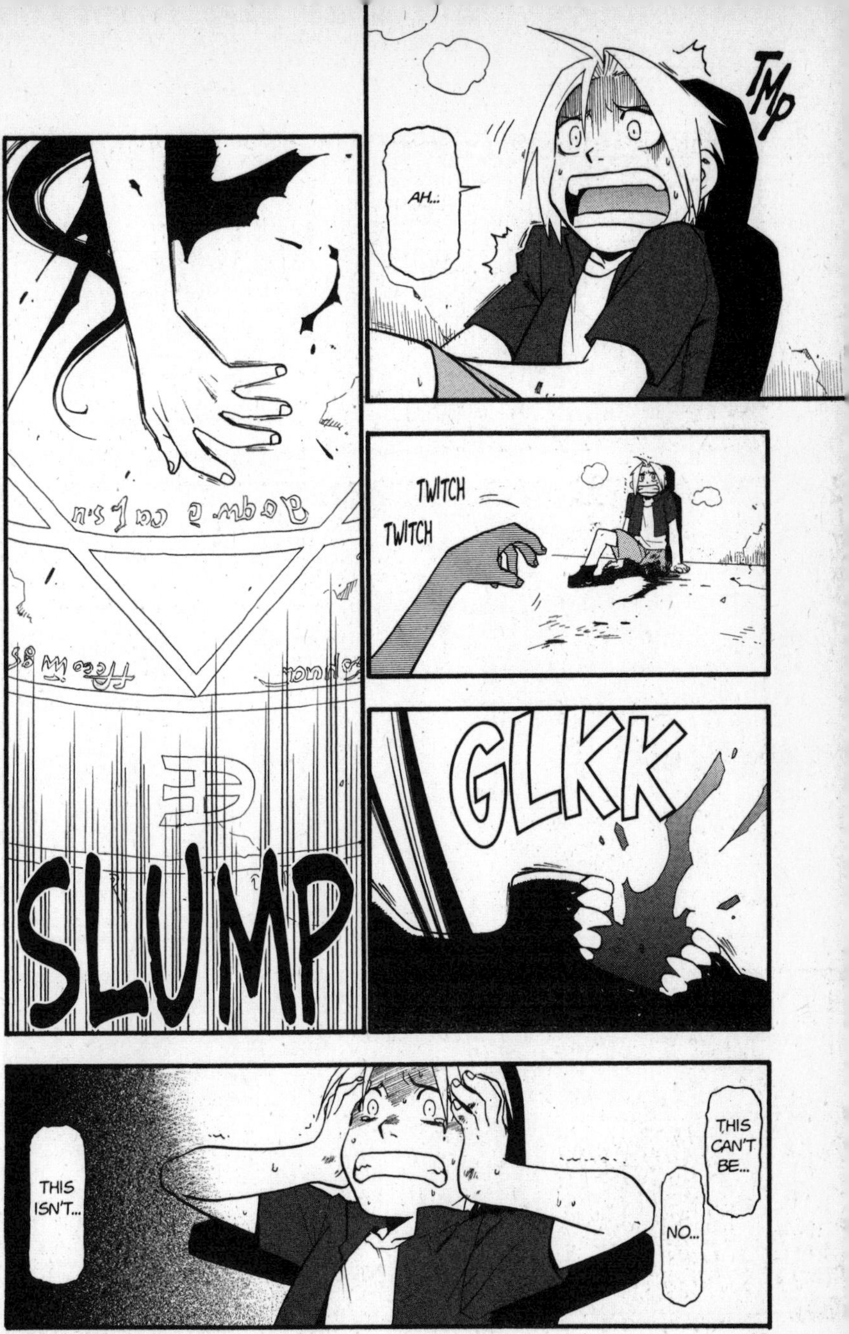
TMP
AH...
TWITCH
TWITCH
GLKK
SLUMP
THIS CAN'T BE...
NO...
THIS ISN'T...

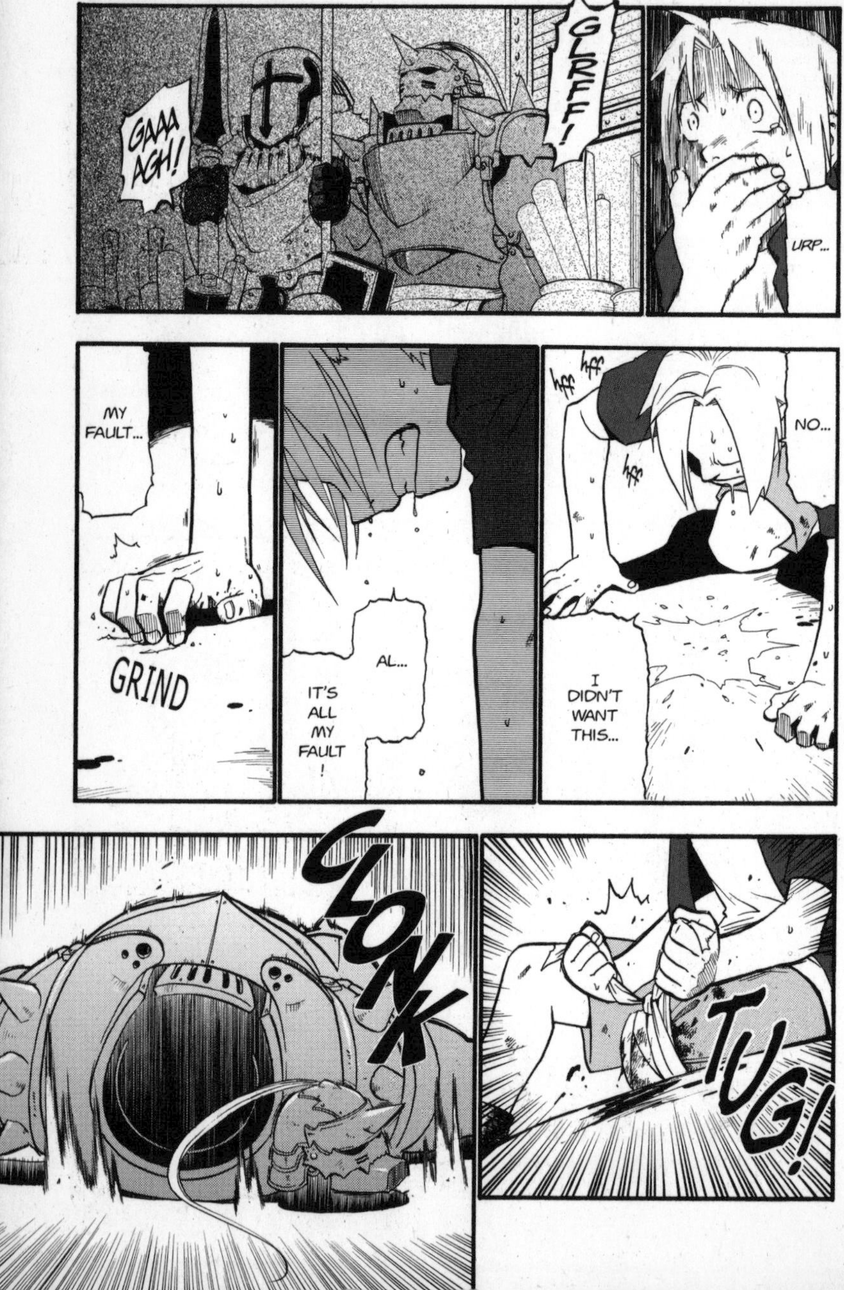
URP...
GLRFF!
GAAA AGH!
hff hff
NO...
hff
I DIDN'T WANT THIS...
AL...
IT'S ALL MY FAULT!
MY FAULT...
GRIND
TUG!
CLONK

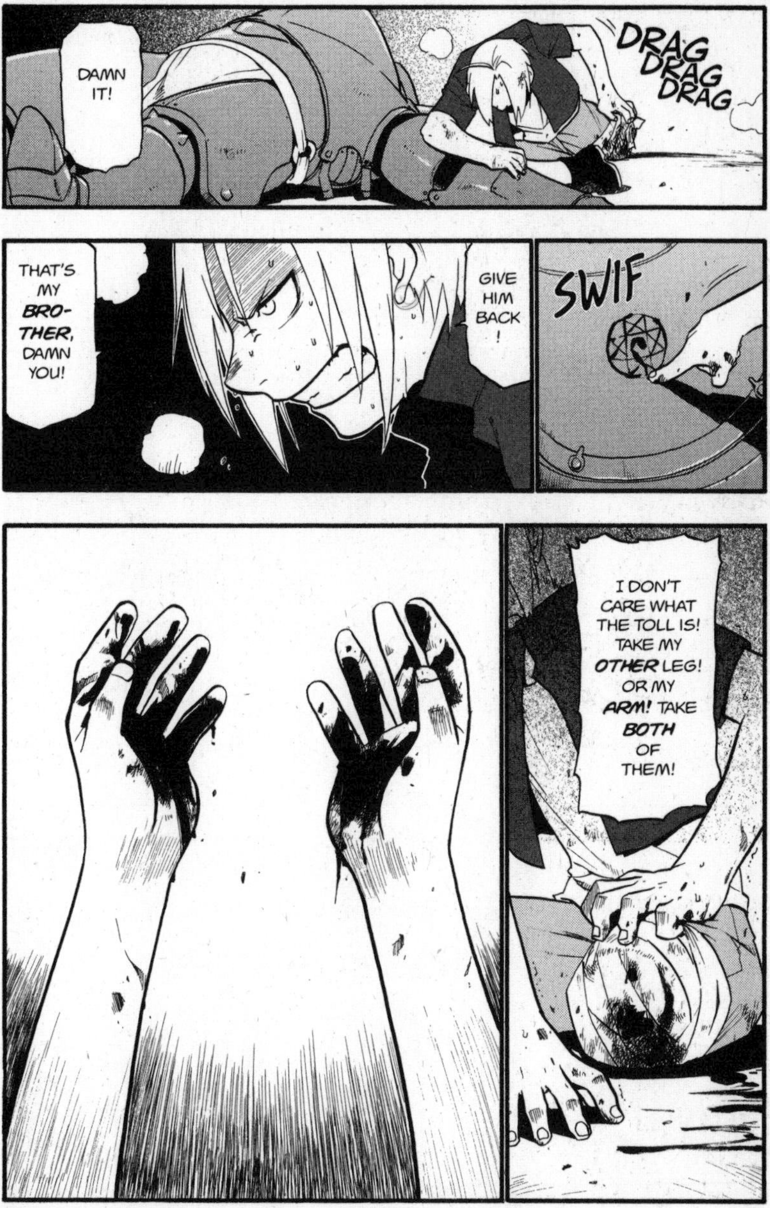
DRAG DRAG DRAG
DAMN IT!
SWIF
GIVE HIM BACK!
THAT'S MY BROTHER, DAMN YOU!
I DON'T CARE WHAT THE TOLL IS! TAKE MY OTHER LEG! OR MY ARM! TAKE BOTH OF THEM!

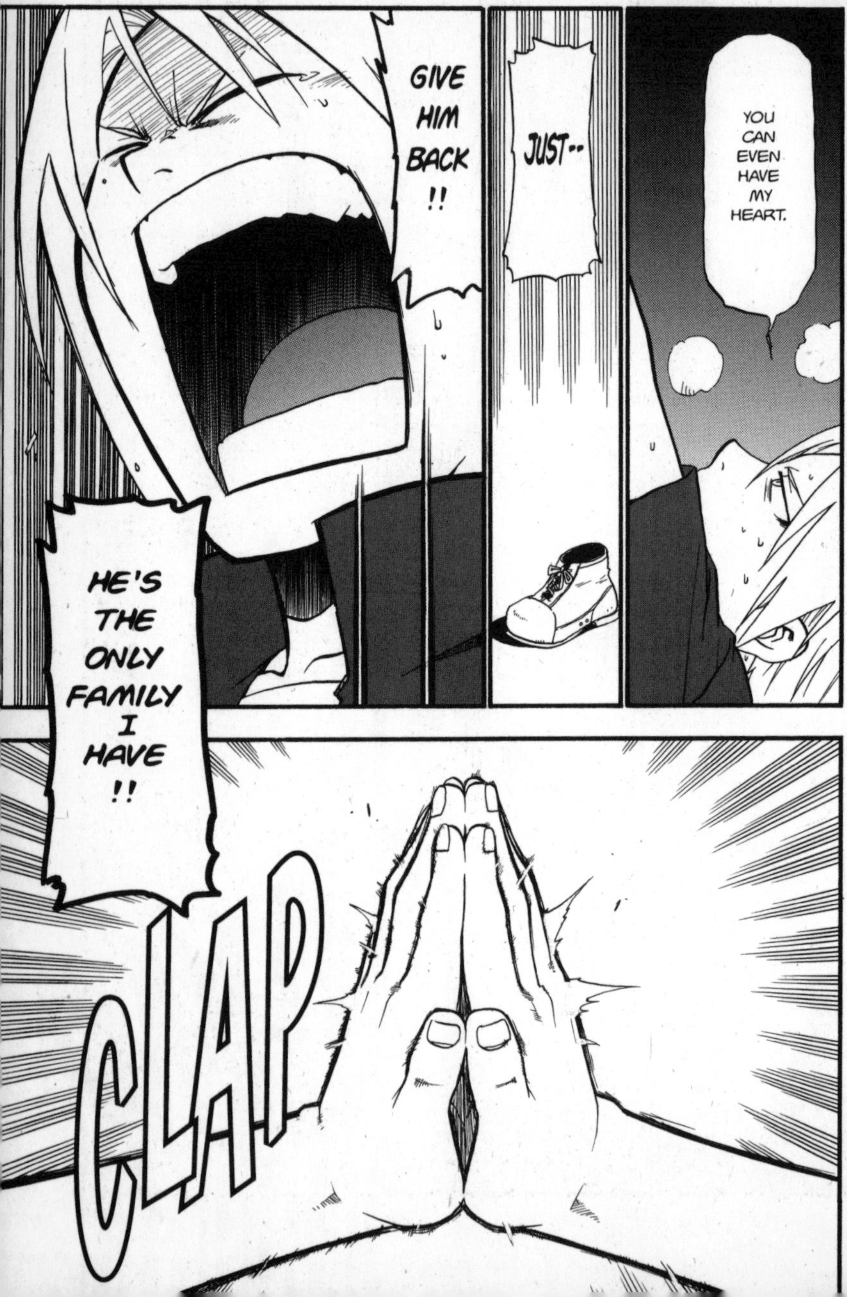
YOU CAN EVEN HAVE MY HEART.
JUST--
GIVE HIM BACK !!
HE'S THE ONLY FAMILY I HAVE !!
CLAP

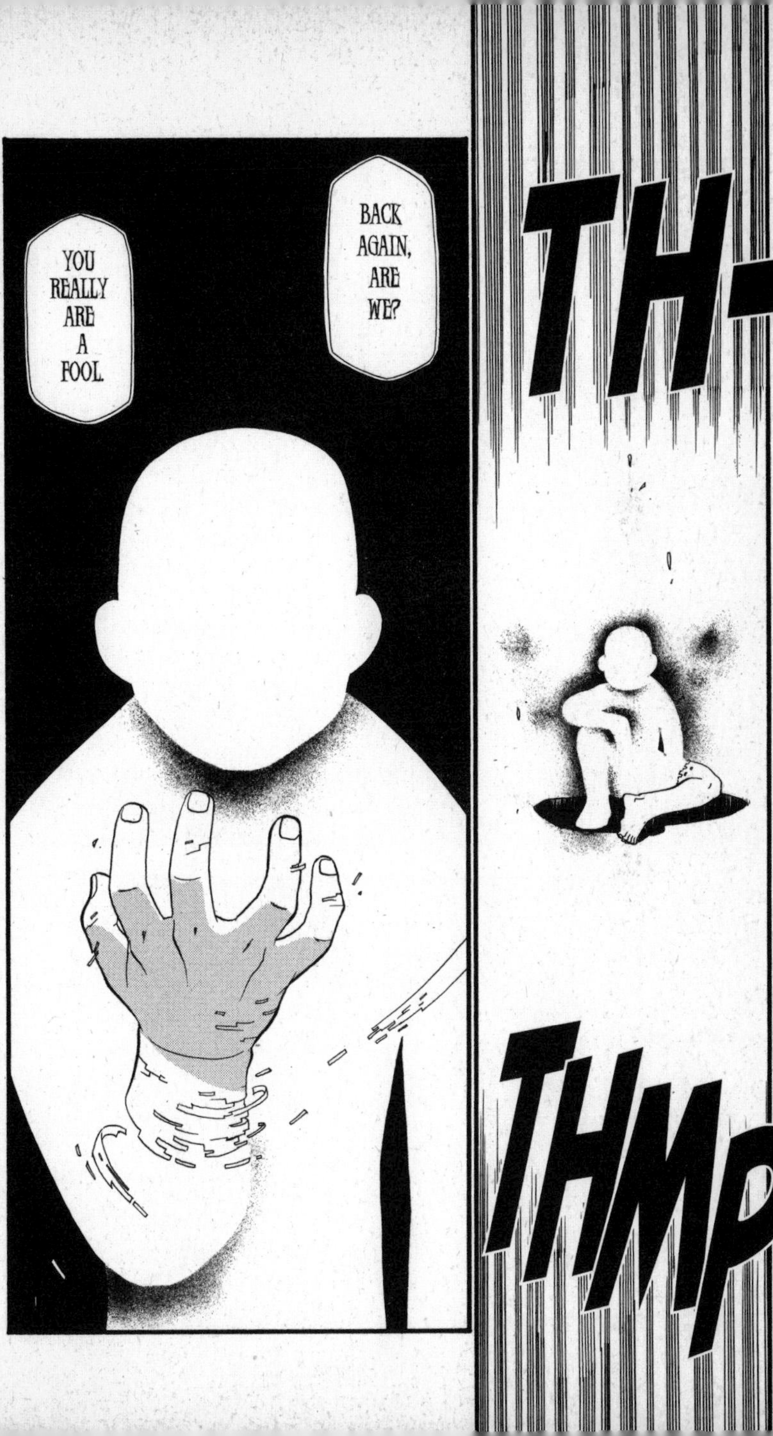
TH-
THMP
BACK AGAIN, ARE WE?
YOU REALLY ARE A FOOL.

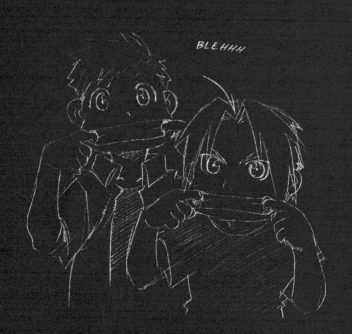

BLEHHH

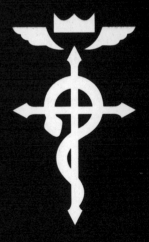

FULLMETAL
ALCHEMIST

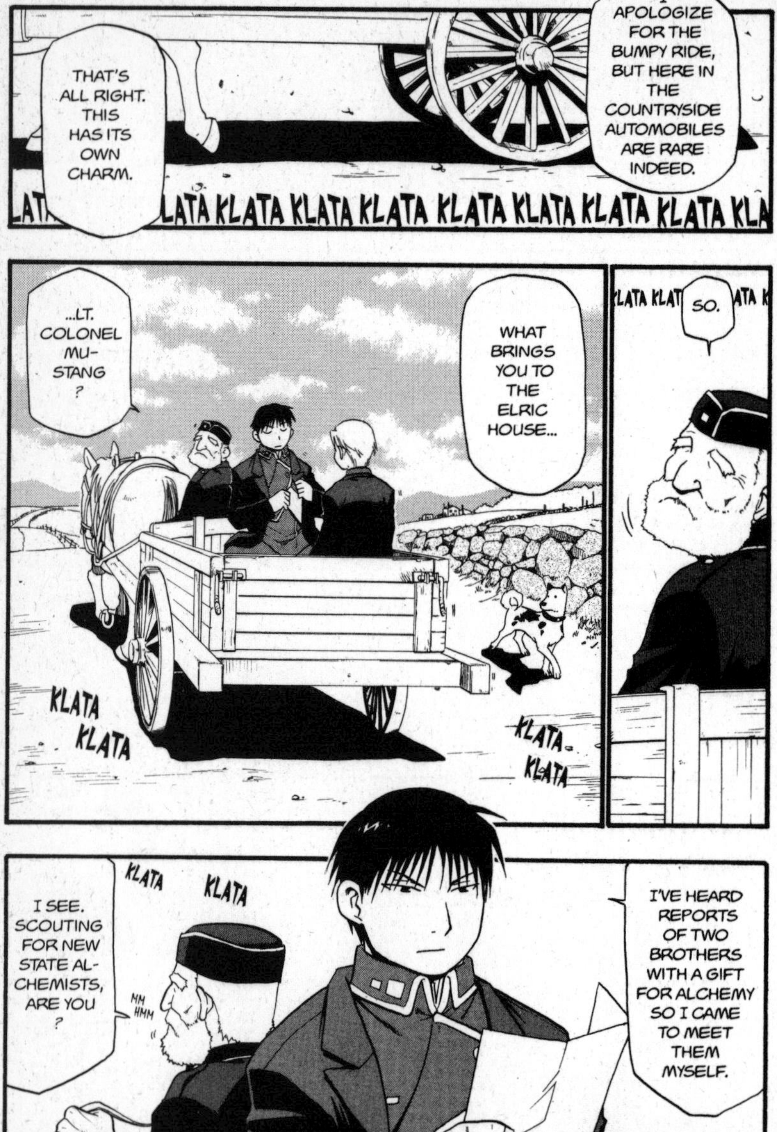
I APOLOGIZE FOR THE BUMPY RIDE, BUT HERE IN THE COUNTRYSIDE AUTOMOBILES ARE RARE INDEED.
THAT'S ALL RIGHT. THIS HAS ITS OWN CHARM.
KLATA KLATA KLATA KLATA KLATA KLATA KLATA KLATA KLATA
KLATA KLATA
SO.
WHAT BRINGS YOU TO THE ELRIC HOUSE...
...LT. COLONEL MU-STANG?
KLATA KLATA
KLATA KLATA
I'VE HEARD REPORTS OF TWO BROTHERS WITH A GIFT FOR ALCHEMY SO I CAME TO MEET THEM MYSELF.
KLATA KLATA
I SEE. SCOUTING FOR NEW STATE AL-CHEMISTS, ARE YOU?
MM HMM

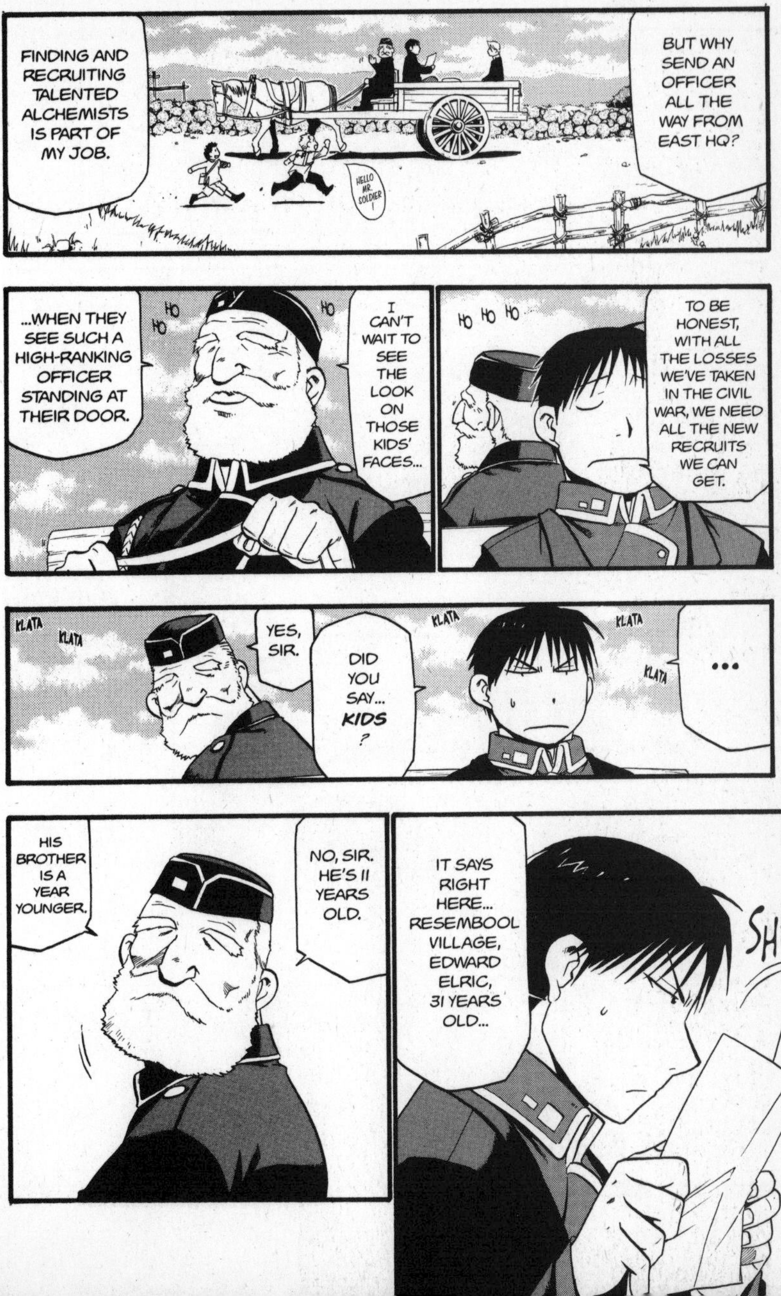
BUT WHY SEND AN OFFICER ALL THE WAY FROM EAST HQ?
FINDING AND RECRUITING TALENTED ALCHEMISTS IS PART OF MY JOB.
HELLO MR. SOLDIER!
TO BE HONEST, WITH ALL THE LOSSES WE'VE TAKEN IN THE CIVIL WAR, WE NEED ALL THE NEW RECRUITS WE CAN GET.
HO HO HO
I CAN'T WAIT TO SEE THE LOOK ON THOSE KIDS' FACES...
HO HO
...WHEN THEY SEE SUCH A HIGH-RANKING OFFICER STANDING AT THEIR DOOR.
...
KLATA
KLATA
KLATA
DID YOU SAY... KIDS?
YES, SIR.
KLATA
KLATA
SHFF
IT SAYS RIGHT HERE... RESEMBOOL VILLAGE, EDWARD ELRIC, 31 YEARS OLD...
NO, SIR. HE'S 11 YEARS OLD.
HIS BROTHER IS A YEAR YOUNGER.

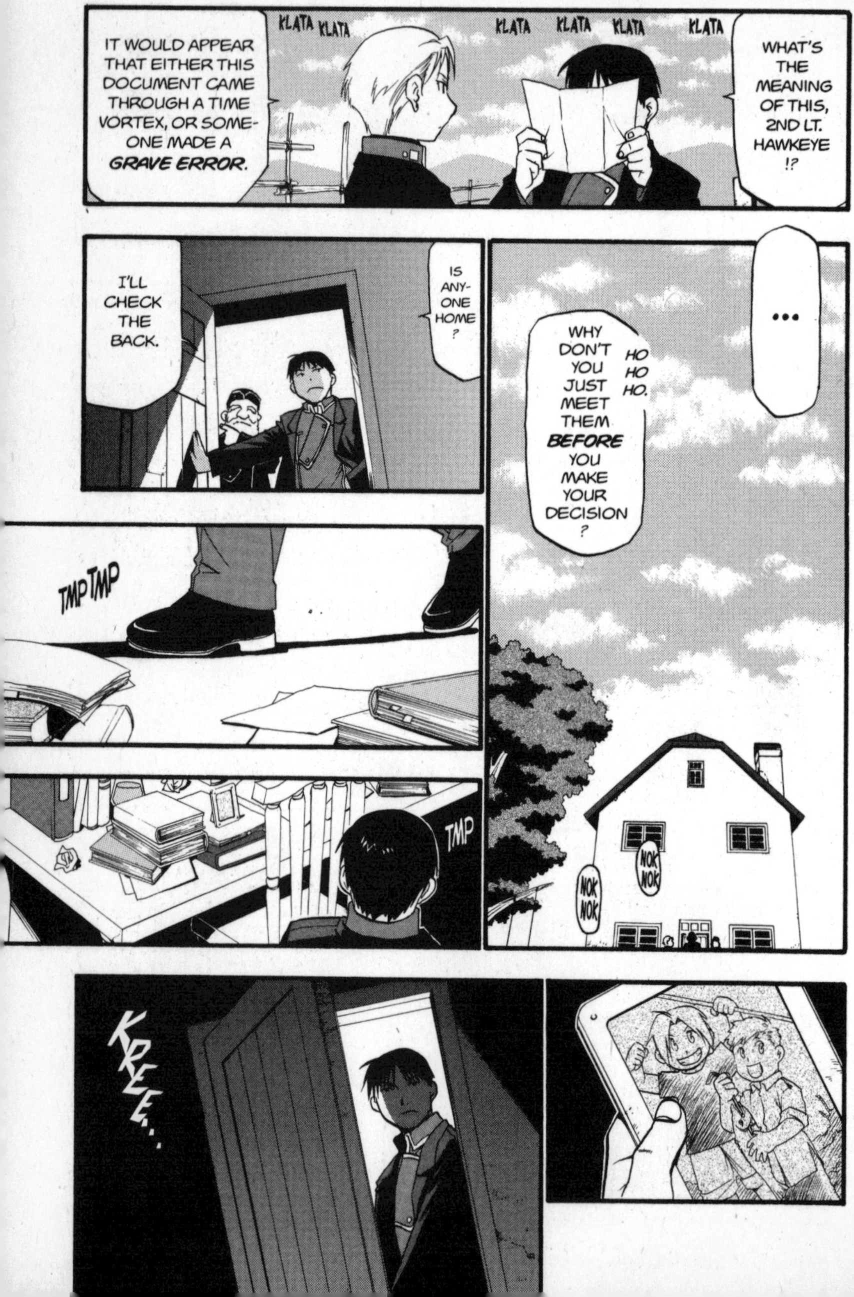

WHAT'S THE MEANING OF THIS, 2ND LT. HAWKEYE!?
KLATA KLATA KLATA KLATA KLATA KLATA
IT WOULD APPEAR THAT EITHER THIS DOCUMENT CAME THROUGH A TIME VORTEX, OR SOME-ONE MADE A GRAVE ERROR.
...
WHY DON'T YOU JUST MEET THEM BEFORE YOU MAKE YOUR DECISION?
HO HO HO.
NOK NOK
NOK NOK
IS ANY-ONE HOME?
I'LL CHECK THE BACK.
TMP TMP
TMP
KREE...

Chapter 24: Fullmetal Alchemist

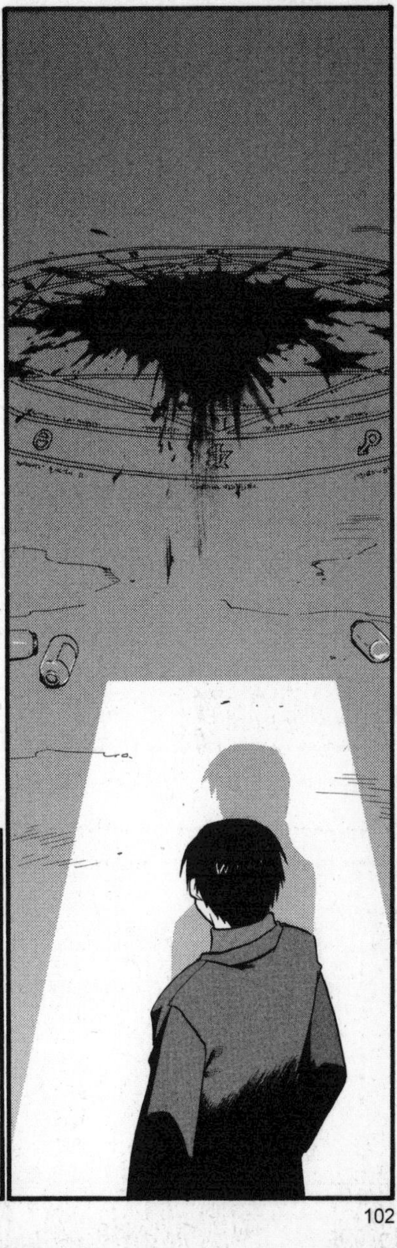

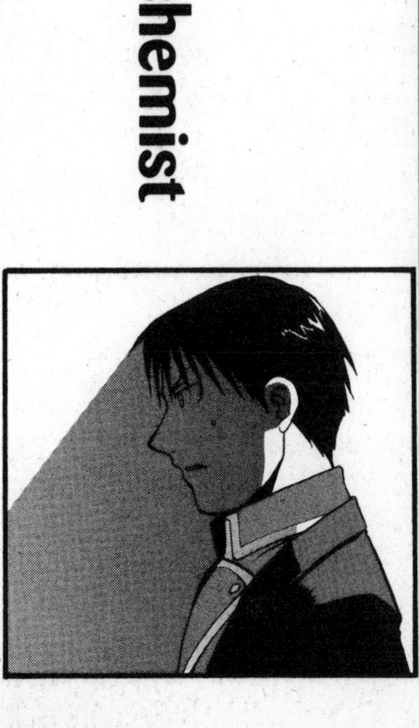

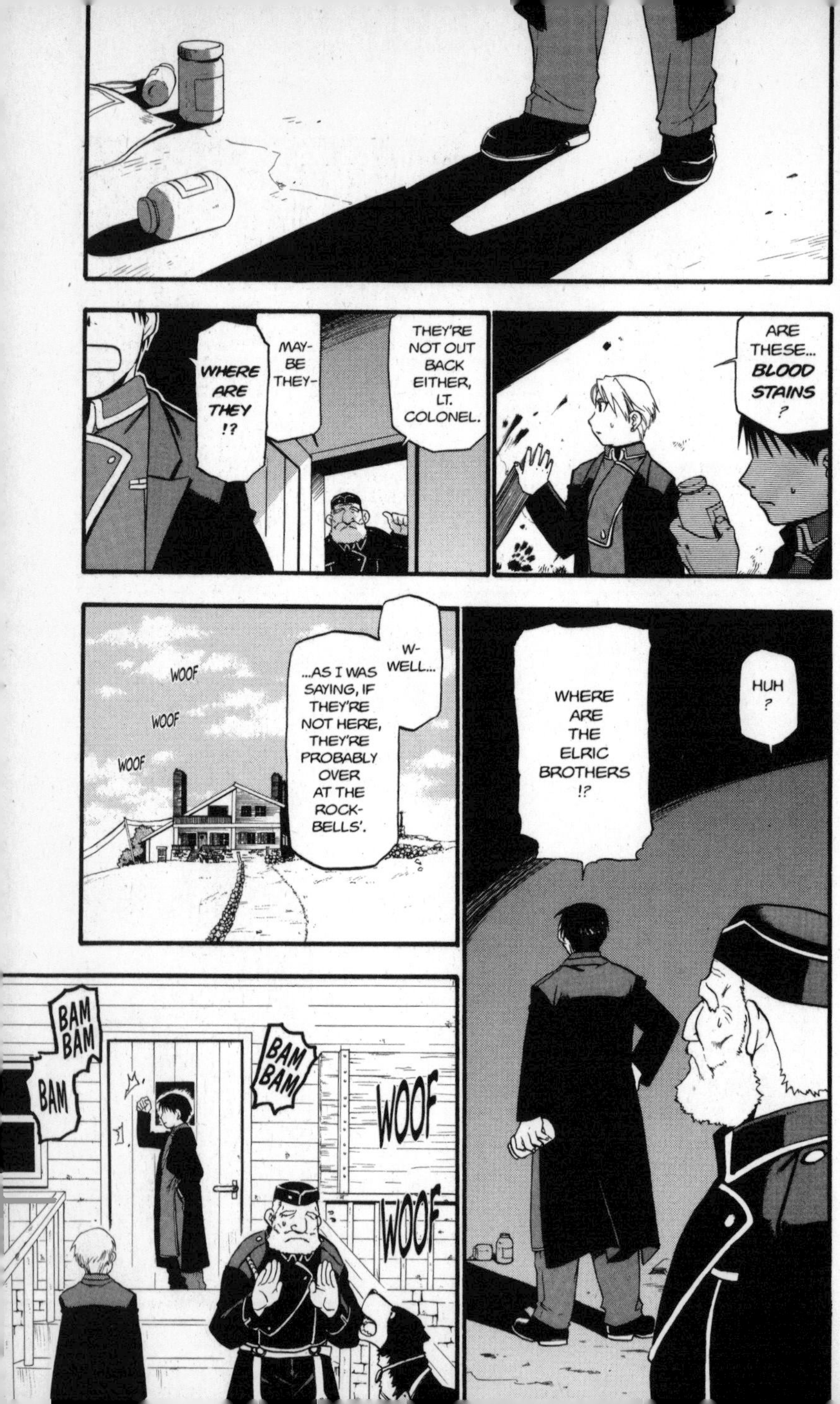
ARE THESE... BLOOD STAINS?
THEY'RE NOT OUT BACK EITHER, LT. COLONEL.
MAY-BE THEY-
WHERE ARE THEY!?
HUH?
WHERE ARE THE ELRIC BROTHERS!?
W-WELL...
...AS I WAS SAYING, IF THEY'RE NOT HERE, THEY'RE PROBABLY OVER AT THE ROCK-BELLS'.
WOOF
WOOF
WOOF
WOOF
WOOF
BAM BAM
BAM BAM
BAM

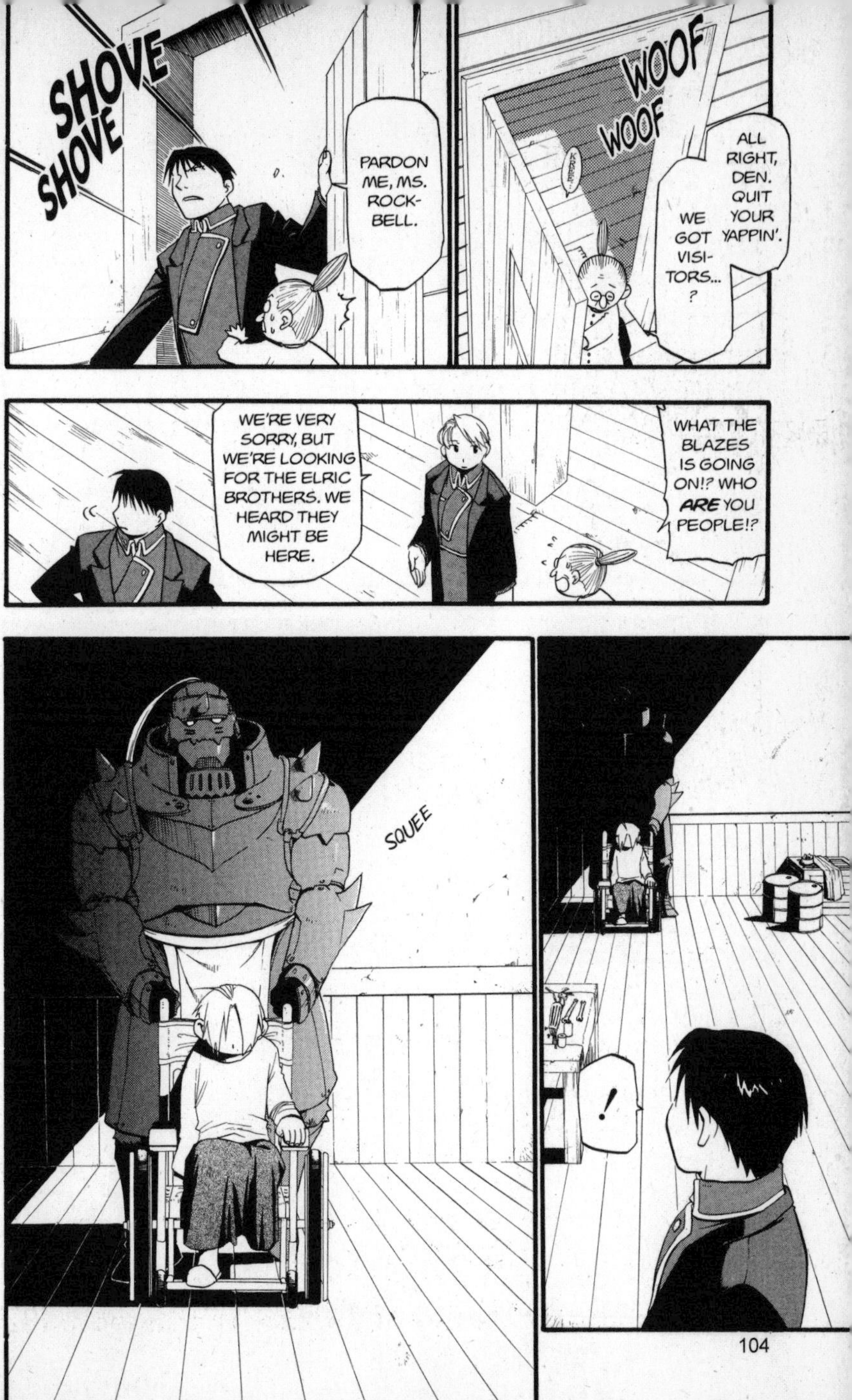
WOOF
WOOF
ALL RIGHT, DEN. QUIT YOUR YAPPIN'.
WE GOT VISITORS... ?
KREE...
SHOVE
SHOVE
PARDON ME, MS. ROCKBELL.
WHAT THE BLAZES IS GOING ON!? WHO ARE YOU PEOPLE!?
WE'RE VERY SORRY, BUT WE'RE LOOKING FOR THE ELRIC BROTHERS. WE HEARD THEY MIGHT BE HERE.
!
SQUEE

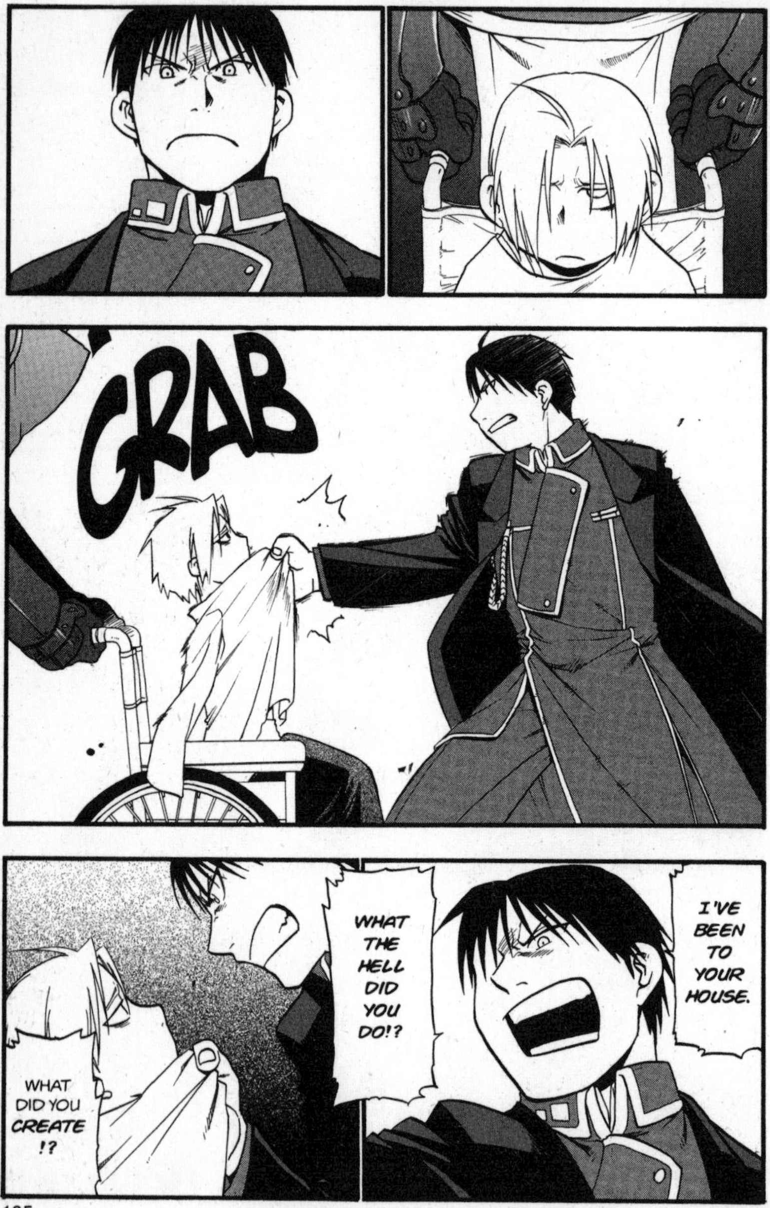
GRAB
I'VE BEEN TO YOUR HOUSE.
WHAT THE HELL DID YOU DO!?
WHAT DID YOU CREATE!?

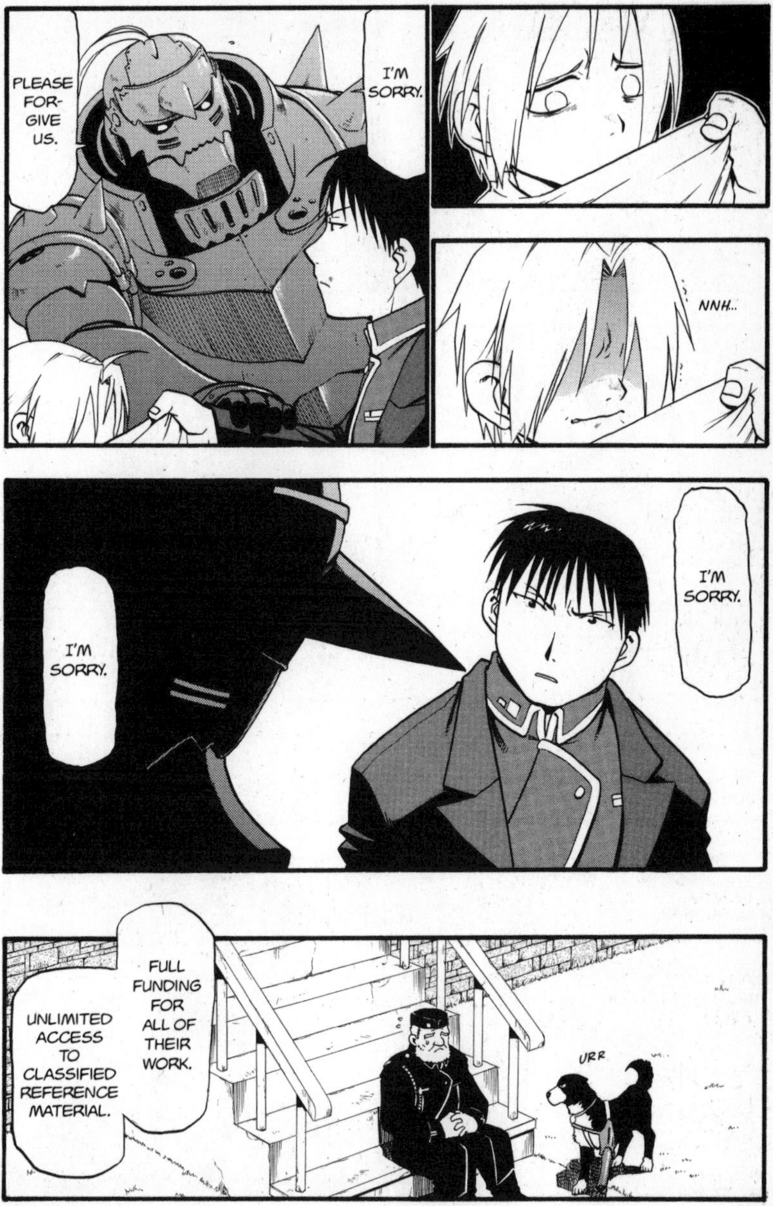
NNH...
I'M SORRY.
PLEASE FOR-GIVE US.
I'M SORRY.
I'M SORRY.
FULL FUNDING FOR ALL OF THEIR WORK.
UNLIMITED ACCESS TO CLASSIFIED REFERENCE MATERIAL.
URR

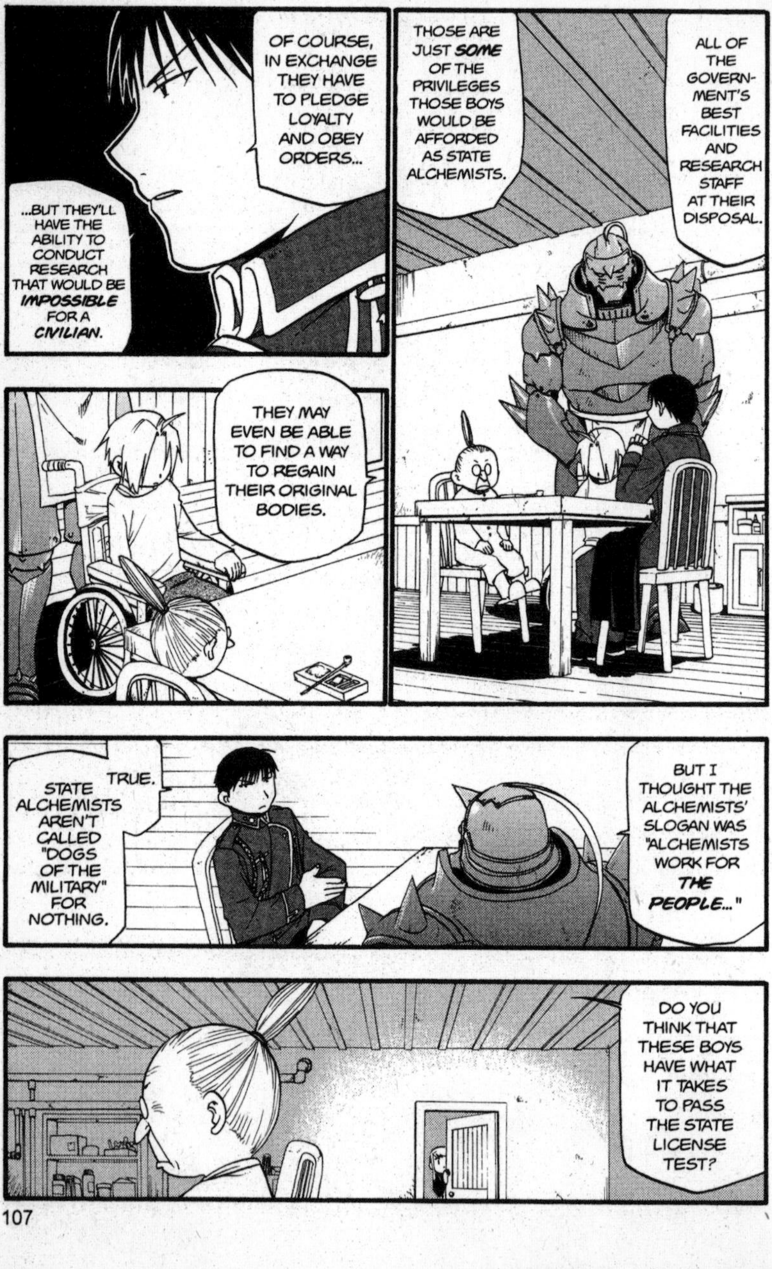
ALL OF THE GOVERNMENT'S BEST FACILITIES AND RESEARCH STAFF AT THEIR DISPOSAL.
THOSE ARE JUST **SOME** OF THE PRIVILEGES THOSE BOYS WOULD BE AFFORDED AS STATE ALCHEMISTS.
OF COURSE, IN EXCHANGE THEY HAVE TO PLEDGE LOYALTY AND OBEY ORDERS...
...BUT THEY'LL HAVE THE ABILITY TO CONDUCT RESEARCH THAT WOULD BE ***IMPOSSIBLE*** FOR A ***CIVILIAN.***
THEY MAY EVEN BE ABLE TO FIND A WAY TO REGAIN THEIR ORIGINAL BODIES.
BUT I THOUGHT THE ALCHEMISTS' SLOGAN WAS "ALCHEMISTS WORK FOR ***THE PEOPLE...***"
TRUE.
STATE ALCHEMISTS AREN'T CALLED "DOGS OF THE MILITARY" FOR NOTHING.
DO YOU THINK THAT THESE BOYS HAVE WHAT IT TAKES TO PASS THE STATE LICENSE TEST?

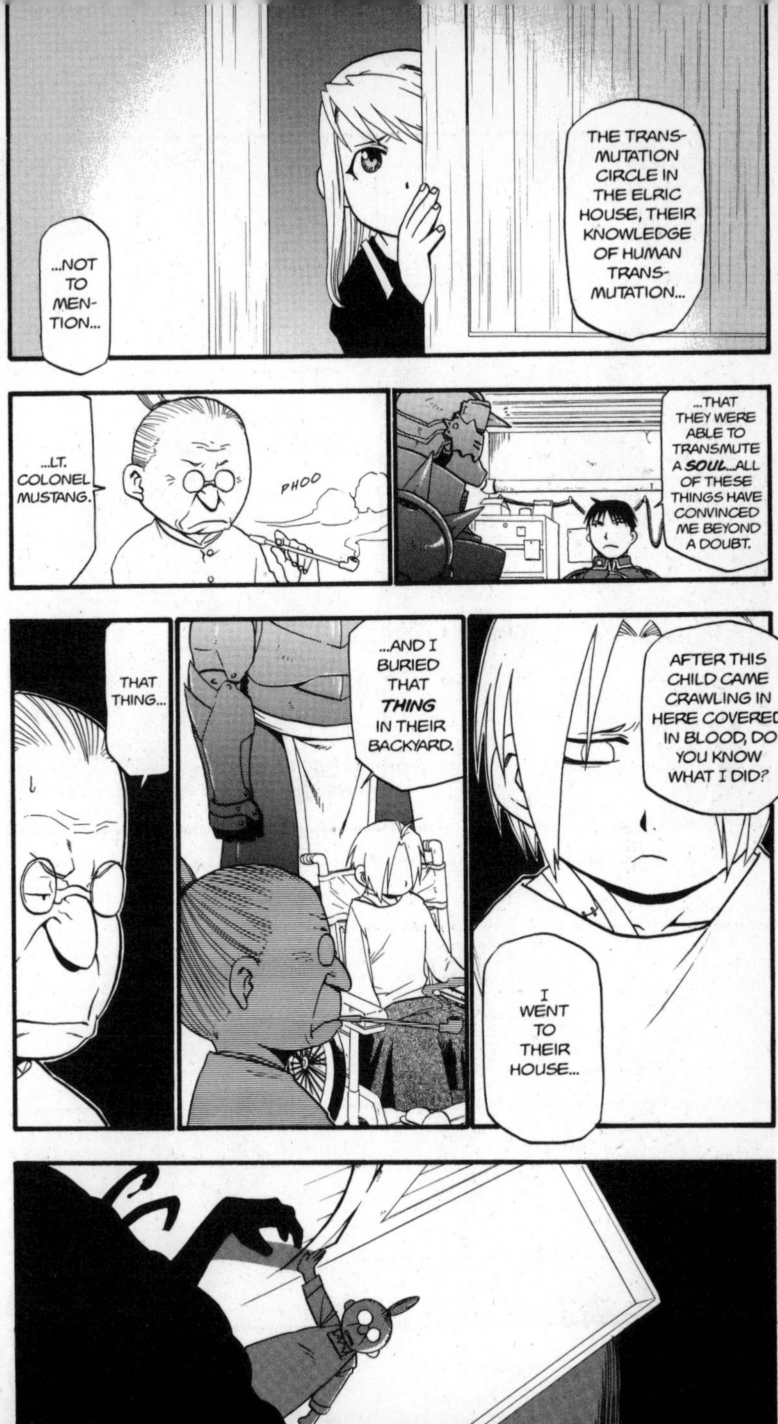
THE TRANS-MUTATION CIRCLE IN THE ELRIC HOUSE, THEIR KNOWLEDGE OF HUMAN TRANS-MUTATION...
...NOT TO MEN-TION...
...THAT THEY WERE ABLE TO TRANSMUTE A SOUL...ALL OF THESE THINGS HAVE CONVINCED ME BEYOND A DOUBT.
...LT. COLONEL MUSTANG.
PHOO
AFTER THIS CHILD CAME CRAWLING IN HERE COVERED IN BLOOD, DO YOU KNOW WHAT I DID?
I WENT TO THEIR HOUSE...
...AND I BURIED THAT THING IN THEIR BACKYARD.
THAT THING...

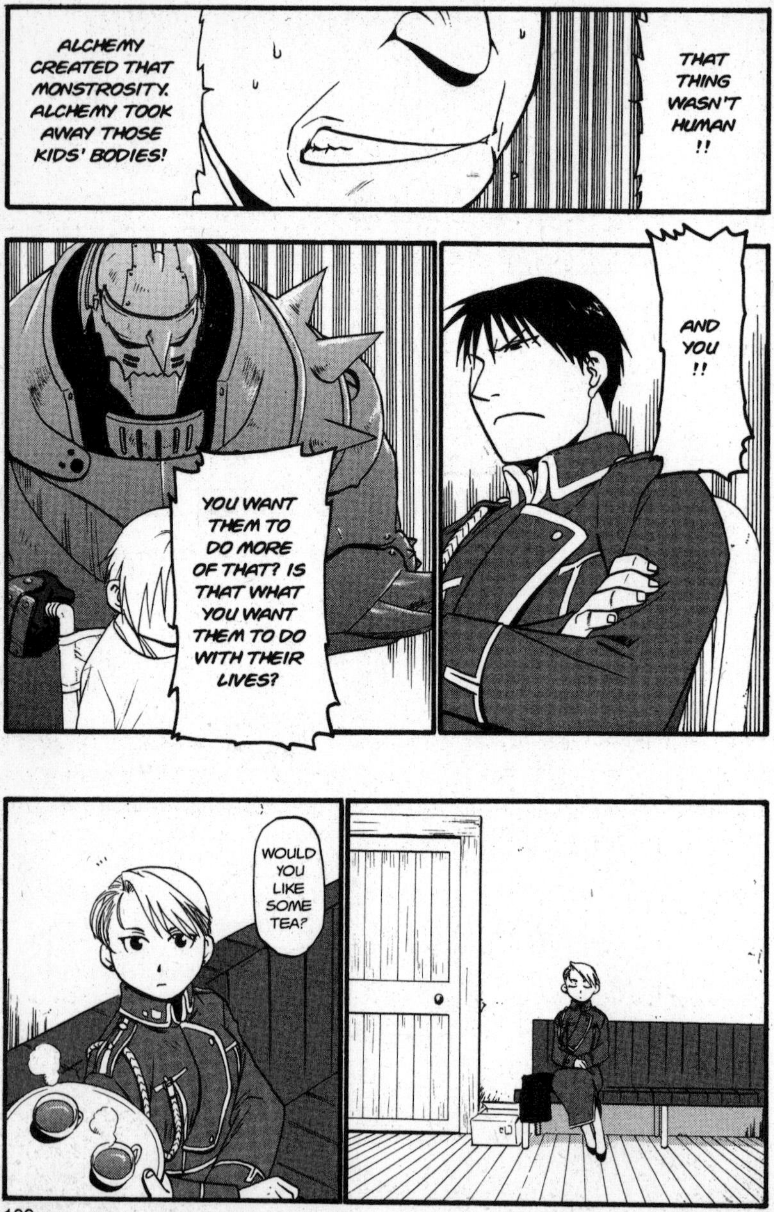
THAT THING WASN'T HUMAN!!
ALCHEMY CREATED THAT MONSTROSITY. ALCHEMY TOOK AWAY THOSE KIDS' BODIES!
AND YOU!!
YOU WANT THEM TO DO MORE OF THAT? IS THAT WHAT YOU WANT THEM TO DO WITH THEIR LIVES?
WOULD YOU LIKE SOME TEA?

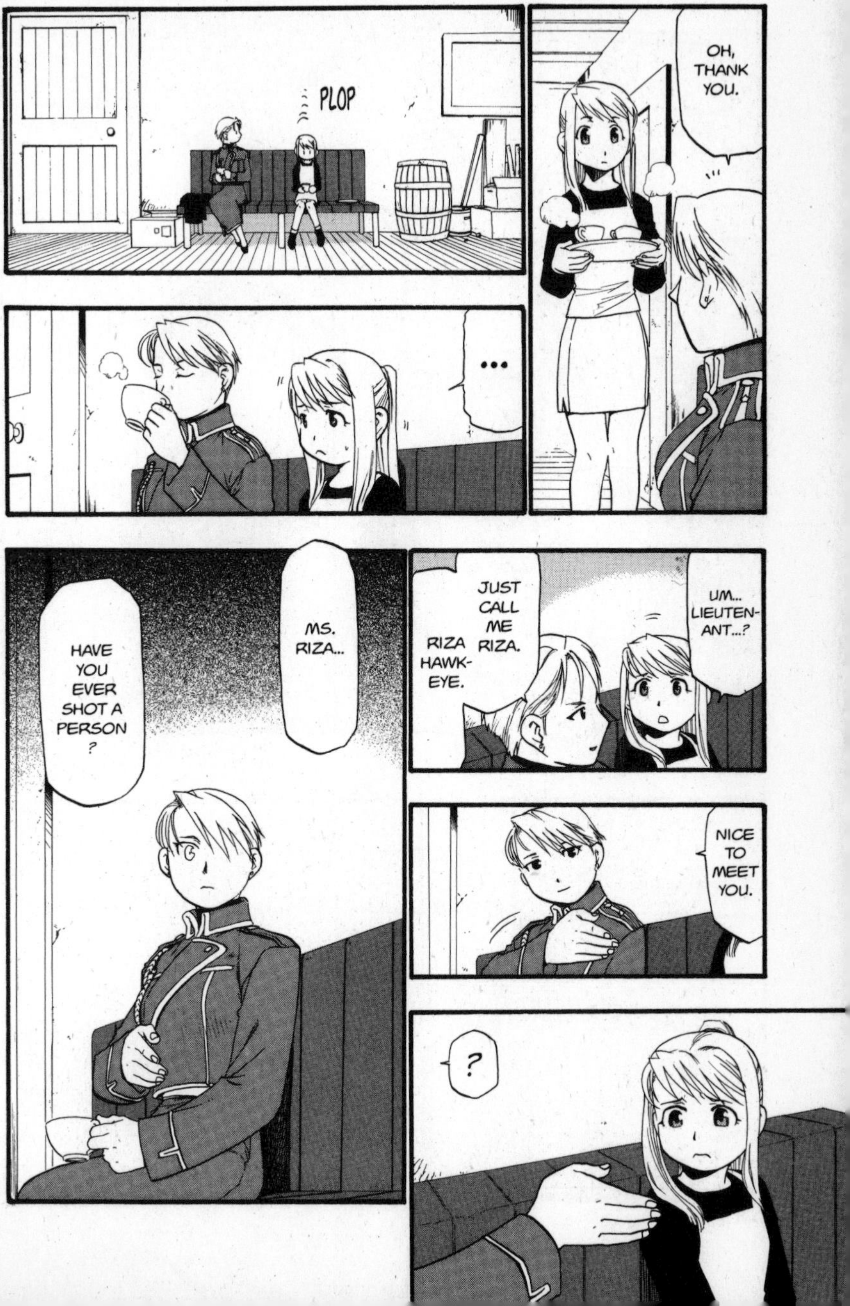
OH, THANK YOU.
PLOP
...
UM... LIEUTEN-ANT...?
JUST CALL ME RIZA.
RIZA HAWK-EYE.
NICE TO MEET YOU.
?
MS. RIZA...
HAVE YOU EVER SHOT A PERSON?

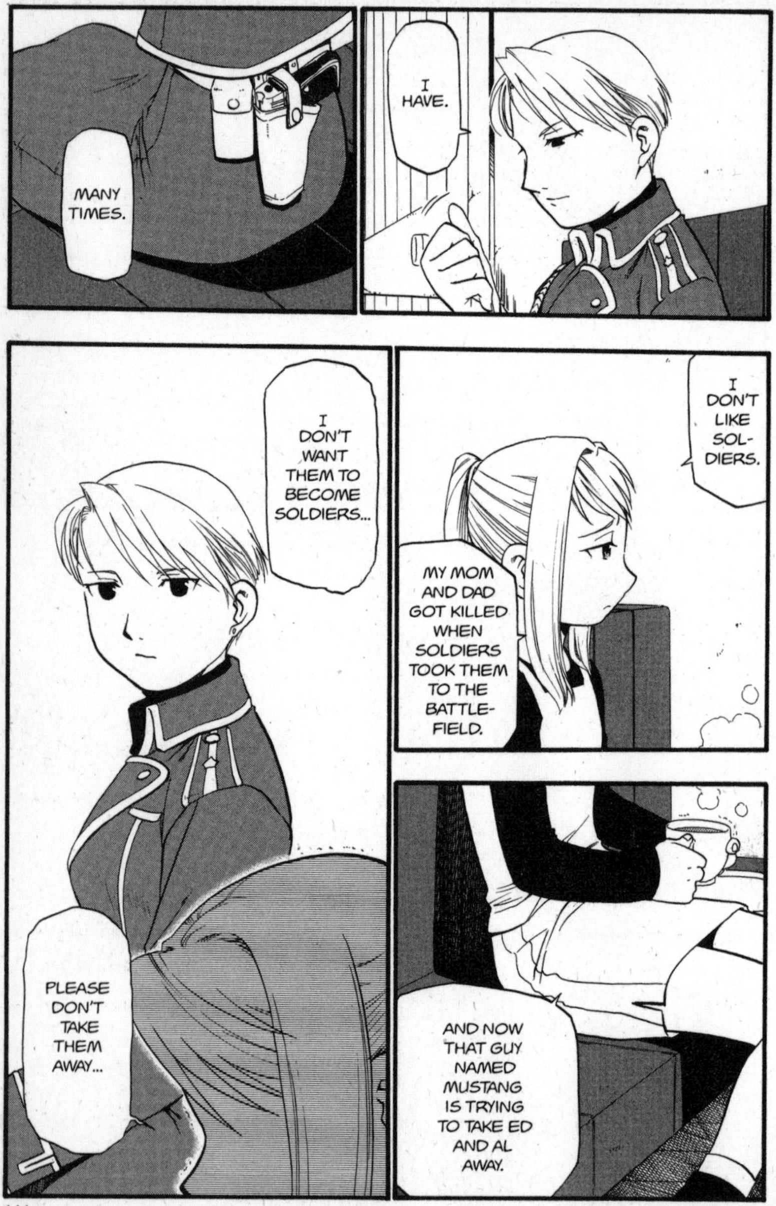
I HAVE.
MANY TIMES.
I DON'T LIKE SOL-DIERS.
MY MOM AND DAD GOT KILLED WHEN SOLDIERS TOOK THEM TO THE BATTLE-FIELD.
AND NOW THAT GUY NAMED MUSTANG IS TRYING TO TAKE ED AND AL AWAY.
I DON'T WANT THEM TO BECOME SOLDIERS...
PLEASE DON'T TAKE THEM AWAY...

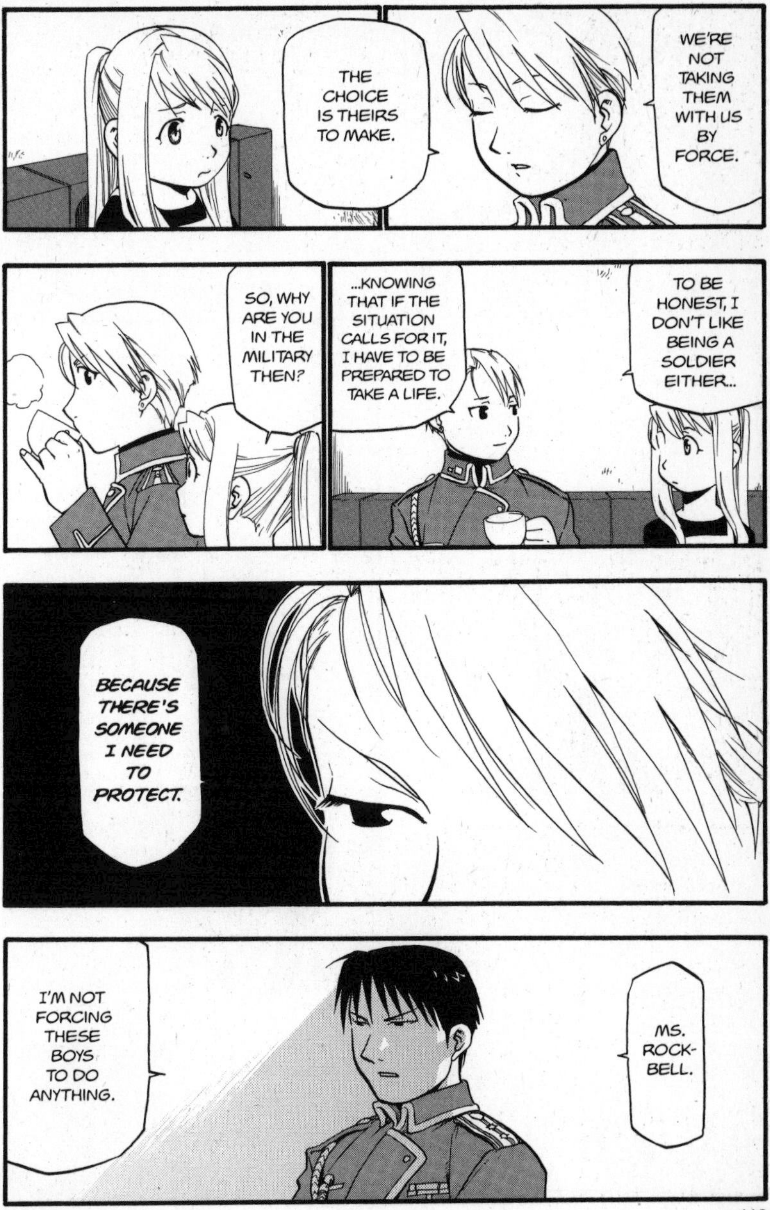
WE'RE NOT TAKING THEM WITH US BY FORCE.
THE CHOICE IS THEIRS TO MAKE.
TO BE HONEST, I DON'T LIKE BEING A SOLDIER EITHER...
...KNOWING THAT IF THE SITUATION CALLS FOR IT, I HAVE TO BE PREPARED TO TAKE A LIFE.
SO, WHY ARE YOU IN THE MILITARY THEN?
BECAUSE THERE'S SOMEONE I NEED TO PROTECT.
MS. ROCK-BELL.
I'M NOT FORCING THESE BOYS TO DO ANYTHING.

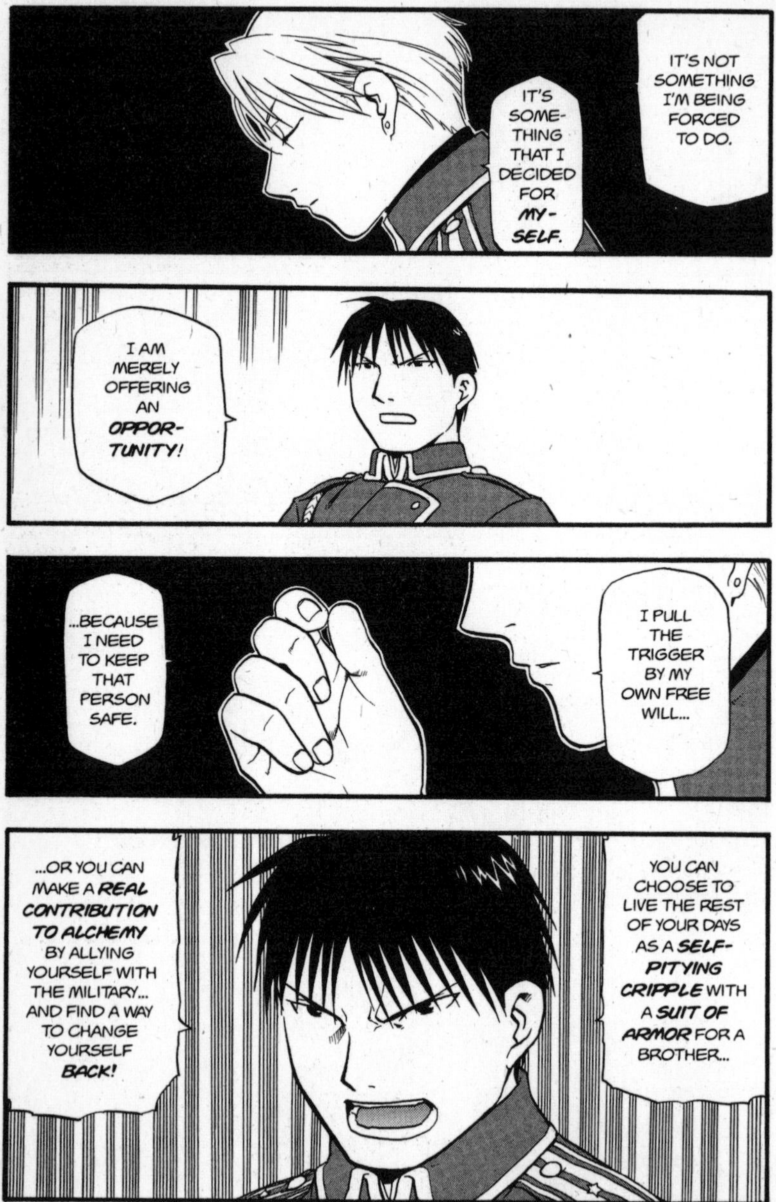
IT'S NOT SOMETHING I'M BEING FORCED TO DO.
IT'S SOMETHING THAT I DECIDED FOR MYSELF.
I AM MERELY OFFERING AN OPPORTUNITY!
I PULL THE TRIGGER BY MY OWN FREE WILL...
...BECAUSE I NEED TO KEEP THAT PERSON SAFE.
YOU CAN CHOOSE TO LIVE THE REST OF YOUR DAYS AS A SELF-PITYING CRIPPLE WITH A SUIT OF ARMOR FOR A BROTHER...
...OR YOU CAN MAKE A REAL CONTRIBUTION TO ALCHEMY BY ALLYING YOURSELF WITH THE MILITARY... AND FIND A WAY TO CHANGE YOURSELF BACK!

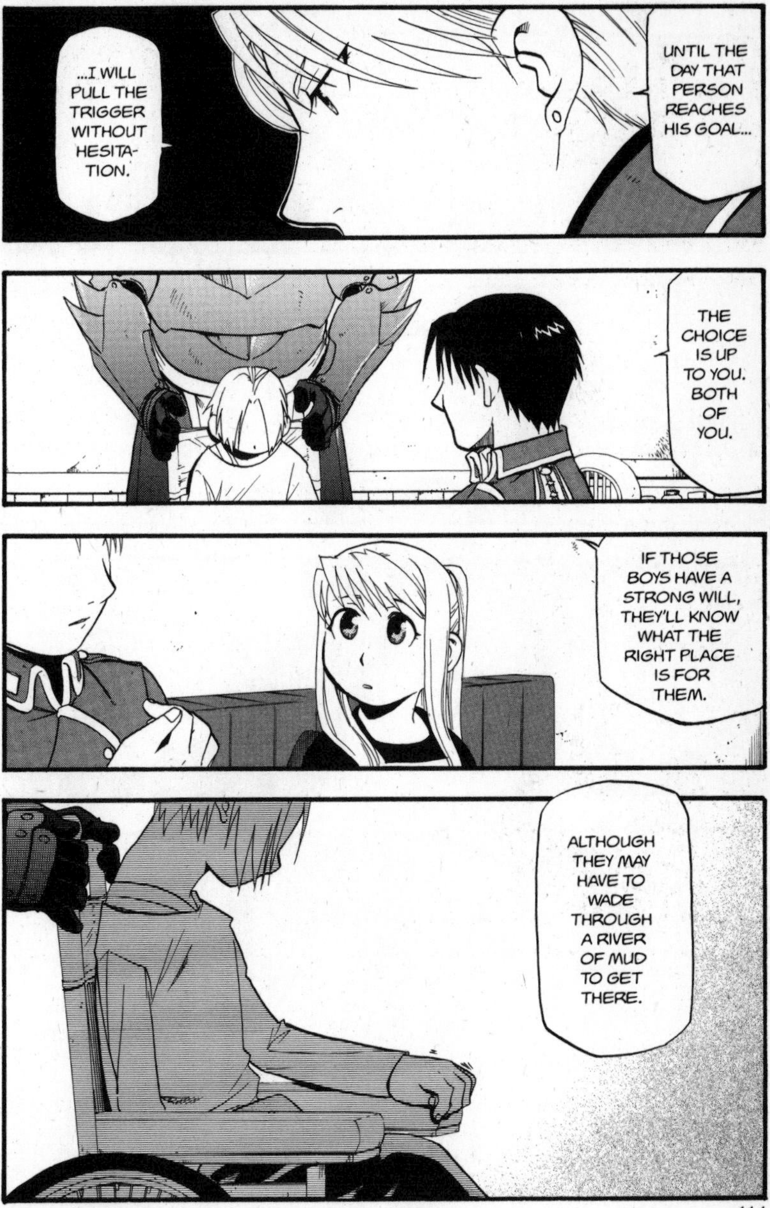
UNTIL THE DAY THAT PERSON REACHES HIS GOAL...
...I WILL PULL THE TRIGGER WITHOUT HESITATION.
THE CHOICE IS UP TO YOU. BOTH OF YOU.
IF THOSE BOYS HAVE A STRONG WILL, THEY'LL KNOW WHAT THE RIGHT PLACE IS FOR THEM.
ALTHOUGH THEY MAY HAVE TO WADE THROUGH A RIVER OF MUD TO GET THERE.

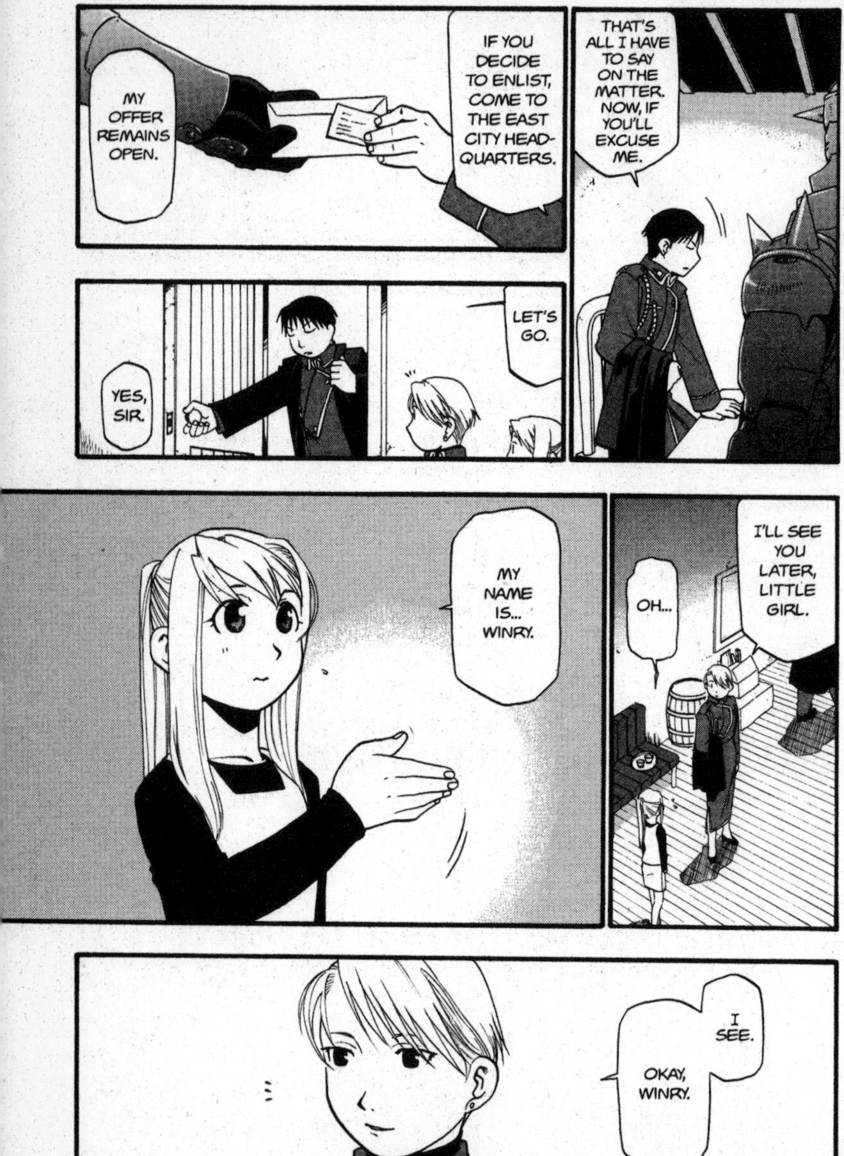
IF YOU DECIDE TO ENLIST, COME TO THE EAST CITY HEAD-QUARTERS.
MY OFFER REMAINS OPEN.
THAT'S ALL I HAVE TO SAY ON THE MATTER. NOW, IF YOU'LL EXCUSE ME.
LET'S GO.
YES, SIR.
I'LL SEE YOU LATER, LITTLE GIRL.
OH...
MY NAME IS... WINRY.
I SEE.
OKAY, WINRY.

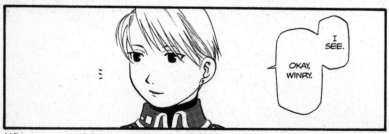

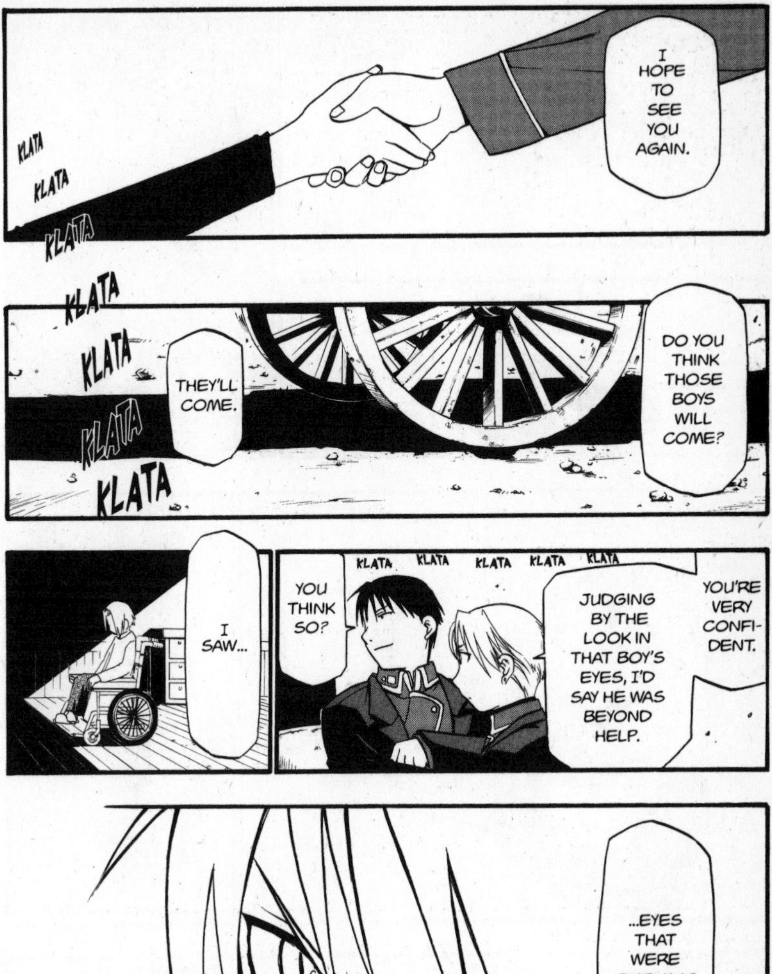

I HOPE TO SEE YOU AGAIN.
KLATA KLATA KLATA KLATA KLATA KLATA KLATA
DO YOU THINK THOSE BOYS WILL COME?
THEY'LL COME.
KLATA KLATA KLATA KLATA KLATA
YOU'RE VERY CONFI-DENT.
JUDGING BY THE LOOK IN THAT BOY'S EYES, I'D SAY HE WAS BEYOND HELP.
YOU THINK SO?
I SAW...
...EYES THAT WERE BURNING LIKE FIRE.

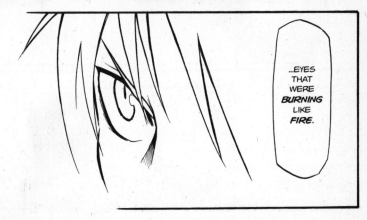

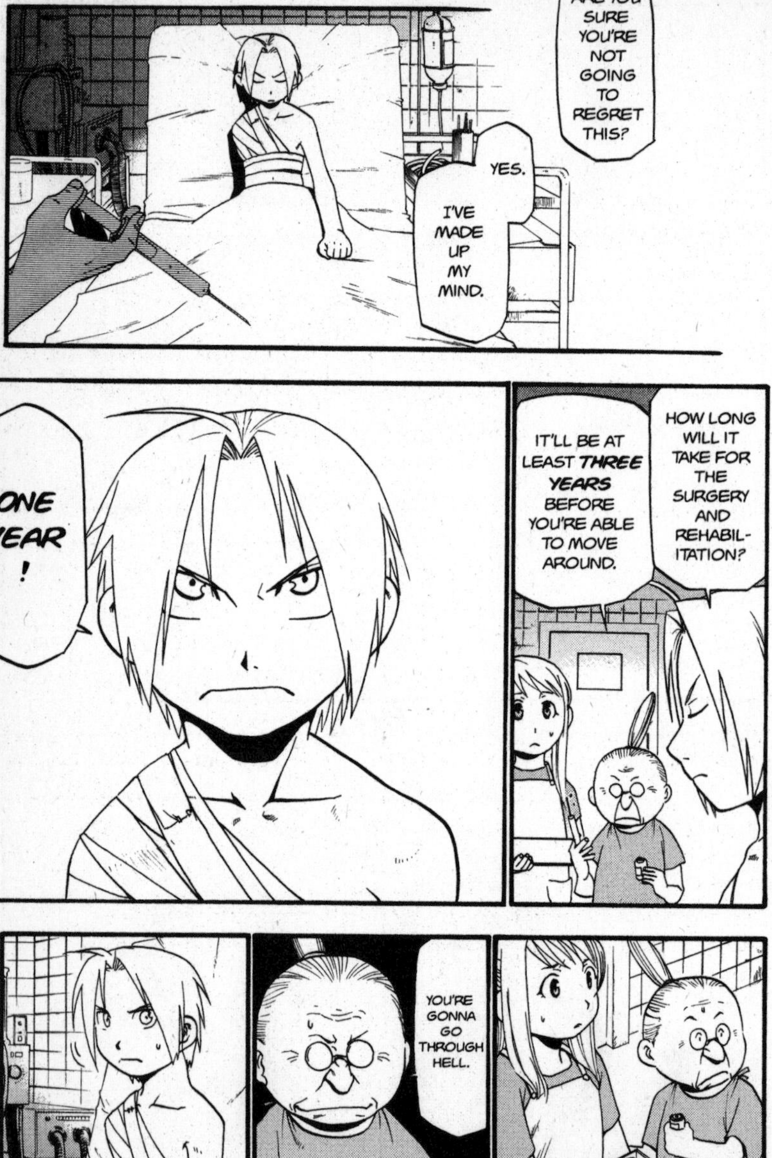
ARE YOU SURE YOU'RE NOT GOING TO REGRET THIS?
YES.
I'VE MADE UP MY MIND.
HOW LONG WILL IT TAKE FOR THE SURGERY AND REHABIL-ITATION?
IT'LL BE AT LEAST *THREE YEARS* BEFORE YOU'RE ABLE TO MOVE AROUND.
ONE YEAR!
YOU'RE GONNA GO THROUGH HELL.

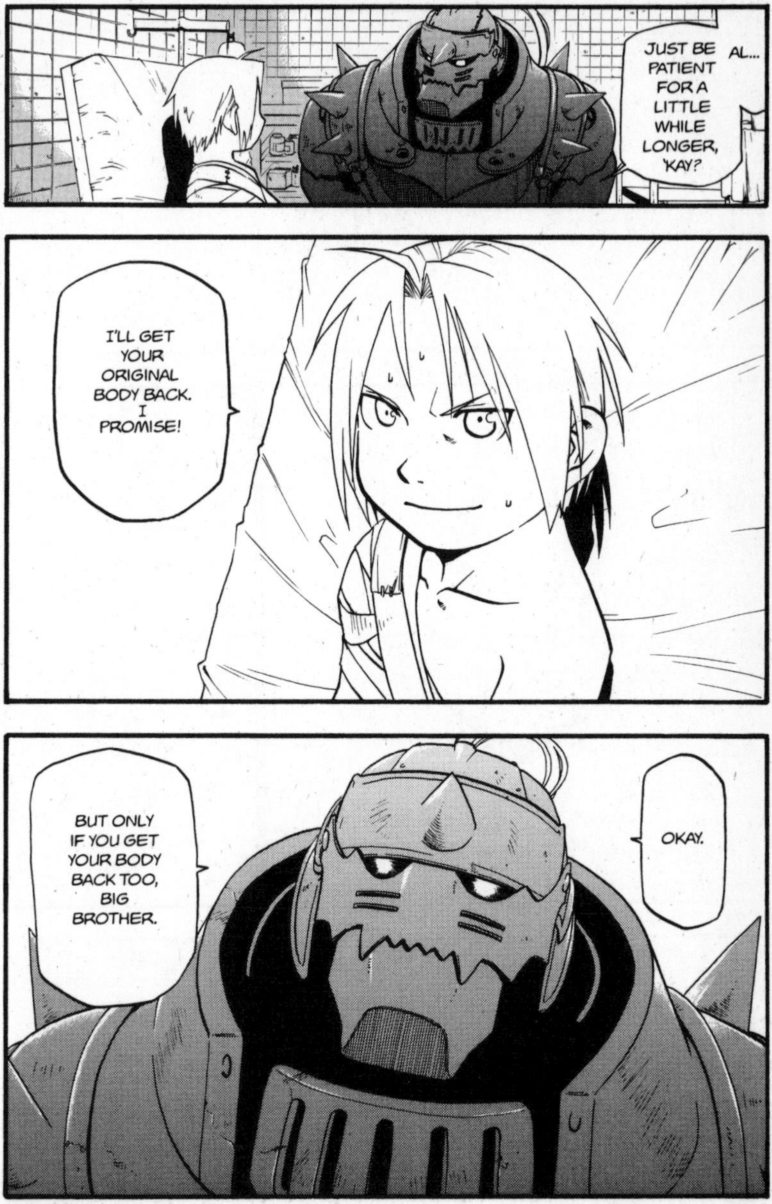
AL...
JUST BE PATIENT FOR A LITTLE WHILE LONGER, 'KAY?
I'LL GET YOUR ORIGINAL BODY BACK. I PROMISE!
OKAY.
BUT ONLY IF YOU GET YOUR BODY BACK TOO, BIG BROTHER.

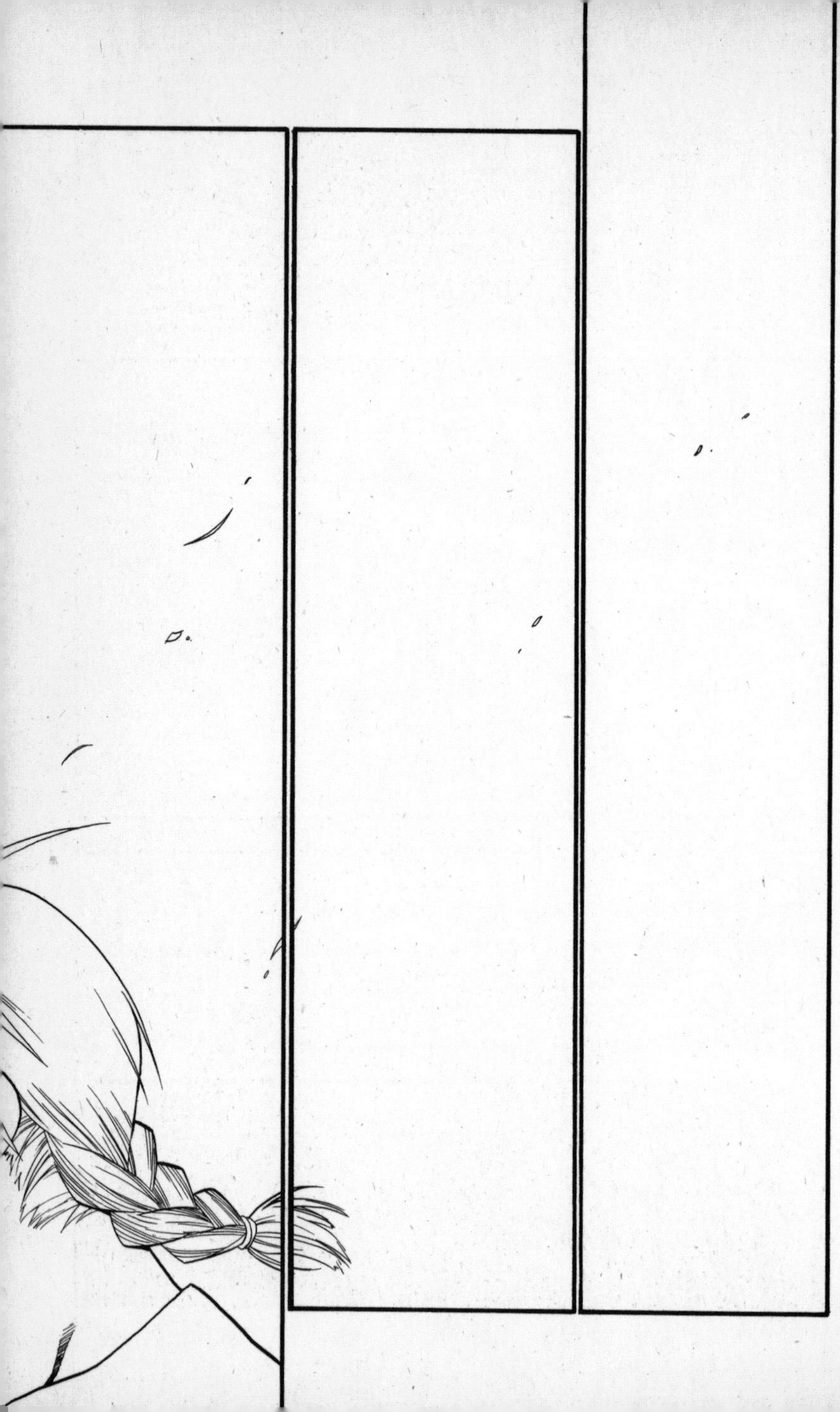

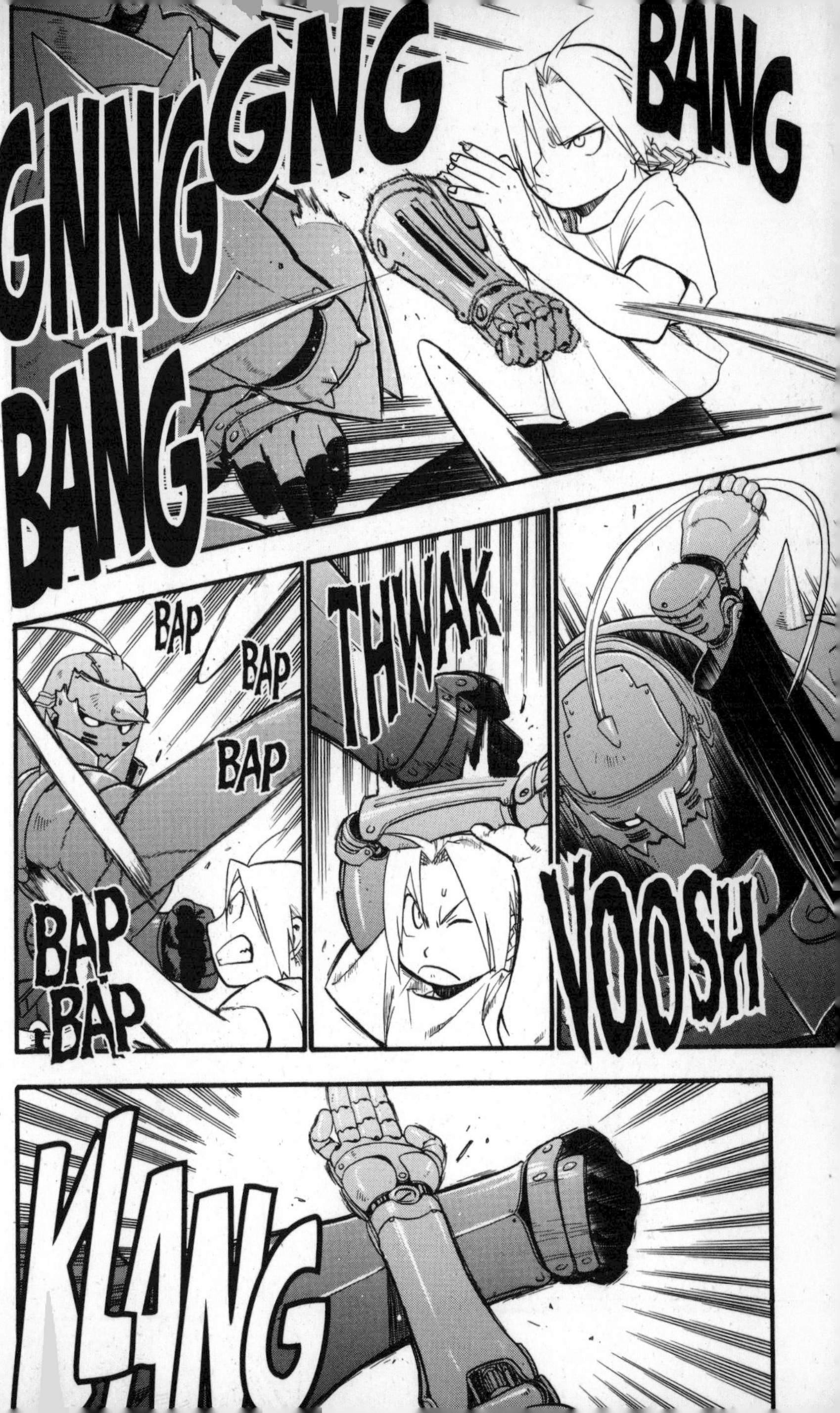
BANG
GNG
GNNG
BANG
VOOSH
THWAK
BAP
BAP
BAP
BAP
BAP
KLANG

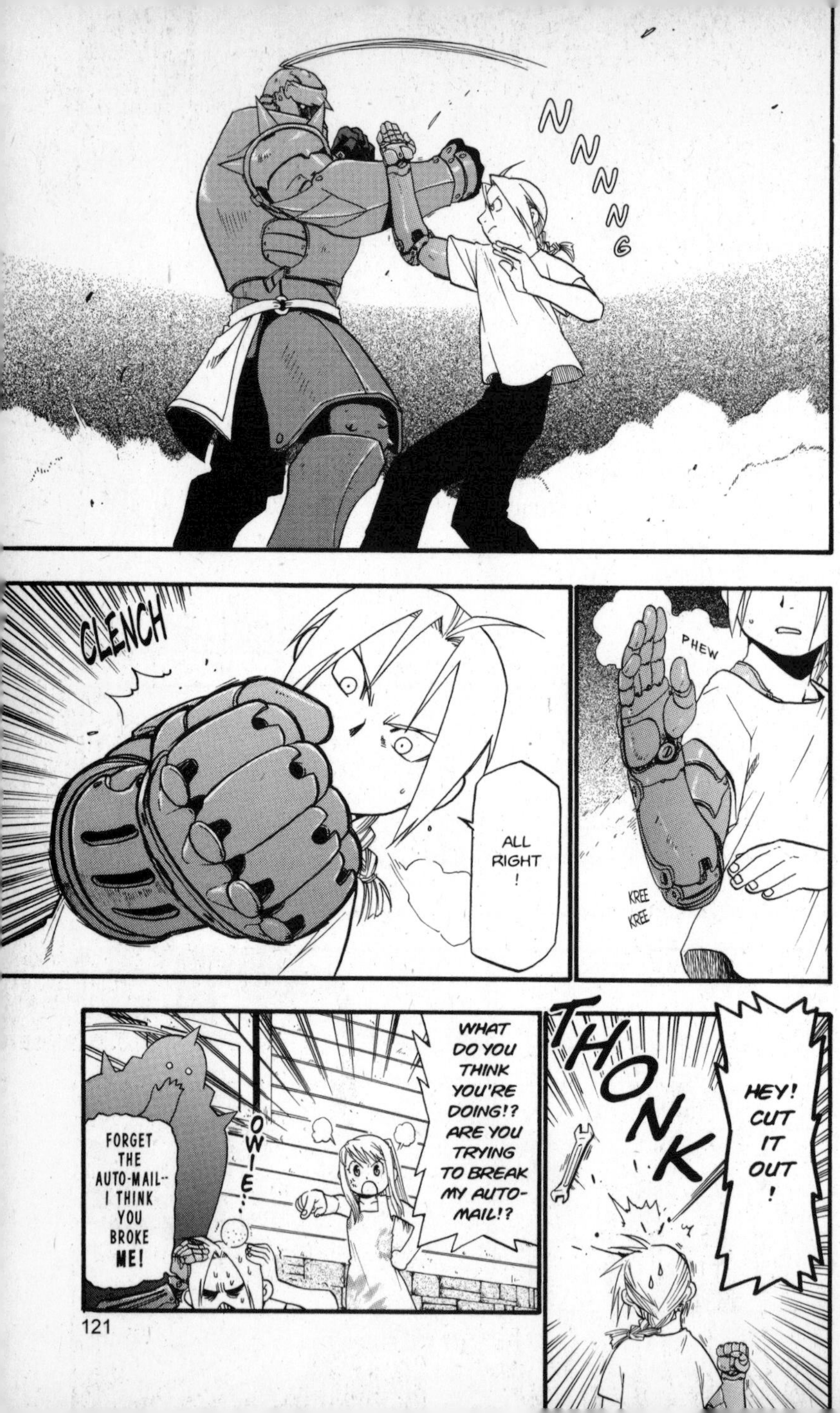
NNNNG
PHEW
KREE KREE
CLENCH
ALL RIGHT!
THONK
HEY! CUT IT OUT!
WHAT DO YOU THINK YOU'RE DOING!? ARE YOU TRYING TO BREAK MY AUTO-MAIL!?
OWIE...
FORGET THE AUTO-MAIL-- I THINK YOU BROKE ME!

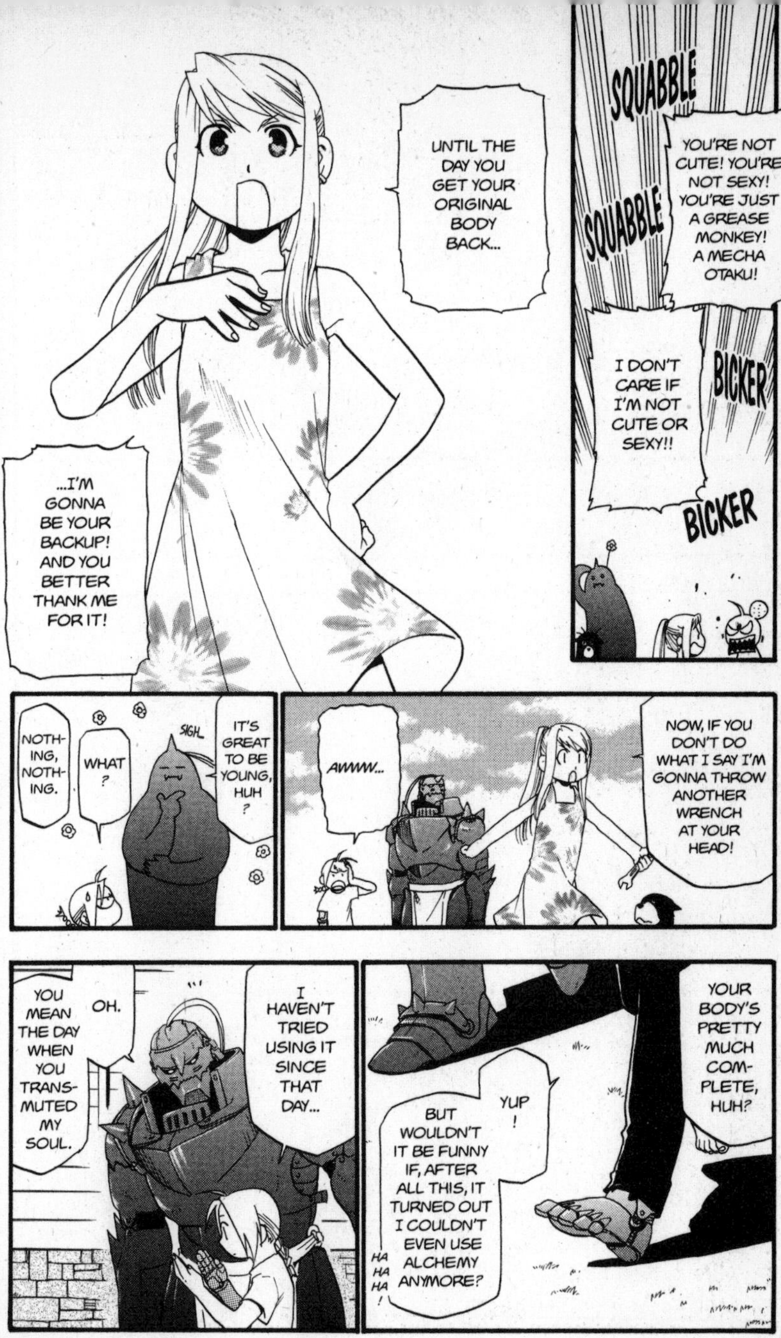
SQUABBLE
SQUABBLE
YOU'RE NOT CUTE! YOU'RE NOT SEXY! YOU'RE JUST A GREASE MONKEY! A MECHA OTAKU!
I DON'T CARE IF I'M NOT CUTE OR SEXY!!
BICKER
BICKER
UNTIL THE DAY YOU GET YOUR ORIGINAL BODY BACK...
...I'M GONNA BE YOUR BACKUP! AND YOU BETTER THANK ME FOR IT!
NOW, IF YOU DON'T DO WHAT I SAY I'M GONNA THROW ANOTHER WRENCH AT YOUR HEAD!
AWWW...
IT'S GREAT TO BE YOUNG, HUH?
SIGH
WHAT?
NOTH-ING, NOTH-ING.
YOUR BODY'S PRETTY MUCH COM-PLETE, HUH?
YUP!
BUT WOULDN'T IT BE FUNNY IF, AFTER ALL THIS, IT TURNED OUT I COULDN'T EVEN USE ALCHEMY ANYMORE?
HA HA HA!
I HAVEN'T TRIED USING IT SINCE THAT DAY...
OH.
YOU MEAN THE DAY WHEN YOU TRANS-MUTED MY SOUL.

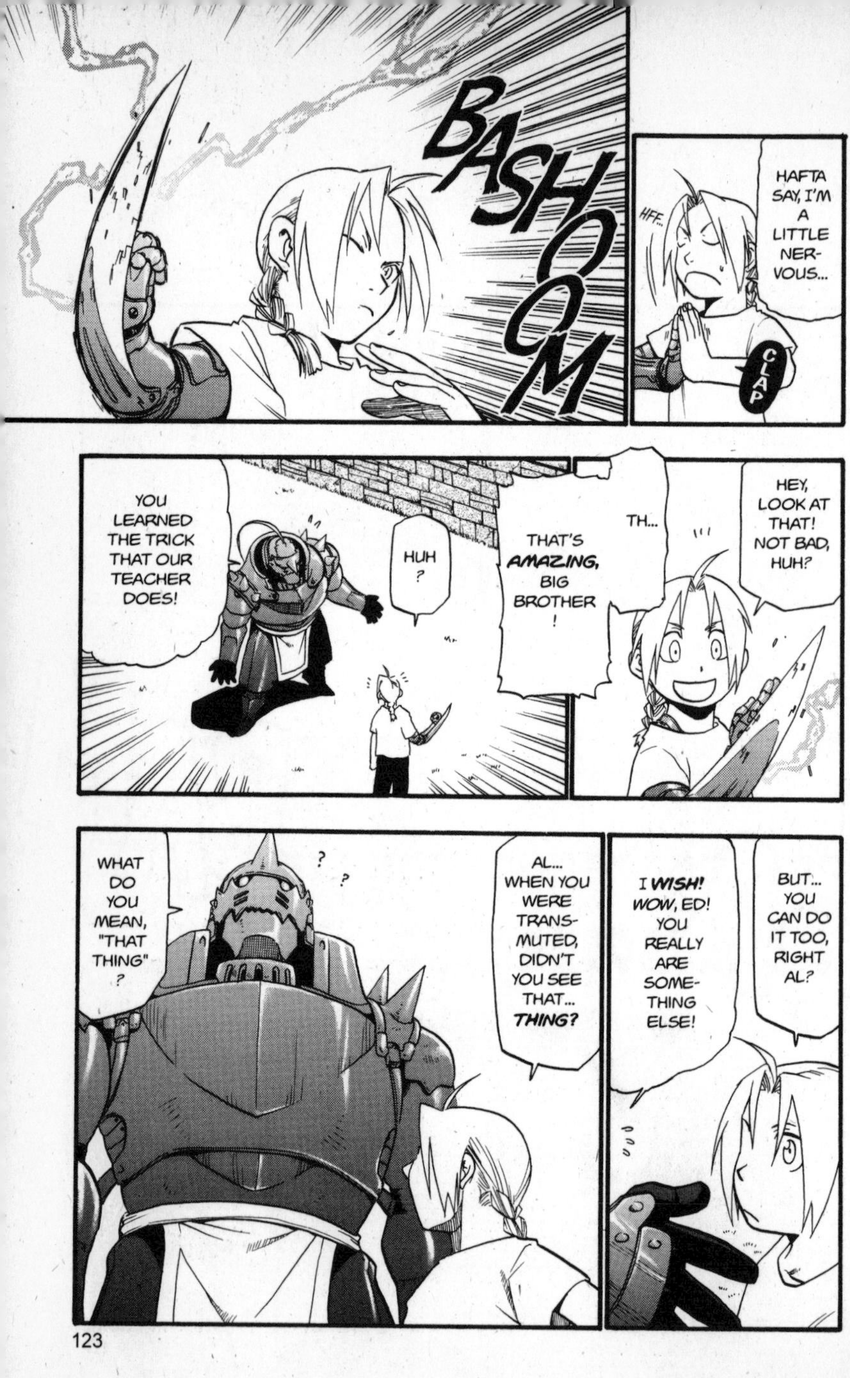
HAFTA SAY, I'M A LITTLE NER-VOUS...
HFF...
CLAP
BASHOOOM
HEY, LOOK AT THAT! NOT BAD, HUH?
TH...
THAT'S **AMAZING,** BIG BROTHER!
HUH?
YOU LEARNED THE TRICK THAT OUR TEACHER DOES!
BUT... YOU CAN DO IT TOO, RIGHT AL?
I **WISH! WOW,** ED! YOU REALLY ARE SOME-THING ELSE!
AL... WHEN YOU WERE TRANS-MUTED, DIDN'T YOU SEE THAT... **THING?**
? ?
WHAT DO YOU MEAN, "THAT THING"?

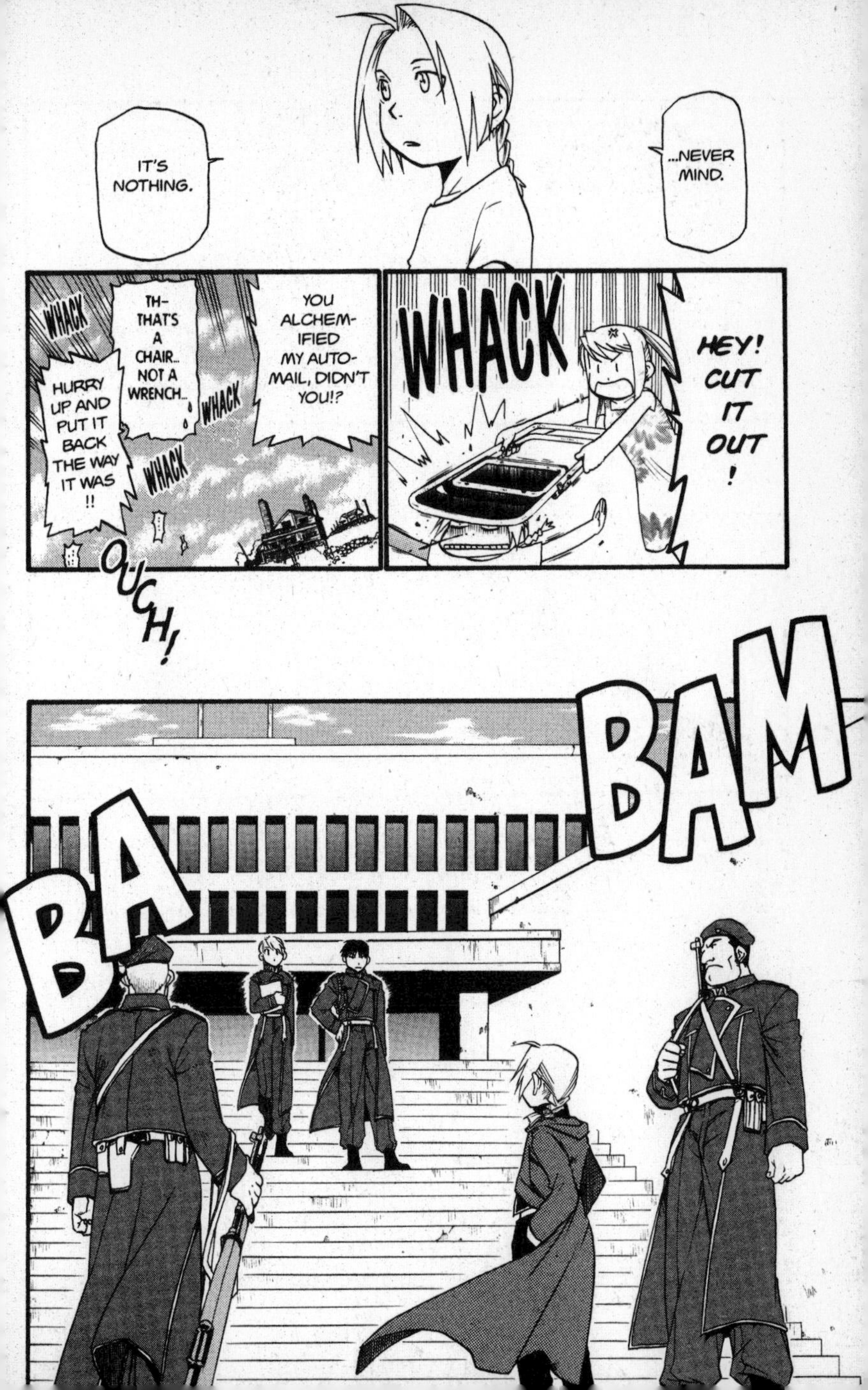
...NEVER MIND.
IT'S NOTHING.
WHACK
HEY! CUT IT OUT!
YOU ALCHEMIFIED MY AUTOMAIL, DIDN'T YOU!?
TH-THAT'S A CHAIR... NOT A WRENCH...
WHACK
WHACK
HURRY UP AND PUT IT BACK THE WAY IT WAS!!
WHACK
OUCH!
BA BAM

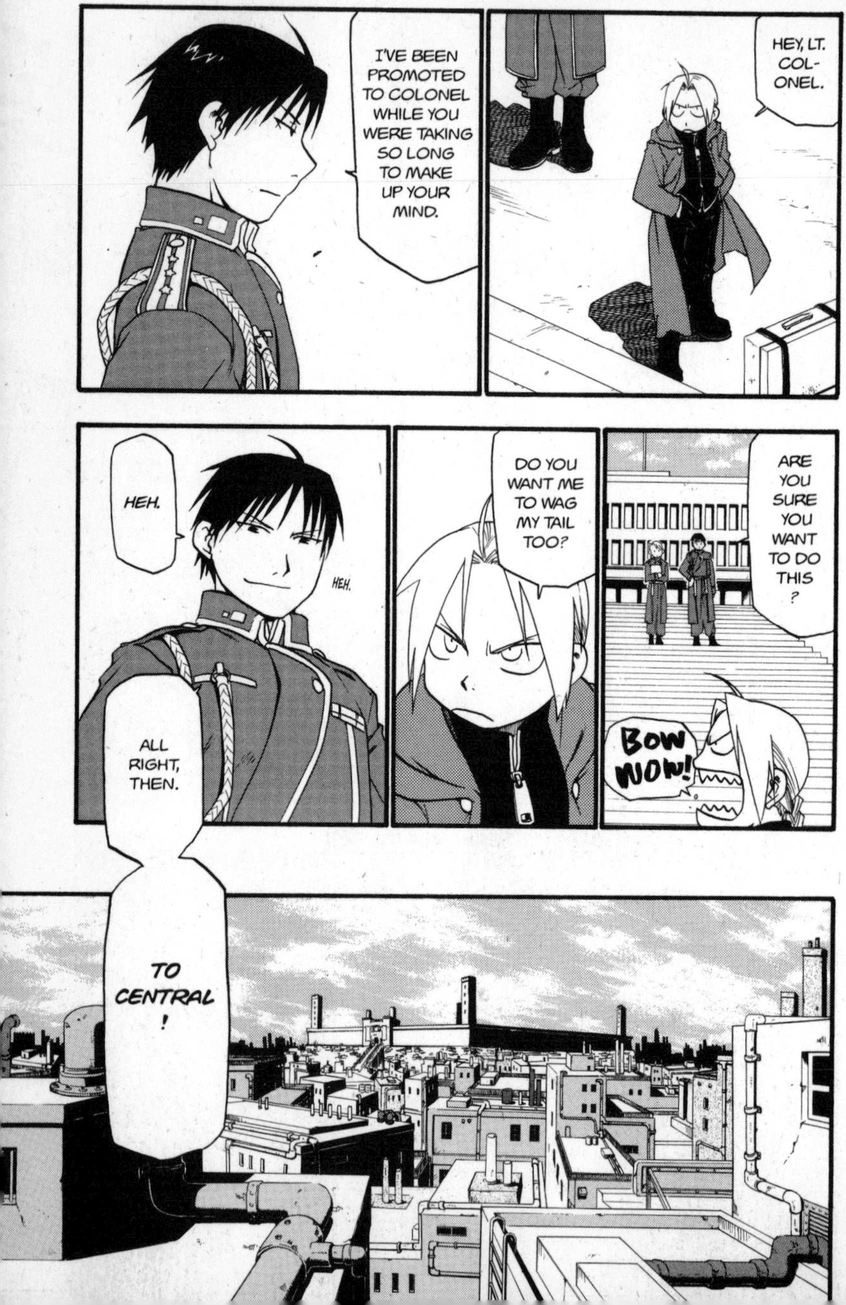
HEY, LT. COLONEL.
I'VE BEEN PROMOTED TO COLONEL WHILE YOU WERE TAKING SO LONG TO MAKE UP YOUR MIND.
ARE YOU SURE YOU WANT TO DO THIS?
BOW WOW!
DO YOU WANT ME TO WAG MY TAIL TOO?
HEH.
HEH.
ALL RIGHT, THEN.
TO CENTRAL!

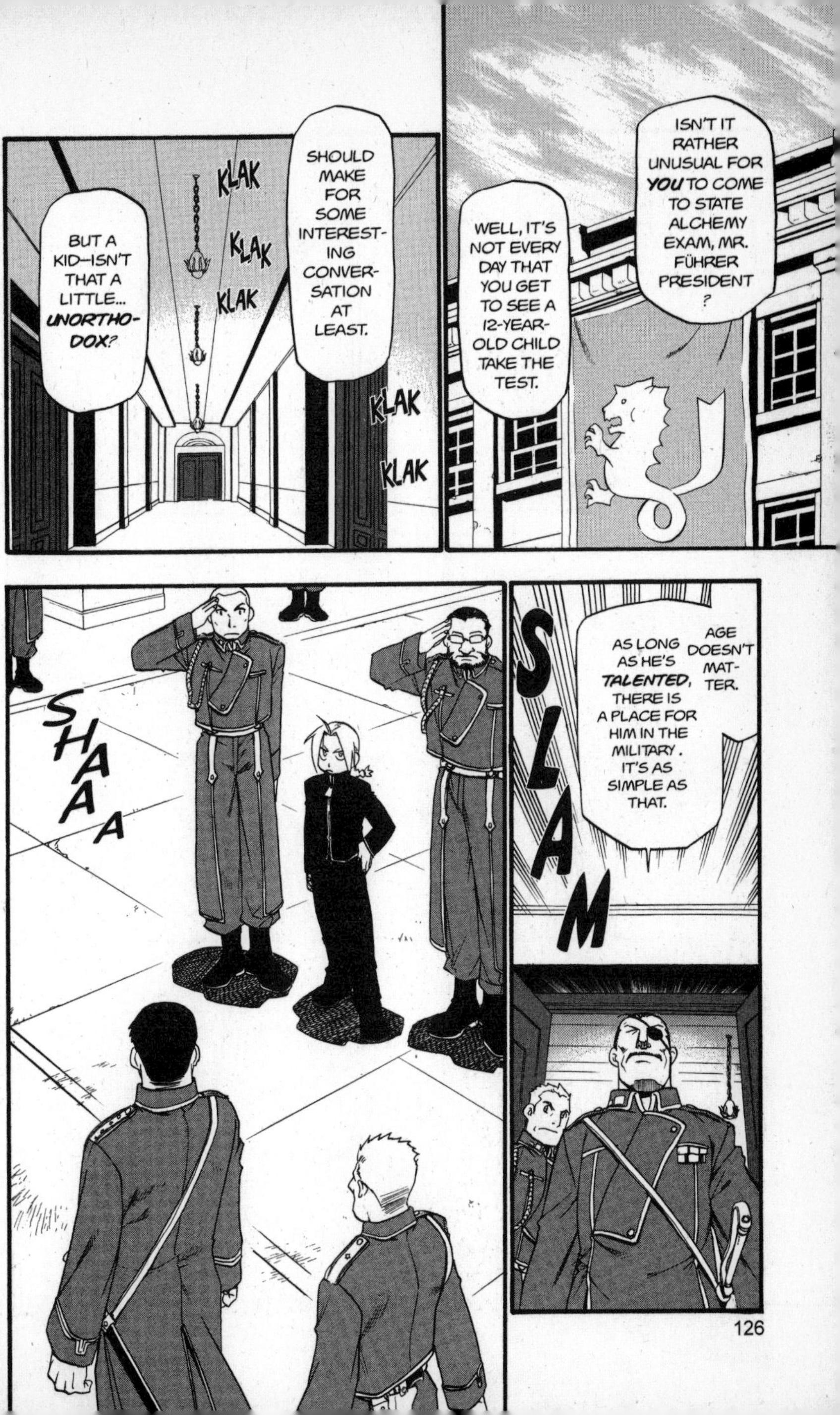
ISN'T IT RATHER UNUSUAL FOR YOU TO COME TO STATE ALCHEMY EXAM, MR. FÜHRER PRESIDENT ?
WELL, IT'S NOT EVERY DAY THAT YOU GET TO SEE A 12-YEAR-OLD CHILD TAKE THE TEST.
SHOULD MAKE FOR SOME INTERESTING CONVERSATION AT LEAST.
KLAK
KLAK
KLAK
BUT A KID--ISN'T THAT A LITTLE... UNORTHODOX?
KLAK
KLAK
SLAM
AGE DOESN'T MATTER.
AS LONG AS HE'S TALENTED, THERE IS A PLACE FOR HIM IN THE MILITARY. IT'S AS SIMPLE AS THAT.
SHAAAA

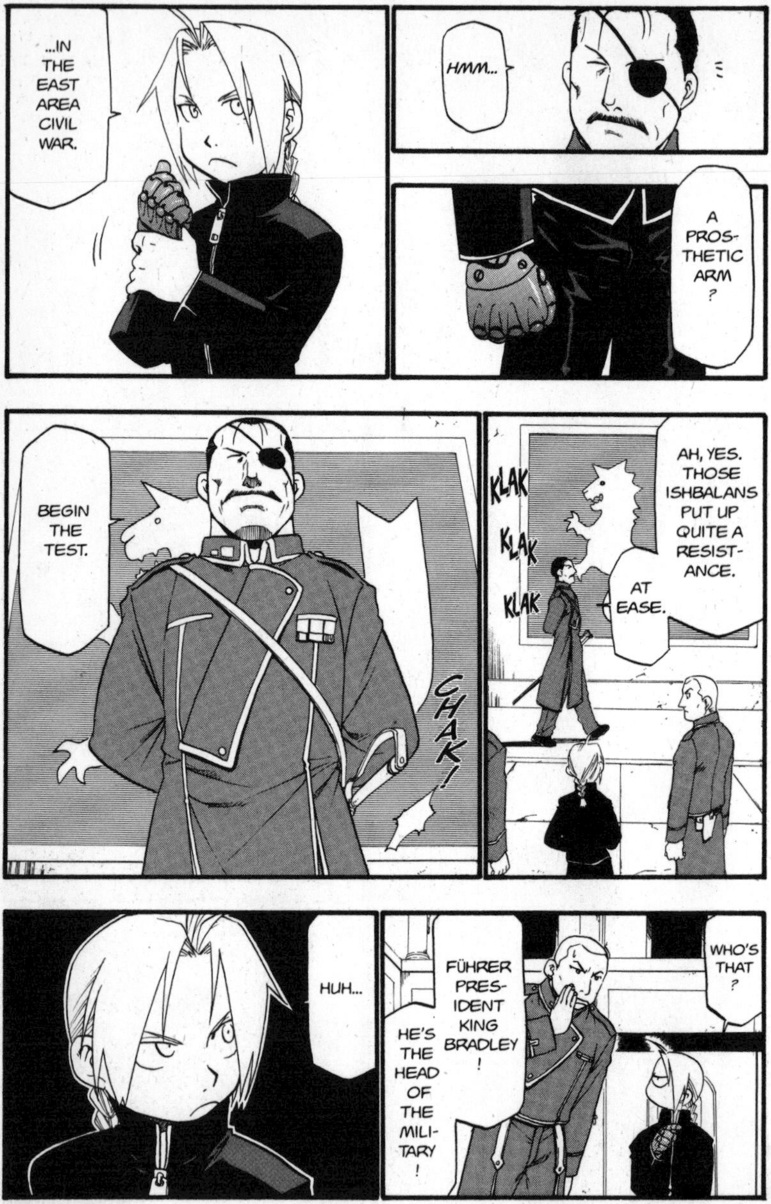
HMM...
A PROSTHETIC ARM?
...IN THE EAST AREA CIVIL WAR.
KLAK KLAK KLAK
AH, YES. THOSE ISHBALANS PUT UP QUITE A RESISTANCE.
AT EASE.
BEGIN THE TEST.
CHAK!
WHO'S THAT?
FÜHRER PRESIDENT KING BRADLEY!
HE'S THE HEAD OF THE MILITARY!
HUH...

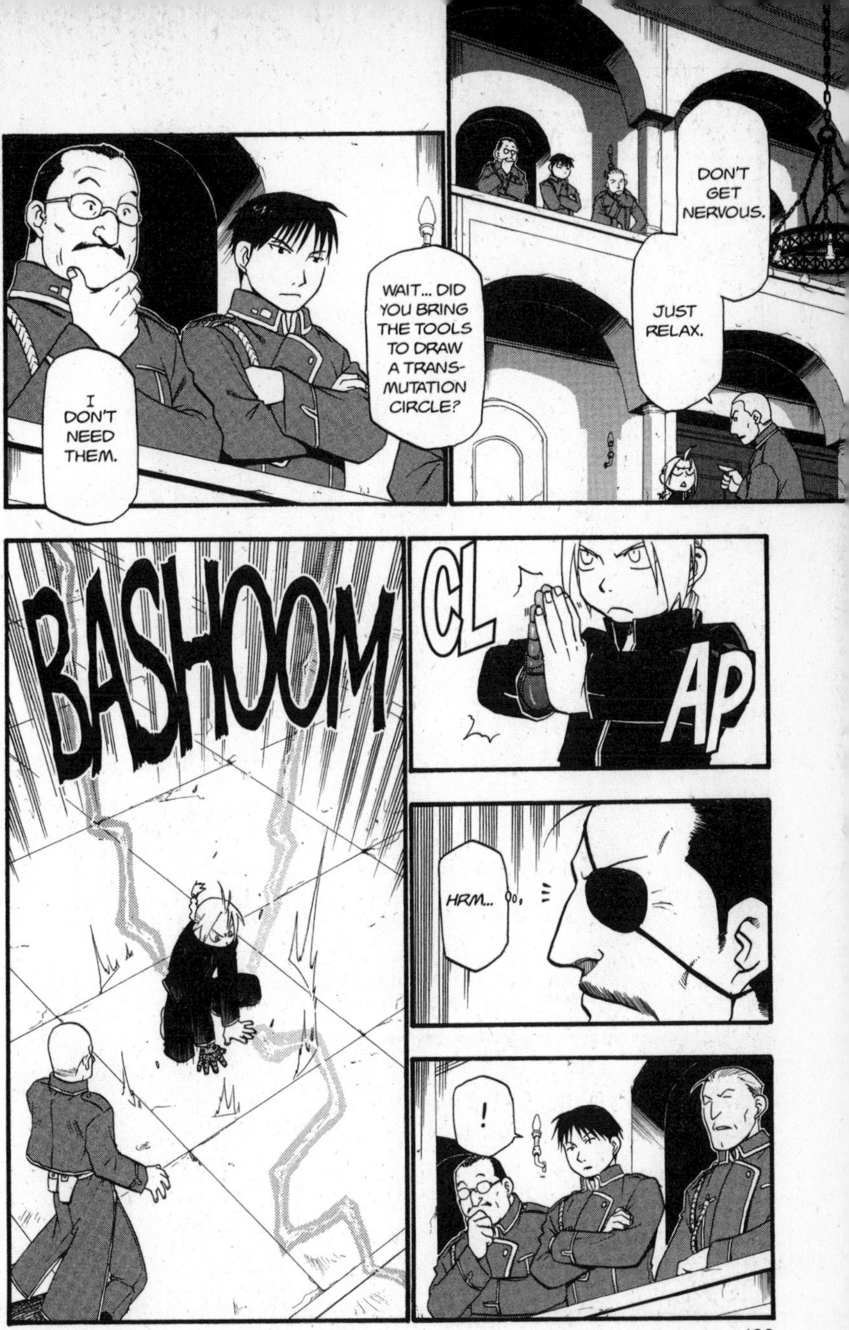
DON'T GET NERVOUS.
JUST RELAX.
WAIT... DID YOU BRING THE TOOLS TO DRAW A TRANS-MUTATION CIRCLE?
I DON'T NEED THEM.
CLAP
HRM...
!
BASHOOM

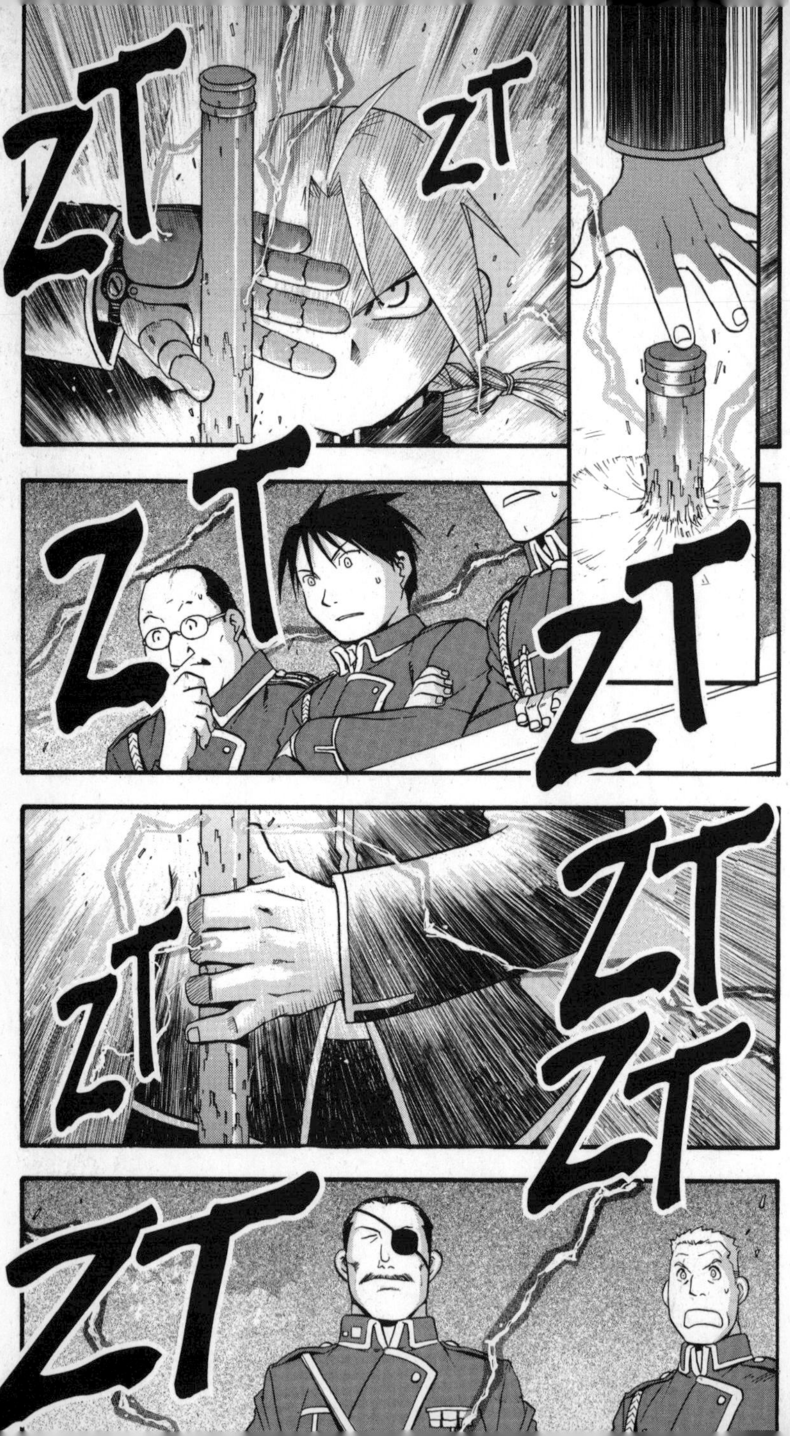
ZT
ZT
ZT
ZT
ZT
ZT
ZT
ZT

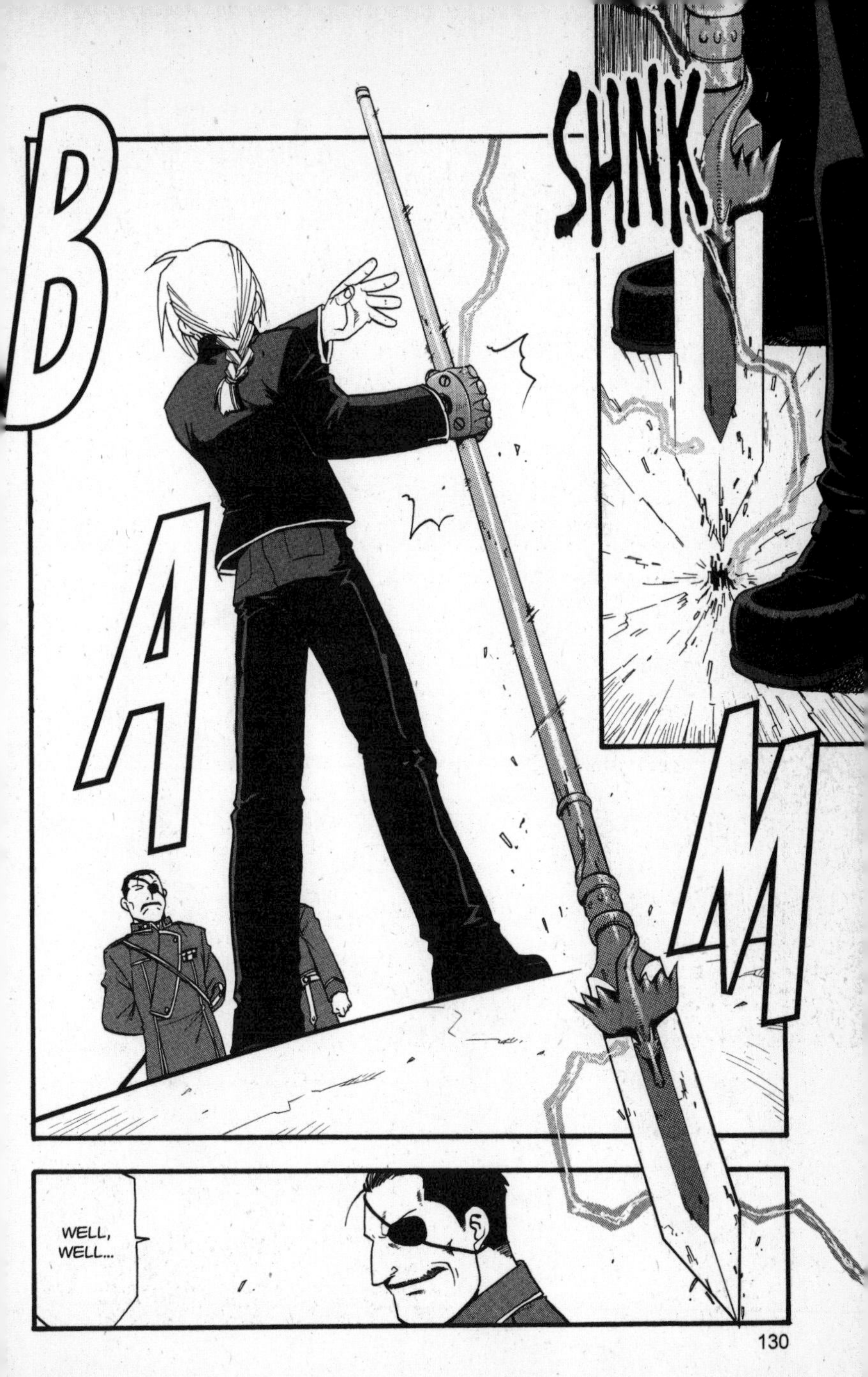
SHNK
BAM
WELL, WELL...

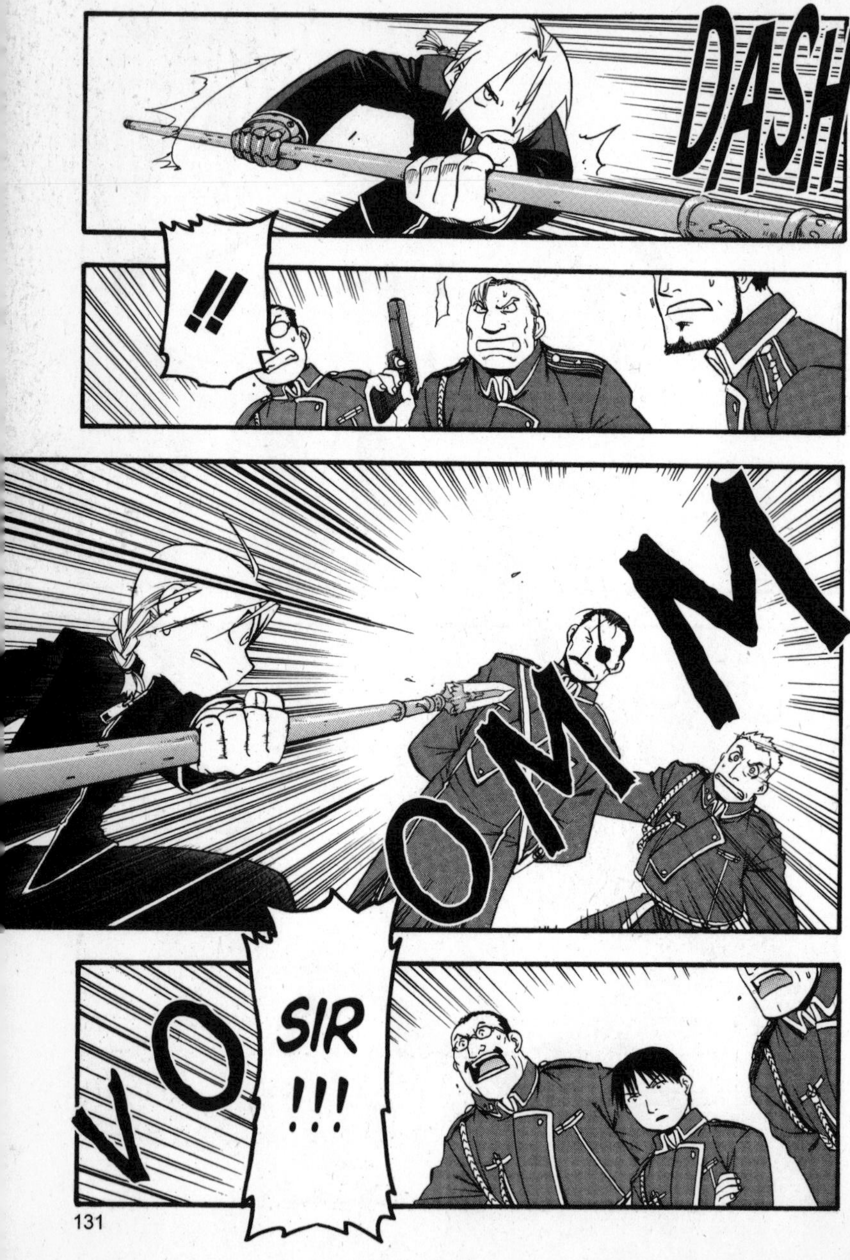
DASH
!!
VOOMM
SIR !!!

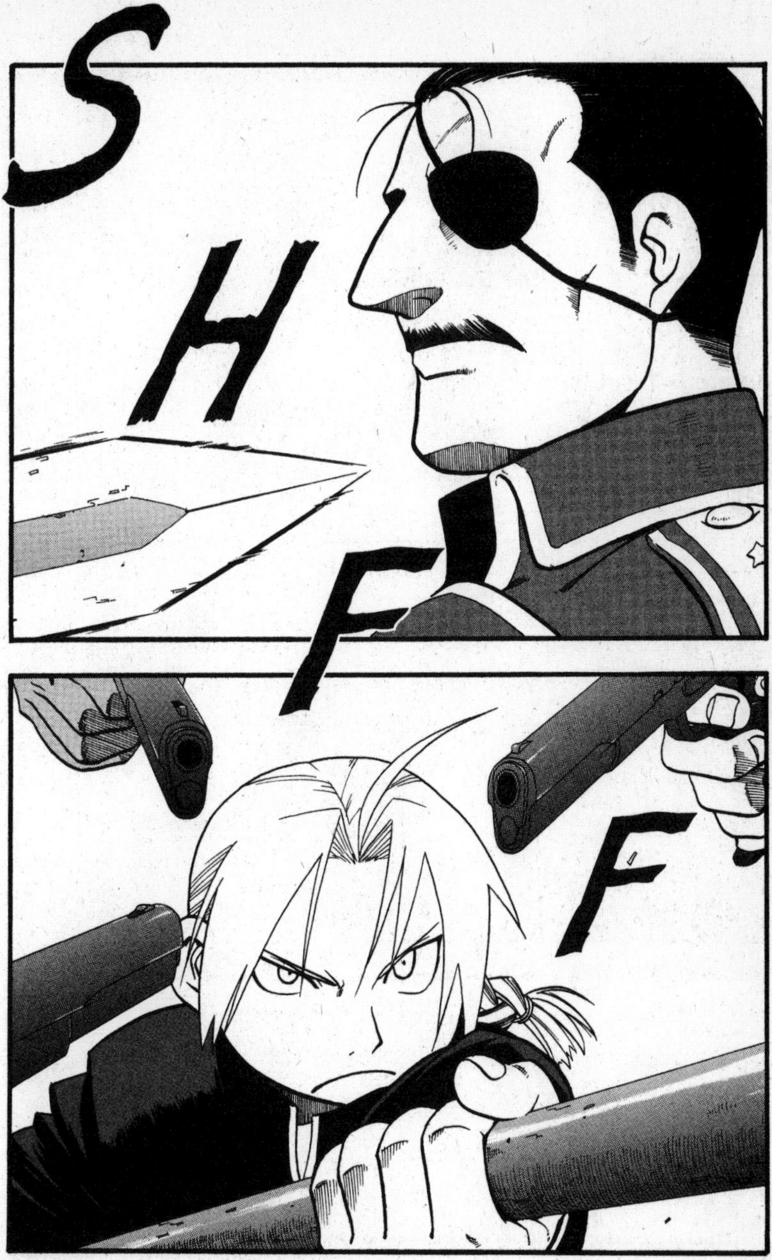
SHFF

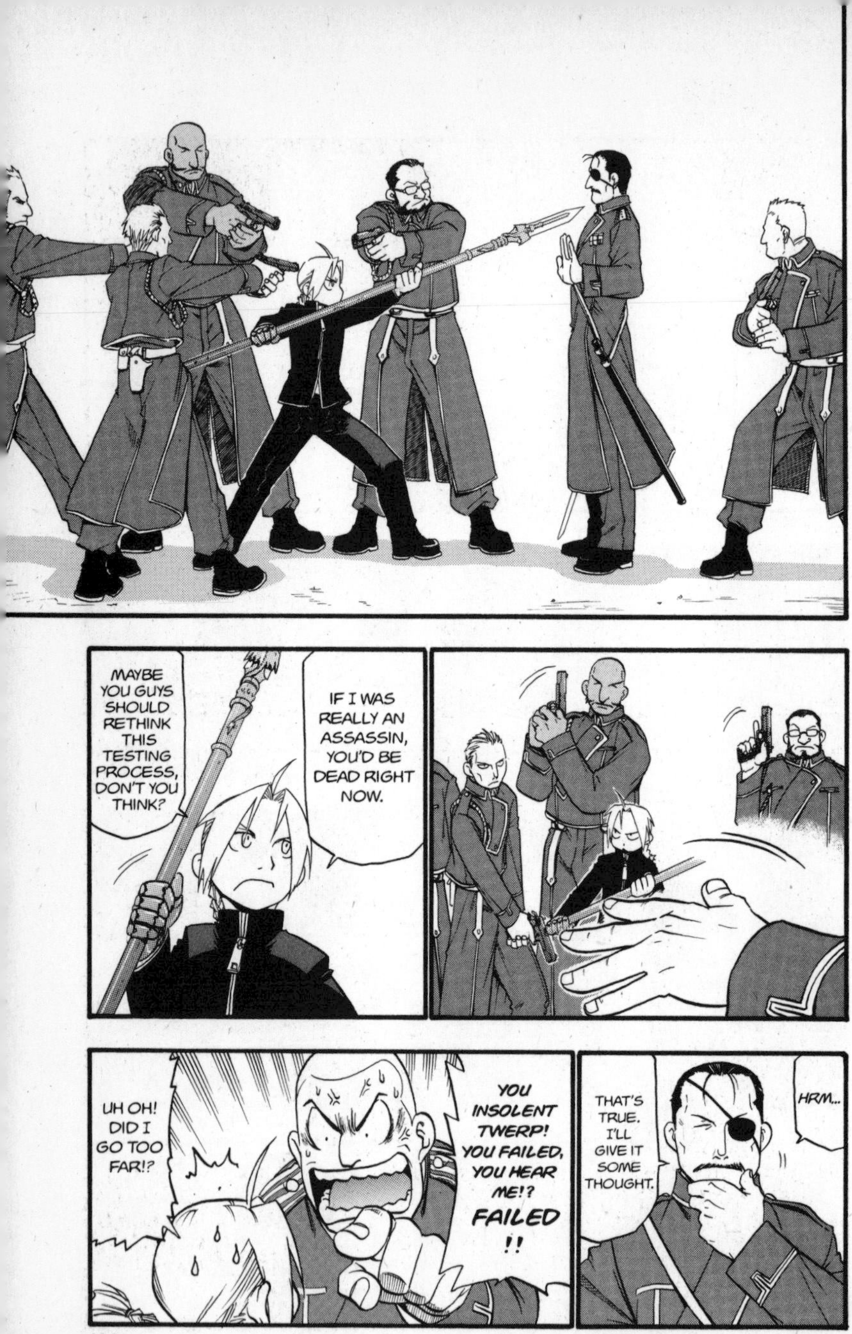
IF I WAS REALLY AN ASSASSIN, YOU'D BE DEAD RIGHT NOW.
MAYBE YOU GUYS SHOULD RETHINK THIS TESTING PROCESS, DON'T YOU THINK?
HRM...
THAT'S TRUE. I'LL GIVE IT SOME THOUGHT.
YOU INSOLENT TWERP! YOU FAILED, YOU HEAR ME!? FAILED!!
UH OH! DID I GO TOO FAR!?

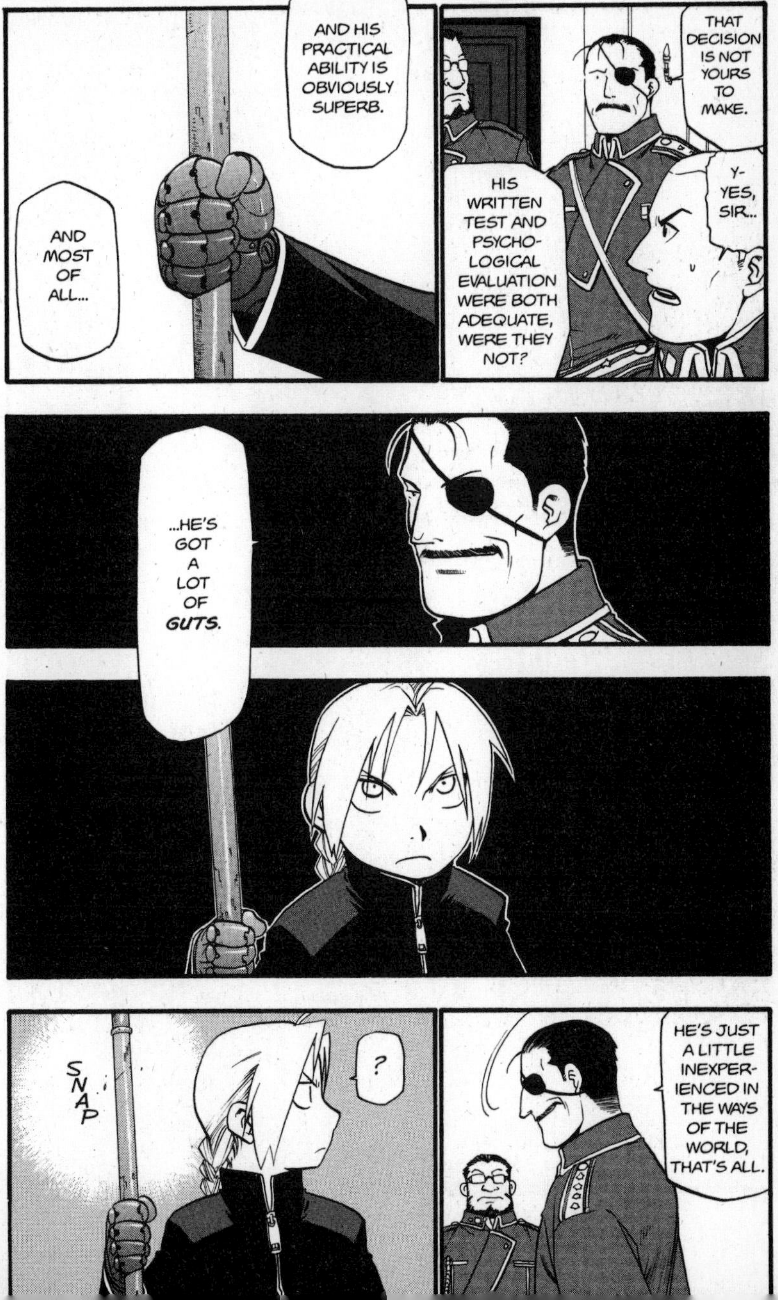
THAT DECISION IS NOT YOURS TO MAKE.
Y-YES, SIR..
HIS WRITTEN TEST AND PSYCHOLOGICAL EVALUATION WERE BOTH ADEQUATE, WERE THEY NOT?
AND HIS PRACTICAL ABILITY IS OBVIOUSLY SUPERB.
AND MOST OF ALL...
...HE'S GOT A LOT OF **GUTS**.
HE'S JUST A LITTLE INEXPERIENCED IN THE WAYS OF THE WORLD, THAT'S ALL.
?
SNAP

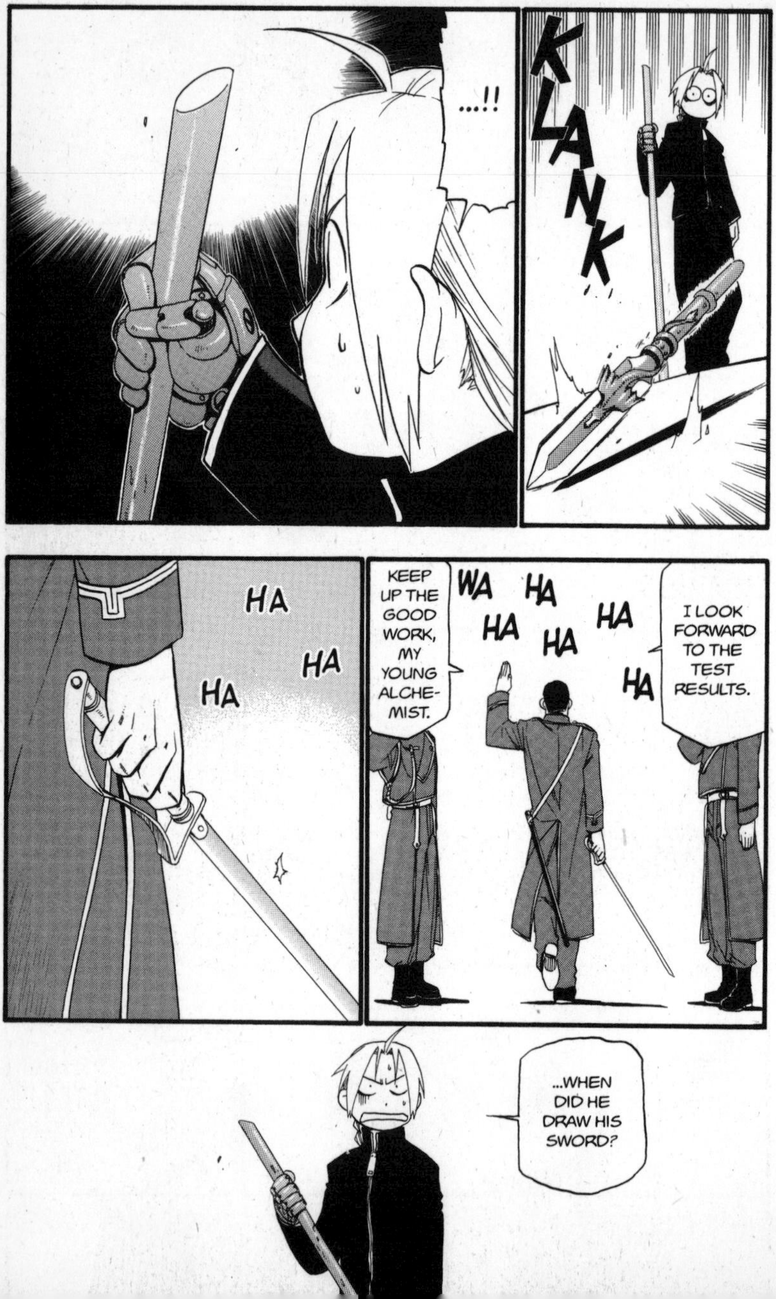
KLANK
...!!
I LOOK FORWARD TO THE TEST RESULTS.
WA HA HA HA HA HA HA
KEEP UP THE GOOD WORK, MY YOUNG ALCHEMIST.
HA HA HA
...WHEN DID HE DRAW HIS SWORD?

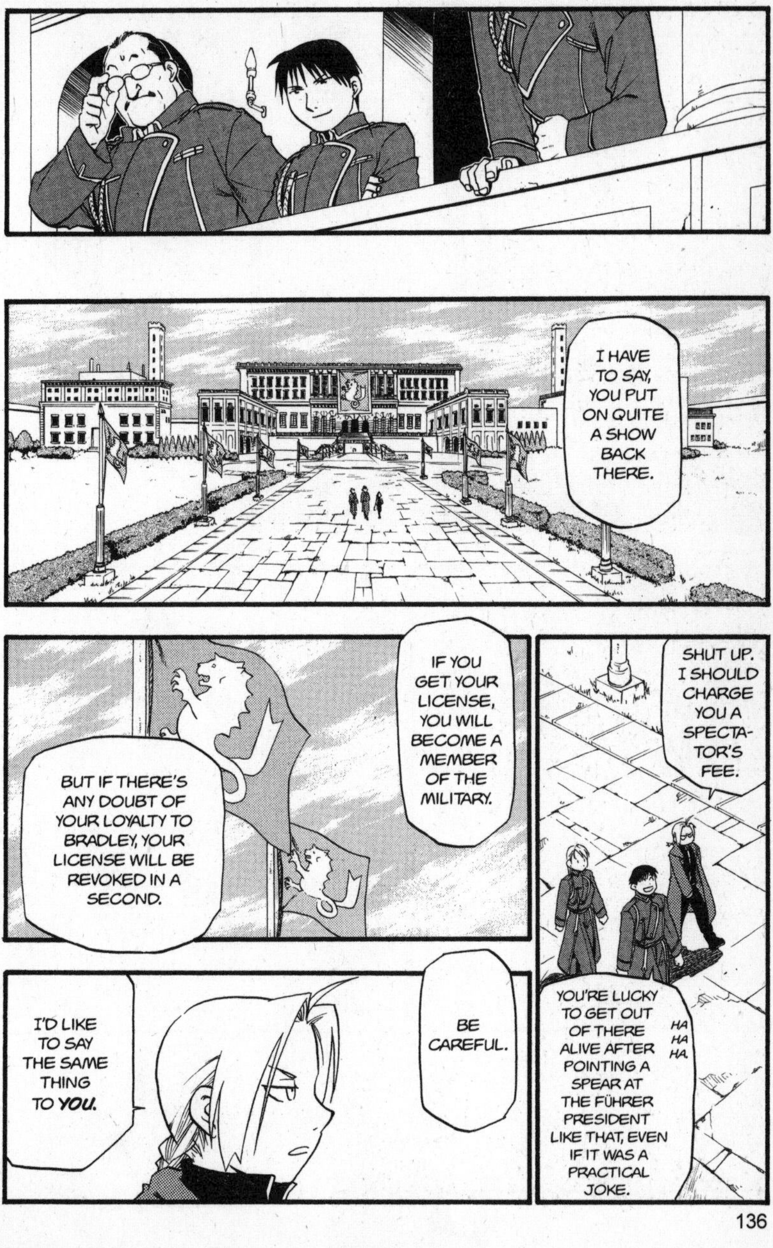

I HAVE TO SAY, YOU PUT ON QUITE A SHOW BACK THERE.
SHUT UP. I SHOULD CHARGE YOU A SPECTA-TOR'S FEE.
HA HA HA.
YOU'RE LUCKY TO GET OUT OF THERE ALIVE AFTER POINTING A SPEAR AT THE FÜHRER PRESIDENT LIKE THAT, EVEN IF IT WAS A PRACTICAL JOKE.
IF YOU GET YOUR LICENSE, YOU WILL BECOME A MEMBER OF THE MILITARY.
BUT IF THERE'S ANY DOUBT OF YOUR LOYALTY TO BRADLEY, YOUR LICENSE WILL BE REVOKED IN A SECOND.
BE CAREFUL.
I'D LIKE TO SAY THE SAME THING TO ***YOU.***

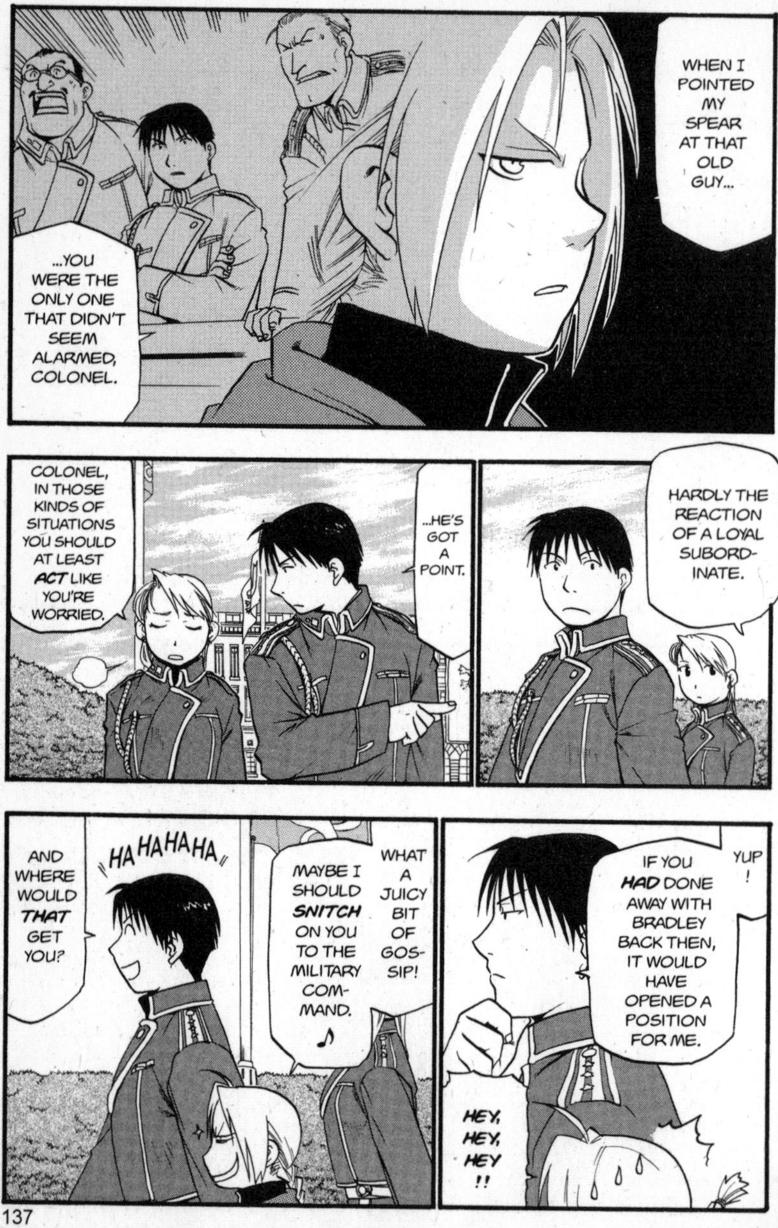
WHEN I POINTED MY SPEAR AT THAT OLD GUY...
...YOU WERE THE ONLY ONE THAT DIDN'T SEEM ALARMED, COLONEL.
HARDLY THE REACTION OF A LOYAL SUBORD-INATE.
...HE'S GOT A POINT.
COLONEL, IN THOSE KINDS OF SITUATIONS YOU SHOULD AT LEAST ACT LIKE YOU'RE WORRIED.
YUP!
IF YOU HAD DONE AWAY WITH BRADLEY BACK THEN, IT WOULD HAVE OPENED A POSITION FOR ME.
HEY, HEY, HEY!!
WHAT A JUICY BIT OF GOS-SIP!
MAYBE I SHOULD SNITCH ON YOU TO THE MILITARY COM-MAND. ♪
HAHAHAHA
AND WHERE WOULD THAT GET YOU?

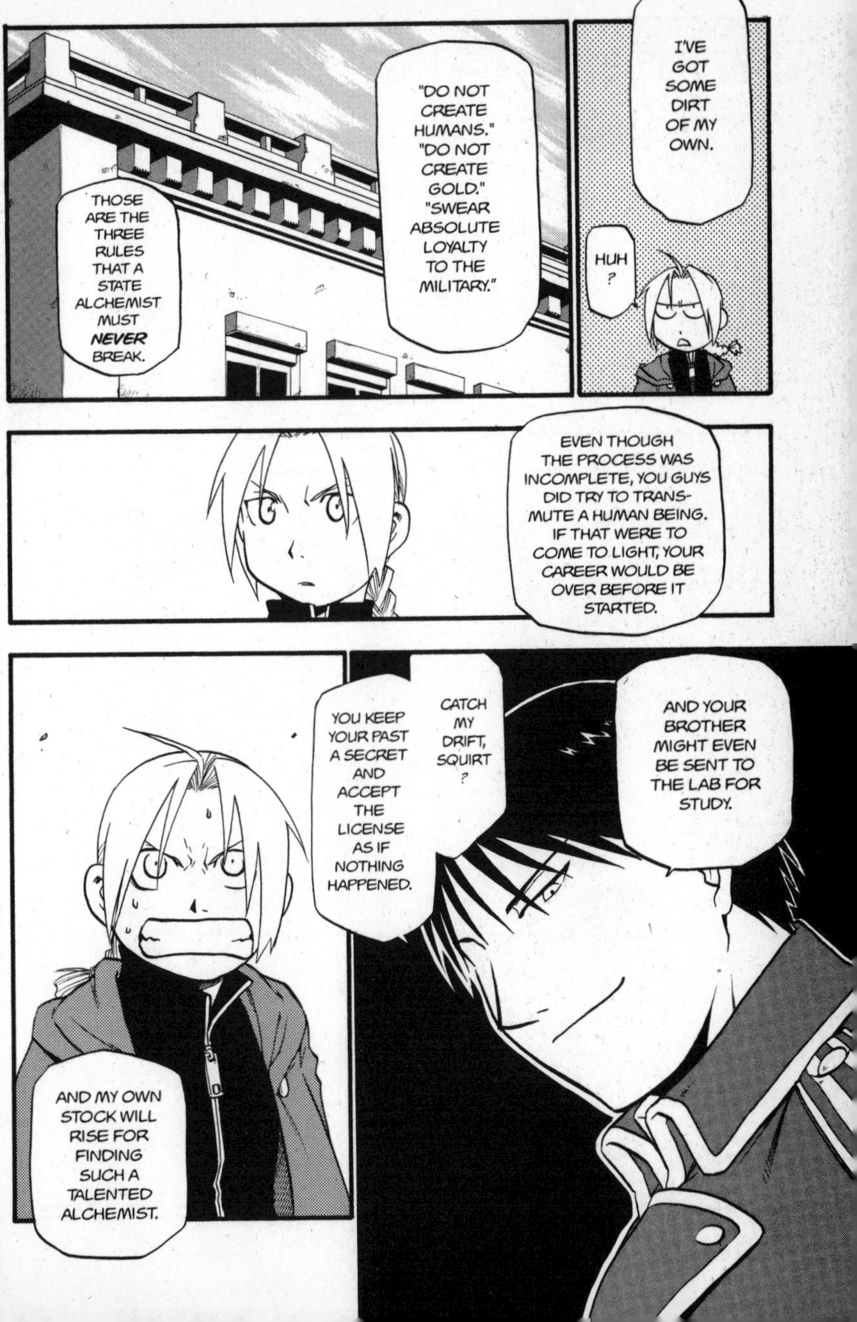
I'VE GOT SOME DIRT OF MY OWN.
HUH?
"DO NOT CREATE HUMANS." "DO NOT CREATE GOLD." "SWEAR ABSOLUTE LOYALTY TO THE MILITARY."
THOSE ARE THE THREE RULES THAT A STATE ALCHEMIST MUST ***NEVER*** BREAK.
EVEN THOUGH THE PROCESS WAS INCOMPLETE, YOU GUYS DID TRY TO TRANS-MUTE A HUMAN BEING. IF THAT WERE TO COME TO LIGHT, YOUR CAREER WOULD BE OVER BEFORE IT STARTED.
AND YOUR BROTHER MIGHT EVEN BE SENT TO THE LAB FOR STUDY.
CATCH MY DRIFT, SQUIRT?
YOU KEEP YOUR PAST A SECRET AND ACCEPT THE LICENSE AS IF NOTHING HAPPENED.
AND MY OWN STOCK WILL RISE FOR FINDING SUCH A TALENTED ALCHEMIST.

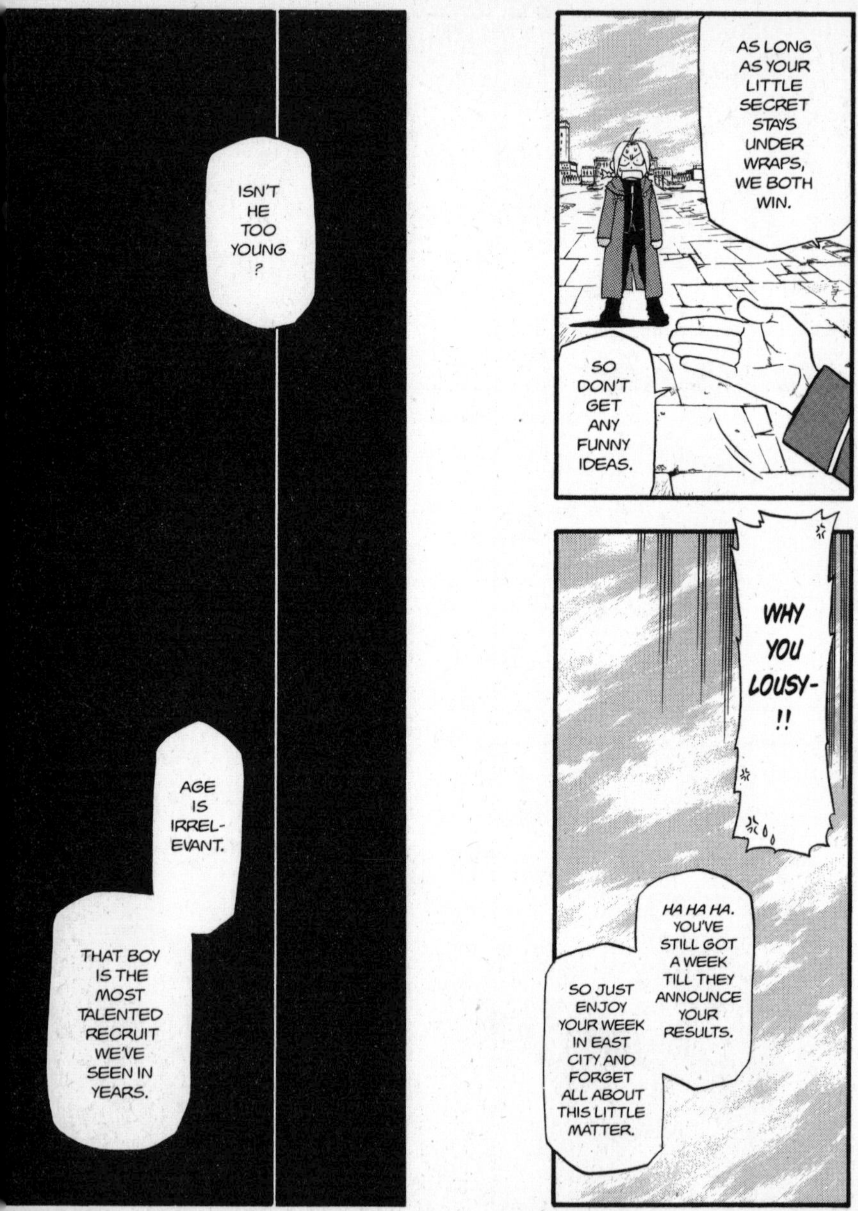
AS LONG AS YOUR LITTLE SECRET STAYS UNDER WRAPS, WE BOTH WIN.
SO DON'T GET ANY FUNNY IDEAS.
WHY YOU LOUSY-!!
HA HA HA. YOU'VE STILL GOT A WEEK TILL THEY ANNOUNCE YOUR RESULTS.
SO JUST ENJOY YOUR WEEK IN EAST CITY AND FORGET ALL ABOUT THIS LITTLE MATTER.
ISN'T HE TOO YOUNG?
AGE IS IRREL-EVANT.
THAT BOY IS THE MOST TALENTED RECRUIT WE'VE SEEN IN YEARS.

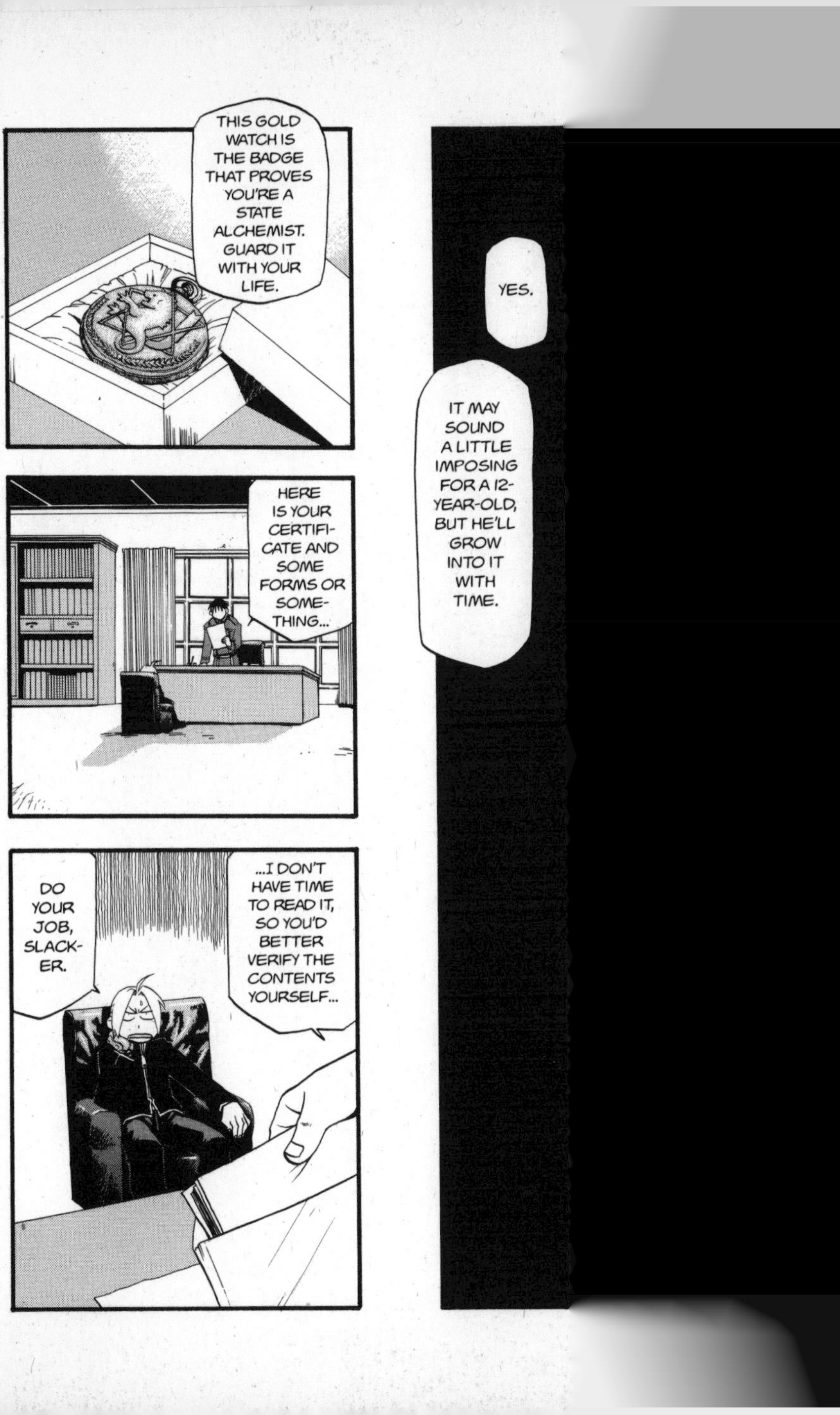
YES.
IT MAY SOUND A LITTLE IMPOSING FOR A 12-YEAR-OLD, BUT HE'LL GROW INTO IT WITH TIME.
THIS GOLD WATCH IS THE BADGE THAT PROVES YOU'RE A STATE ALCHEMIST. GUARD IT WITH YOUR LIFE.
HERE IS YOUR CERTIFICATE AND SOME FORMS OR SOMETHING...
...I DON'T HAVE TIME TO READ IT, SO YOU'D BETTER VERIFY THE CONTENTS YOURSELF...
DO YOUR JOB, SLACKER.

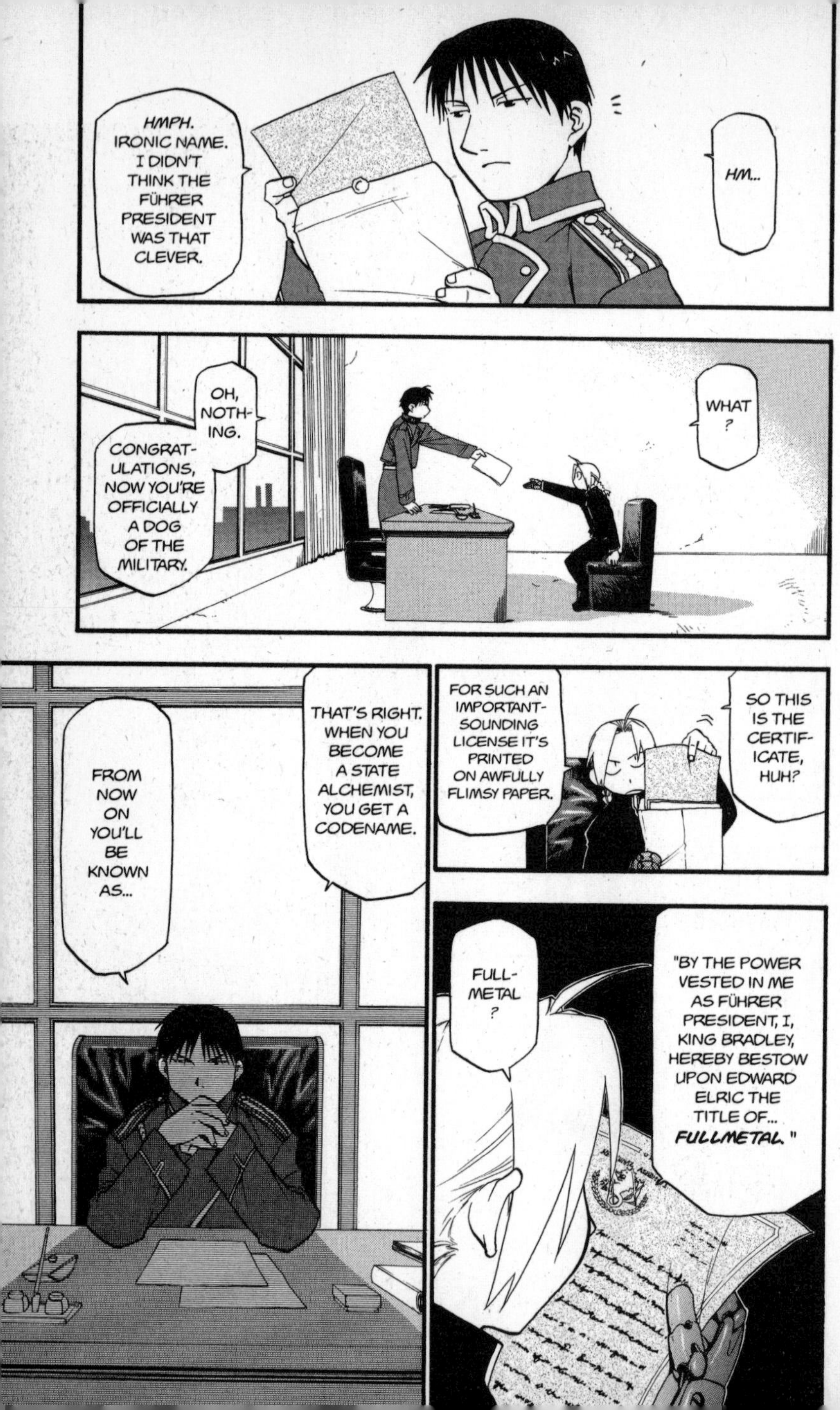
HM...
HMPH. IRONIC NAME. I DIDN'T THINK THE FÜHRER PRESIDENT WAS THAT CLEVER.
WHAT?
OH, NOTHING.
CONGRATULATIONS, NOW YOU'RE OFFICIALLY A DOG OF THE MILITARY.
SO THIS IS THE CERTIFICATE, HUH?
FOR SUCH AN IMPORTANT-SOUNDING LICENSE IT'S PRINTED ON AWFULLY FLIMSY PAPER.
"BY THE POWER VESTED IN ME AS FÜHRER PRESIDENT, I, KING BRADLEY, HEREBY BESTOW UPON EDWARD ELRIC THE TITLE OF... FULLMETAL."
FULLMETAL?
THAT'S RIGHT. WHEN YOU BECOME A STATE ALCHEMIST, YOU GET A CODENAME.
FROM NOW ON YOU'LL BE KNOWN AS...

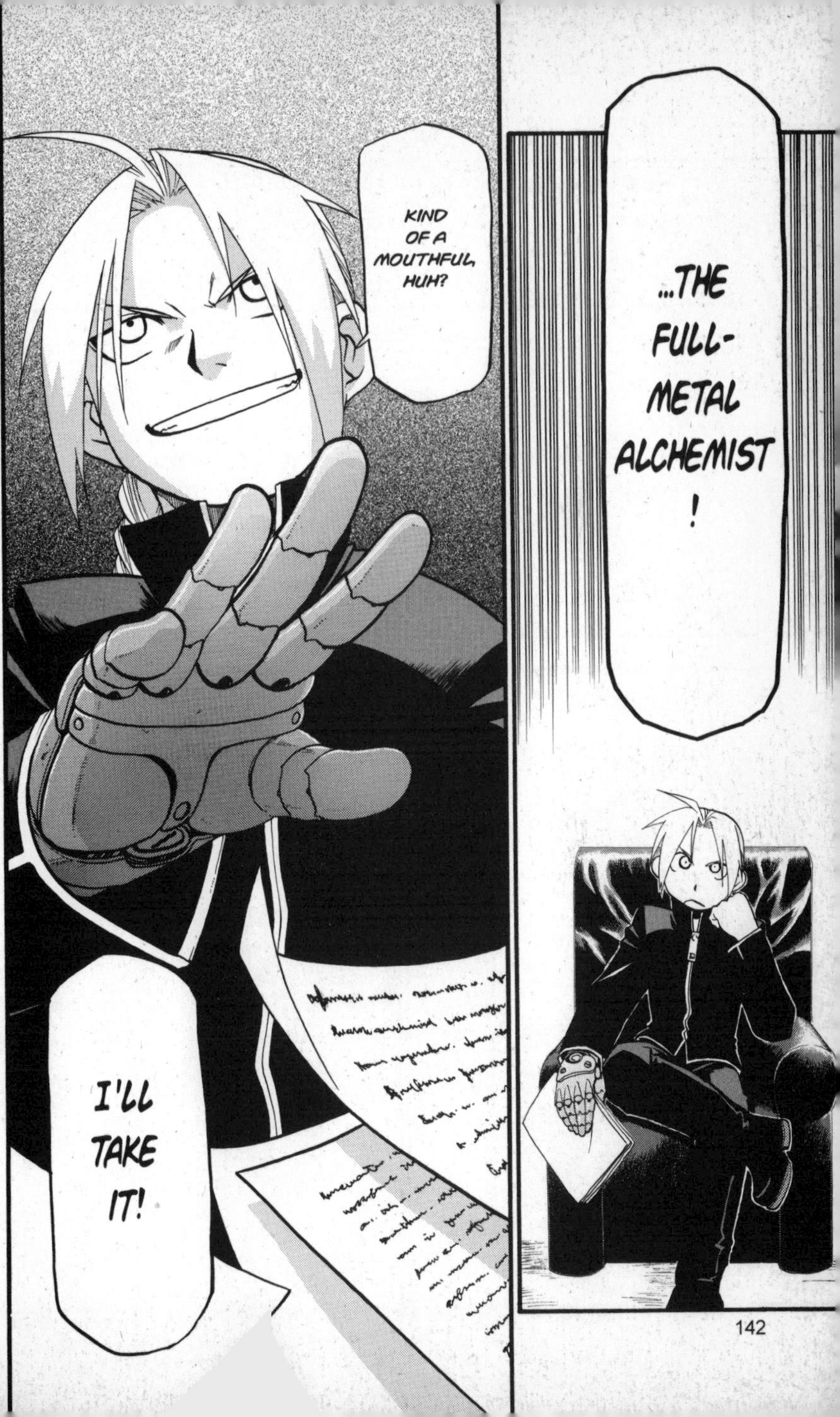
...THE FULL-METAL ALCHEMIST !
KIND OF A MOUTHFUL, HUH?
I'LL TAKE IT!

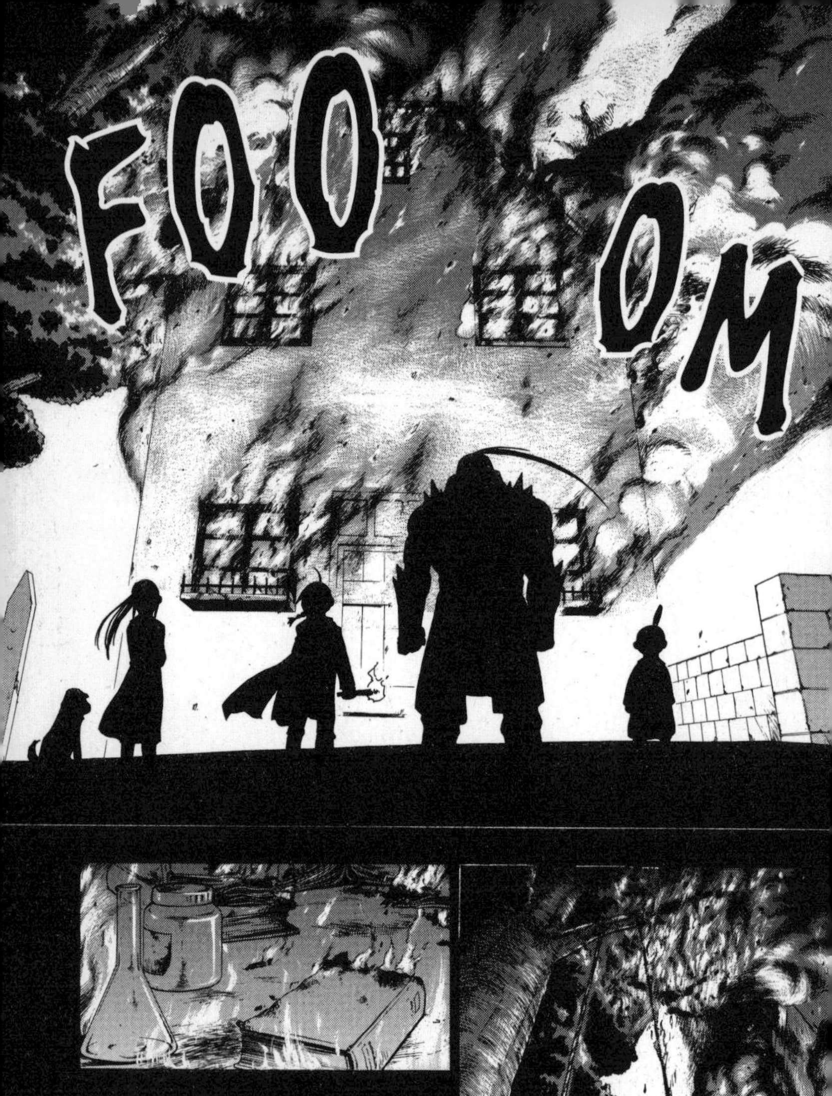
FOOOM
KRKL
SNAP

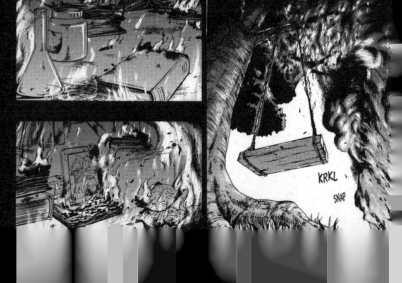

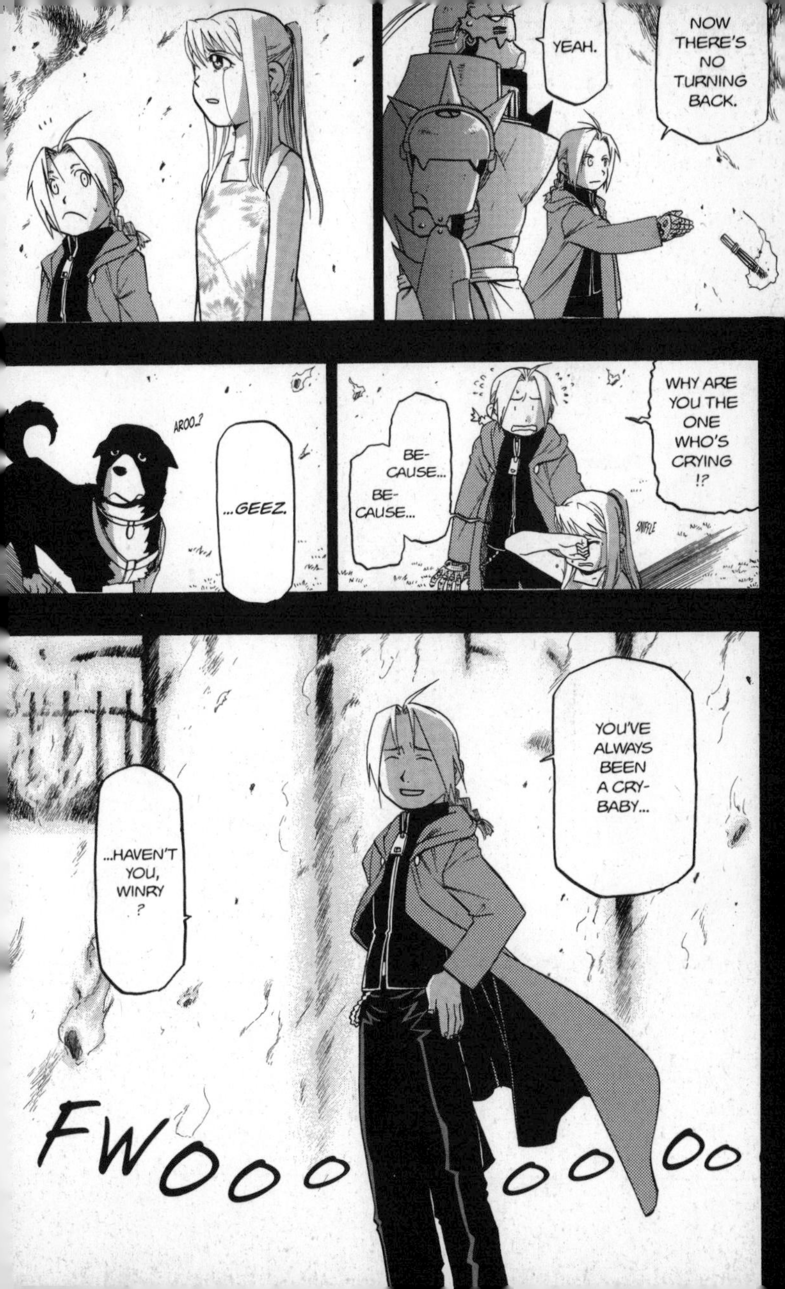
NOW THERE'S NO TURNING BACK.
YEAH.
WHY ARE YOU THE ONE WHO'S CRYING !?
BE-CAUSE... BE-CAUSE...
SNIFFLE
...GEEZ.
AROO..?
YOU'VE ALWAYS BEEN A CRY-BABY...
...HAVEN'T YOU, WINRY ?
FWOOOOOOOOO

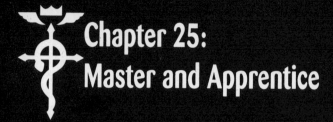

Chapter 25:
Master and Apprentice

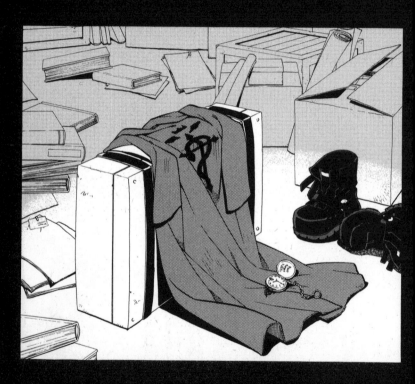

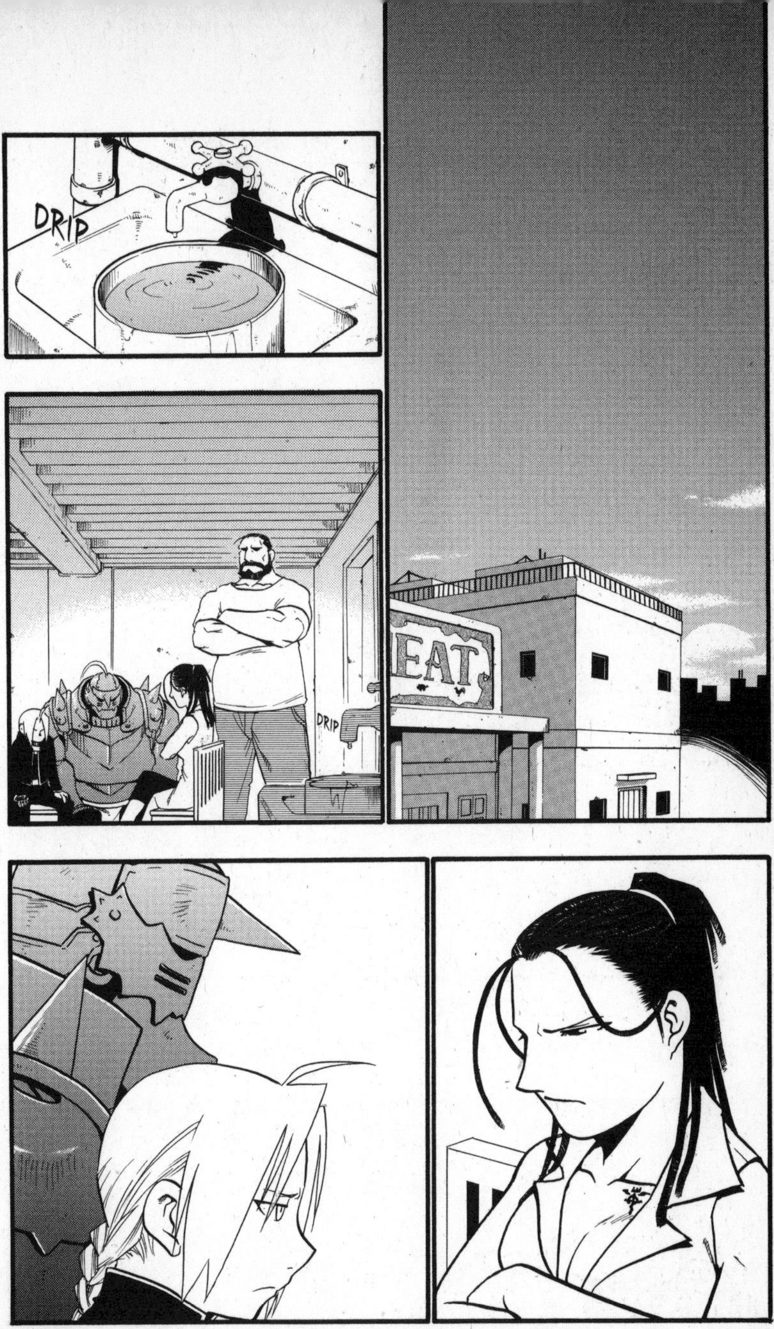
EAT
DRIP
DRIP

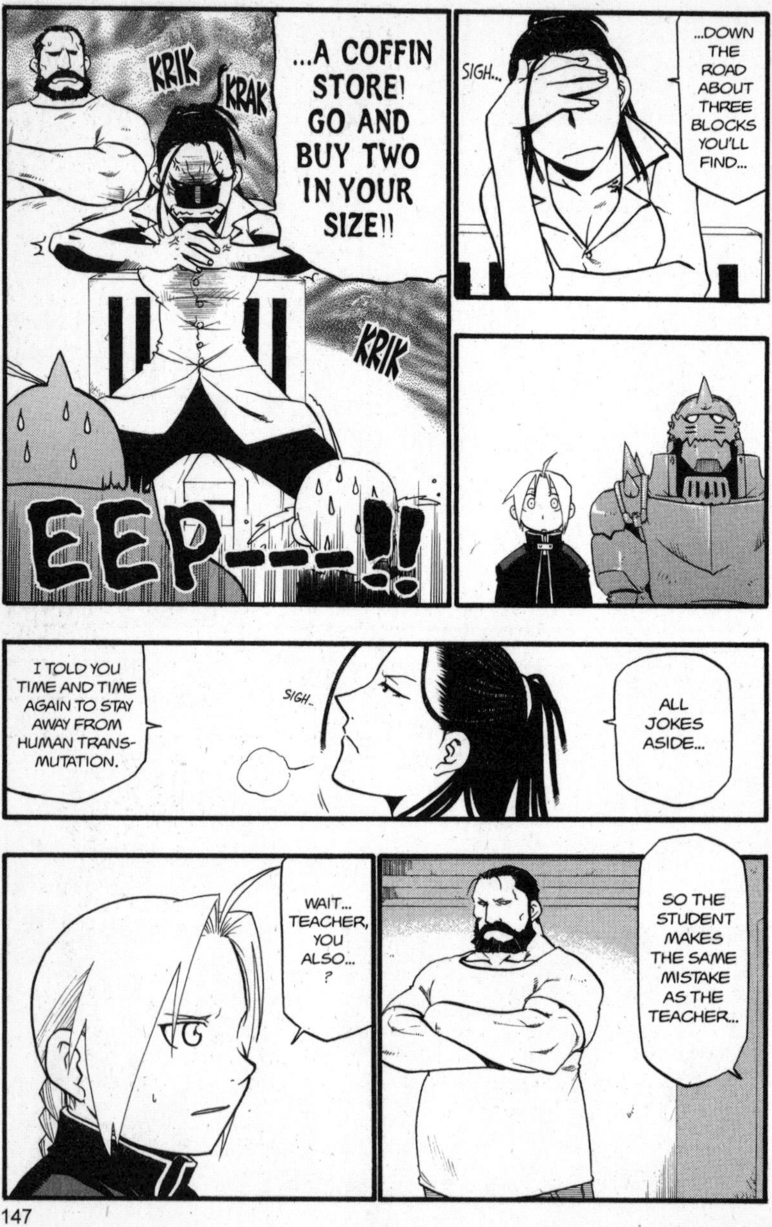
...DOWN THE ROAD ABOUT THREE BLOCKS YOU'LL FIND...
SIGH...
...A COFFIN STORE! GO AND BUY TWO IN YOUR SIZE!!
KRIK
KRAK
KRIK
EEP---!!
ALL JOKES ASIDE...
SIGH...
I TOLD YOU TIME AND TIME AGAIN TO STAY AWAY FROM HUMAN TRANS-MUTATION.
SO THE STUDENT MAKES THE SAME MISTAKE AS THE TEACHER...
WAIT... TEACHER, YOU ALSO...?

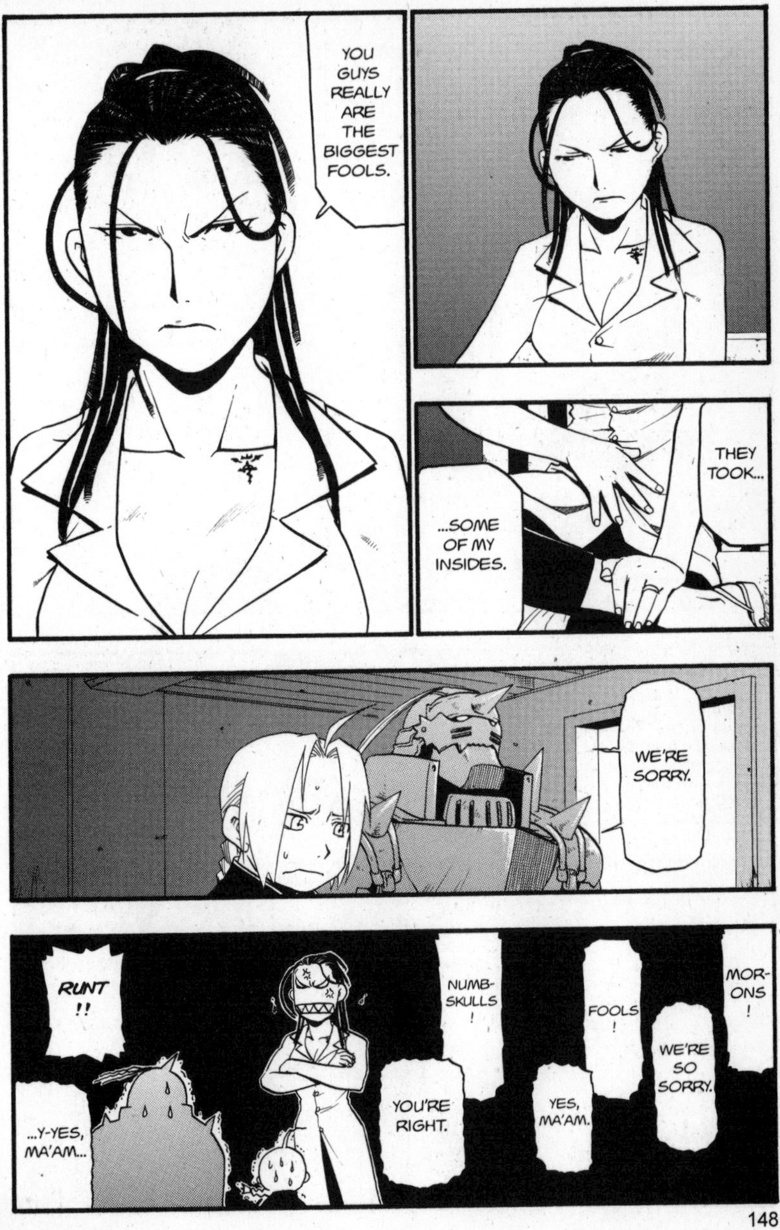
THEY TOOK...
...SOME OF MY INSIDES.
YOU GUYS REALLY ARE THE BIGGEST FOOLS.
WE'RE SORRY.
MOR-ONS!
WE'RE SO SORRY.
FOOLS!
YES, MA'AM.
NUMB-SKULLS!
YOU'RE RIGHT.
RUNT!!
...Y-YES, MA'AM...

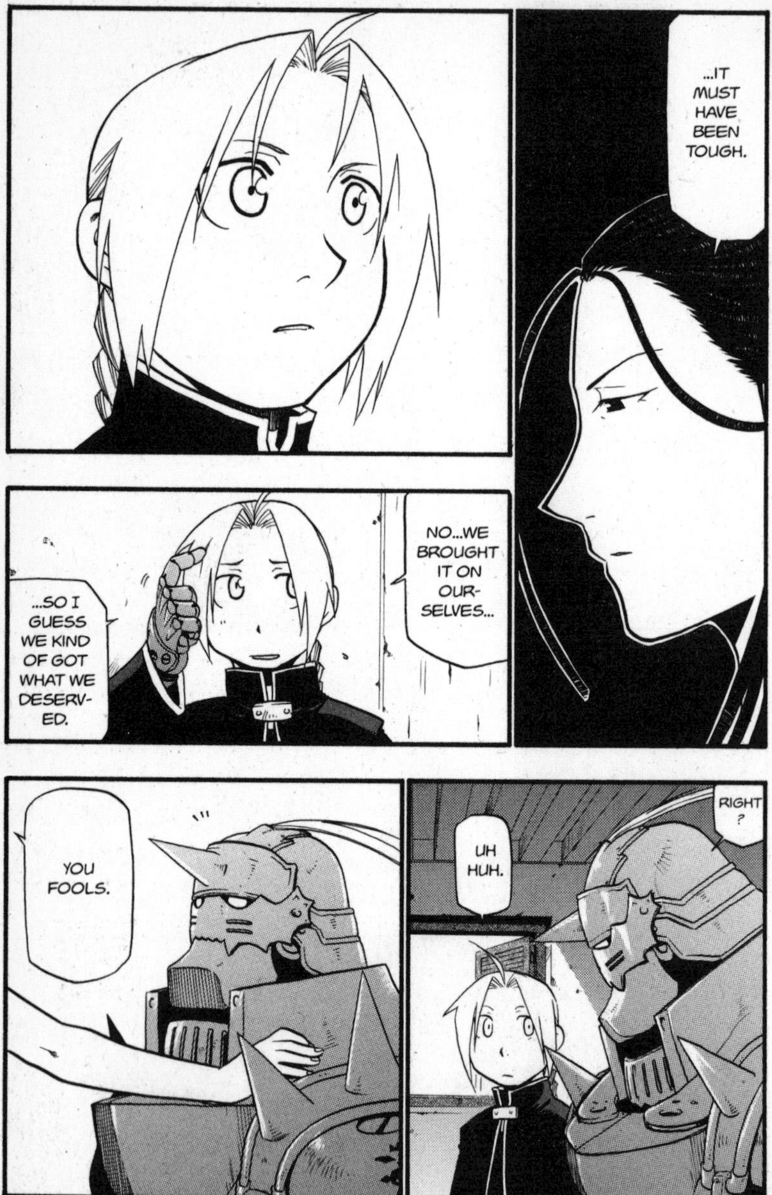
...IT MUST HAVE BEEN TOUGH.
NO...WE BROUGHT IT ON OURSELVES...
...SO I GUESS WE KIND OF GOT WHAT WE DESERVED.
RIGHT?
UH HUH.
YOU FOOLS.

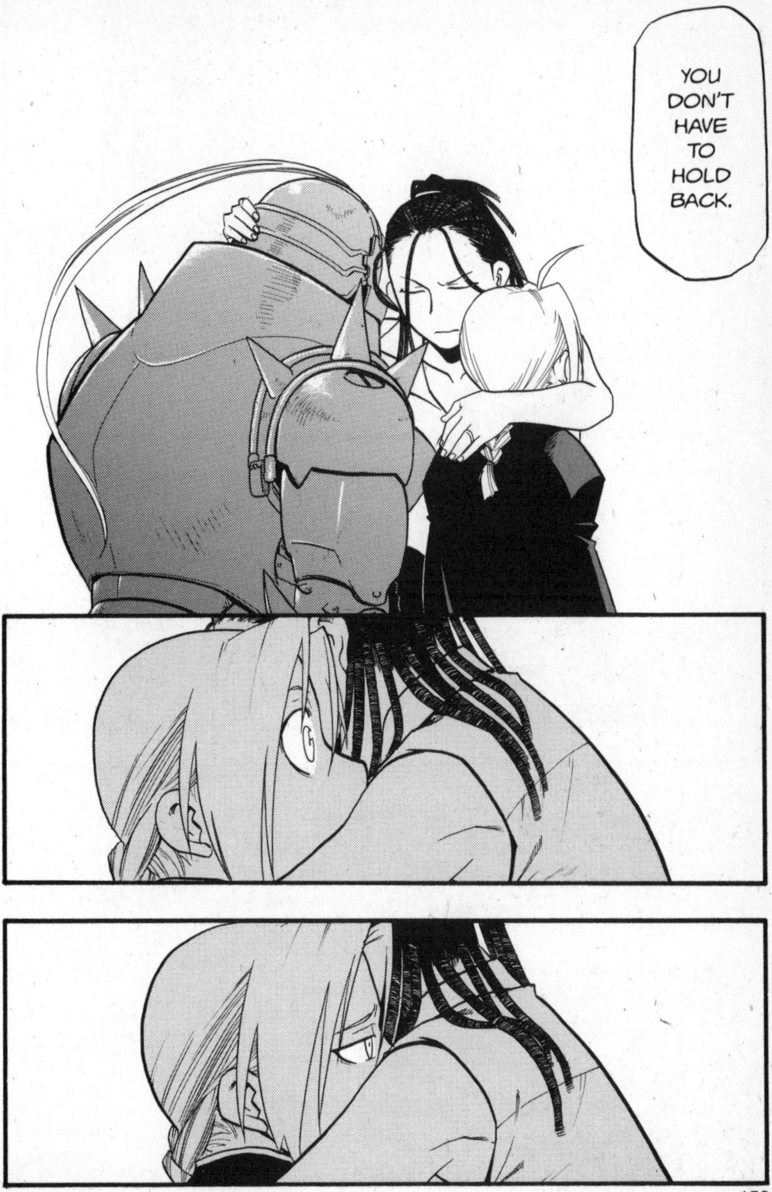
YOU DON'T HAVE TO HOLD BACK.

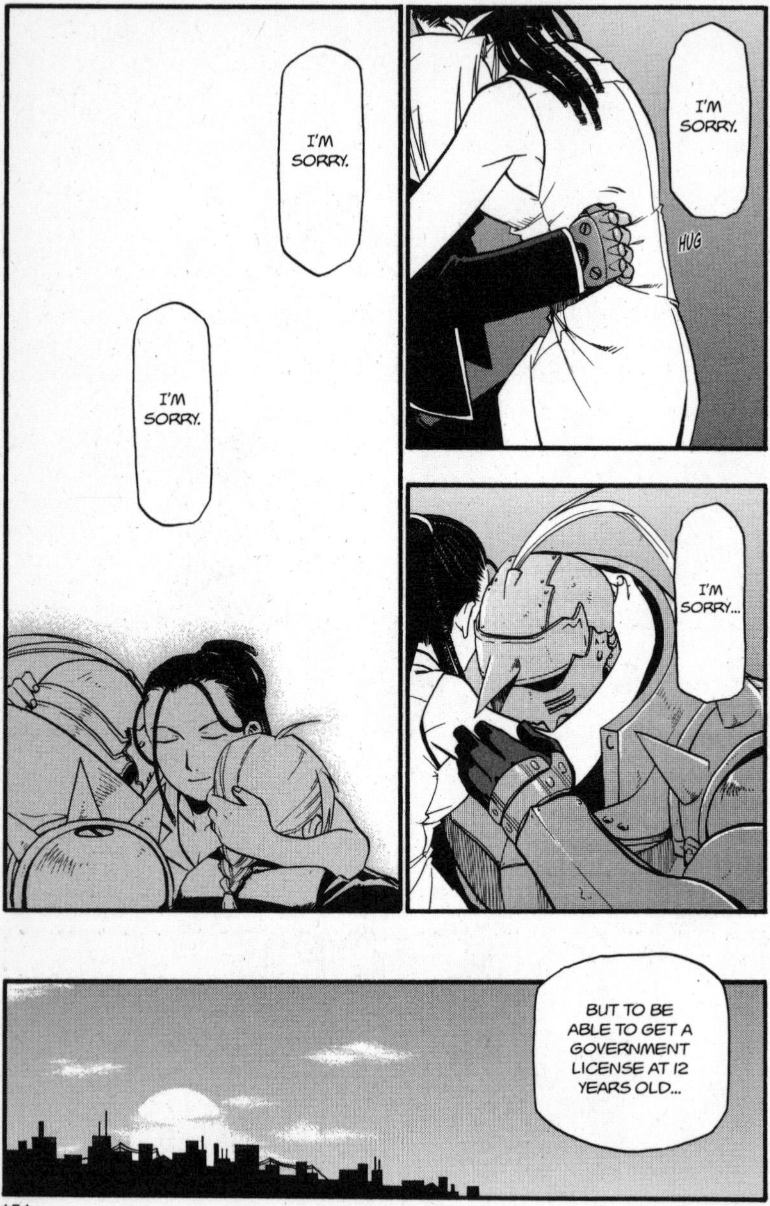

I'M SORRY.
HUG
I'M SORRY...
I'M SORRY.
I'M SORRY.
BUT TO BE ABLE TO GET A GOVERNMENT LICENSE AT 12 YEARS OLD...

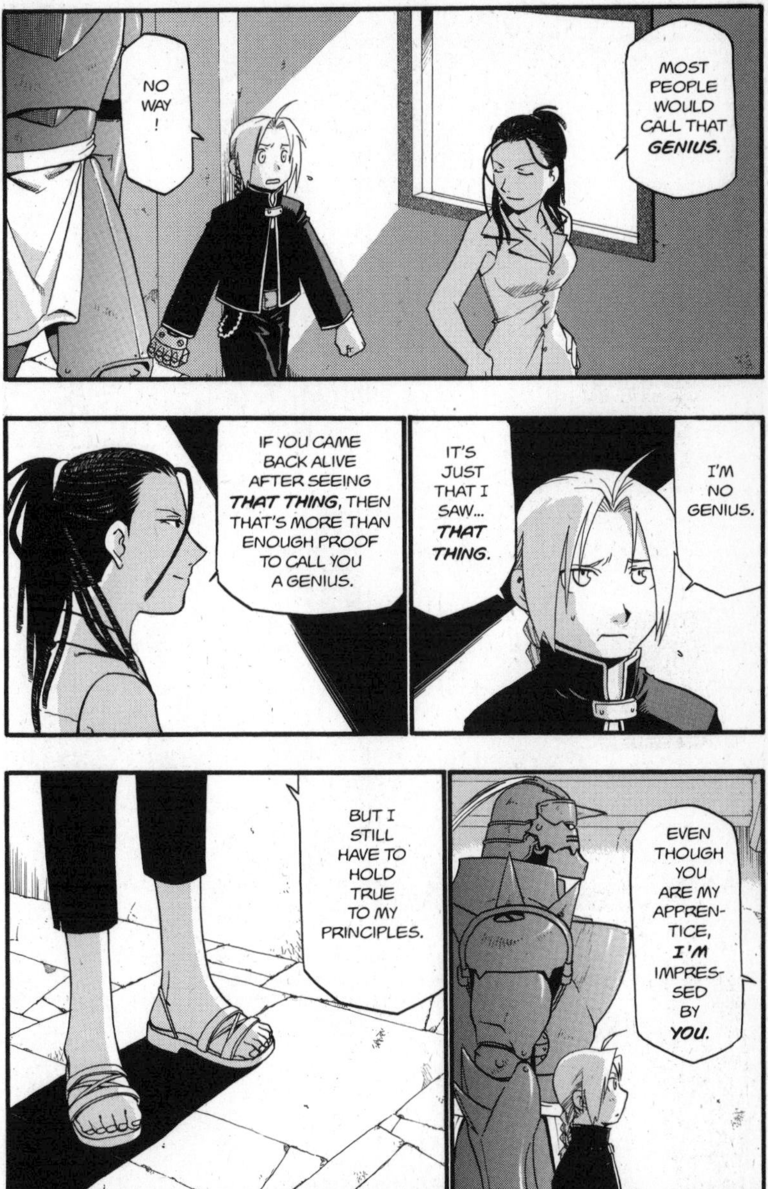
MOST PEOPLE WOULD CALL THAT **GENIUS.**
NO WAY !
I'M NO GENIUS.
IT'S JUST THAT I SAW... **THAT THING.**
IF YOU CAME BACK ALIVE AFTER SEEING **THAT THING**, THEN THAT'S MORE THAN ENOUGH PROOF TO CALL YOU A GENIUS.
EVEN THOUGH YOU ARE MY APPRENTICE, **I'M** IMPRESSED BY **YOU.**
BUT I STILL HAVE TO HOLD TRUE TO MY PRINCIPLES.

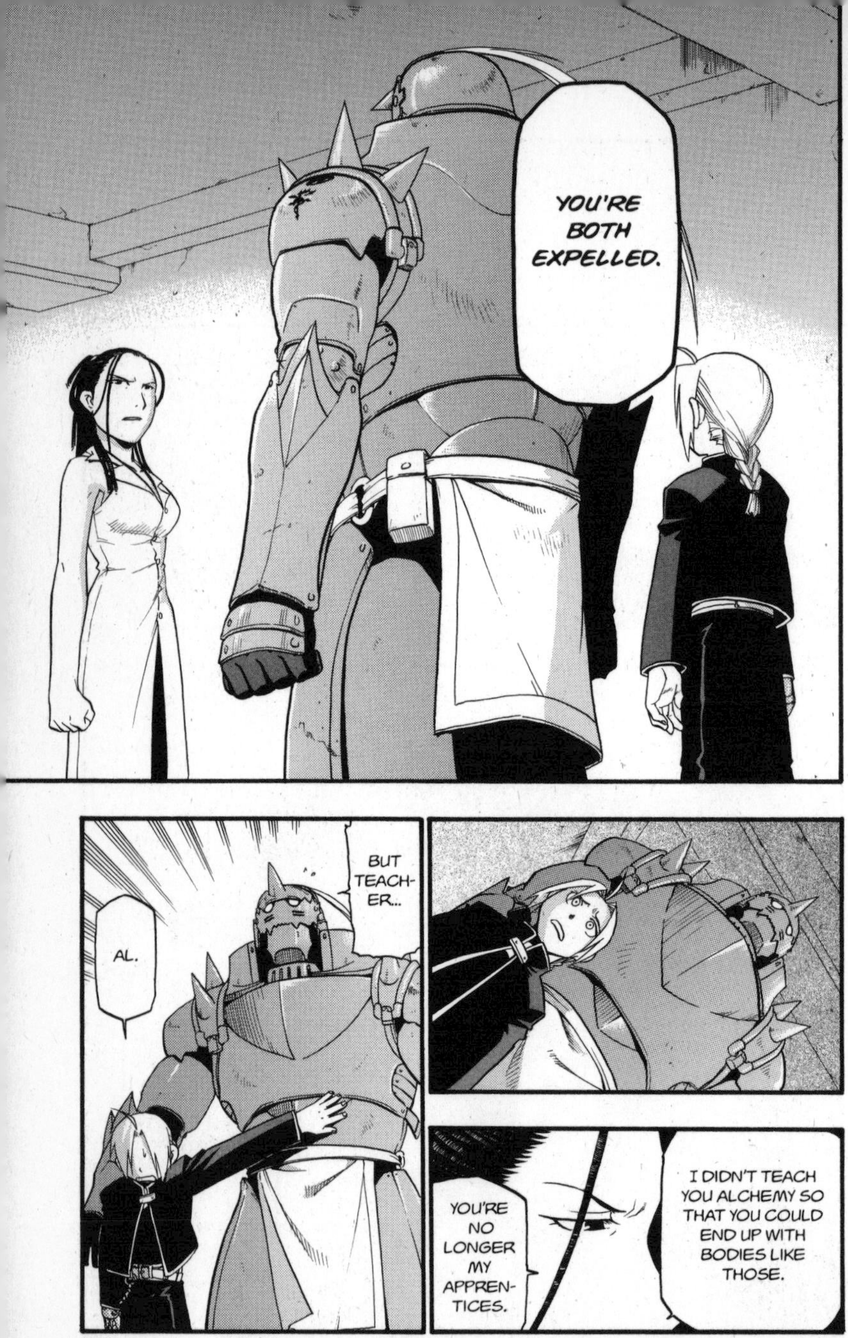
YOU'RE BOTH EXPELLED.
I DIDN'T TEACH YOU ALCHEMY SO THAT YOU COULD END UP WITH BODIES LIKE THOSE.
YOU'RE NO LONGER MY APPRENTICES.
BUT TEACHER...
AL.

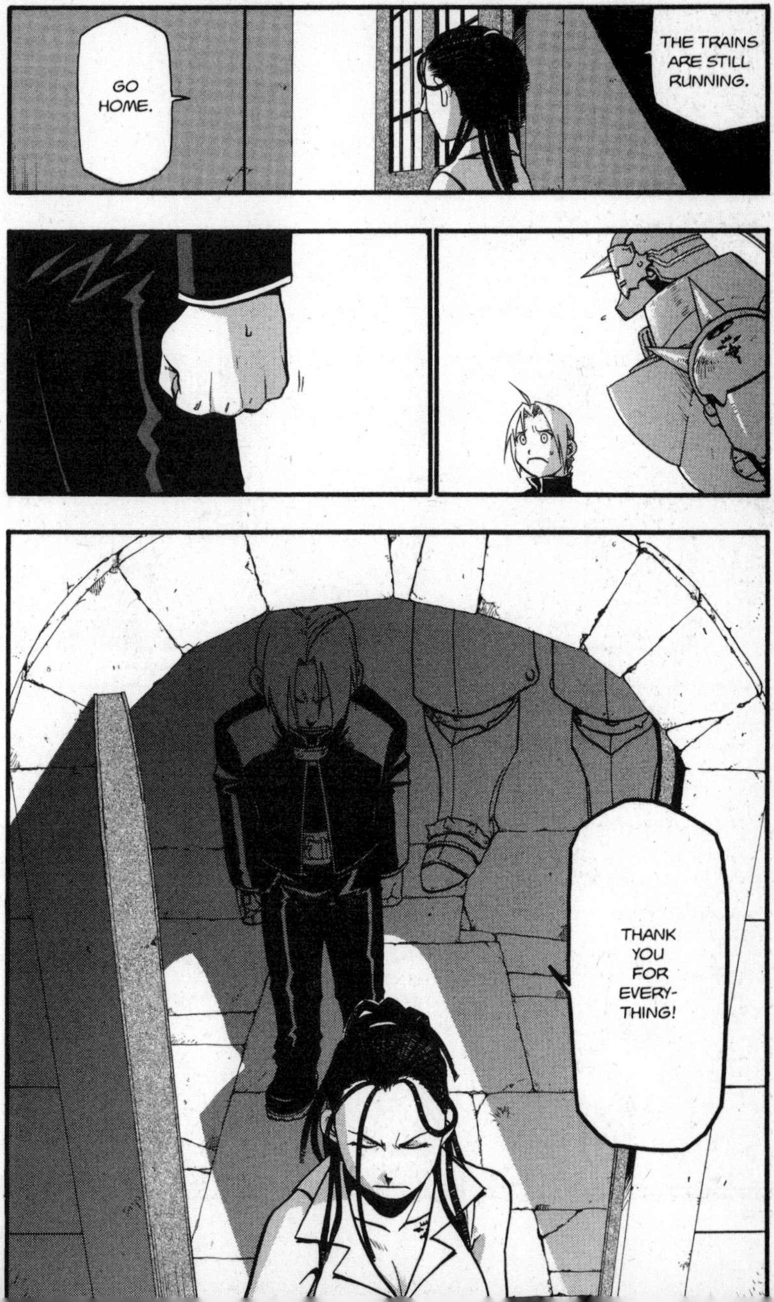
THE TRAINS ARE STILL RUNNING.
GO HOME.
THANK YOU FOR EVERYTHING!

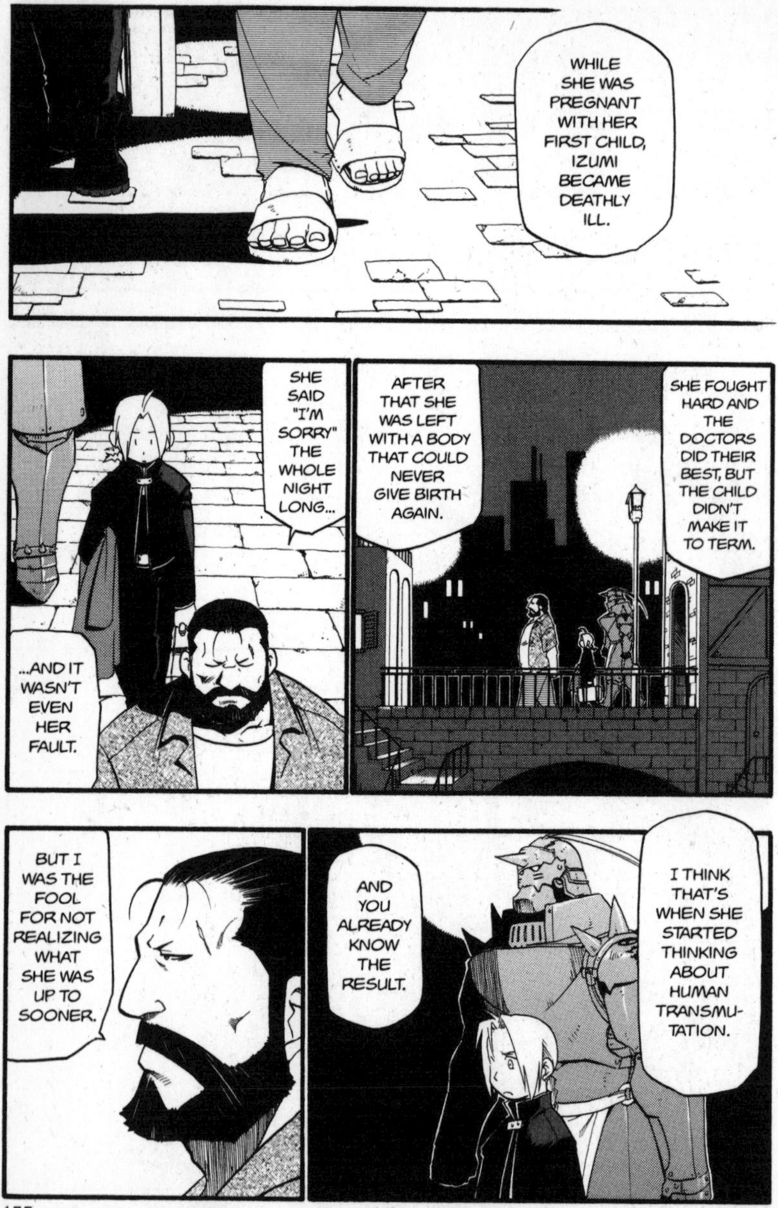
WHILE SHE WAS PREGNANT WITH HER FIRST CHILD, IZUMI BECAME DEATHLY ILL.
SHE FOUGHT HARD AND THE DOCTORS DID THEIR BEST, BUT THE CHILD DIDN'T MAKE IT TO TERM.
AFTER THAT SHE WAS LEFT WITH A BODY THAT COULD NEVER GIVE BIRTH AGAIN.
SHE SAID "I'M SORRY" THE WHOLE NIGHT LONG...
...AND IT WASN'T EVEN HER FAULT.
I THINK THAT'S WHEN SHE STARTED THINKING ABOUT HUMAN TRANSMU-TATION.
AND YOU ALREADY KNOW THE RESULT.
BUT I WAS THE FOOL FOR NOT REALIZING WHAT SHE WAS UP TO SOONER.

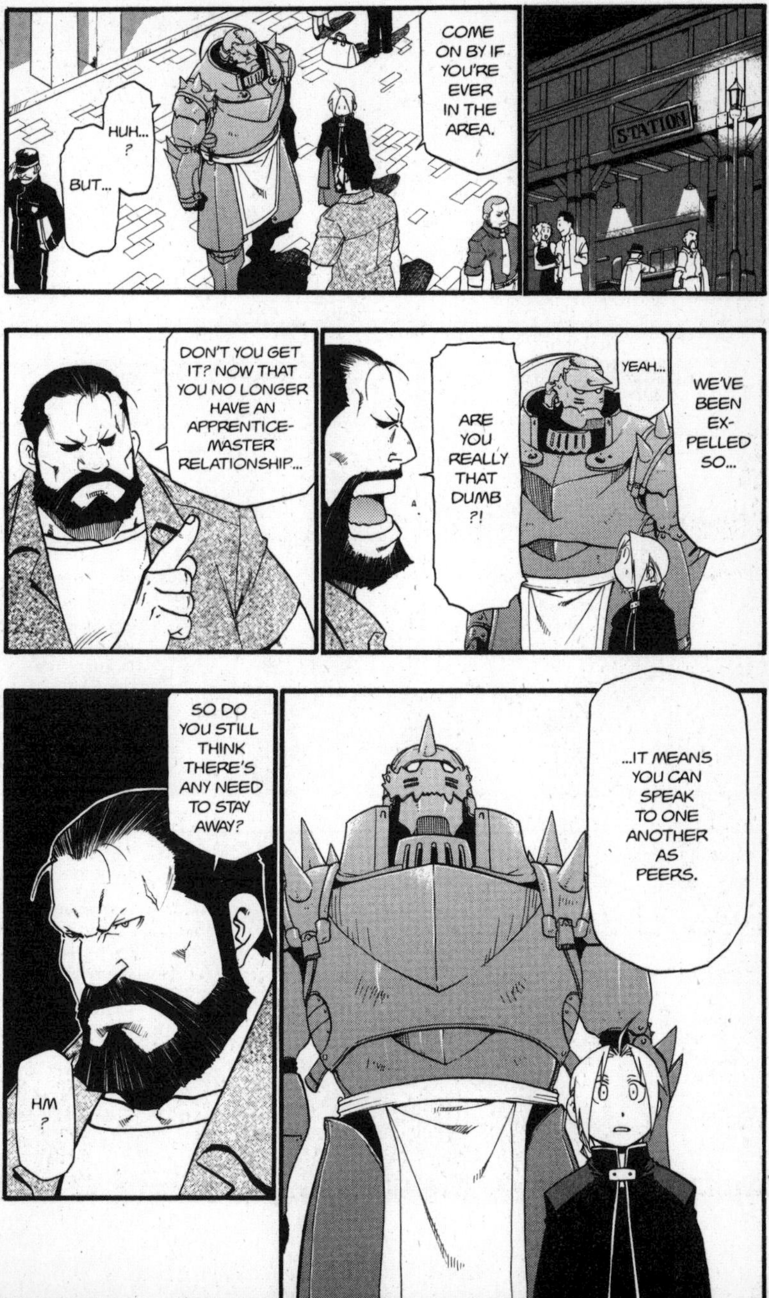
STATION
COME ON BY IF YOU'RE EVER IN THE AREA.
HUH... ?
BUT...
YEAH...
WE'VE BEEN EX-PELLED SO...
ARE YOU REALLY THAT DUMB ?!
DON'T YOU GET IT? NOW THAT YOU NO LONGER HAVE AN APPRENTICE-MASTER RELATIONSHIP...
...IT MEANS YOU CAN SPEAK TO ONE ANOTHER AS PEERS.
SO DO YOU STILL THINK THERE'S ANY NEED TO STAY AWAY?
HM ?

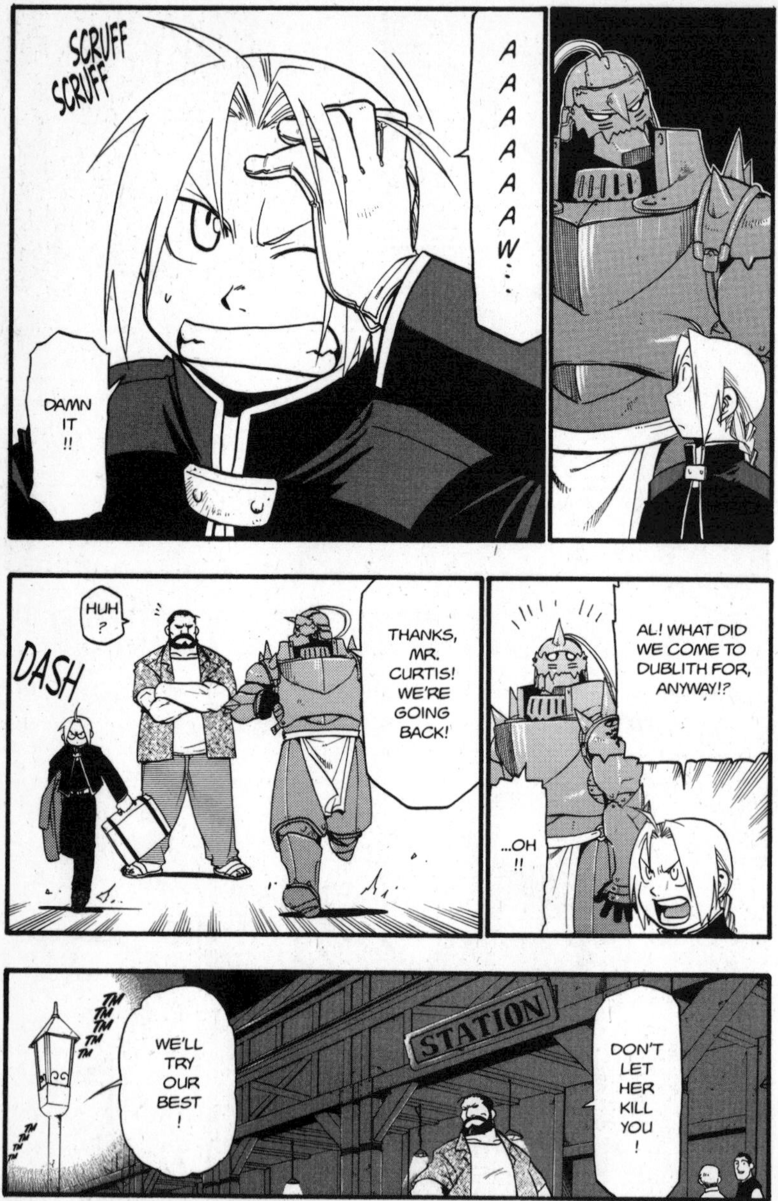
AAAAAAW...
SCRUFF SCRUFF
DAMN IT!!
AL! WHAT DID WE COME TO DUBLITH FOR, ANYWAY!?
...OH!!
THANKS, MR. CURTIS! WE'RE GOING BACK!
HUH?
DASH
DON'T LET HER KILL YOU!
STATION
WE'LL TRY OUR BEST!
TM TM TM TM TM
TM TM TM TM

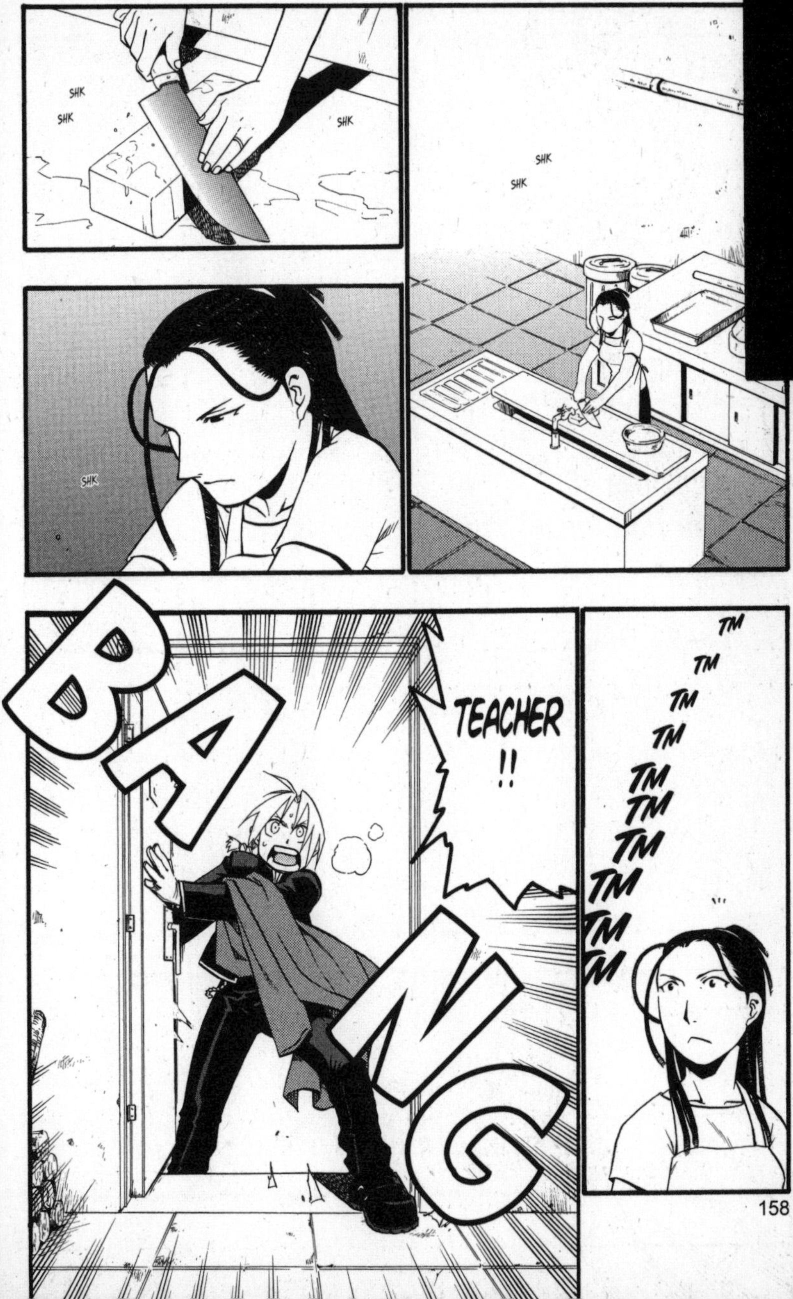
SHK
SHK
SHK
SHK
SHK
SHK
TM
TM
TM
TM
TM
TM
TM
TM
TM
TM
BANG
TEACHER!!

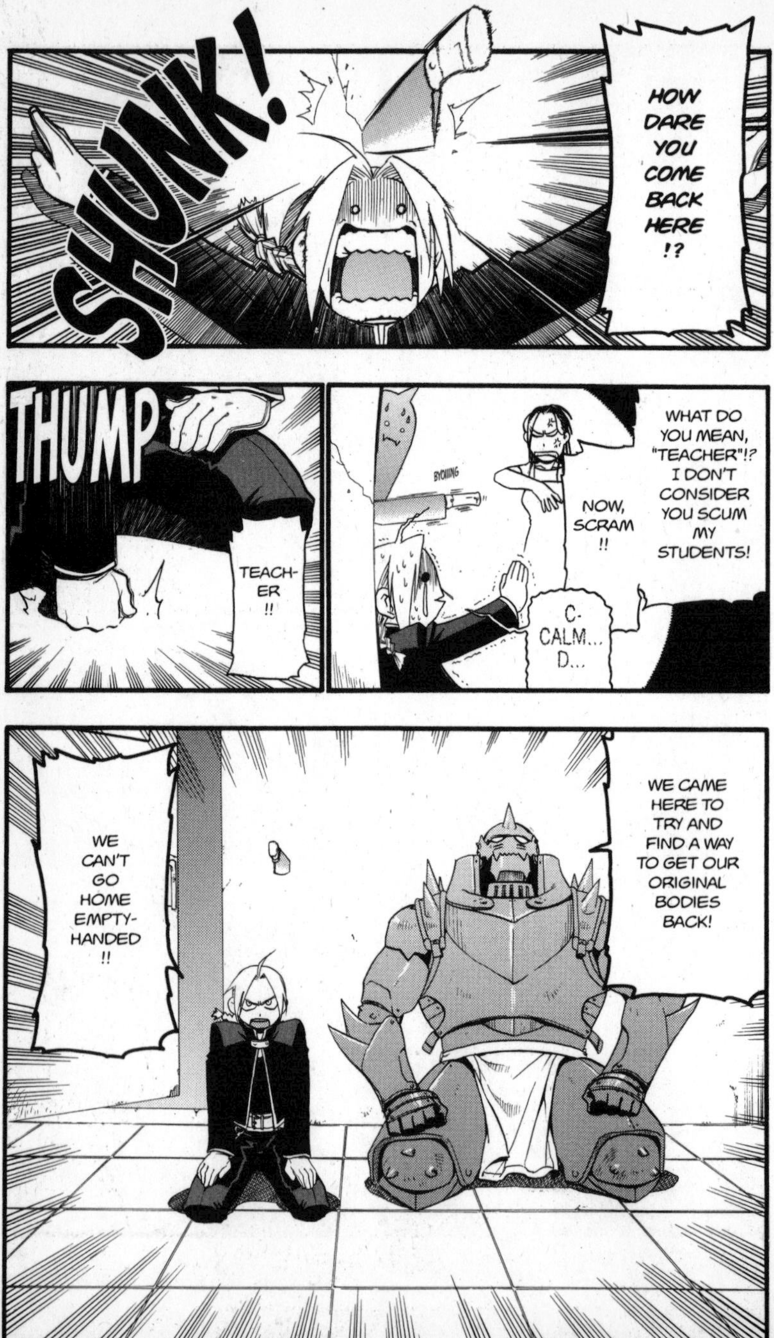
HOW DARE YOU COME BACK HERE!?
SHUNK!
WHAT DO YOU MEAN, "TEACHER"!? I DON'T CONSIDER YOU SCUM MY STUDENTS!
NOW, SCRAM!!
BYOIIING
C- CALM... D...
THUMP
TEACHER!!
WE CAME HERE TO TRY AND FIND A WAY TO GET OUR ORIGINAL BODIES BACK!
WE CAN'T GO HOME EMPTY-HANDED!!

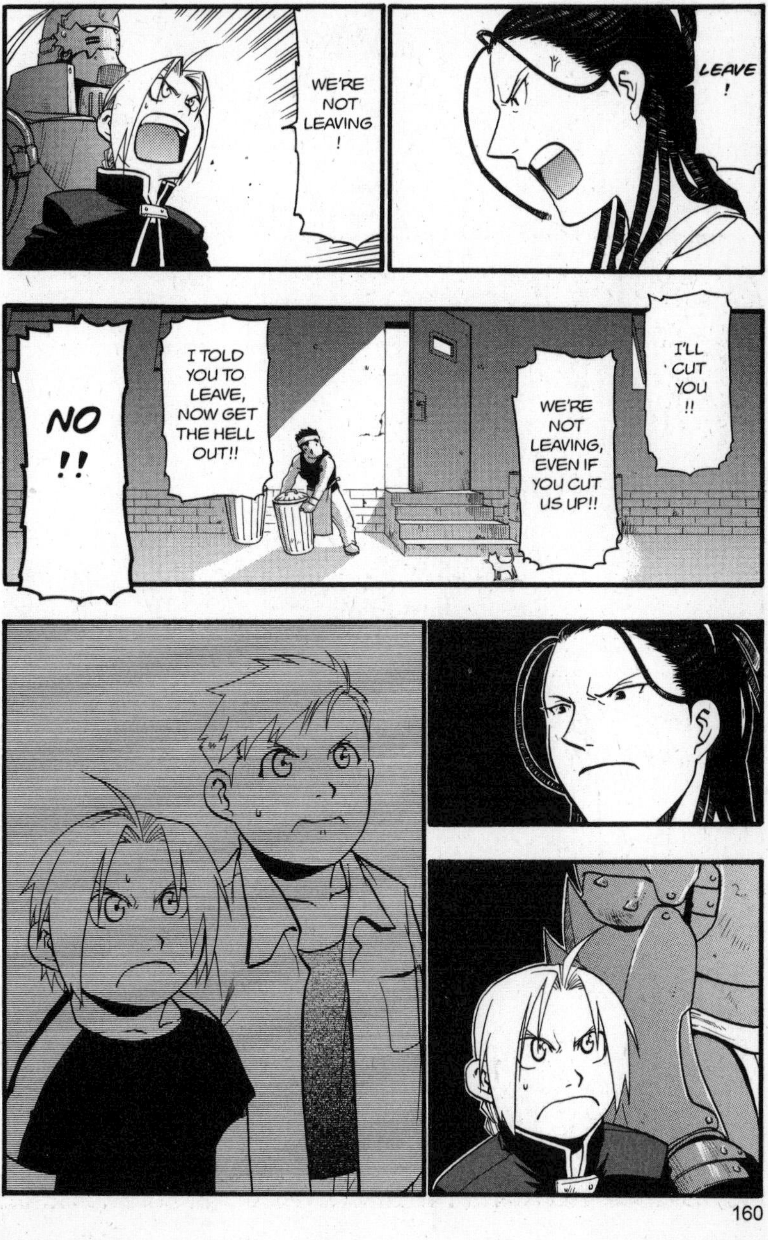
LEAVE!
WE'RE NOT LEAVING!
I'LL CUT YOU!!
WE'RE NOT LEAVING, EVEN IF YOU CUT US UP!!
I TOLD YOU TO LEAVE, NOW GET THE HELL OUT!!
NO!!

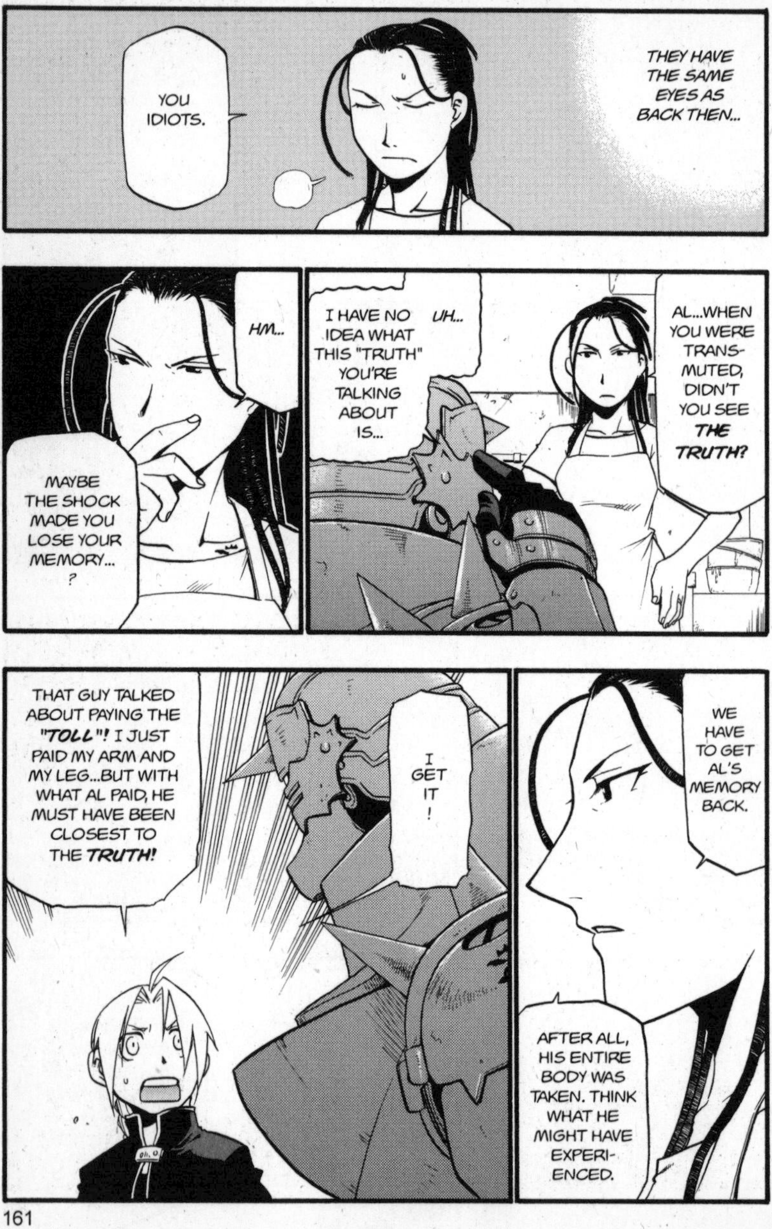
THEY HAVE THE SAME EYES AS BACK THEN...
YOU IDIOTS.
AL...WHEN YOU WERE TRANS-MUTED, DIDN'T YOU SEE **THE TRUTH?**
UH...
I HAVE NO IDEA WHAT THIS "TRUTH" YOU'RE TALKING ABOUT IS...
HM...
MAYBE THE SHOCK MADE YOU LOSE YOUR MEMORY...?
WE HAVE TO GET AL'S MEMORY BACK.
AFTER ALL, HIS ENTIRE BODY WAS TAKEN. THINK WHAT HE MIGHT HAVE EXPERI-ENCED.
I GET IT!
THAT GUY TALKED ABOUT PAYING THE "**TOLL**"! I JUST PAID MY ARM AND MY LEG...BUT WITH WHAT AL PAID, HE MUST HAVE BEEN CLOSEST TO THE **TRUTH!**

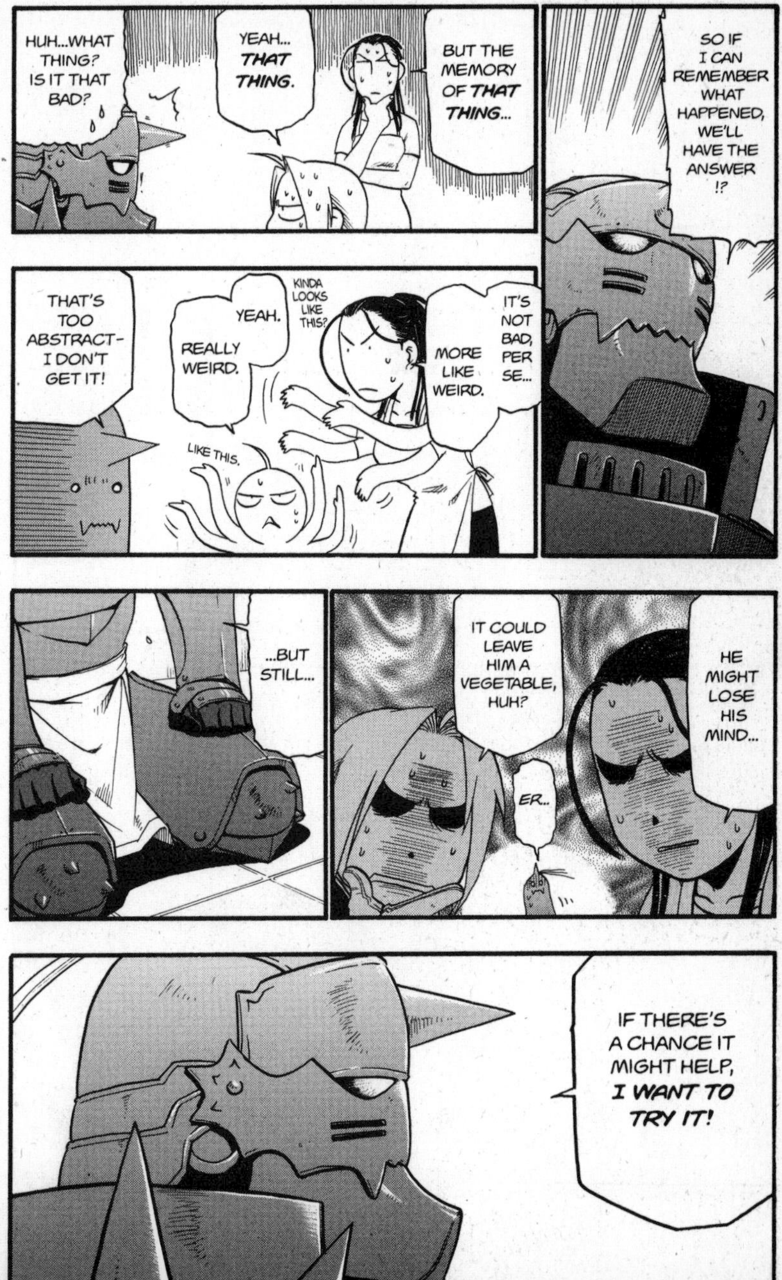
SO IF I CAN REMEMBER WHAT HAPPENED, WE'LL HAVE THE ANSWER!?
BUT THE MEMORY OF *THAT THING*...
YEAH... *THAT THING*.
HUH...WHAT THING? IS IT THAT BAD?
IT'S NOT BAD, PER SE...
MORE LIKE WEIRD.
KINDA LOOKS LIKE THIS?
YEAH.
REALLY WEIRD.
LIKE THIS.
THAT'S TOO ABSTRACT- I DON'T GET IT!
HE MIGHT LOSE HIS MIND...
IT COULD LEAVE HIM A VEGETABLE, HUH?
ER..
...BUT STILL...
IF THERE'S A CHANCE IT MIGHT HELP, ***I WANT TO TRY IT!***

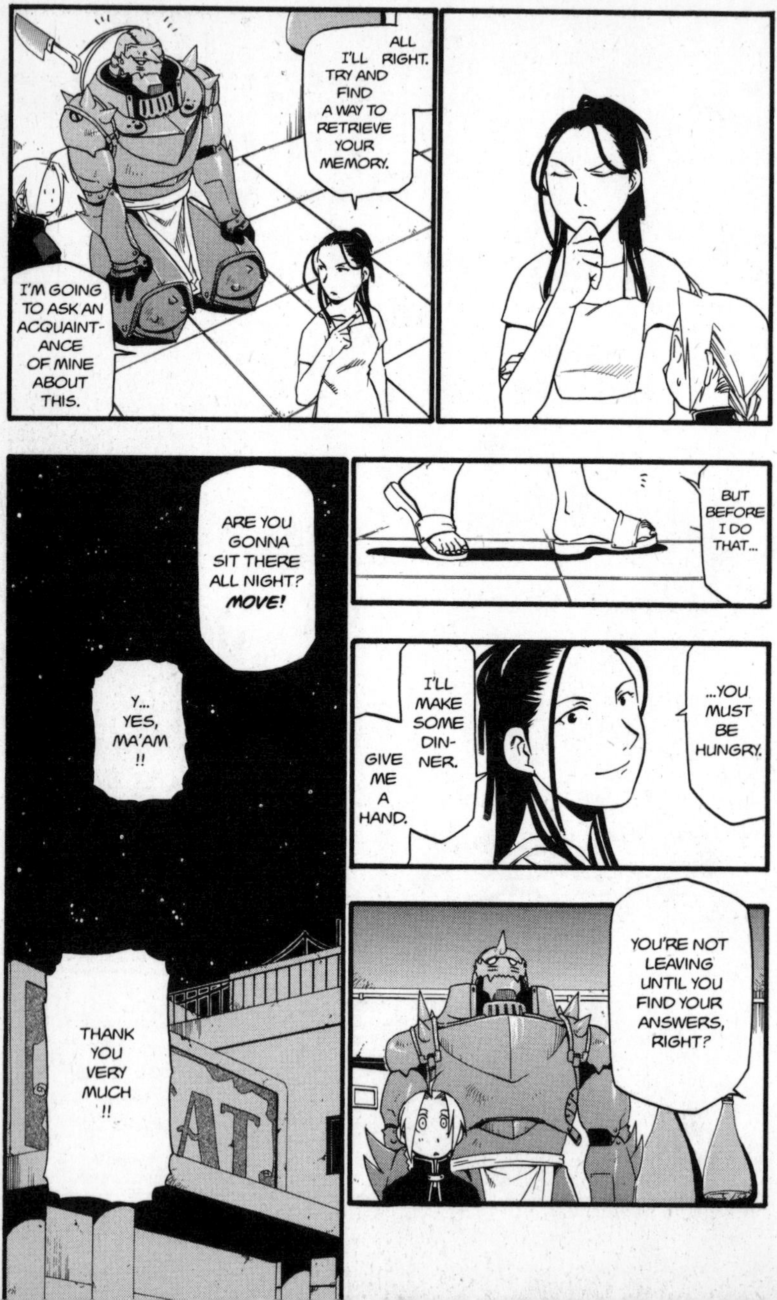

ALL RIGHT. I'LL TRY AND FIND A WAY TO RETRIEVE YOUR MEMORY.
I'M GOING TO ASK AN ACQUAINTANCE OF MINE ABOUT THIS.
BUT BEFORE I DO THAT...
...YOU MUST BE HUNGRY.
I'LL MAKE SOME DINNER.
GIVE ME A HAND.
YOU'RE NOT LEAVING UNTIL YOU FIND YOUR ANSWERS, RIGHT?
ARE YOU GONNA SIT THERE ALL NIGHT? ***MOVE!***
Y... YES, MA'AM!!
THANK YOU VERY MUCH!!

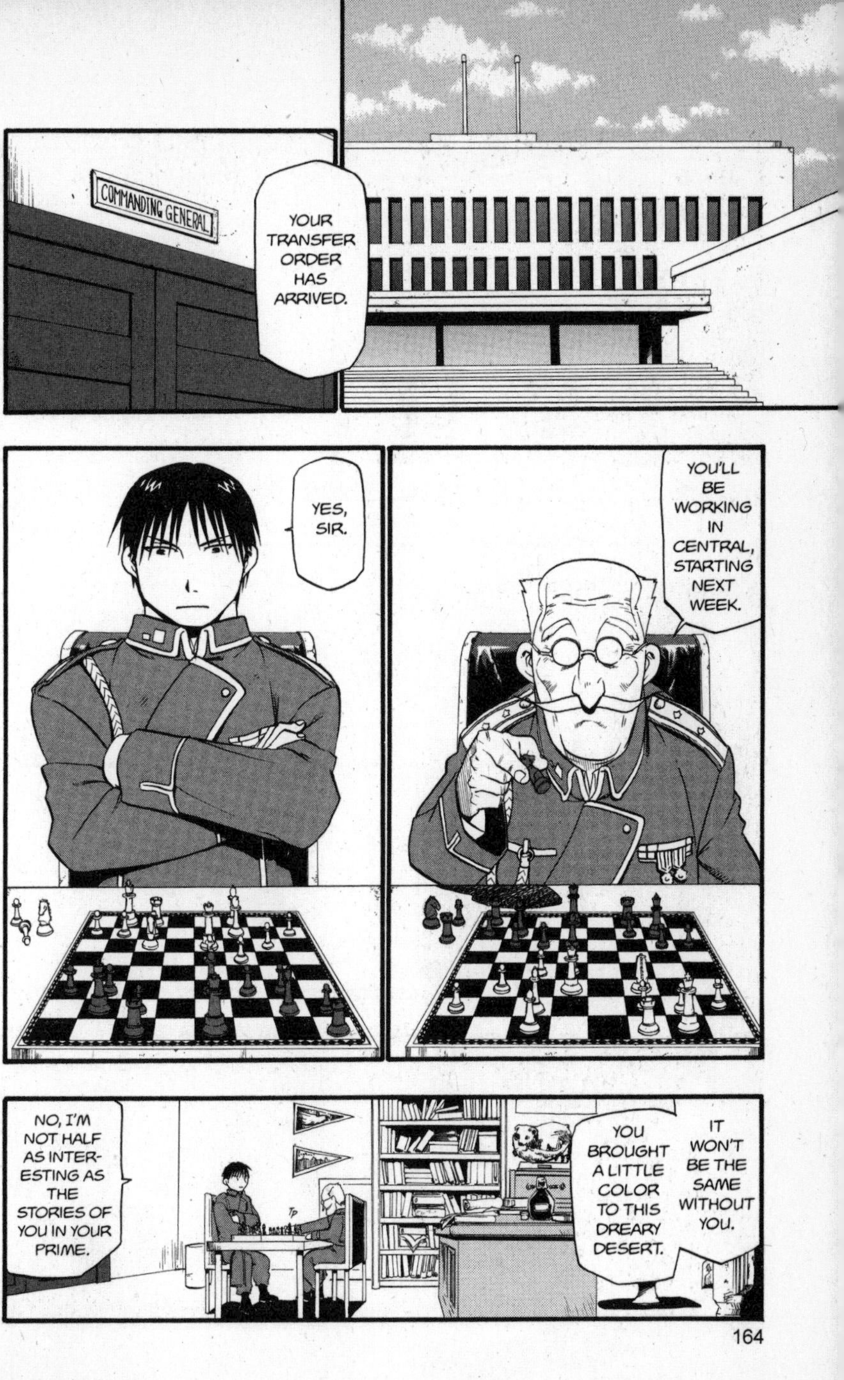
YOUR TRANSFER ORDER HAS ARRIVED.
COMMANDING GENERAL
YOU'LL BE WORKING IN CENTRAL, STARTING NEXT WEEK.
YES, SIR.
IT WON'T BE THE SAME WITHOUT YOU.
YOU BROUGHT A LITTLE COLOR TO THIS DREARY DESERT.
NO, I'M NOT HALF AS INTER-ESTING AS THE STORIES OF YOU IN YOUR PRIME.

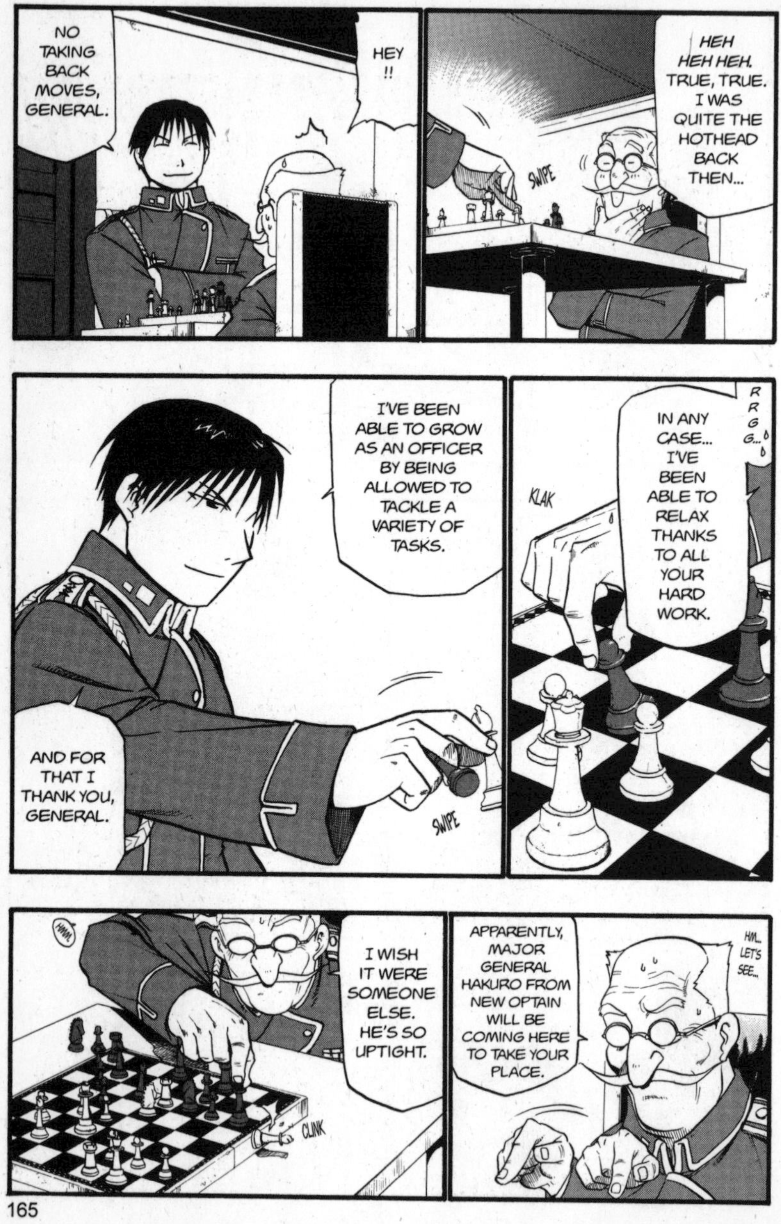
HEH HEH HEH. TRUE, TRUE. I WAS QUITE THE HOTHEAD BACK THEN...
SWIPE
HEY !!
NO TAKING BACK MOVES, GENERAL.
RRGG...
IN ANY CASE... I'VE BEEN ABLE TO RELAX THANKS TO ALL YOUR HARD WORK.
KLAK
I'VE BEEN ABLE TO GROW AS AN OFFICER BY BEING ALLOWED TO TACKLE A VARIETY OF TASKS.
AND FOR THAT I THANK YOU, GENERAL.
SWIPE
HM... LET'S SEE...
APPARENTLY, MAJOR GENERAL HAKURO FROM NEW OPTAIN WILL BE COMING HERE TO TAKE YOUR PLACE.
HMM
I WISH IT WERE SOMEONE ELSE. HE'S SO UPTIGHT.
CLINK

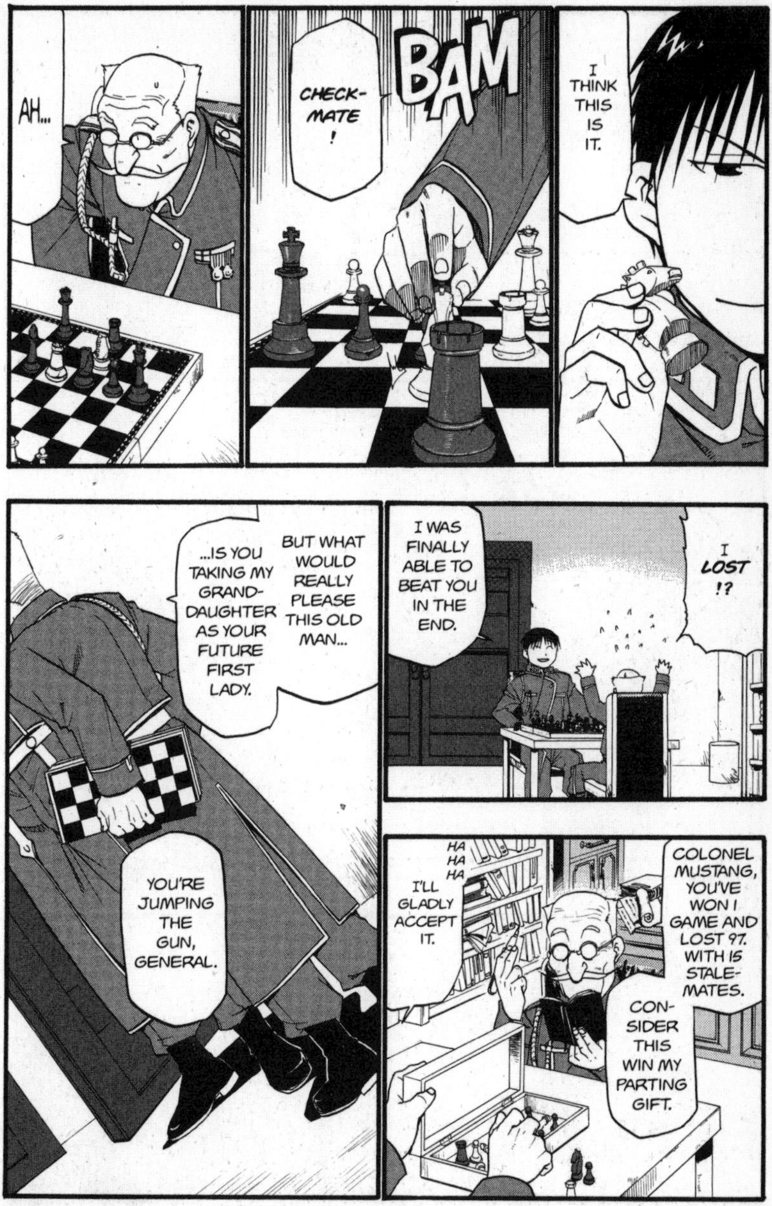
I THINK THIS IS IT.
BAM
CHECK-MATE!
AH...
I LOST!?
I WAS FINALLY ABLE TO BEAT YOU IN THE END.
COLONEL MUSTANG, YOU'VE WON 1 GAME AND LOST 97. WITH 15 STALE-MATES.
CON-SIDER THIS WIN MY PARTING GIFT.
HA HA HA
I'LL GLADLY ACCEPT IT.
BUT WHAT WOULD REALLY PLEASE THIS OLD MAN...
...IS YOU TAKING MY GRAND-DAUGHTER AS YOUR FUTURE FIRST LADY.
YOU'RE JUMPING THE GUN, GENERAL.

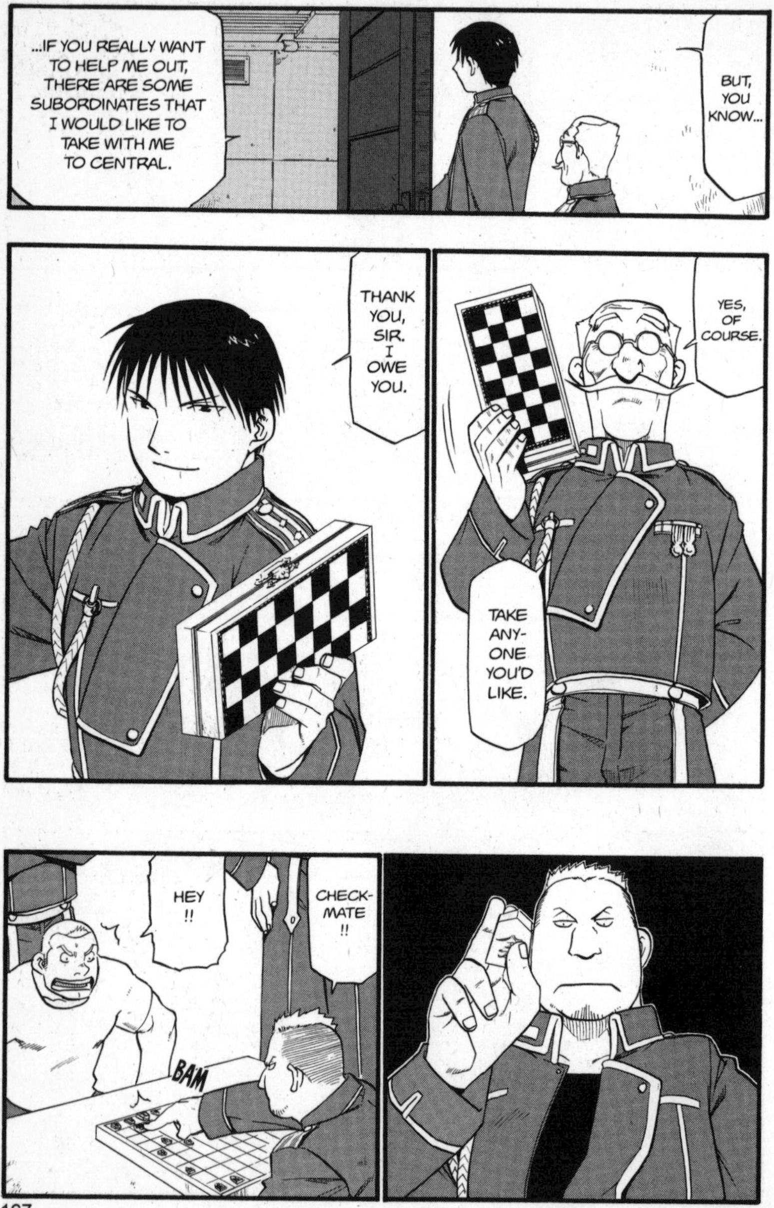
BUT, YOU KNOW...
...IF YOU REALLY WANT TO HELP ME OUT, THERE ARE SOME SUBORDINATES THAT I WOULD LIKE TO TAKE WITH ME TO CENTRAL.
YES, OF COURSE.
TAKE ANY-ONE YOU'D LIKE.
THANK YOU, SIR. I OWE YOU.
CHECK-MATE !!
HEY !!
BAM

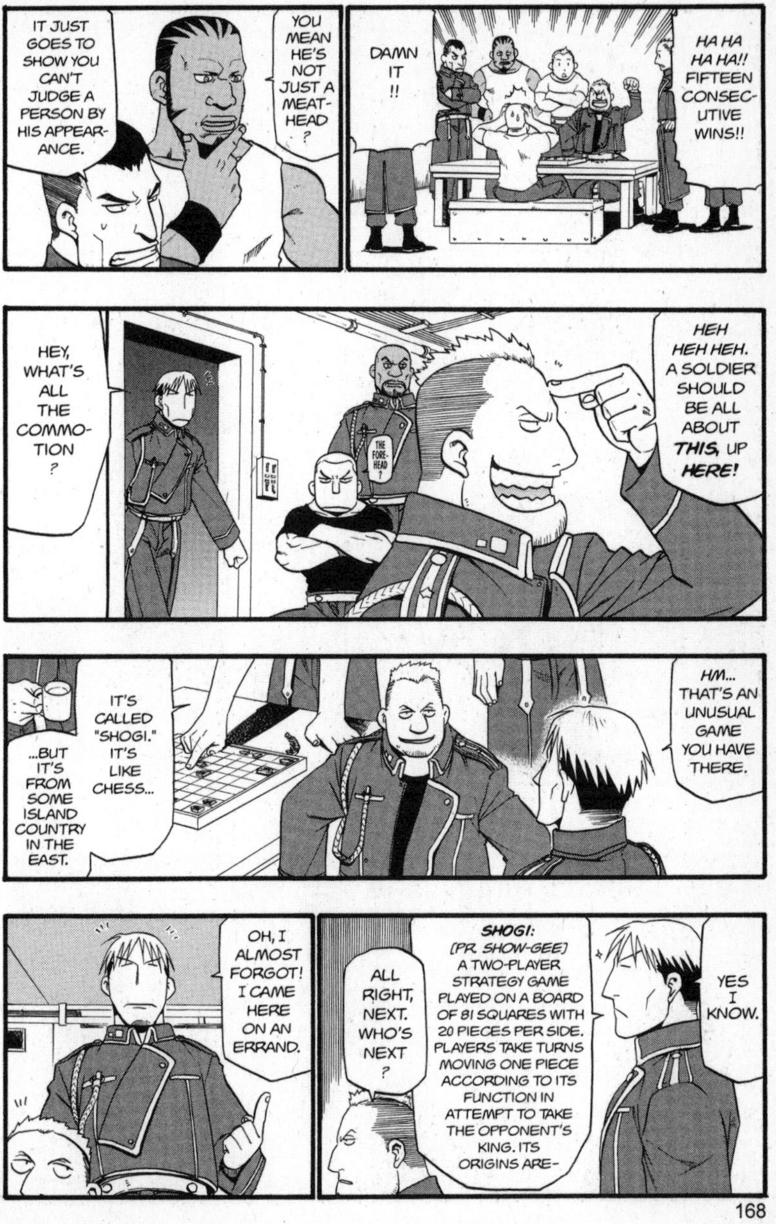

HA HA HA HA!! FIFTEEN CONSECUTIVE WINS!!
DAMN IT !!
YOU MEAN HE'S NOT JUST A MEAT-HEAD ?
IT JUST GOES TO SHOW YOU CAN'T JUDGE A PERSON BY HIS APPEARANCE.
HEH HEH HEH. A SOLDIER SHOULD BE ALL ABOUT THIS, UP HERE!
THE FORE-HEAD ?
HEY, WHAT'S ALL THE COMMOTION ?
HM... THAT'S AN UNUSUAL GAME YOU HAVE THERE.
IT'S CALLED "SHOGI." IT'S LIKE CHESS...
...BUT IT'S FROM SOME ISLAND COUNTRY IN THE EAST.
YES I KNOW.
SHOGI: [PR. SHOW-GEE] A TWO-PLAYER STRATEGY GAME PLAYED ON A BOARD OF 81 SQUARES WITH 20 PIECES PER SIDE. PLAYERS TAKE TURNS MOVING ONE PIECE ACCORDING TO ITS FUNCTION IN ATTEMPT TO TAKE THE OPPONENT'S KING. ITS ORIGINS ARE-
ALL RIGHT, NEXT. WHO'S NEXT ?
OH, I ALMOST FORGOT! I CAME HERE ON AN ERRAND.

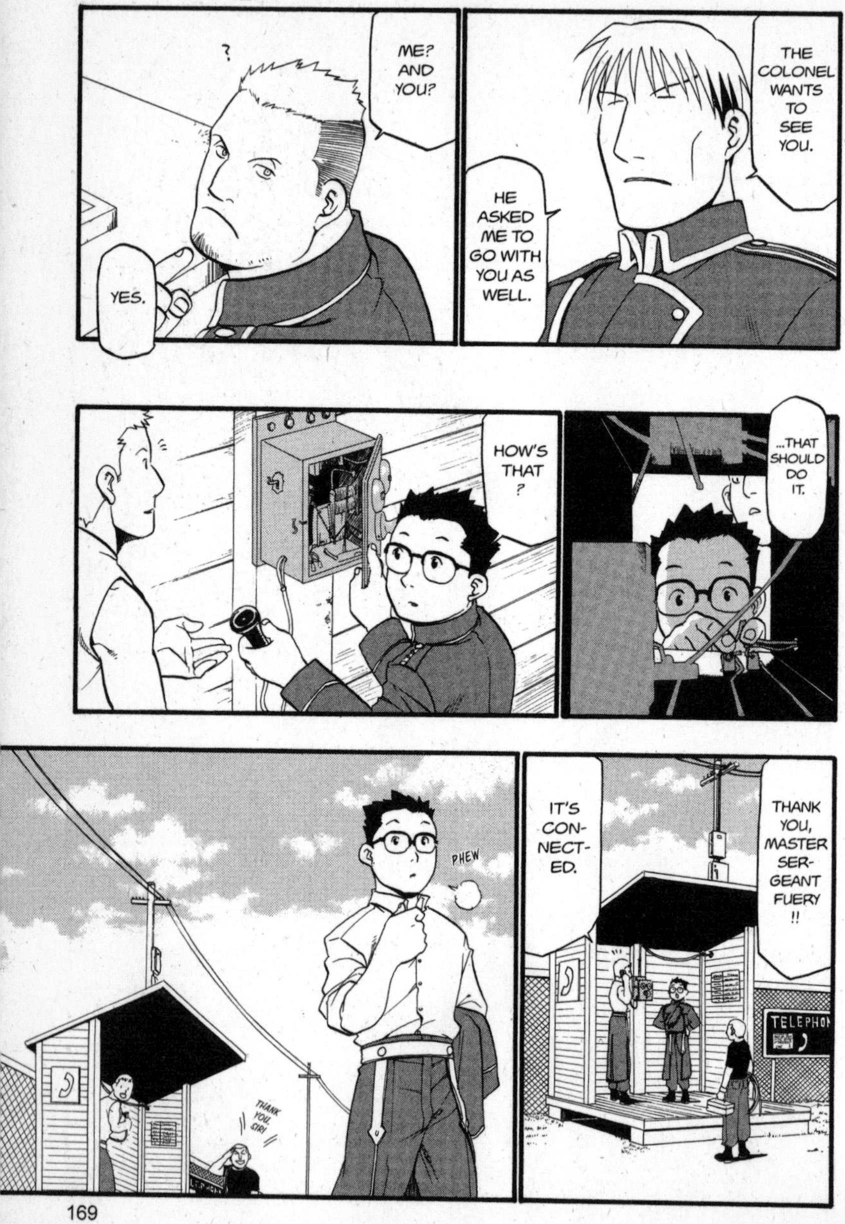
THE COLONEL WANTS TO SEE YOU.
HE ASKED ME TO GO WITH YOU AS WELL.
?
ME? AND YOU?
YES.
...THAT SHOULD DO IT.
HOW'S THAT?
THANK YOU, MASTER SERGEANT FUERY!!
IT'S CONNECTED.
TELEPHON
PHEW
THANK YOU, SIR!

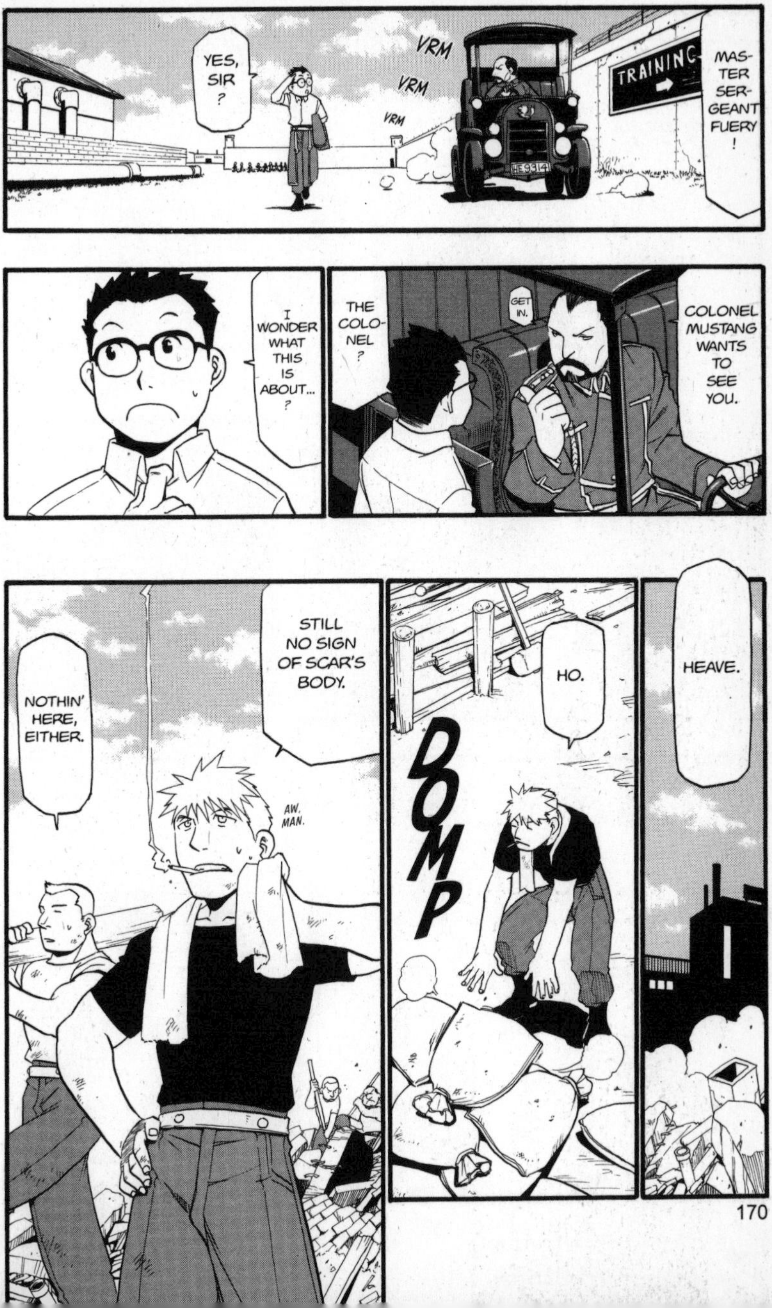
MASTER SERGEANT FUERY!
TRAINING
VRM
VRM
VRM
YES, SIR?
COLONEL MUSTANG WANTS TO SEE YOU.
GET IN.
THE COLONEL?
I WONDER WHAT THIS IS ABOUT...?
HEAVE.
HO.
DOMP
STILL NO SIGN OF SCAR'S BODY.
NOTHIN' HERE, EITHER.
AW. MAN.

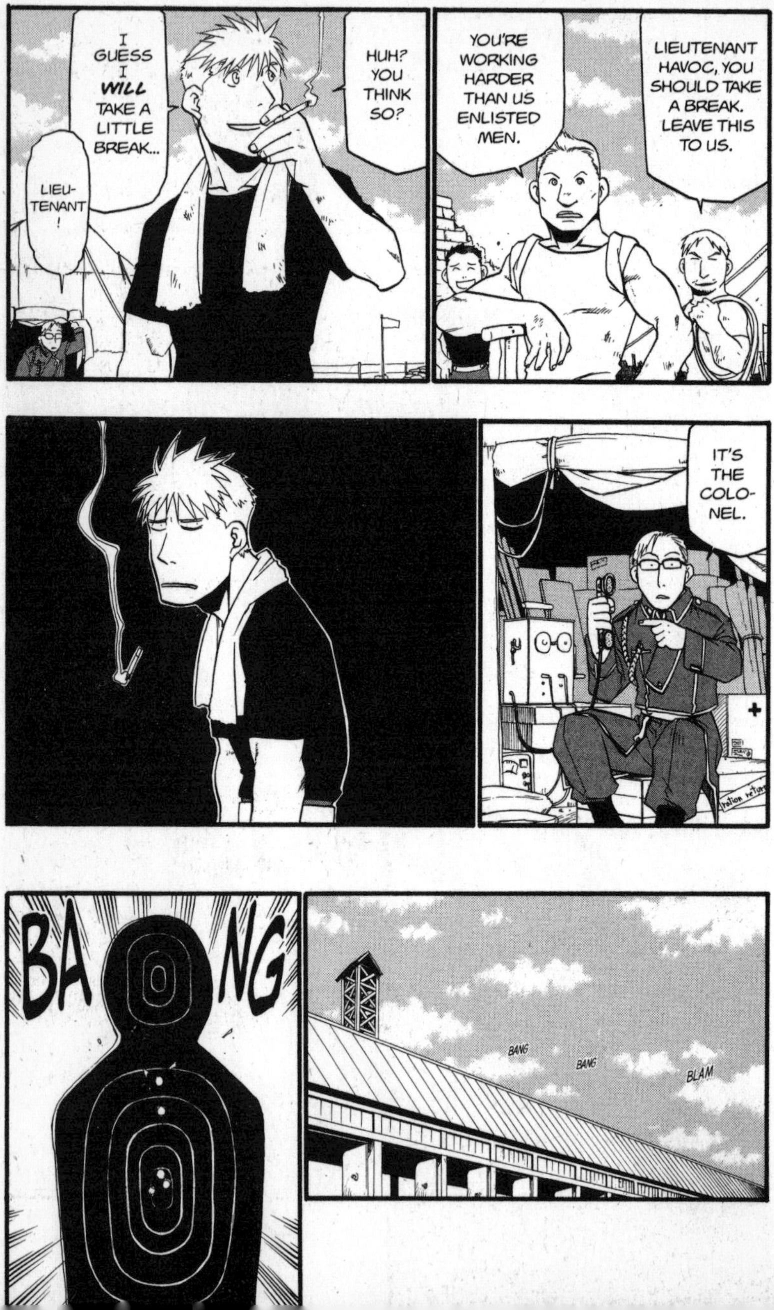
LIEUTENANT HAVOC, YOU SHOULD TAKE A BREAK. LEAVE THIS TO US.
YOU'RE WORKING HARDER THAN US ENLISTED MEN.
HUH? YOU THINK SO?
I GUESS I WILL TAKE A LITTLE BREAK...
LIEU-TENANT!
IT'S THE COLO-NEL.
BANG
BANG
BLAM
BANG

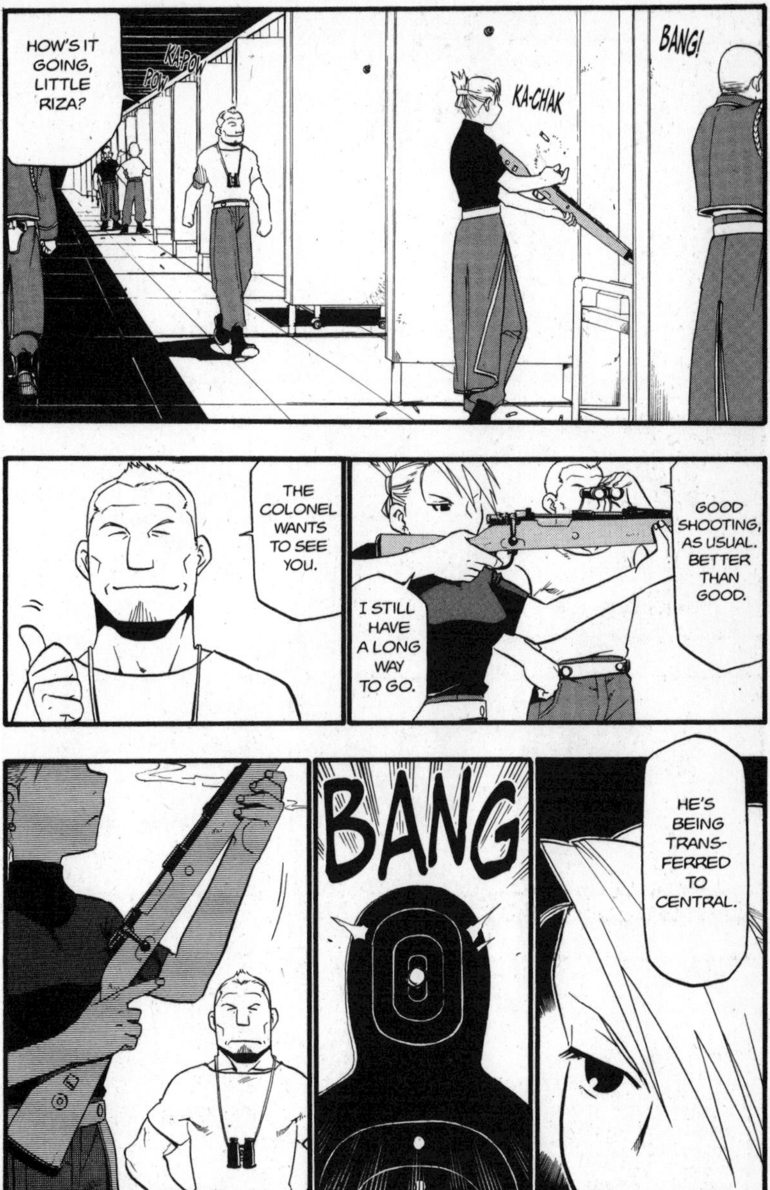
BANG!
KA-CHAK
KA-POW
POW
HOW'S IT GOING, LITTLE RIZA?
GOOD SHOOTING, AS USUAL. BETTER THAN GOOD.
I STILL HAVE A LONG WAY TO GO.
THE COLONEL WANTS TO SEE YOU.
HE'S BEING TRANS-FERRED TO CENTRAL.
BANG

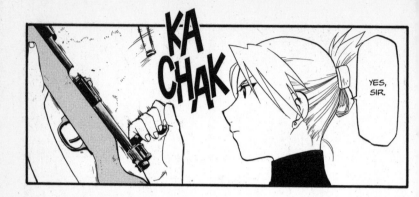

YES, SIR.

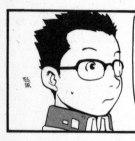

MASTER SERGEANT KAIN FUERY.

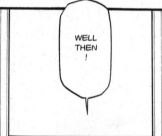

WELL THEN!

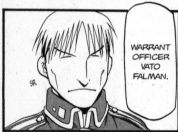

WARRANT OFFICER VATO FALMAN.

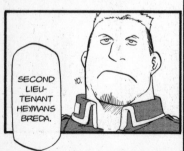

SECOND LIEUTENANT HEYMANS BREDA.

YO.

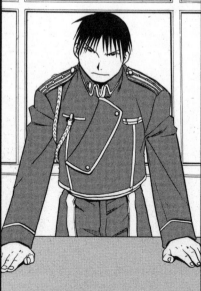

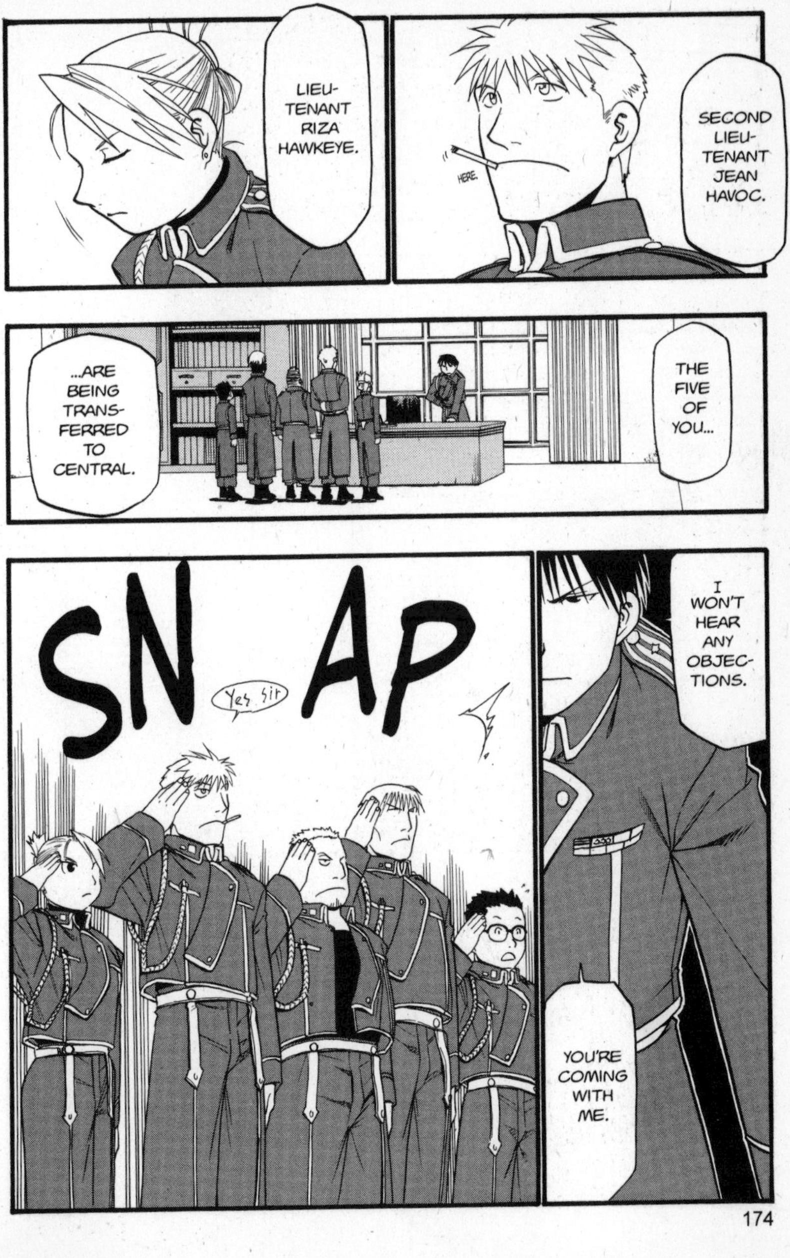
SECOND LIEUTENANT JEAN HAVOC.
HERE.
LIEUTENANT RIZA HAWKEYE.
THE FIVE OF YOU...
...ARE BEING TRANSFERRED TO CENTRAL.
I WON'T HEAR ANY OBJECTIONS.
YOU'RE COMING WITH ME.
SNAP
Yes sir

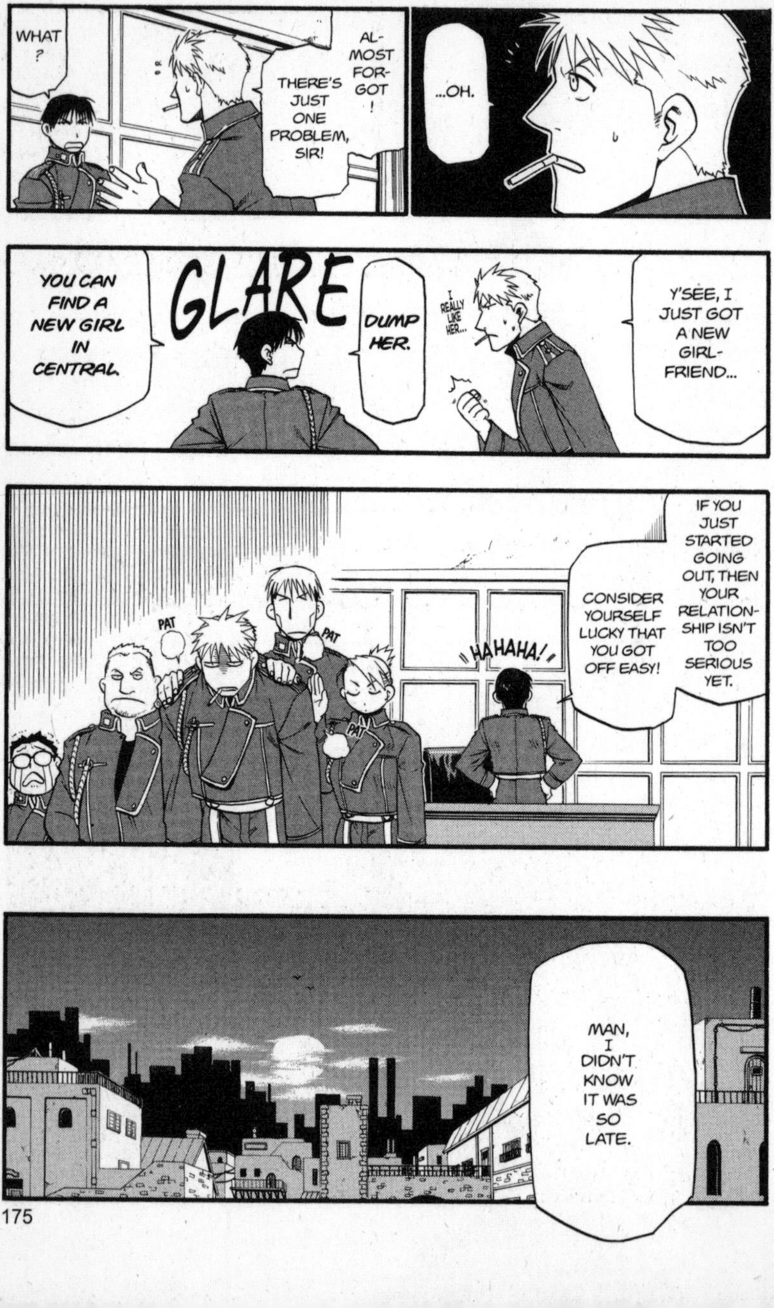
...OH.
ALMOST FORGOT!
THERE'S JUST ONE PROBLEM, SIR!
WHAT?
Y'SEE, I JUST GOT A NEW GIRLFRIEND...
I REALLY LIKE HER...
DUMP HER.
GLARE
YOU CAN FIND A NEW GIRL IN CENTRAL.
IF YOU JUST STARTED GOING OUT, THEN YOUR RELATIONSHIP ISN'T TOO SERIOUS YET.
CONSIDER YOURSELF LUCKY THAT YOU GOT OFF EASY!
HAHAHA!
PAT
PAT
PAT
MAN, I DIDN'T KNOW IT WAS SO LATE.

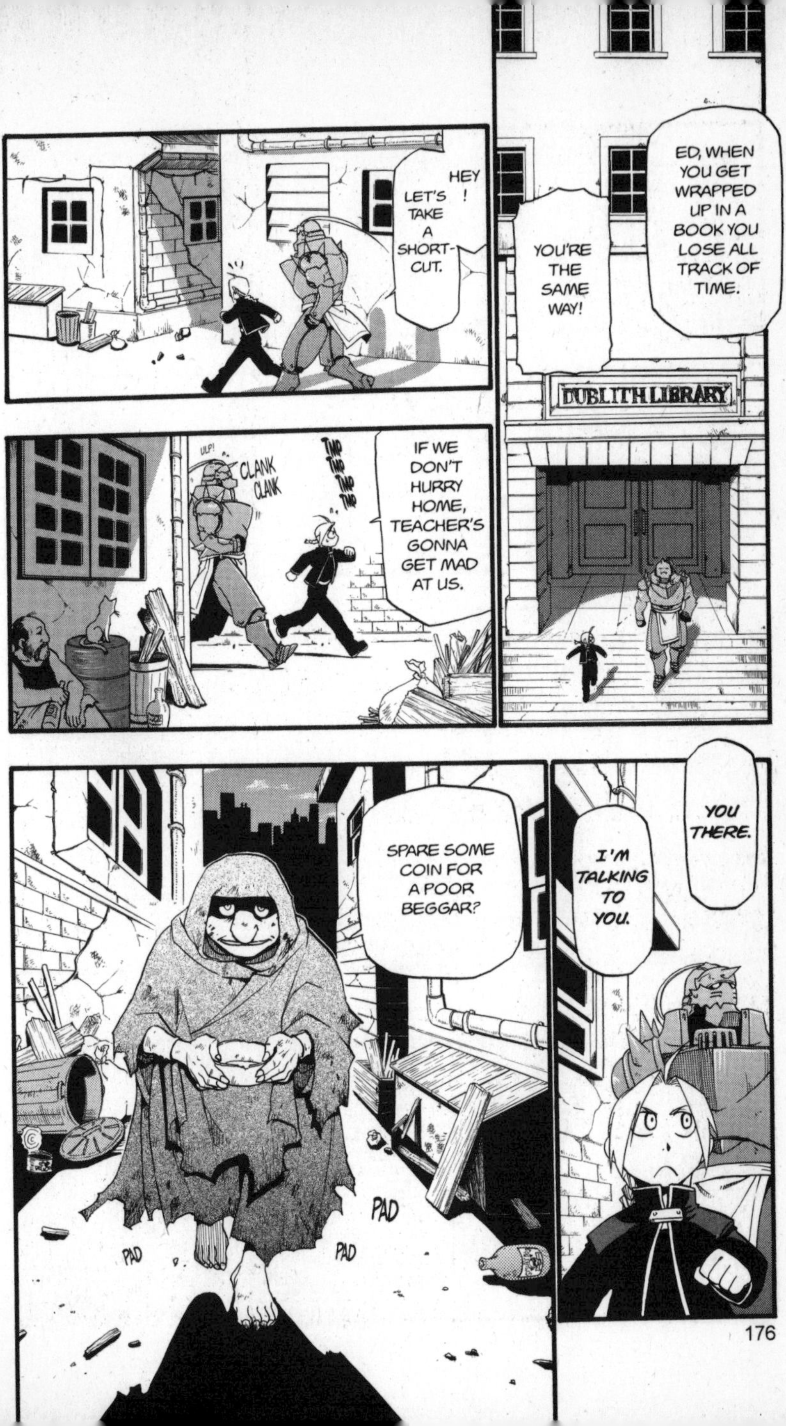
ED, WHEN YOU GET WRAPPED UP IN A BOOK YOU LOSE ALL TRACK OF TIME.
YOU'RE THE SAME WAY!
DUBLITH LIBRARY
HEY! LET'S TAKE A SHORT-CUT.
IF WE DON'T HURRY HOME, TEACHER'S GONNA GET MAD AT US.
TMP TMP TMP TMP
CLANK CLANK
ULP!
YOU THERE.
I'M TALKING TO YOU.
SPARE SOME COIN FOR A POOR BEGGAR?
PAD
PAD
PAD

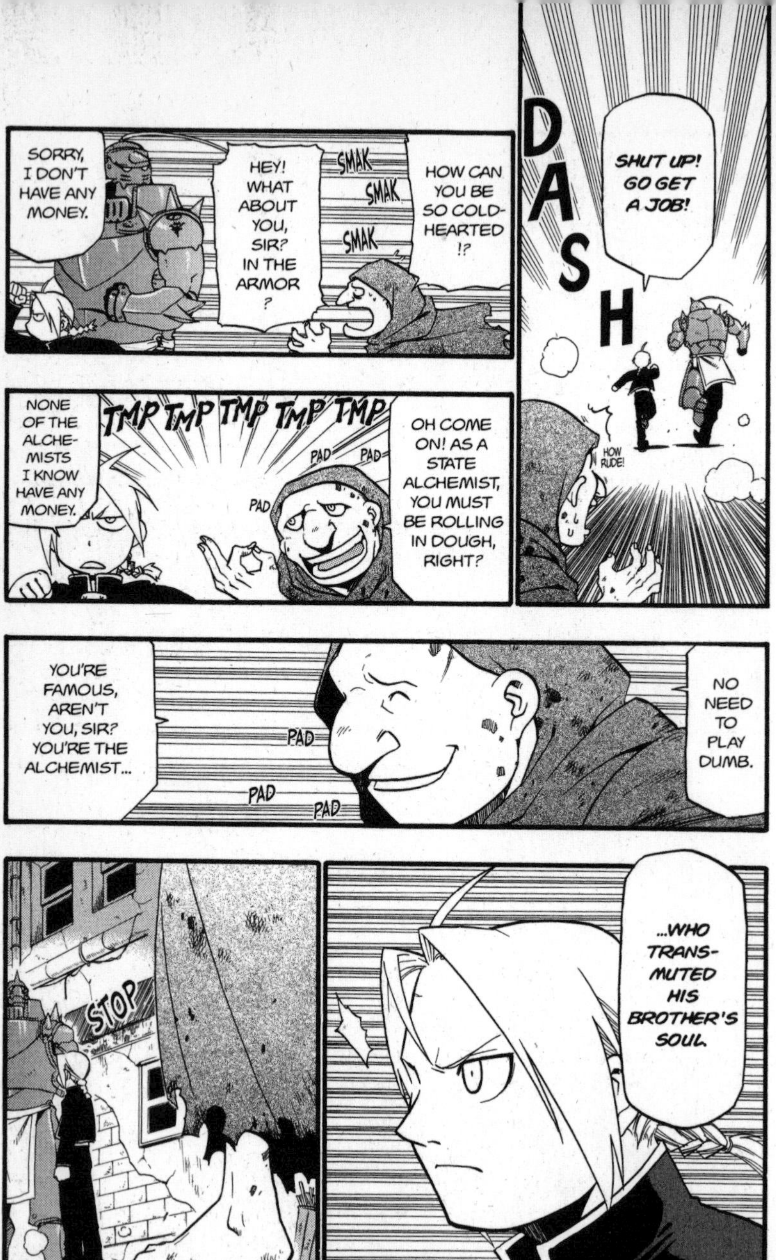
D A S H
SHUT UP! GO GET A JOB!
HOW RUDE!
HOW CAN YOU BE SO COLD-HEARTED !?
SMAK
SMAK
SMAK
HEY! WHAT ABOUT YOU, SIR? IN THE ARMOR ?
SORRY, I DON'T HAVE ANY MONEY.
OH COME ON! AS A STATE ALCHEMIST, YOU MUST BE ROLLING IN DOUGH, RIGHT?
PAD PAD PAD
TMP TMP TMP TMP TMP
NONE OF THE ALCHE-MISTS I KNOW HAVE ANY MONEY.
NO NEED TO PLAY DUMB.
PAD
PAD
PAD
YOU'RE FAMOUS, AREN'T YOU, SIR? YOU'RE THE ALCHEMIST...
...WHO TRANS-MUTED HIS BROTHER'S SOUL.
STOP

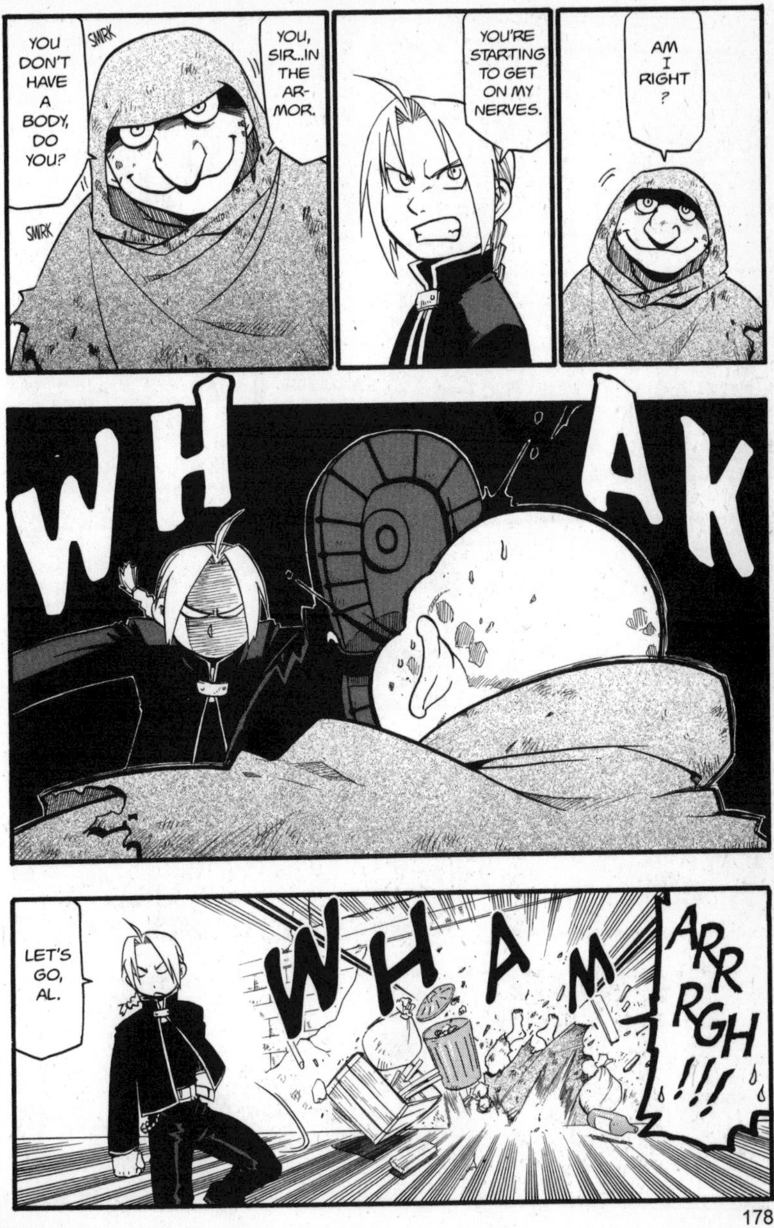
AM I RIGHT?
YOU'RE STARTING TO GET ON MY NERVES.
YOU, SIR...IN THE AR-MOR.
SMIRK
YOU DON'T HAVE A BODY, DO YOU?
SMIRK
WH
AK
ARRRGH!!!
WHAM
LET'S GO, AL.

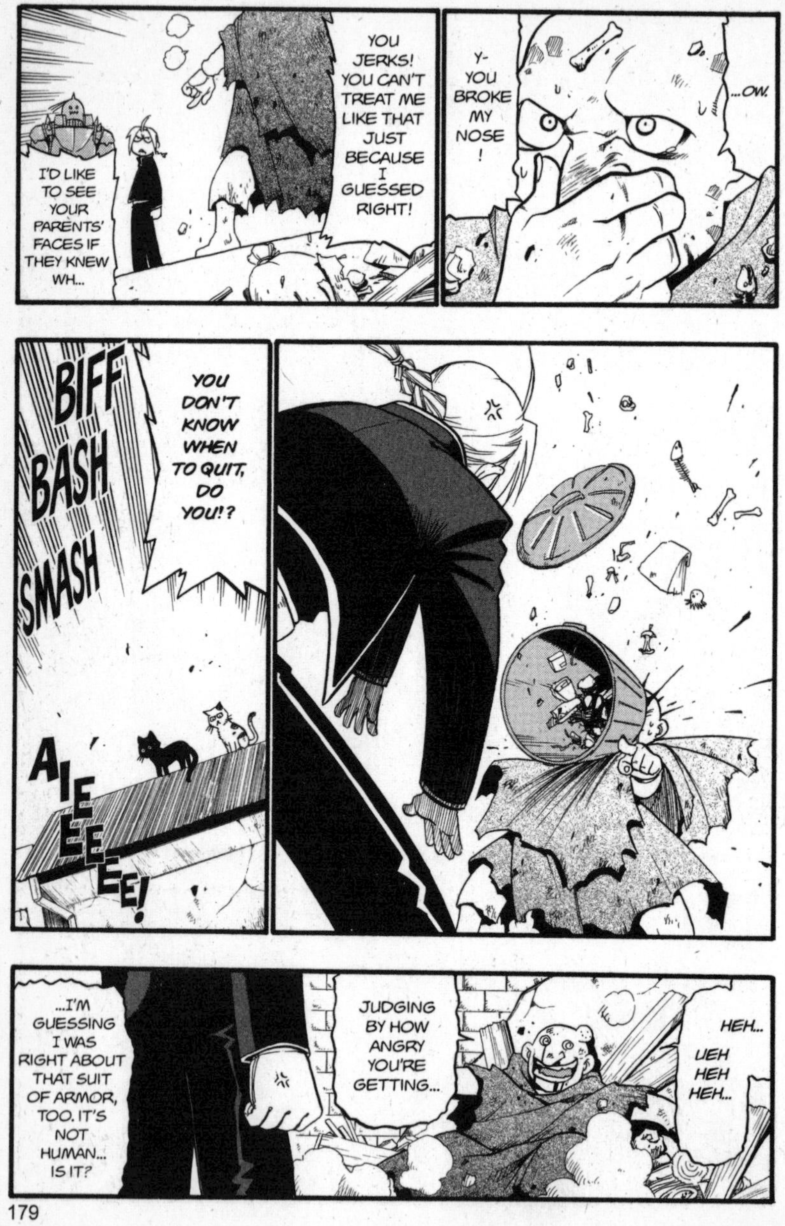
...OW.
Y-YOU BROKE MY NOSE!
YOU JERKS! YOU CAN'T TREAT ME LIKE THAT JUST BECAUSE I GUESSED RIGHT!
I'D LIKE TO SEE YOUR PARENTS' FACES IF THEY KNEW WH...
YOU DON'T KNOW WHEN TO QUIT, DO YOU!?
BIFF
BASH
SMASH
AIEEEEEE!
HEH...
UEH HEH HEH...
JUDGING BY HOW ANGRY YOU'RE GETTING...
...I'M GUESSING I WAS RIGHT ABOUT THAT SUIT OF ARMOR, TOO. IT'S NOT HUMAN... IS IT?

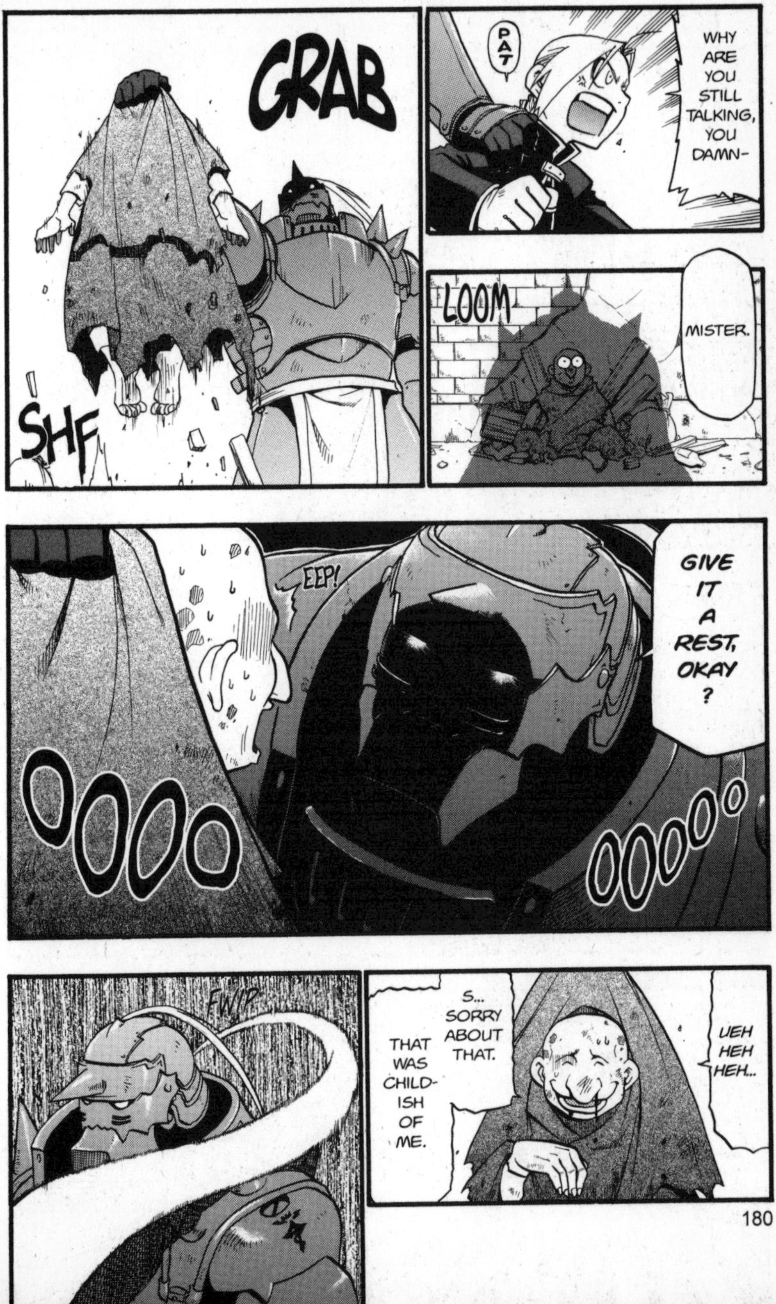
PAT
WHY ARE YOU STILL TALKING, YOU DAMN-
LOOM
MISTER.
GRAB
SHF
GIVE IT A REST, OKAY?
EEP!
OOOOO
OOOO
UEH HEH HEH...
S... SORRY ABOUT THAT.
THAT WAS CHILD-ISH OF ME.
FWIP

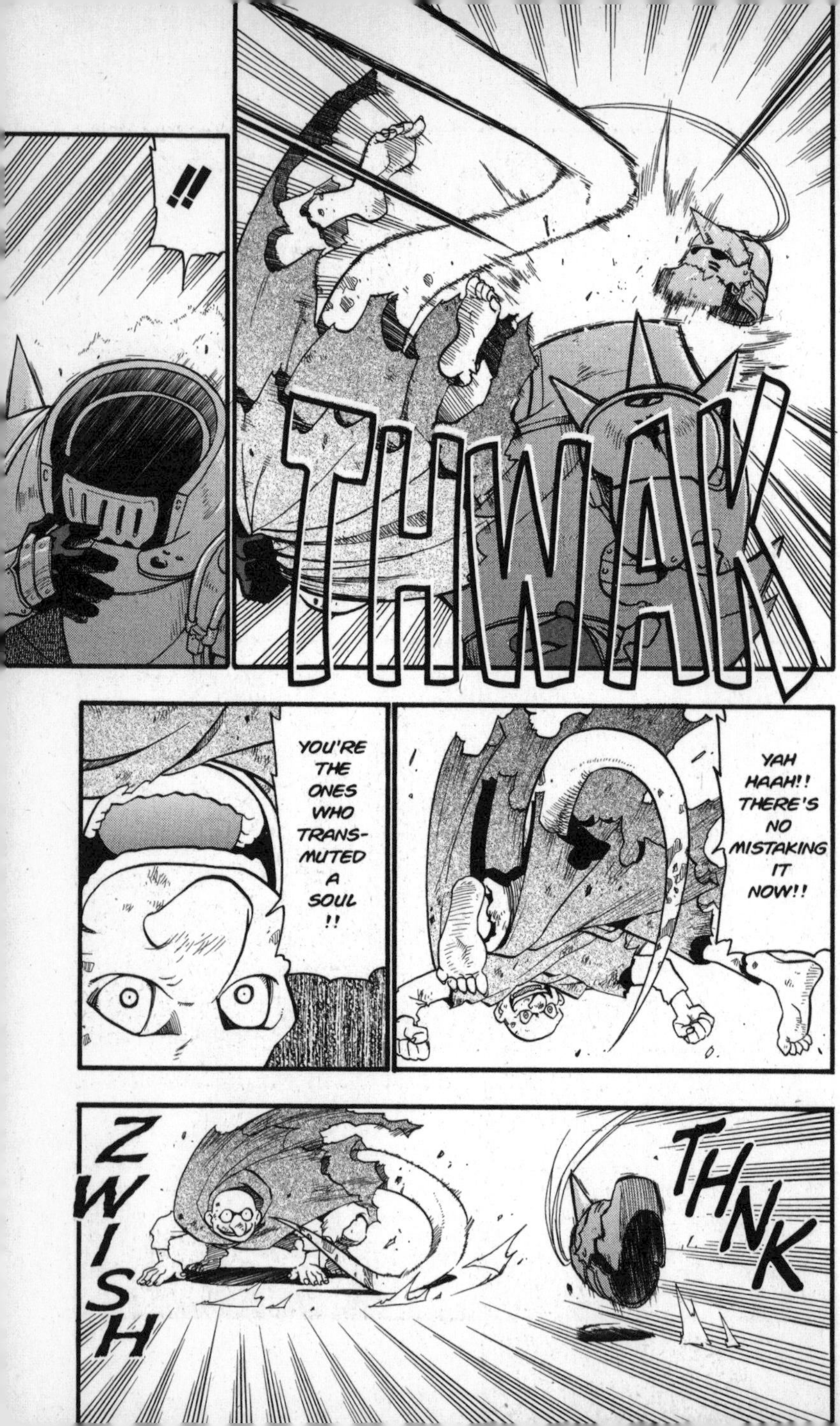
THWAK
!!
YAH HAAH!! THERE'S NO MISTAKING IT NOW!!
YOU'RE THE ONES WHO TRANS-MUTED A SOUL!!
THNK
ZWISH

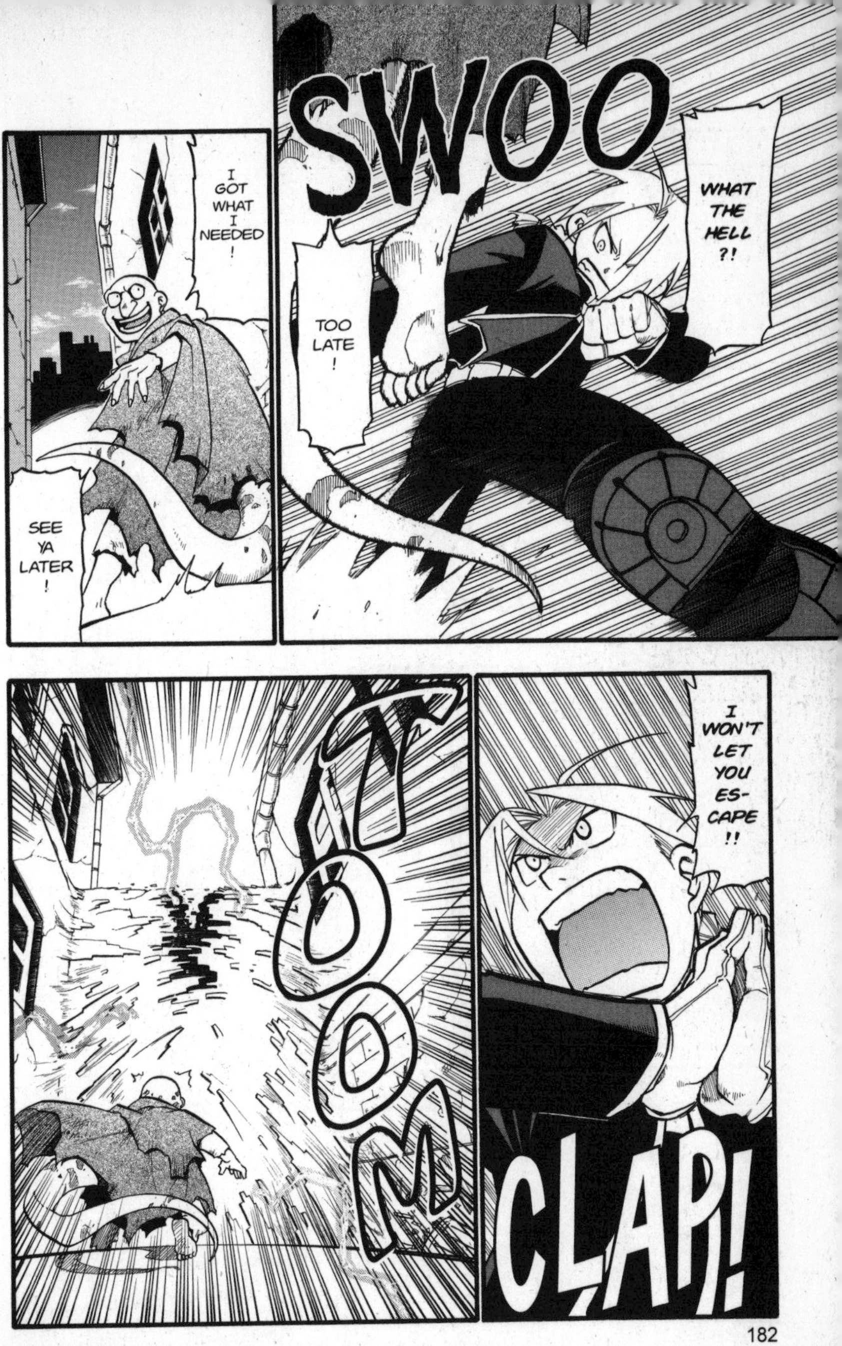
SWOO
WHAT THE HELL ?!
TOO LATE !
I GOT WHAT I NEEDED !
SEE YA LATER !
I WON'T LET YOU ES-CAPE !!
CLAP!
TOOM

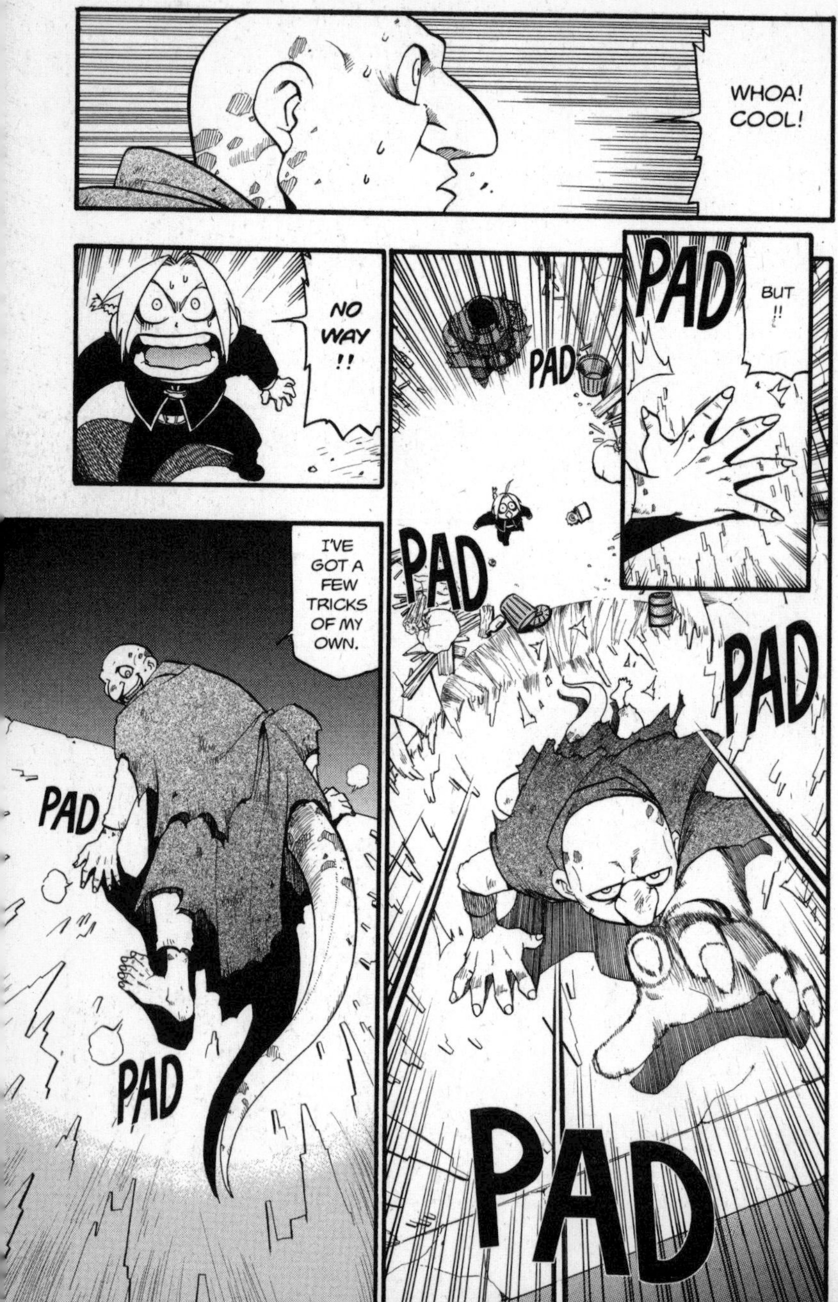
WHOA! COOL!
PAD
BUT !!
PAD
PAD
PAD
PAD
NO WAY !!
I'VE GOT A FEW TRICKS OF MY OWN.
PAD
PAD

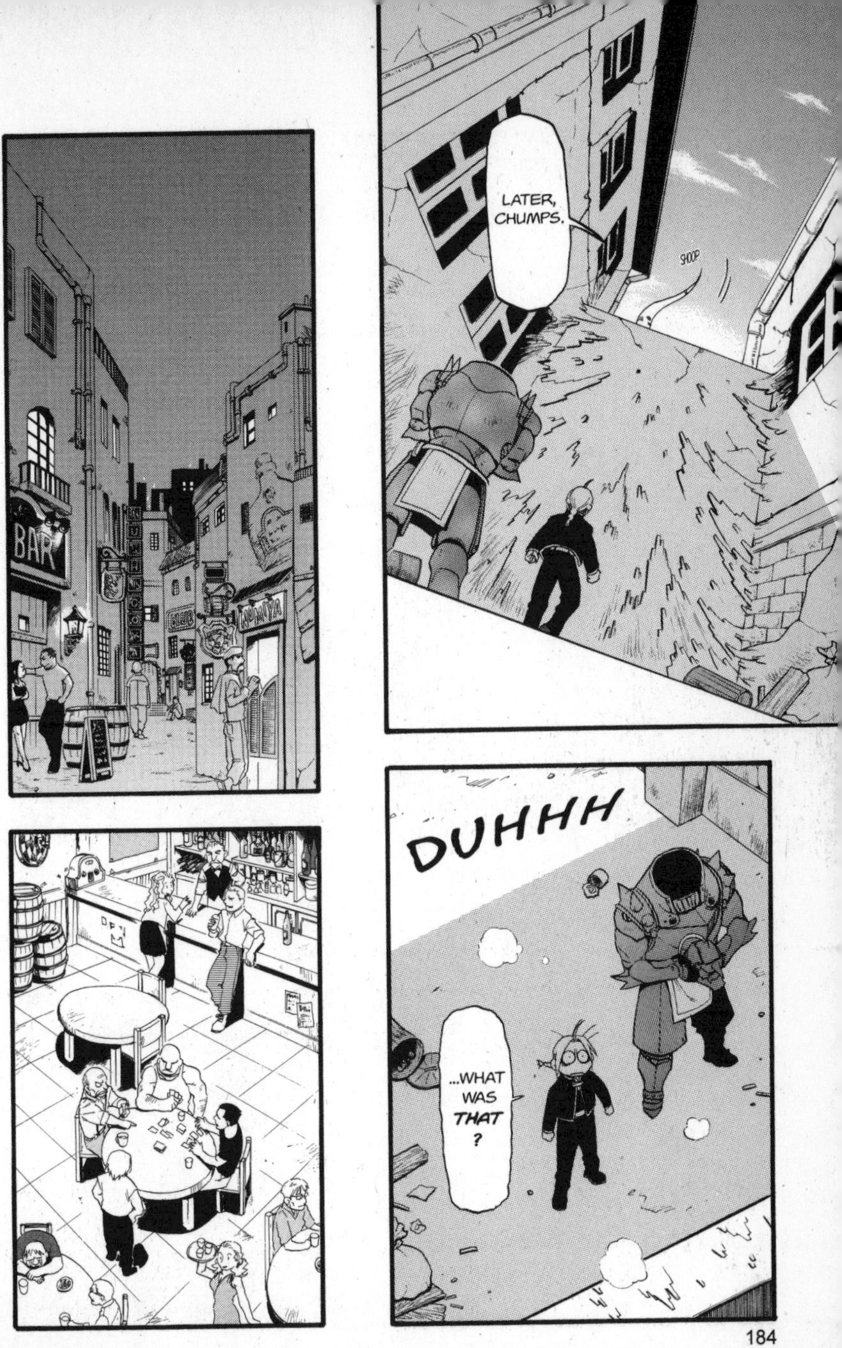
LATER, CHUMPS.
SHOOP
BAR
DUHHH
...WHAT WAS *THAT* ?

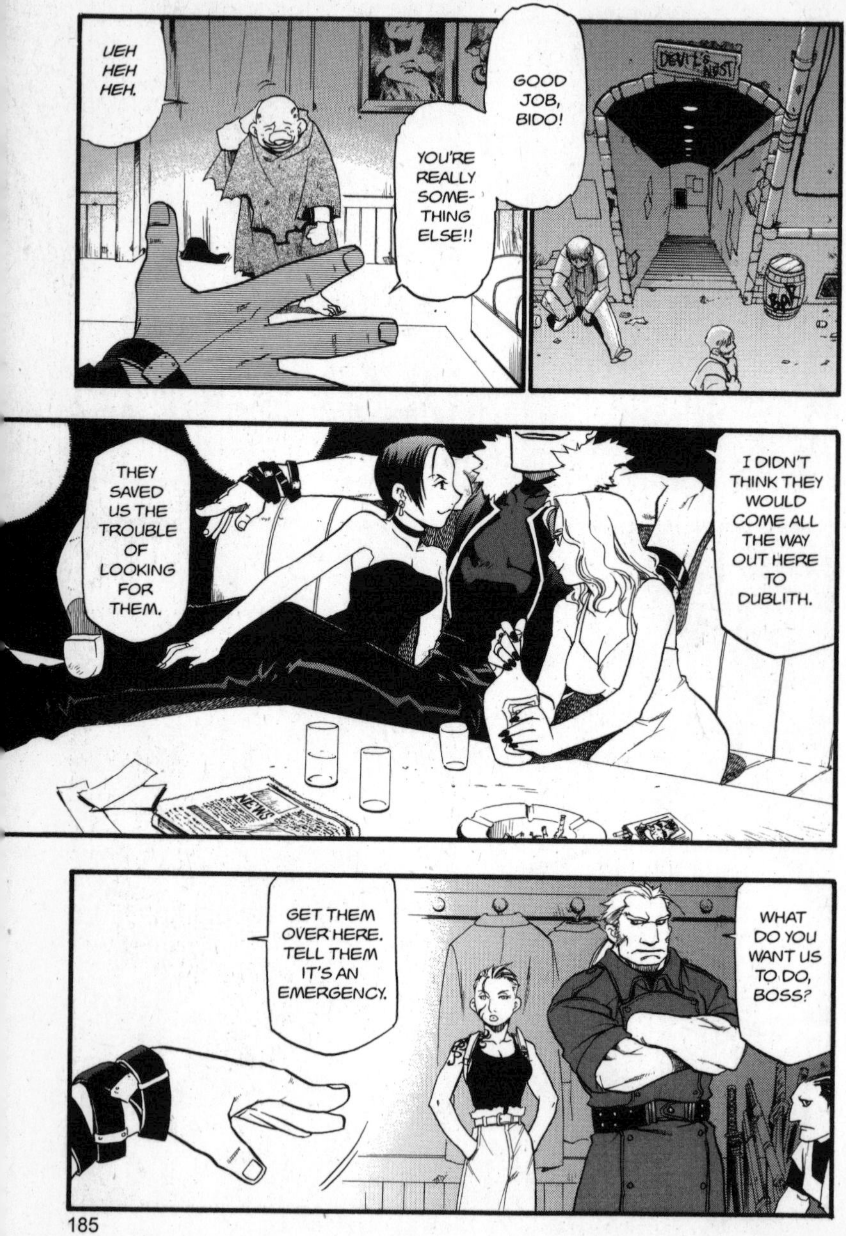
DEVIL'S NEST
BAR
GOOD JOB, BIDO!
YOU'RE REALLY SOME-THING ELSE!!
UEH HEH HEH.
I DIDN'T THINK THEY WOULD COME ALL THE WAY OUT HERE TO DUBLITH.
THEY SAVED US THE TROUBLE OF LOOKING FOR THEM.
NEWS
WHAT DO YOU WANT US TO DO, BOSS?
GET THEM OVER HERE. TELL THEM IT'S AN EMERGENCY.

THIS MANGA WAS ORIGINALLY PRINTED IN MONTHLY **SHONEN GANGAN**, MAY THROUGH AUGUST 2003.

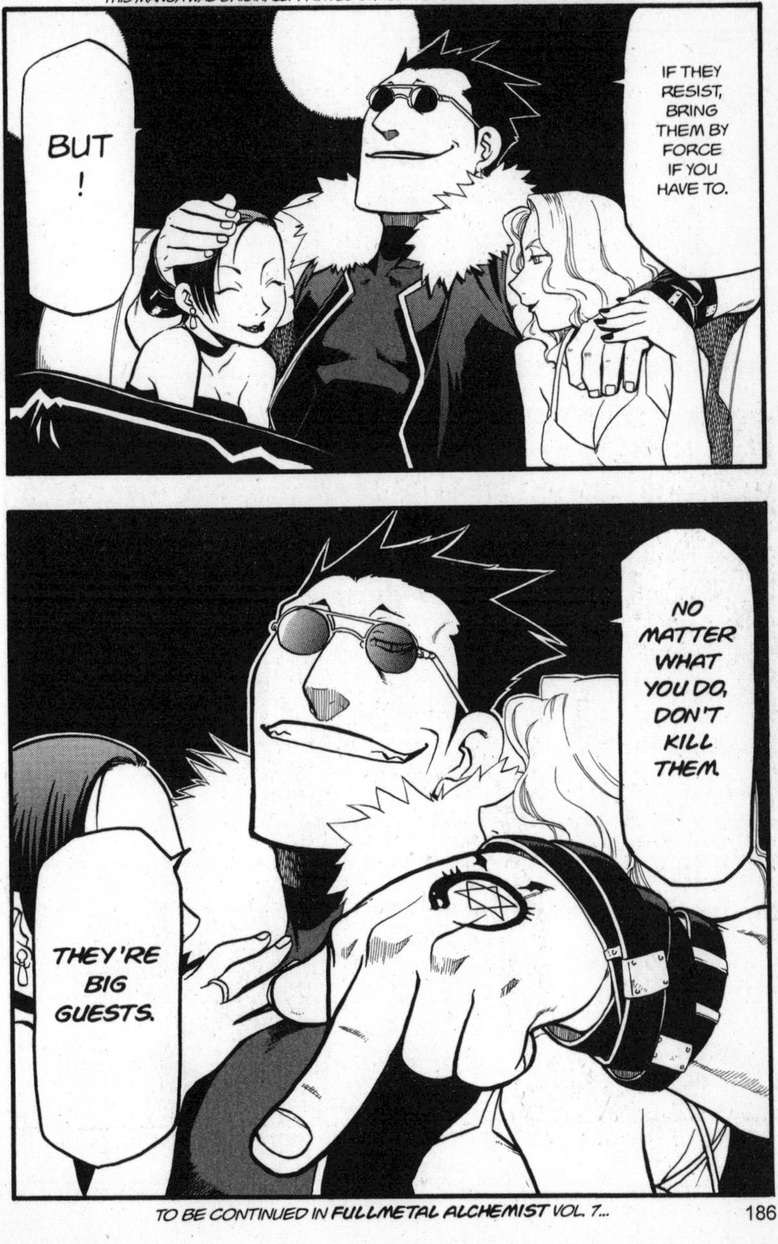
IF THEY RESIST, BRING THEM BY FORCE IF YOU HAVE TO.
BUT !
NO MATTER WHAT YOU DO, DON'T KILL THEM.
THEY'RE BIG GUESTS.

TO BE CONTINUED IN **FULLMETAL ALCHEMIST** VOL. 7...

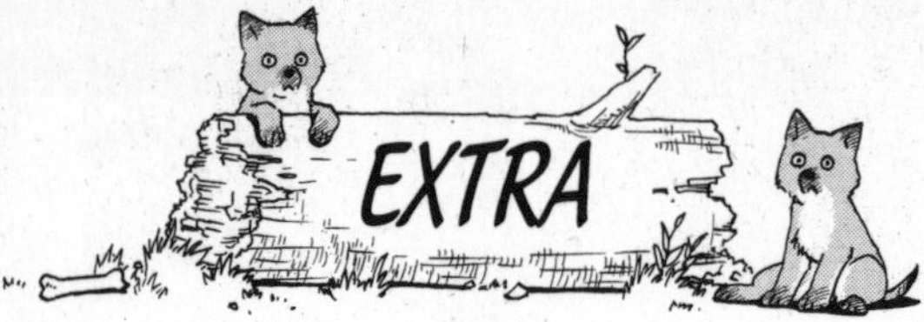
EXTRA

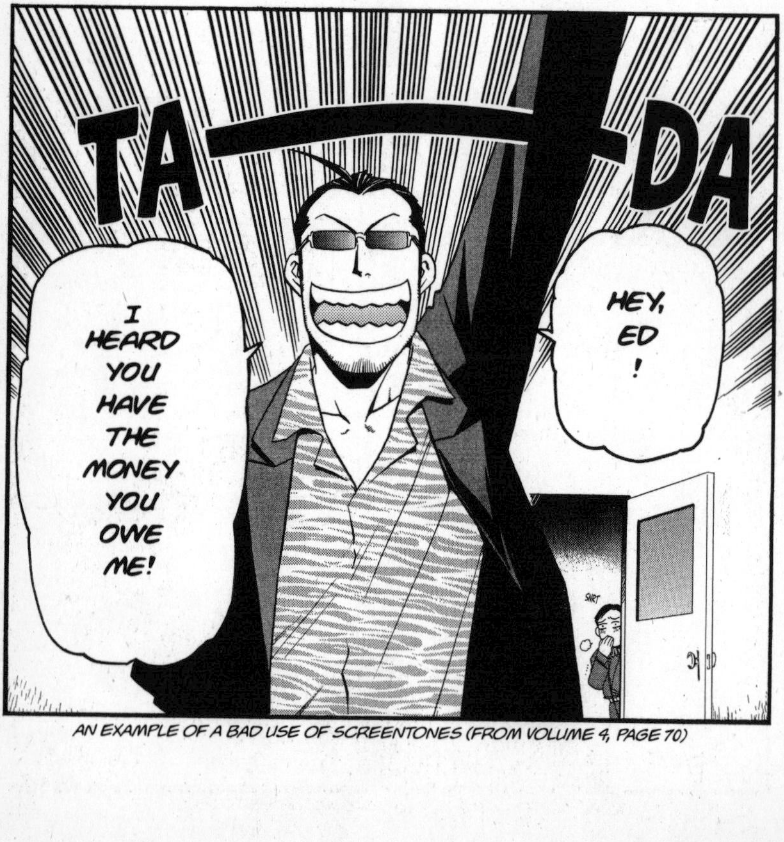
TA—DA
HEY, ED!
I HEARD YOU HAVE THE MONEY YOU OWE ME!

AN EXAMPLE OF A BAD USE OF SCREENTONES (FROM VOLUME 4, PAGE 70)

I COULDN'T GO TO THE OCEAN THIS YEAR

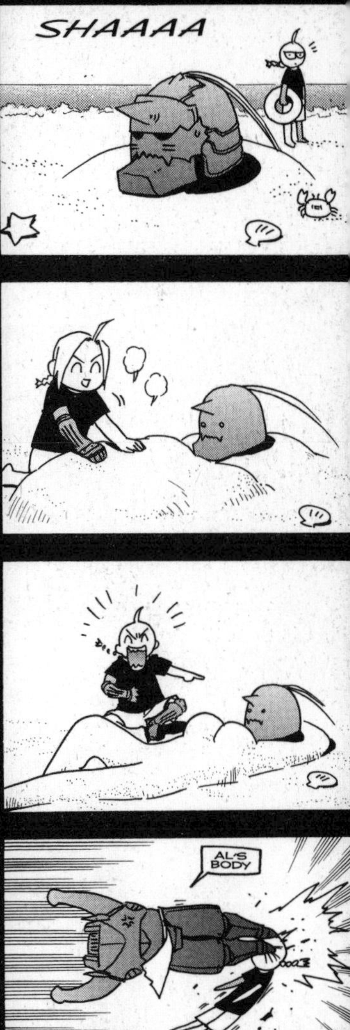
SHAAAA
AL'S BODY

YOU TOO?

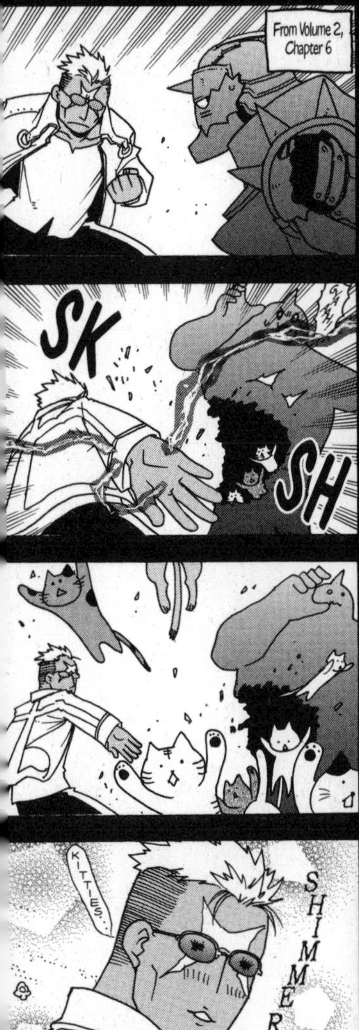
From Volume 2, Chapter 6
SK
SH
KITTIES...
SHIMMER

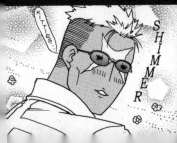

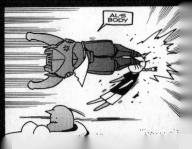

EARS, EARS, EARS

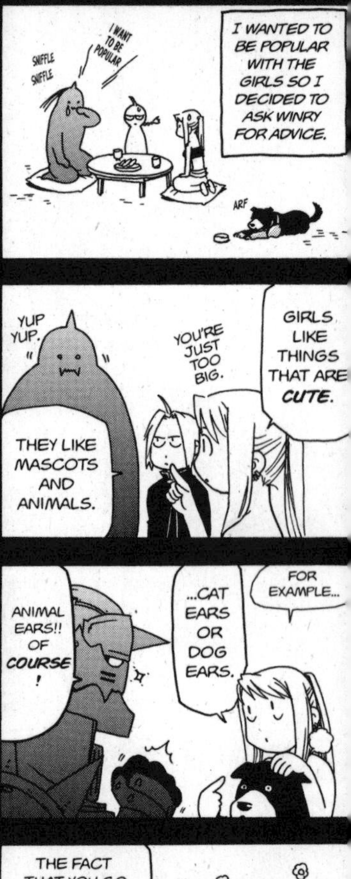
I WANTED TO BE POPULAR WITH THE GIRLS SO I DECIDED TO ASK WINRY FOR ADVICE.
I WANT TO BE POPULAR
SNIFFLE SNIFFLE
ARF
GIRLS LIKE THINGS THAT ARE CUTE.
YOU'RE JUST TOO BIG.
YUP YUP.
THEY LIKE MASCOTS AND ANIMALS.
FOR EXAMPLE...
...CAT EARS OR DOG EARS.
ANIMAL EARS!! OF COURSE!
THE FACT THAT YOU GO STRAIGHT FOR THE ELEPHANT EARS SHOWS YOU'RE HOPELESS.

FULLMETAL ALCHEMIST 6

SPECIAL THANKS TO...

KEISUI TAKAEDA-SAN
SANKICHI HINODEYA-SAN
MASANARI YUBEKA-SAN
JUNSHI BABA-SAN
AIYAABALL-SAN
RIKA SUGIYAMA-SAN
POKUTE-SAN
RENJURO KINDAICHI-SENSEI
YOICHI SHIMOMURA-SHI (MANAGER)

AND YOU!!

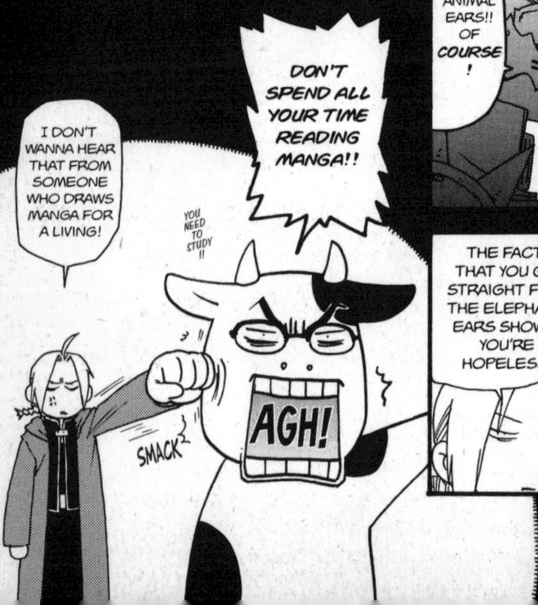
DON'T SPEND ALL YOUR TIME READING MANGA!!
I DON'T WANNA HEAR THAT FROM SOMEONE WHO DRAWS MANGA FOR A LIVING!
YOU NEED TO STUDY!!
AGH!
SMACK

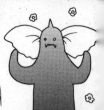

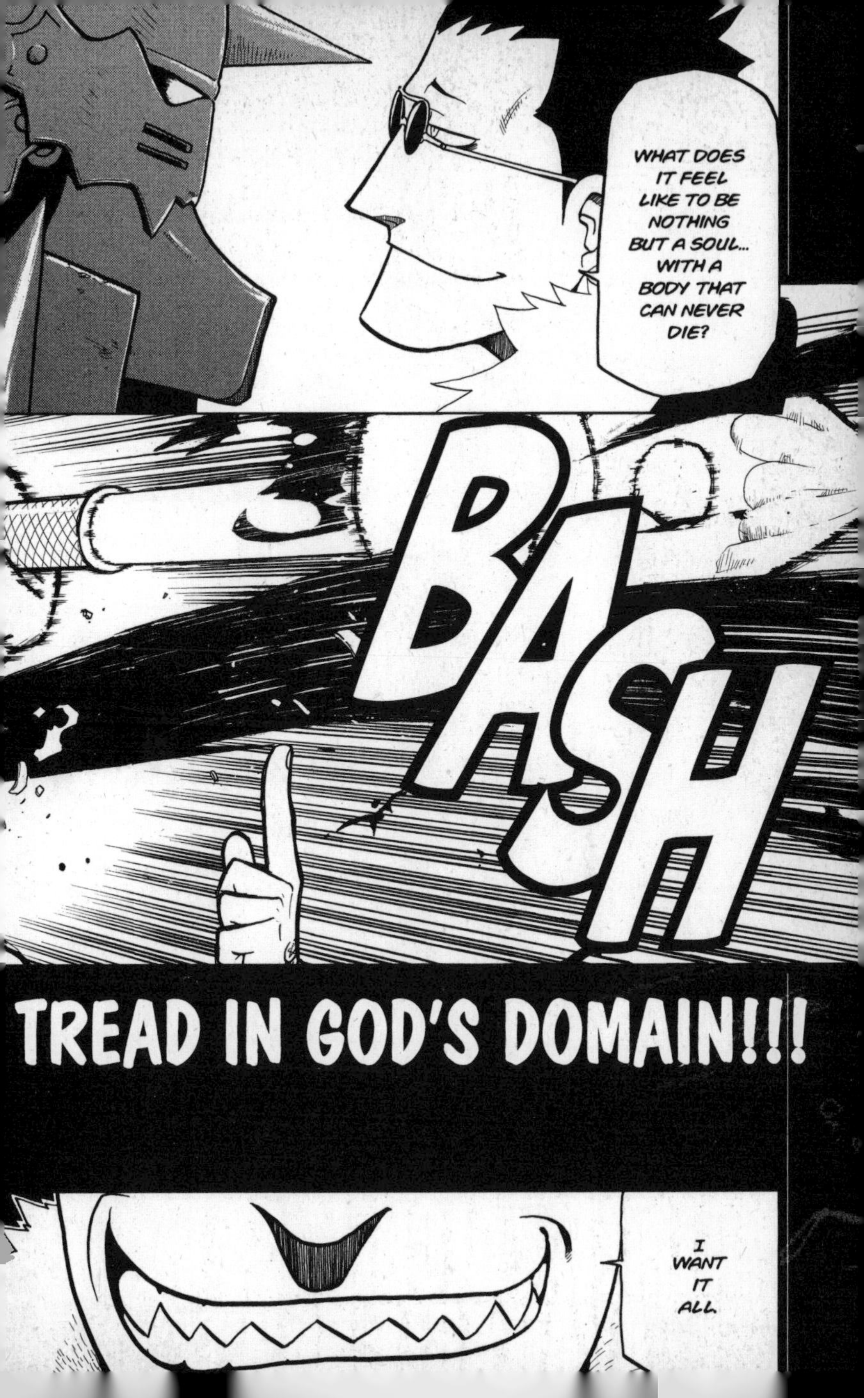
WHAT DOES IT FEEL LIKE TO BE NOTHING BUT A SOUL... WITH A BODY THAT CAN NEVER DIE?
BASH
TREAD IN GOD'S DOMAIN!!!
I WANT IT ALL.

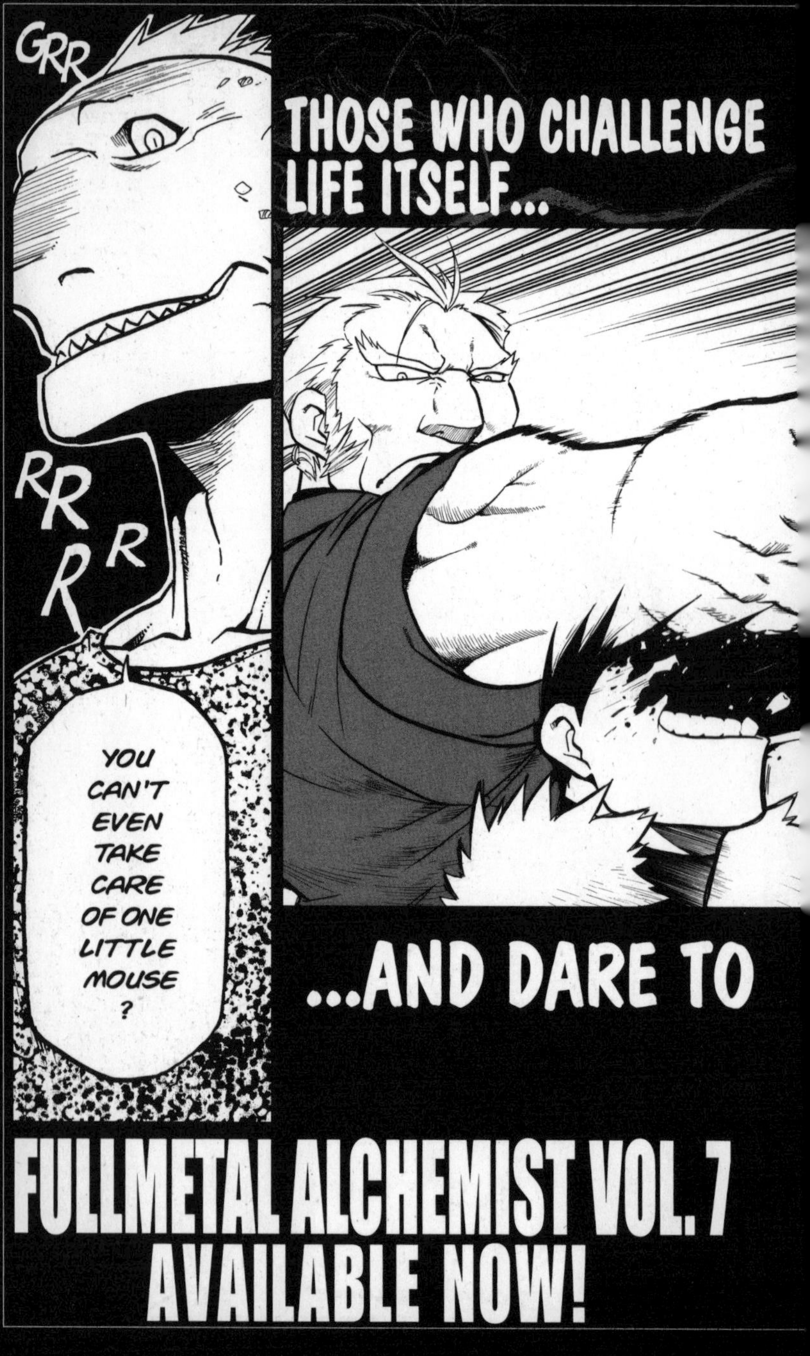
THOSE WHO CHALLENGE LIFE ITSELF...
...AND DARE TO
GRR
RRRR
YOU CAN'T EVEN TAKE CARE OF ONE LITTLE MOUSE?
FULLMETAL ALCHEMIST VOL. 7
AVAILABLE NOW!

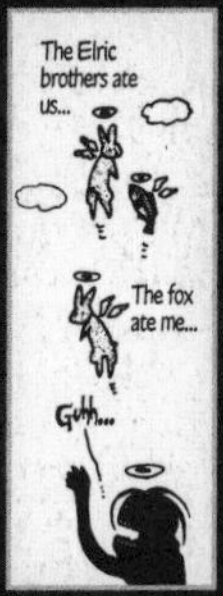
The Elric brothers ate us...
The fox ate me...
Guh...

In Memoriam

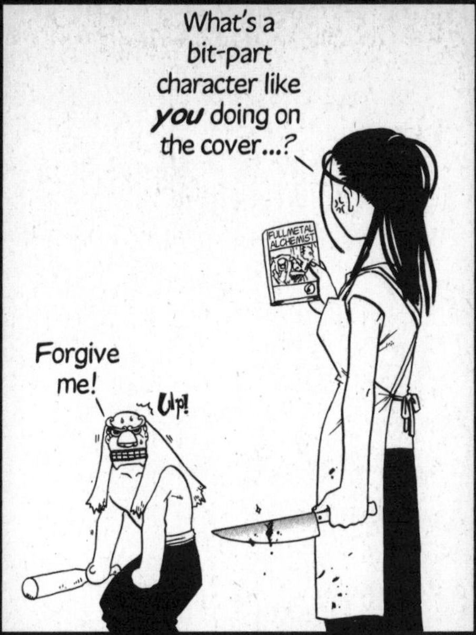
What's a bit-part character like *you* doing on the cover...?
FULLMETAL ALCHEMIST
Forgive me!
Ulp!

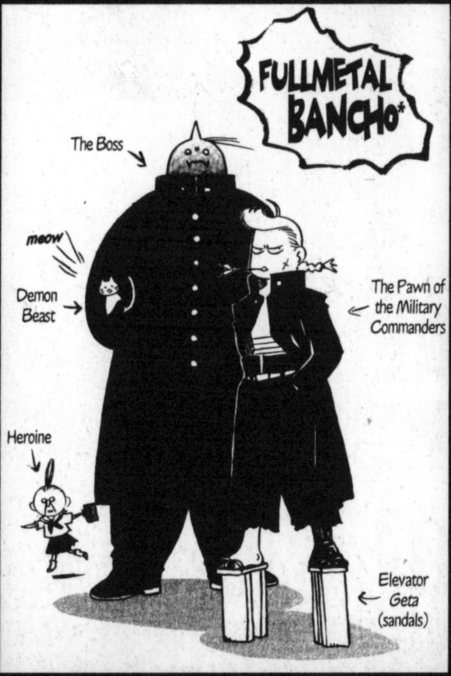
FULLMETAL BANCHO*
The Boss
meow
Demon Beast
The Pawn of the Military Commanders
Heroine
Elevator Geta (sandals)

*Bancho=A stereotypical Japanese delinquent. A 1970s term.

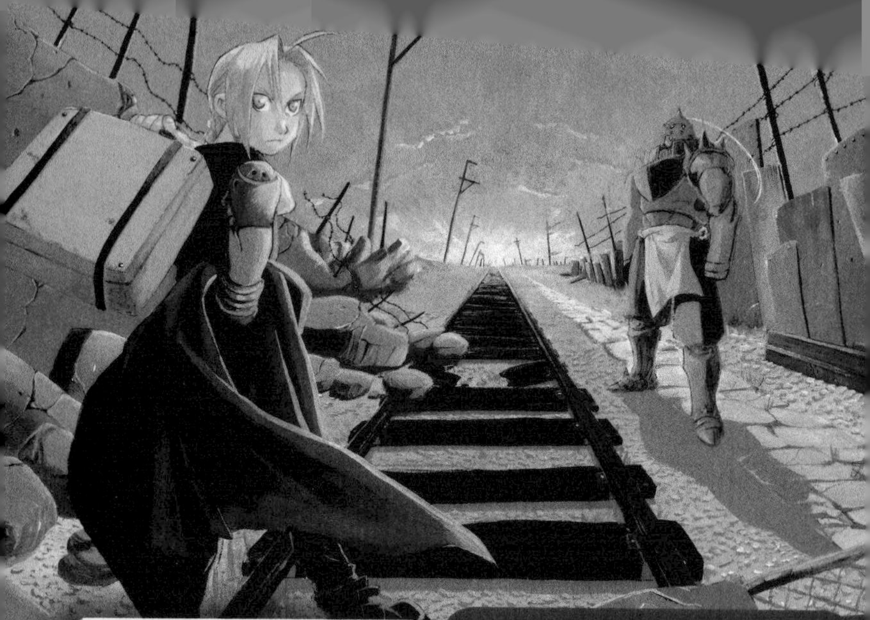

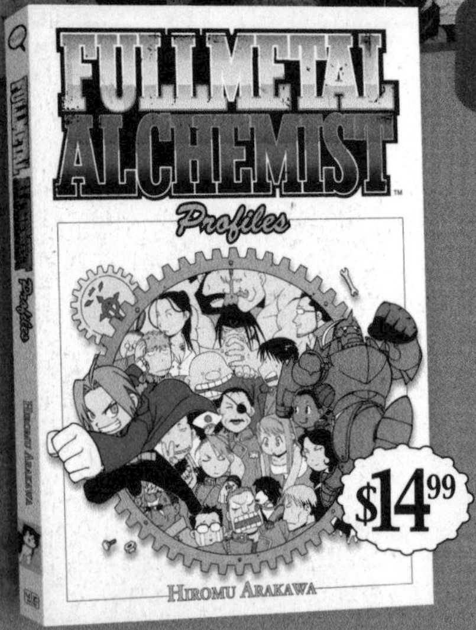
FULLMETAL ALCHEMIST
Profiles
HIROMU ARAKAWA
$14.99

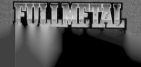

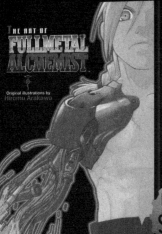
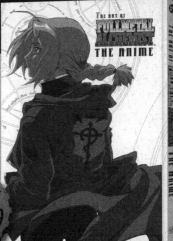

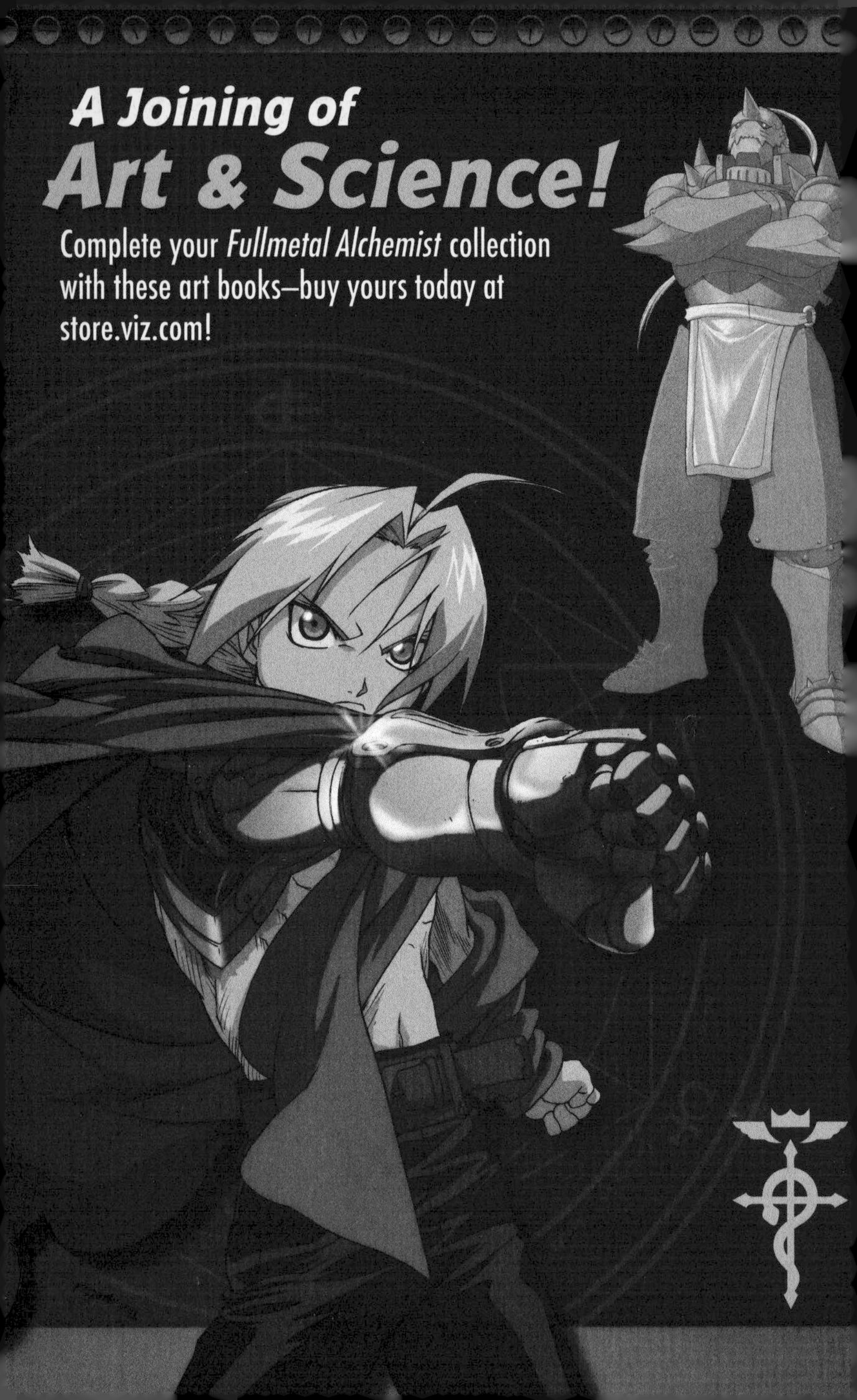
A Joining of
Art & Science!
Complete your Fullmetal Alchemist collection with these art books—buy yours today at store.viz.com!

Without a Past?

From the original manga artist of SPRIGGAN—get armed with the manga and anime today!

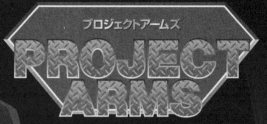

プロジェクトアームズ

PROJECT ARMS

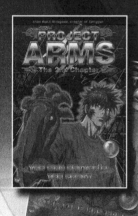

Anime only $24.98

DVD VIDEO

viz media

www.viz.com
store.viz.com

What's a Future

Ryo thought he was normal until he learned his arm was secretly replaced with a powerful weapon. But he soon learns that there are others—teens like him—with mechanical limbs and no idea how the weapons were implanted. Now a secret organization is after the only living samples of this technology and wants to obtain their power by any means possible...

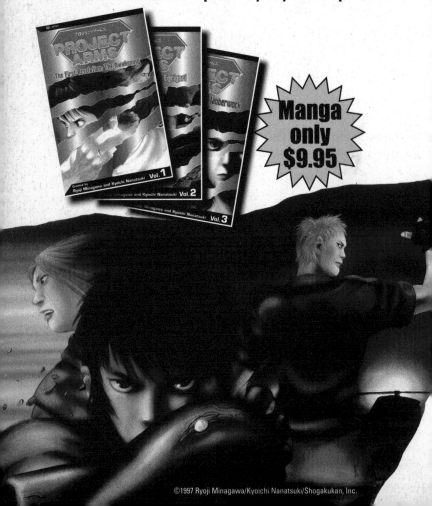

Manga only $9.95

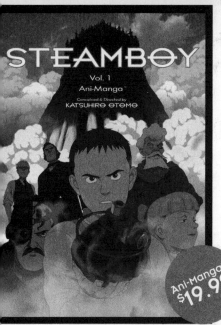
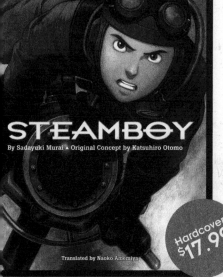

The Evolution of Science... The Downfall of Man?

Based on the hit movie from Katsuhiro Otomo

STEAMBOY

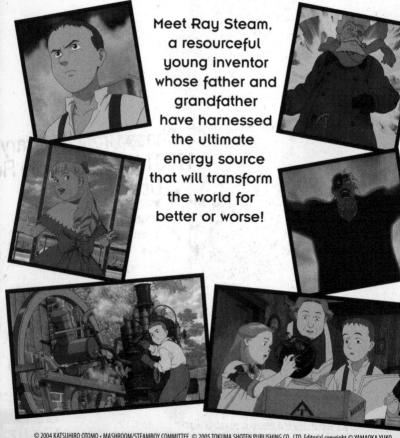

Meet Ray Steam, a resourceful young inventor whose father and grandfather have harnessed the ultimate energy source that will transform the world for better or worse!

LOVE MAN

LET US KNOW WHAT YOU THINK!

OUR MANGA SURVEY IS NOW
AVAILABLE ONLINE. PLEASE VISIT:
VIZ.COM/MANGASURVEY

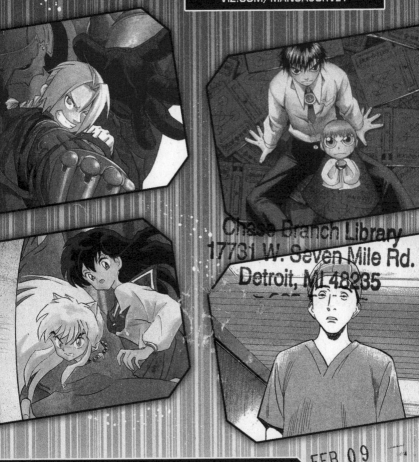

HELP US MAKE THE MANGA
YOU LOVE BETTER!